W9-BHW-567

KENTUCKY HARMONY.

OR

A CHOICE COLLECTION OF PSALM TUNES HYMNS AND ANTHEMS;

IN THREE PARTS

TAKEN FROM THE MOST EMINENT AUTHORS, AND WELL ADAPTED TO CHRISTIAN CHURCHES, SINGING SCHOOLS, OR PRIVATE SOCIETIES.

SELECTED, BY

ANANIAS DAVISSON.

FOURTH EDITION.

PRINTED, and sold by the *AUTHOR*, in Harrisonburg Virginia; and by one of the principal Booksellers in each of the following places, viz. Staunton, Lexington and Abington Va. Knoxville, E. Tennessee, Nashville, W. Tennessee, Louisville Kentucky, and St. Louis Missouri.

N. B. All description of Music printing can be done at this office, upon as reasonable terms as any in the United States.

1821.

Die

allgemein nützliche

Choral-Music,

enthaltend:

auserlesene Melodien, welche bey allen Religions-Verfassungen gebräuchlich sind.

Auf zwey Stimmen gesetzt.

Begleitet, mit einer Vorrede, über die Music, oder Tonkunst: und mit einer, zum Grunde der Vocal-Music vollständigen Einleitung.

Eingerichtet

zum Gebrauch des öffentlichen Gottesdienstes, Sing-Schulen und Privat-Uebungen.

Verfasset von Joseph Funk.

Meine Lippen, und meine Seele, die du erlöset hast, sind fröhlich und lobsingen dir. Psm: 71, 23.

Harrisonburg, gedruckt bey Laurentz Wartmann, Rockingham County, Virginia.

A

SUPPLEMENT

TO THE

Kentucky Harmony

BY

ANANIAS DAVISSON. A. K. H.

COPY RIGHT SECURED.

PRINTED, and sold by the AUTHOR, in Harrisonburg Virginia; and sold by one of the principle Booksellers in each of the following places, viz. Richmond and Staunton, Va. Knoxville, E. Tennessee, Nashville, W. Tennessee, Lexington, Kentucky, and Louisville, Missouri.

1820.

THREE TITLE-PAGES

TOP: *Title-page of Ananias Davisson's* Kentucky Harmony, *fourth edition, published first presumably about the year 1815 in Harrisonburg, Virginia.* MIDDLE: ***Title-page** of Joseph Funk's German* Choral-Music, *Harrisonburg, Virginia, 1816.* BOTTOM: *Title-page of the* Supplement to the Kentucky Harmony, *by Ananias Davisson, Harrisonburg, Virginia, 1820.*

WHITE SPIRITUALS IN THE SOUTHERN UPLANDS

The Story of the Fasola Folk, Their Songs, Singings, and "Buckwheat Notes"

GEORGE PULLEN JACKSON

Dover Publications, Inc., New York

This Dover edition, first published in 1965, is an unabridged and unaltered republication of the work first published by the University of North Carolina Press, Chapel Hill, in 1933.

International Standard Book Number: 0-486-21425-7
Library of Congress Catalog Card Number: 65-24348

Manufactured in the United States of America
Dover Publications, Inc.
180 Varick Street
New York, N. Y. 10014

TO MY MOTHER

ANN JANE JACKSON

AND

MY FATHER

GEORGE FREDERICK JACKSON

WHO BESTOWED ON ME

THE LOVE OF MUSIC

Since I the poet's pen have took,
And swelled my notes into a book;
Let every tongue, by art refined,
Mingle its softest notes with mine.

—Zion's Songster, 1831

FOREWORD

When the late Cecil J. Sharp and Mrs. Olive Dame Campbell went folk-song hunting into the southern Appalachians, the English folk-lorist was surprised that the people usually "misunderstood our requirements and would give us hymns instead" of the secular ballads that had survived from English and Scottish tradition. He did not want "hymns." Other collectors of songs in the southern highlands have specialized less. Mrs. Ethel Park Richardson, for example, included in her *American Mountain Songs* eleven religious folk-songs which she called by their right names, "spirituals." For they were not "hymns." Mr. R. W. Gordon, Professor Newman I. White, and Dr. Guy B. Johnson have recognized the spirituals of the white people as a type in folk-song and have made substantial contributions to its lore. But when we see John Tasker Howard, in his excellent *Our American Music,* referring to the camp-meeting spirituals from 1800 on as "gospel hymns" we are forced to conclude that the concept of the folk-genre in question is still nebulous in the minds of many.

The fact that even the scholars know little or nothing of the religious folk-songs is probably the result of two general conditions. One is that many students of cultural phenomena shy away from them in the belief that they are organic with "psalmody" or "hymnody," and hence not a part of folk-lore at all, not important or even interesting. This was probably Mr. Sharp's attitude of mind. Another condition is that even those who have known of the spirituals and have felt their possible importance, have lacked material for their study. Mrs. Richardson thought a supply of the spirituals might be found in "the old books" that one learns of merely through "hearsay." That these old books are more than hearsay has been shown by the late Louis F. Benson and by the other scholars mentioned above. But even their source material was far from complete.

It has been my good fortune, and good fun, incidentally, to have uncovered a goodly batch of the aged handbooks of spiritual folk-song which seem to have completely escaped all other collectors and all other diggers into American institutions. How and where I found them, what strange sorts of songs they contained, whence the unique notation in which the songs are recorded, who made, collected, and sang them, how, when, and where they came into being, and how and where their singing persists at present—these are a few of the problems which have claimed my interest for a number of years and have provided matter for discussion in *White Spirituals*.

My acknowledgments of help are due largely to those who have furnished me with the rare old books of song. I am especially grateful to Mr. Carl Engel and Mr. W. R. Gordon of the Library of Congress; to Miss Mary Baugham, librarian of the Kennedy Free Library in Spartanburg, South Carolina; to Miss Mary U. Rothrock, librarian of the Lawson McGhee Public Library in Knoxville, Tennessee; and to the Ruebush brothers, Will H., James H., and Joe K., of Dayton, Virginia, whose books and files of the *Musical Million* have been documents of immense value in my undertaking.

My greatest inspiration has come from the southern "country singers," scores of them, whom I have met at "singings" and the bigger conventions, people who seemed glad to let me sing, talk, and eat with them and become their friend. It is therefore one of my earnest hopes in sending this book out that these singers may find in it a welcome story of their beloved "science" and that some others may, through it, come to a deeper and broader knowledge of, and respect for, the American rurals and their lyric-religious folk-ways.

George Pullen Jackson.

Nashville, Tennessee
June, 1932

TABLE OF CONTENTS

PART II

Fasola Offspring, the Dorayme Folk

LIST OF ILLUSTRATIONS

The illustrations, except a few placed in the text, face the page indicated.

PART I

THE OLD FASOLA FOLK

A PAGE FROM THE OLDEST KNOWN SHAPE-NOTE BOOK

The Easy Instructor, *compiled in 1798 by William Little and William Smith, Philadelphia, edition of 1802 (?). The melody is on the second staff from the bottom.*

CHAPTER I

BEGINNINGS OF AMERICAN GROUP SINGING IN NEW ENGLAND

A Survival in Culture

The word "fasola" is not of my making. Neither is it to be found in any dictionary. But ask almost any real country person of mature years anywhere in the wide stretches of the southern states—the hilly and mountainous regions principally, which make up the far greater part of that section—if he knows anything about fasola singers, and he will very likely be able to direct you to one of them, or perhaps to a group in a "singin'."

I lived in cities of that section for many years and was in touch with its musical life and thought as they exist in urban environments, long before I heard of these country singers. My eventual learning of them was a pure accident, the result of a chance conversation with Dr. John W. Barton of Ward-Belmont School, one of those all too rare individuals who see deeply, even into their own culture. And my discovery of them was the result of my own zeal. Dr. Barton described one of the fasola "singin'-all-day-and-dinner-on-the-grounds" conventions which he had observed in Texas and told of the singers' claims to an art of song which had come down in direct line from the earliest music of the world, as that earliest music had been revealed in the Bible and by subsequent history. He told also of their strange notation and of a music theory, singing schools, teachers, and song books which were exclusively the rurals' own, making these people, in effect, as contrasted to music and musicians as they are known in occidental urban culture, a sort of "lost tonal tribe."

There was, I soon found out, a large ingredient of truth along with the manifest element of romance in the country songsters' claims. There was so much truth, indeed, and truth that has impressed me as being so important and interesting, culturally and historically, and so completely unknown to the archivists of culture-lore, that its story on the following pages can need no apology.

The country singer's emphasis on the genesis of his art led me to check up first on that phase. Where did this "fasola" singing come from? Readers of this book who are careful students of the history of music will perhaps have recognized that the adjective in question is made of the names of those three musical notes with which the common major diatonic scale began in the time of Queen Elizabeth. In those times the primeval *ut re mi fa sol la si* sequence and other manners of note singing had simmered down, among the masses in England, to the three syllables, *fa, sol,* and *la,* with a *mi* thrown in to serve in a comparatively rare melodic emergency. To fill out the seven notes of the octave these early Britishers sang, ascending, *fa sol la,* repeated them for the next three notes, and then added *mi* as their "leading" tone or pointer to the coming *fa* which completed the octave. So the series with which we are more or less familiar nowadays as *do re mi fa sol la ti do* was sung *fa sol la fa sol la mi fa* in Shakespeare's England, and is still so taught and practised among those who belong to this lost tonal tribe in America.

The realization of the existence of this little "survival in culture" is not startling. Such cultural "antiques" have come to be expected in the rural Southeast. It may take on importance and arouse more interest, however, when we learn—as we shall in the course of the following pages—that this now antiquated solmization was and is associated, precisely as the country singers assert, with a likewise surviving primitive vocal-musical theory and practice, and with a great body of song constructed in manners that have been forgotten, as it seems, everywhere else for generations; and that it is graphically represented in a notation form of which present-day urban musical folk know nothing. And this interest may broaden when it is known also that the people who foregather regularly in voluntary choral groups to learn and to sing these old songs and the countless other lays that are their direct offspring, can be reckoned by hundreds of thousands.

The Singing Movement in Early New England

New England seems to have been the section where Old England's manner of solmization entered the New World, where organized song fostering among the masses first sprang up and throve, and whence these practices spread in time to the country at large. And all signs observable among our southern country singers point to this far northeastern section as the chief source of their singing cult.

In seeking reasons for this musical primacy of New England, we must bear in mind that song fostering of this sort was from the start a democratic affair, and religious. The earliest singing schools and their successors for over a century used no songs but those which could be transferred to the "meeting house" without offense. It can be seen, therefore, that the comparatively democratic and deeply and autonomously religious settlers of New England were of the kind that might well be expected to initiate such a song movement.

But even in New England the singing movement, as an independent cultural undertaking, was not destined to obtain without a struggle. It is a sorry picture that the historians of music have painted of the sacred-musical side of early New England colonial life. In the seventeenth-century church they sang few tunes, and the few they did use were tolerated rather than prized and fostered. The spoken gospel was the thing. "Part singing" sank to one part, the droned melody which church folk could sing, to their own satisfaction at least, without any musical instruction at all. The words were "lined out" by the leader much as they are now in the most primitive Negro congregations in the South, and the singing of the dozen or so possible tunes proceeded in a sort of everybody-for-himself manner much like the responsive readings in some churches today.

The First Tune Books Compiled in the Colonies

But in the early part of the eighteenth century a new spirit in music became manifest. The year 1721 marked the beginning of what might be called a musical revolt; and this revolt, like so many others, was due to the spirit of youth pitted against tradition. In that year two young college-bred men, John Tufts and Thomas Walter, published separately two song books and sent them out among a people that had been starved for music all too long.

The radical innovations of Tufts' twenty-three-page book, *An Introduction to the Singing of Psalm Tunes* (Boston, 1721), were that it added twenty-five tunes to the unbelievably meager body of song of the New England congregations up to that time; that it was the first tune book compiled in the colonies, and that it pointed the people to a new (to them) way of singing by note, instead of by rote, which had been the only orthodox way.[1] Tufts' "notes," however, were not the symbols current on the European continent at that time. They were simply the initial letters of the four syllables, *fa sol la mi,* placed on the five staff-lines and the spaces between. As for length of note, "F" indicated a quarter note, "F." a half note, and "F:" a whole note. Vertical bar-lines were used simply at the end of a musical phrase, not between measures. A sample of this notation is given in the illustration on page 2.

Thomas Walter's book, *Grounds and Rules of Musick* (Boston, 1721), was even more revolutionary, for while it was insignificant in size, it was the very first American song book to use regular notes[2] and the sole American-made book of this type in use in the English-speaking colonies for forty years after its first appearance. It enjoyed several editions and was not long in completely displacing the Tufts book.

With the work of these musical pioneers and their followers throughout the rest of the eighteenth century, singing gradually released itself from the hegemony of the churches and became the possession of the people, churchman and outsider alike. Presently it became, in the eyes of religious conservatives, quite worldly indeed, for even though the songs themselves were still nominally "sacred," the whole environment of their learning and fostering was what some might call delightfully secular.

The Singing Schools

This secular environment was that of "singing schools" which throve from about 1770. Gould tells us that these

[1] The hornet's nest stirred up by Tufts and Walter is indicated by the often cited outbreak of a writer in the *New England Chronicle* in 1723: "Truly, I have a great jealousy that, if we once begin to sing by note, the next thing will be to pray by rule and preach by rule; and then comes popery."

[2] Walter used the diamond-headed and square notes (◊ ⊟) that were usual in Europe during the eighteenth century.

schools were music's declaration of independence.[3] "Ministers, Christians, and all good men, and men of correct taste in regard to music, looked on sometimes grieved and sometimes vexed. But they had let go their hold, and the multitude had the whole management of it and sung what and when they pleased," this during what Gould calls the musical "dark age," 1770 to 1800.

The singing-school teacher, according to Gould, was often a man who "steeped his talents in spirit." He would come to a town and start a popular subscription to pay for the school. A wealthy man would often refuse to have any part in it, declaring, in sentiments that are not yet entirely obsolete, that "if anyone wishes to learn to sing, let him pay for it," by taking private lessons, of course. A hall in a tavern was the usual place of meeting. The landlord made the rental cheap in consideration of the patronage which his barroom enjoyed during recess and afterwards. The singers brought their own candles, used improvised benches on which to lay the books and to set the candles, and sat in a semicircle two or three rows deep. The pupils were taught the clefs, syllables or notes, keys, note lengths (semibreve, minim, crochet, quaver, semiquaver, demisemiquaver). Then they sang a song through by note (syllables), part by part, and time after time. And not until it was thoroughly learned were they allowed to sing the words. The music was usually in three parts—air, bass, and counter. The air "lead," or tune, was sung by males of the higher-voiced type, the bass by the deep-voiced males, and the counter (a sort of tenor part) by the females. Everybody beat time with the right hand while singing. The beating was usually merely up and down. But three-part time demanded, and sometimes got, a three-part beating: (1) fingers on the table, (2) flat hand on table, and (3) hand raised.

[3] Nathaniel D. Gould, *History of Sacred Music in America*, pp. 76 ff.

The singing-school term seldom exceeded twenty-four afternoons and evenings. The sessions were three hours long. The objective of all this activity was realized in the final "exhibition" which was held in the "meeting house." Here the whole class showed what it had learned. And in the exhibition singing, all that remained of the solmization practice of the singing school was the chord that was sung before the piece started. (There were few organs in New England churches in the eighteenth century.) Gould avers that a good time was had by all and that ardent spirit was the usual interlude,—even in the meeting-house, though perhaps not at service—partaken of by all, from the clergy down. When the singing master left for other fields, his pupils swelled the ranks of the church choir.

The "Dark Age"

Gould's "dark age" (he did not have the democratic slant on music) was one of steadily increasing development of singing schools and song books. The Revolutionary War and its accompanying antipathy to all things British lent impetus to the tendency to desert the old imported tunes and to substitute for them the newly fabricated domestic article. Hence many a singing-school teacher became a maker of tunes, and tune books multiplied. Every book opened with a set of "rudiments" which were intended to make the art of singing learnable by those "of meanest capacities." That this was fortunate will be realized when it is remembered that the task confronting the singing teachers was nothing less than the education, by this method alone, of a pioneering nation whose minds must have been musically a perfect blank.

Under these circumstances it was understandable that each teacher should strive to make his teaching method and material a little easier, and therefore a little more popular and successful than that of his competitors. The hardest part of learning to sing was, naturally, getting acquainted with the notation, and thus it came about that some teachers, especially those who were in musically virgin territory, became emboldened to try to improve on the traditional notation system.

It so happened that one of the earliest of these notational "helps to read" became eventually the standard musical symbolism of American rurals in general and of the rural South in particular. I refer to what is called the "character" or "shape" notation which is even now used exclusively and in its original form by the fasola folk and, in a further developed form, by other legions of rural southerners. This notation, although it soon became highly significant as an easily learned musical alphabet for the singer of simple songs, developed in time an even greater influence in separating rural from urban music, folk-singing from art-singing; and these facts justify a few paragraphs as to the origin, material, and trend of the notation.

CHAPTER II

EARLY SHAPE-NOTE SINGING SCHOOLS: THEIR SPREAD TO THE WEST AND SOUTH

Early Musical "Helps to Read"

The singing-school teachers' reasoning, as a basis for their notational improvement in the interests of beginning singers, was fundamentally sound. They saw rightly that the singer, in beginning to learn a new tune or a harmonic part, looked up the key signature, located the tonic, and then orientated the successive notes in the light of his knowledge of scale structure, his feeling for the size of pitch intervals and for tonal relationship or melodic character. The teachers saw, in other words, that the singer's establishment of the tonic *fa* and its related notes—and this without the help of harmonic instruments—was a process involving reasoning, reckoning, and musical feeling. And they concluded that a system of giving to each note-head a characteristic shape—one that would reduce the reasoning and reckoning processes by showing instantly that the particular note in question was *fa, sol, la,* or *mi,* leaving the singer simply to the exercise of his melodic feeling—would simplify his learning to sing.

I have not positively identified the author of the scheme of shaped note-heads in question. The authorship lies probably with either the New England singing-school teacher, Andrew Law, or the two partners in song-book compiling, William Little and William Smith. The few who have given any thought to the subject credit the scheme to Law, but I feel that this is a false conclusion.

Metcalf declares, "A musical magazine" and "a new form

of musical notation . . . are the additions made by Andrew Law to the literature of American psalmody."[1] Law was born in 1748. He taught singing school many years in the round-note form of music. But the year 1803, when he was fifty-five years old, seems to be the date of the first appearance of shape-notation in his books; and "the fourth edition [of Law's *Music Primer*] printed in Cambridge, Massachusetts, by W. Hillard in 1803, appears to have been the first one to contain his new system of notation." Metcalf bases his conclusion on Law's claims in that edition of the *Primer,* where we read, "This book exhibits a new plan of printing music. Four kinds of characters are used, and are situated between the single bars that divide the time, in the same manner as if they were on lines. . . . their situations mark perfectly the height and distance of their sounds . . . without the assistance of lines. These four kinds of characters also denote the four syllables, mi, faw, sol, law, which are used in singing. The diamond has the name of mi; the square of faw; the round of sol; and the quarter of a diamond [right-angle triangle] of law." An example of Law's notation may be seen opposite page 22. In ascribing priority to Law, Metcalf agrees with Gilson, who declared that "the first man who altered the form of notes . . . appears to have been Andrew Law."[2] Grove's *Dictionary* leans on Metcalf, but places without warrant the first appearance of Law's shapes at "about 1800."[3]

Now a word as to the priority claims of William Little and William Smith.[4] A song book published by them and using

[1] Frank J. Metcalf, *American Writers and Compilers of Sacred Music* (New York, Abingdon Press, 1915), pp. 68 ff.

[2] F. H. Gilson, *The History of Shaped or Character Notes.*

[3] *American Supplement,* p. 386.

[4] I have learned nothing about the identity of either Smith or Little. They may have lived, as Carl Engel thinks, in Philadelphia. But the 1802 edition of their *Easy Instructor* was printed in Albany and sold "in N. Y. City, Schnectady [*sic*], Utica, Lansingburgh, Troy, and New-Haven."

the same shapes as those in Law's *Primer,* but with the retention of staff-lines, is called *The Easy Instructor; or A New Method of teaching Sacred Harmony, containing the rudiments of music on an improved plan, wherein the naming and timing of the notes are familiarized to the weakest capacity.* The *Easy Instructor* was copyrighted in 1802. But Carl Engel, former chief of the music division of the Library of Congress, is of the opinion that it was published for the first time in 1798 in Philadelphia. This opinion he bases probably on the Philadelphia Urania Society's official recommendation of the notation "novelty" used by Little and Smith printed in the *Easy Instructor* and dated August 15, 1798.

Until further data are found, therefore, we shall have to ascribe the shape-note idea to the Little and Smith partnership. Neither Law nor the Philadelphia compilers seem to have been very cocky in claiming authorship. It was perhaps too early, for the system had not yet proved its worth.

But there is one thing that has been overlooked by all who have inquired into this matter, namely, that each of the claimants had a perfect right to claim a "new method," for there was a decided difference between the two notations, entirely aside from the fact that one used the staff-lines and the other did not. I refer to the *sequence* of the shapes in the diatonic scale. In Law's notation the ascending sequence, beginning with what would be our *do,* was square, round, triangle, etc.; whereas the sequence in the Little and Smith scale is triangle, round, square, etc. This may be verified by referring to samples of both notations on page 14 below. And it is important to state here that it was the Little and Smith sequence, and not the Andrew Law sequence, which subsequently found wide use in the West and the South. But it is passing strange that the subsequent compilers of shape-note

Four-Shape Notation, Sequence used by Little and Smith:

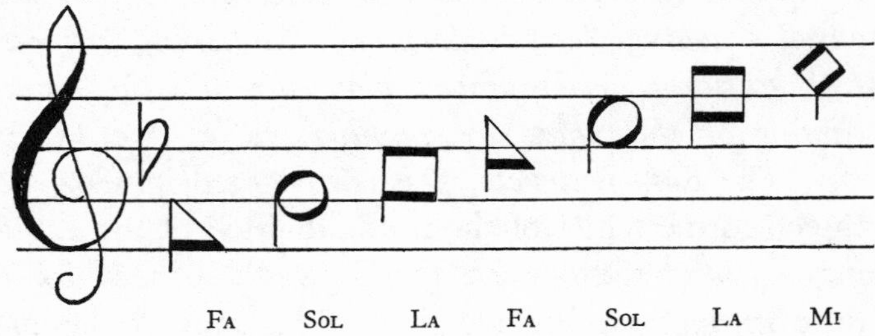

Four-Shape Notation, Sequence used by Andrew Law:

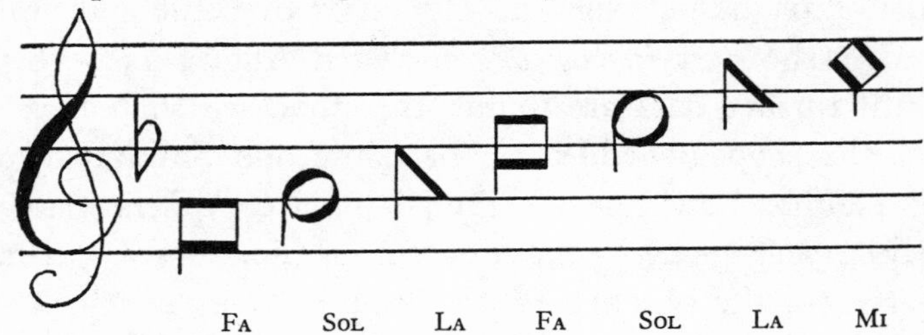

song books in the South were, with one exception, silent as to the source of the notable innovation. They seemed to accept the "patent notes" without question, much as they would accept the alphabet in written language. The one exception to this rule was William Hauser.[5] Fifty years after the first appearance of the *Easy Instructor,* Hauser speaks, in his Georgia *Hesperian Harp,* of "the glorious Patent notes of William Little and William Smith."[6]

Gould tells of the decline in the use of song books printed in the shape notation. Such books, "if used at all, have been crowded to the far West, mostly out of sight and hearing."[7] That was in 1853. Metcalf said as to the survival of the note shapes (he looks upon them as Law's and does not mention

[5] See p. 70 below.
[6] P. vi.
[7] *Op. cit.,* p. 55.

Little and Smith), "The new notation did not last long, though it may have obtained some vogue."[8] And Waldo S. Pratt, editor of the *American Supplement* to Grove's *Dictionary*, assures us that this attempt to simplify music reading was "equally transient" with that of John Tufts.[9]

In the face of all this authoritative negation, my immediate task becomes all the more important. It is the task of showing that Gould, Metcalf, and Pratt were not conversant with all the facts in the case. It is the task of proving that this very four-shape notation is still used by tens of thousands of singers, that an early extension of the notation to seven shapes (including the old four) has become the musical symbolism of millions, and that its popularity remains unabated today over vast stretches of the United States.

This proof must begin with some mention of the geography of early shape-note usage and of the direction in which this usage spread from New England and the states of New York and (eastern) Pennsylvania.

Early Shape-note Singing Schools: Their Spread to the West

I have found no authoritative data as to the popularity of these rural musical helps-to-read in New England proper. But scattered bits of information indicate that they found for a time a far greater welcome in most rural parts of those far-eastern states than the historians of music have led us to believe. It is sure, however, that it was the "Yankee singing-school master" from those parts who carried the rural music method west and south.

The motivating elements in this musical trend were various. The trend was naturally in line with migration as

[8] *Op. cit.*, p. 74.
[9] P. 158.

a whole. The shape-note method fostered by the masters was ideally suited, in its simplicity, to the crude and musically traditionless settlers in those new sections. Little by little the urban and even the rural parts of the East were getting and approving certain musical notions, largely from Europe, which made the tenure of the domestic singing school and its master uncertain. Among these notions was the *do re mi* solmization which soon arrived to combat the traditional and thus far universal *fa sol la* method of the Yankees. In Boston and other cities in the 1820's the public school children were being taught music along the advanced educational lines suggested by Pestalozzi. From Europe came also Better Music than the American masses could make or sing generally, democratically. Into the churches came the organs which, with their great tone volume, put a crimp in the hard-learned and dearly loved harmonic vocalism of the singing-school folk and relieved the church-going masses of the necessity of doing much more than following the organ's lead and singing the melody part. And even the melody was being taken away from the men, for urban leaders were beginning to give the important tune part to the women,[10] thus lowering in rank the men, the mainstays of the singing schools. So the intransigent singing-school master had no choice. He had to leave for unspoiled parts.

For the first three decades of the nineteenth century the errant master of primitive song had things pretty much his own way. He became an institution in what was then called the "West" and the "South." His singing schools and his fasola shape-notes were in vogue in all the open stretches. But even there he was destined eventually to meet his troubles. To the west, such cities as Pittsburgh, Cleveland, Cincinnati, and St. Louis were soon springing up. The Better

[10] Louis C. Elson, *History of American Music*, p. 21.

Music boys saw this growth, and they were not long in following up the advantages (to themselves) of nascent urban conditions. So they too went west. And the shape-noters had to "move on" again. The case of Timothy B. Mason, one of the Better Music boosters, may serve to make this development clearer.

Early in the 1830's Mason pilgrimaged from the musically urbane Boston—with its Handel and Haydn Society, its Boston Academy of Music, the notable Lowell Mason (Timothy's brother), the Pestalozzian methods for juvenile learners-to-sing, the *do re mi* solmization, and other freshly imported contributions to the advance of the art—to Cincinnati. There he found everybody singing and enjoying the Billings and Company "fuguing songs" and all the rest of the old-time, native New England singing-school stock-in-trade, and using books printed in the popular shape-notes. Burning with musical-misisonary zeal, as it would appear, he set about compiling an orthodox instruction and song book that was to counteract all this tonal paganism. The *Ohio Sacred Harp*[11] was an excellent collection, with twenty pages of "Introduction to Vocal Music" and two hundred twenty pages of song. The "Editors' Advertisement" was signed by both Lowell and T. B. Mason. In the "Introduction to Vocal Music" we find signs of the Masons' opposition to shape-notes and to the traditional English system of solmization with which it was linked. "The most correct method of solmization," the authors declare, "is to apply a distinct syllable to each note of the scale, viz.: the syllable DO to *one,* RE (ray) to *two,* MI to *three,* FA to *four,* SOL to *five,* LA to *six,* and SI (see) to *seven.* Indeed, by pursuing the common method of only *four* syllables, sing-

[11] It seems that this book or a revision of it appeared later entitled "Masons' Sacred Harp or Eclectic Harmony." Grove's *Dictionary, American Supplement,* mentions its eighteenth edition as of Boston, 1836. A copy in my possession was published in Cincinnati, Truman and Smith, 1840.

ers are almost always superficial. It is therefore recommended to all who wish to be thorough, to pursue the system of seven syllables, disregarding the different forms of the notes."

This *Ohio Sacred Harp* appeared in the shape-notes which its authors advised singers to "disregard," and subsequent editions came out in both types of notation. The "Publishers' Advertisement" in my shape-note copy of 1840 makes the equivocal situation clearer: "The publishers would further remark," the notice reads, "that the Sacred Harp is printed in patent notes (contrary to the wishes of the authors) under the belief that it will prove much more acceptable to a majority of singers in the West and South. [Signed] Truman and Smith." In order to be quite positive that no one should suspect the two notable Masons of musical provincialism, the disavowal is repeated on page 2: "The proprietors of Masons' Sacred Harp have (contrary to the express views and wishes of the authors) prepared," etc. Another tradition of the country singing schools was opposed in the *Sacred Harp;* I refer to the custom of having the men sing the melody. The Masons delivered the following edict on page 20: "This part [they called it the "treble or leading melody"] is always to be sung by female voices, and by them alone."

Timothy Mason did even more along the line of bringing Cincinnati's music practices up to date and, inevitably, making the indigenous singing schools decidedly *out* of date. He introduced orchestral instruments into his Second Presbyterian Church, and he and the minister, Dr. Beecher, sponsored the advent of an organ in that church in 1837, the very first organ to be installed west of the Alleghenies. Timothy Mason was apparently as great an enthusiast as his illustrious brother for juvenile-music teaching along Pestalozzian lines, and he followed that method in his Cincinnati "Eclectic Academy of

Music." Thus Mason carried on what Gould called "the work of reformation in the West,"[12] and the doings in Cincinnati were probably typical of the musical trend in other western cities.

On top of these disturbances of the musical *status quo,* came such tradition-breaking distractions as the California gold fever, the war with Mexico, general prosperity, mass immigrations of comparatively urban Germans into this very territory, bringing their advanced instrumental and vocal practices, and, finally, the vogue of a new form of secular concert music that was brought to the people by trouping "bell-ringers," "tumbler-players," and "family" concertizers whose sole purpose was to amuse, and whose music had the effect of giving the people tunes to whistle and sing without their having to expend any energy in learning them. No longer were singing schools needed. All one had to do was to go to the concert and learn by ear, much as do the victims of the present-day "song pluggers" and "jazz crooners."

Urban Sentiment and Musical Reform

The development of urban sentiment antipathetic to the singing schools in the territory under consideration in the 1840's is well shown by an article which I found in the Cincinnati *Musician and Intelligencer:*

"The most mortifying feature and grand cause of the low estate of scientific music among us," declared the writer of the article, one Miss Augusta Brown, after having made some allusions to Europe's tonal superiorities, "is the presence of common Yankee singing schools, so called. We of course can have no allusion to the educated professors of vocal music, from New England, but to the genuine Yankee singing masters, who profess to make an accomplished amateur in one

[12] *Op. cit.,* p. 143.

month, and a regular professor of music (not in seven years, but) in one quarter, and at the expense, to the initiated person, usually one dollar. Hundreds of country idlers, too lazy or too stupid for farmers or mechanics, 'go to singing school for a spell,' get diplomas from others scarcely better qualified than themselves, and then with their brethren, the far famed 'Yankee Peddlars,' itinerate to all parts of the land, to corrupt the taste and pervert the judgment of the unfortunate people who, for want of better, have to put up with them. We have heard of one of these cute geniuses, who 'set up' in a town way down east as cobbler! On his sign, under the announcement of his profession, as a provider for the wants of the bodily understanding, was the following choice couplet, setting forth, as a musician, he did not neglect to provide also for the wants of the mental.

> 'Delightful task! to mend the tender boot,
> And teach the young idea how to flute.'

"Cobbling and music! We just ask how any musical nerve can stand that?" And feeling that she had still been a bit hard on New England, Miss Brown hastened to add that that section had, to be sure, produced a host of illustrious men in all the arts and sciences. "Even in music," she asked rhetorically, "has she [New England] not given us Billings and Holden? A blessing be on their memories."[13]

Cobbling and music! Richard Wagner had not yet made it easy for Miss Brown to learn about how Hans Sachs had turned the trick. But she certainly should have known that Oliver Holden was a carpenter and that the self-educated William Billings was a rural Yankee singing-school teacher and, even though not a cobbler himself, had considerable truck

[13] Vol. II (1848), No. 1, pp. 21 ff.

with the repairers of men's soles in that he was a tanner of hides.

Under the adverse conditions indicated in the foregoing paragraphs, the singing-school master and his humble institution had a hard time of it. Gould tells us that the "buckwheat notes" were not "all eaten up" in 1853, but that their use was then restricted probably to "the great west." And while this statement is not true,[14] the fact remains that the old-time singing school with its old-style notation was crippled, and lost its influence north of the Ohio far sooner than in the parts of which I shall speak presently. But before leaving the subject of the "musical reform" to the north of the Ohio, I wish to recall Gould's disappointment that this reform, which seemed to promise so many blessings to the people as a whole, failed to keep its promise. The one great purpose of learning to sing in those times was that congregational singing should improve. And Gould felt he had to admit that in 1853, despite Mason, Beecher, Colburn, Pestalozzi, *et al,* congregational singing was poorer and church choirs were smaller.[15] The music historian did not place the blame, but one can sense his feeling that the masses had had their *own* music taken away, and that they had not yet been able to assimilate the Better Music which was foreign to them. He might have recalled also that the singing-school masters and other natives had made their own songs, and that now the Better Music of the noted composers had made them first conscious of their own deficiencies and then unproductive, ashamed of home-made music. Gould might have reflected also that the majestic organs were absolute monarchs, reducing to musical serfdom all attempts at vocal harmonizing.

[14] I have information that singing schools, using shape-notes, are still found in the southern parts of Ohio, Indiana, and Illinois. But all definite information as to their extent is ungathered.

[15] *Op. cit.*, p. 237.

Fasola Singing Schools Trek Southward

The factors I have mentioned above as those which alienated the northern masses from their own naïve form of song fostering were not active in the rural South. Economic prosperity, European musical influences, urban-continental-nordic immigration, the growth of cities—from all of these the upland southerner was, naturally, exempt. Organs could not have been hauled along his primitive roads, over his hills and mountains, even if he had greatly desired them. So when the singing schools came into the South, they stuck.

The remote source of these singing schools was, as we have seen, New England. Their immediate source seems to have been Philadelphia and eastern Pennsylvania. During the eighteenth century Philadelphia had been a busy port of debarkation. Hundreds of thousands entered the new continent there. First came the English Quakers; then the Scotch-Irish, and various German groups who were also distinguished by their religious complexions—Lutherans, Moravians, Mennonites, and Dunkers. These groups varied greatly in their attitudes toward song in church worship. But they all seem to have agreed that singing in other surroundings, in singing schools for example, was a very good thing. When the shape-notation appeared, bound up as it was from the start with religious song and showing no taint of secularism or heterodoxy, the mixed separatistic population which radiated from eastern Pennsylvania received it with open arms. So the Yankee music masters—Wyeth, Little, Smith, and Law, for example, who were active in those parts, joined forces with the Pennsylvanians for the fostering of popular song.[16]

[16] Metcalf tells (*op. cit.*, p. 67) that Andrew Law, an ordained minister, was recommended by the Philadelphia Presbytery "to preach in the South." The third edition of his *Musical Primer* (shape-notes) was printed in Philadelphia and, as Metcalf believes, in 1812. "Allegheny College of Meadville, Pennsylvania, . . . honored him with a LL.D. in 1821." Metcalf quotes John W. Moore, the historian

60 Cheerful.

DELAWARE. No. 50.

Let earth with every isle and sea Rejoice, the Saviour reigns : His word like fire prepares his way, And mountains melt to plains, And mountains,

Cheerful.

OLD 100 No. 51.

Ye nations round the earth, rejoice Before the Lord your sovereign King ; Serve him with cheerful heart and voice, With all your tongues his glory sing.

A PAGE FROM ANDREW LAW'S *ART OF SINGING*

Fourth edition, 1803. The tune is the uppermost series of notes.

From this eastern Pennsylvania district the pioneers began spreading, toward the end of the eighteenth century, in various directions. One of the main directions was to the southwestward into the Valley of Virginia. And with the settlers went, naturally, the music masters. It is therefore not surprising that we should find the southern rural singing-school movement and the shape-note practices with which it was bound up, beginning in the Shenandoah Valley and spreading farther to the south, southwest, and west.

The tidewater sections of the Southeast will have no part in our considerations. Those sections were the territory of the big-planter and Negro-owner type of patrician American. His culture was foreign-influenced and comparatively urban. His music, what there may have been of it, came in as an urban article imported from abroad and from the northeastern cities of America. Instruments were comparatively easy to obtain. These coastwise Americans were therefore not forced, as were those very differently conditioned people in the mountains, mountain valleys, and hill country to the west, either to raise their own voices in song or to submit to musical starvation. So the story of the singing schools and the homespun songs and tune books is not a lowlands story.

On the Trail of the Tune Books

In following the song trail through the South we shall let the southern-made song books lead us. With the books' stories I shall tell, where possible, of the compilers; for those book-makers were always teachers, music propagandists, and usually song composers. Subsequently we shall go on to the

of music, as stating that "as late as 1820 Mr. Law resided in Newark and from thence wrote letters for publication, recommending his system of notation." Metcalf quotes, from F. L. Ritter's *History of Music in America,* the passage in which Ritter declares that "Law's most efficient work was that of a singing teacher . . . in the New England states and in the South." I have been unable to find further indications of his "southern" activities.

consideration of the singers, their institutions, the body of song as such, and some of the individual musical compositions.

From the list on page 25, as complete a list as can be made at present, it may be seen that thirty-eight different books of song appeared in the four-shape notation between the years 1798 and 1855. The list gives us naturally no idea as to the total number of copies printed and used. Some books were popular throughout a large part of that span of fifty-seven years. Others died after a first edition. Nor does the date of the last fasola book, McCurry's *Social Harp* (1855), mean the end of four-shape singing, for the popularity of some of the listed books continued for decades after that date. One of them, the 1844 *Sacred Harp,* is enjoying a wide use today. It was the introduction of *seven*-shape notation practices in the 1840's that put an end in a short time to the making of *new* collections in the four-shape manner and brought books which in time superseded most of the old fasola collections.

Twenty-one of the books listed, those marked with an asterisk, were made by compilers living in the southern states. These compilers aimed primarily at supplying the demands of their own territory. Indeed, the home of the compiler was, in most cases, the center of his book's sphere of influence. It is for this reason and because the present work is concerned with the shape-note singing in the South primarily, that I shall omit all discussion of the northern books and confine my considerations to those in the South, where the bulk of shape-note history has been made.

LIST OF SONG BOOKS IN THE FOUR-SHAPE NOTATION

Year of Publication	Name of Book	Author	Author's Home	Place of Printing
1798.......	Easy Instructor	Wm. Little & Wm. Smith	?	Albany.
1803.......	Musical Primer	Andrew Law	Cheshire, Conn.	Cambridge, Mass.
1810.......	Repository of Sacred Music	John Wyeth	Harrisburg, Pa.	Harrisburg, Pa.
*1815(?).....	Kentucky Harmony	Ananias Davisson	Virginia	Harrisonburg, Va.
*1816.......	Choral-Music	Joseph Funk	Mountain Valley, Va.	Harrisonburg, Va.
1816.......	Columbian Harmonist	Timothy Flint	?	Cincinnati, O.
*1817.......	Kentucky Harmonist	Samuel L. Metcalf	Lexington, Ky.	Cincinnati, O.
*1820.......	Suppl. to Kentucky Harmony	Ananias Davisson	Virginia	Harrisonburg, Va.
*1820.......	Missouri Harmony	Allen D. Carden	St. Louis, Mo.	Cincinnati, O.
*1820.......	Songs of Zion	James P. Carrell	Lebanon, Va.	Harrisonburg, Va.
1821 or 1822	Methodist Harmonist	Printed by Waugh and Mason	?	New York.
1822.......	Sacred Music	Seth Ely	Germantown, Pa.	?
*1824.......	Western Harmony	Allen D. Carden & Samuel J. Rogers	Nashville, Tenn.	Nashville, Tenn.
*1825.......	Columbian Harmony	William Moore	Wilson County, Tenn.	Cincinnati, O.
*1826.......	Western Harmonic Companion	James W. Palmer	Lexington, Ky.	Cincinnati, O.
1829.......	Union Harmony	John Cole	?	Baltimore, Md.
*1831.......	Virginia Harmony	James P. Carrell and David S. Clayton	Lebanon, Virginia	Winchester, Va.
1831.......	Western Lyre	Wm. B. Snyder & W. B. Chappell	?	?
*1831.......	American or Union Harmonist	Wm. R. Rhinehart	Maryland	Chambersburg, Pa.
*1832.......	Genuine Church Music	Joseph Funk	Mountain Valley, Va.	Winchester, Va.
1832.......	Sacred Harp	James H. Hickok	Lewiston, Pa.	?
*1832.......	Lexington Cabinet	Robert Willis	Lexington, Ky.	?
1834.......	Evangelical Musick	J. H. Hickok & G. Fleming	Carlsile, Pa.	?
1834.......	Ohio Sacred Harp	Lowell Mason and Timothy Mason	Boston, Mass. and Cincinnati, O.	Cincinnati, O.
1834.......	Church Harmony	Henry Smith	Chambersburg, Pa.	Chambersburg, Pa.
*1835.......	Southern Harmony	William Walker	Spartanburg, S. C.	New Haven, Conn.
1835.......	Introduction to Sacred Music	Amos S. Hayden	Ohio	Pittsburgh, Pa.
*1836.......	The Valley Harmonist	J. W. Steffey	New Market, Va.	Winchester, Va.
1837.......	The Harmonist	(Printed by Mason & Lane)	?	New York, N. Y.
*1837.......	Union Harmony	William Caldwell	Maryville, Tenn.	Maryville, Tenn.
*1838.......	Knoxville Harmony	John B. Jackson	Madisonville, Tenn.	Madisonville & Pumpkintown, Tenn.
*1844.......	Sacred Harp	B. F. White and E. J. King	Hamilton, Ga.	Philadelphia, Pa.
1844.......	Western Harp	Samuel Wakefield	?	Pittsburgh, Pa.
*1845.......	Southern and Western Harmonist	William Walker	Spartanburg, S. C.	?
1846.......	Southern Melodist	George Hood	Massachusetts	?
1848.......	Sacred Harmony	Samuel Jackson	?	New York, N. Y.
*1848.......	Hesperian Harp......	William Hauser	Wadley, Ga.	Philadelphia, Pa.
*1855.......	Social Harp	John G. McCurry	Andersonville, Ga.	Philadelphia, Pa.

CHAPTER III

IN THE SHENANDOAH VALLEY

Ananias Davisson and the Kentucky Harmony

The first southern rural singing activity seems to have been in northwestern Virginia. The first object there to claim our attention will be the *Kentucky Harmony,* and the first singing-school master, Ananias Davisson, the book's compiler.

As to Ananias Davisson's life I have gathered but little information. William B. Blake wrote in the *Musical Million* (Dayton, Virginia, 1884):

> He was born Feb. 2, 1780. I have not succeeded in discovering the place of his nativity. But I am almost certain it was along the border-line of Maryland and Virginia. He was well and favorably known forty years ago up and down our valley. He was author of Kentucky Harmony, a book characteristic of that period, abounding in minor tunes. He was also author of Supplement to Kentucky Harmony, printed separately from the first-named work. If he published other books, I have never seen them. The Wartmanns of Harrisonburg . . . were his publishers. He spent the evening of his life on his farm at Weyer's Cave, about fourteen miles from Dayton, and died on the 21st of October, 1857, aged 76 years, three months and eleven days. He is buried in the Union Church graveyard, eight miles from Dayton. He was a ruling elder in the Presbyterian church and a man of unaffected piety. On his gravestone appears, in addition to the foregoing dates, this verse:
>
> Father, I give my spirit up,
> I trust it in thy hand;
> My dying flesh shall rest in hope,
> And rise at thy command.[1]

—See Illustration facing page 308.

[1] *Musical Million,* XV (1884), 41. From the title-page of Davisson's book, where we read that it was "printed by the author in Harrisonburg," and from

That the early part, at least, of Davisson's life was devoted to teaching singing schools is clear. In the Preface of the *Kentucky Harmony* he speaks of his "practical knowledge as a teacher of sacred Music." In the Preface of the *Supplement to the Kentucky Harmony,* which appeared in its third edition in 1825, he speaks of himself as a retired singing teacher well past middle life. He was then forty-five.

The copy of the *Kentucky Harmony* which has been placed at my disposal[2] is the fourth edition printed in 1821. The book was copyrighted, however, "on the eleventh day of March in the forty-first year of the Independence of the United States of America," which I reckon as 1817. This copyright date is verified by I. H. Whitty, in *A Record of Virginia Copyright Entries, 1790-1844,* a pamphlet published by the Virginia State Library in 1911. But the fact that the *Kentucky Harmony* was in circulation before 1816 is proved by a note in the German song book, *Choral-Music,* issued in 1816 (see p. 31), to the effect that two of its songs, on page 48, are "von der Kentucky Harmonie genommen." The form of the *Kentucky Harmony* is the then usual oblong, five by eight and three-fourths inches. The title-page is reproduced here as part of the Frontispiece. The first fifteen pages are devoted to Preface, Rudiments, General Observations, "A Remark or Two at the request of several Refined Musicians," "Lessons for Tuning the Voice," and minute directions for the construction of a metronome or a "pendulem [*sic*] that will vibrate once for every beat in the several moods here laid down."

There are 144 pages of tunes, all in four-part harmony. The parts are called—from lowest upward—bass, tenor, counter,

Chute's testimony (see *Musical Million* VI (1875), 71), that James P. Carrell's *Songs of Zion* was "printed by A. Davisson, Harrisonburg, Va.," I should judge that Davisson had his own printing establishment at the time of these publications.

[2] By Joe K. Ruebush, dealer in rare books, Dayton, Virginia.

and treble. And on page 13 we read that "The bass stave [*sic*] is assigned to the gravest voices of men, and the tenor [the melody] to the highest. The counter [is assigned] to the lowest voices of the Ladies, and the treble to the highest of Ladies' voices." This arrangement, by which the men sing the tune and the high-voiced women sing a part that corresponds fairly well to present-day tenor, was, as we have seen, a tradition that went back to the very beginnings of song in America and has lived on in the most conservative shape-note circles to the present day. The bass part is notated in the "F Cliff" and the other three parts are placed on three distinct staves in the "G Cliff."[3] In Part I the songs are short, two to the page. They have but one verse of text each, and that verse runs across the page dividing the two staves for male voices from those sung by females. After the title and the indication of the song's meter, we see at the top, right, the key of the tune. A major key is called a "Sharp Key" and a minor is called a "Flat Key." So "Sharp Key on C" means C Major, and "Flat Key on A" means C Minor. The Part I songs are those "plain and easy tunes commonly used in time of divine worship." In the second part we find "more lengthy and elegant pieces" used in "singing societies." Here may be found one of the richest collections of "fuguing tunes" in all the shape-note song books. Practically every tune on pages 46-109 is of this variety. (See p. 207 below for its description.) And the book closes with a series of anthems, some of which fill as many as eight pages each.

It is not hard to learn where Davisson got his tunes, for

[3] This spelling, and also "clift" are often met with in books of the eighteenth century and earlier, and we shall meet them again in southern books even later than the *Kentucky Harmony*. An editor of the *Sacred Harp* admits, as late as 1911, the orthographic alternatives "cliff or cleft." Davisson also writes of "minums" (minims), and "treble" (triple) time, like many of his contemporaries, and his spelling "faw, sol, law, me" was perfectly orthographic in four-shape-note circles, as it still is today.

his Preface lists the collections of Smith, Little, Wyeth, Billings, Holyoke, Adgate, Atwell, and Peck as reference volumes in his possession, and his Index of Songs lists the composers of all but three. According to this list, fifty-six composers are represented. Davisson claims fifteen of the pieces as his own compositions. He attributes to Shumway ten, Reed and Chapin seven each, Billings and Morgan six each, and Boyd and Timothy Swan five each.

Like so many other compilers of those and later times in the South, Davisson has not mentioned the names of the composers of the texts. I do not know the reason for this omission. It may have been because the texts were, by and large, a fixed and generally taken-for-granted corpus, founded on the changeless psalms, and therefore looked upon as non-individual in source, whereas the tunes were the product of real persons many of whom were still living at the time of the book's publication. And then there is much doubt as to whether those named by Davisson as "authors" were the producers of tunes or words or both. It would take a deal of research to determine this point, and such a study is not in place here. Some of those which Davisson claims as his own songs are, in my judgment, among the best in the book,[4] and the approval of the subsequent compilers of rural song books in the South is shown by their unanimity in adopting, especially, "Idumea," and their use of one or more of Davisson's other songs in practically all the books that have been found. Davisson preferred the minor keys. Two of the songs which he claims, "Golden Hill" and "Idumea," are five-tone melodies and one, "Reflection," is six-tone.

Davisson's ability in selecting for his *Kentucky Harmony*

[4] They are Condescension, Glasgow, Golden Hill, Garland, Idumea, Immensity, Mount Calvary, Reflection, Solemnity, Solitude in the Grove, Tender Thought, Tribulation, Zion's Hill, Lovers' Lamentation, and The Leprous Jew.

those tunes of other composers which made a deep appeal to his particular public is evinced by the extremely large number of those tunes which became stock-in-trade for the southern rural compilers who followed him. In fact, there are many signs that point to this book and to its *Supplement* as being unique in the wide recognition accorded to them as pioneer repositories of a sort of song that the rural South really liked.

Supplement to the Kentucky Harmony

The *Supplement to the Kentucky Harmony* by the same author appeared in 1820. The copy which is at my disposal is of the first edition.[5] On the title-page (see Frontispiece) Davisson is proud to subscribe himself "A. K. H.," "Author of Kentucky Harmony." The fine print on that page tells that the book is "PRINTED, and sold by the AUTHOR, in Harrisonburg, Virginia; and sold by one of the principle [*sic*] Booksellers in each of the following places, viz.: Richmond and Staunton, Va.; Knoxville, E. Tennessee; Nashville, W. Tennessee; Lexington, Kentucky, and Louisville, Missouri [*sic*]." This list of cities, as it appeared a year later in the fourth edition of the *Kentucky Harmony,* left out Lexington, Kentucky, and put in both Louisville and St. Louis. The title-page of the *Supplement,* third edition, 1825, states more precisely that it is sold by L. Tremper, Staunton; Mr. North, Lynchburg, Virginia; Robertson and Elliott, Nashville, W. Tenn.; Crosier and Barton, Knoxville, and J. Lynn, Boatyard, E. Tenn. "And if ageants can be procured in Camden, Christon, and Rauleigh, in the Carolina's it will be done." His hoped-for Louisville and St. Louis customers seem not to have materialized.

[5] Lent me by Joe K. Ruebush, dealer in rare books, Dayton, Virginia. A copy of the third edition, 1825, is in the Lawson McGhee Public Library in Knoxville, Tennessee.

That the *Supplement* is a real one is shown by the fact that the list of songs is entirely different in the two books. In his Preface Davisson states this and announces that the book is made with the special aim to furnish his "Methodist friends" (Davisson, it will be remembered, was a Presbyterian) with "suitable and proper" songs. His "Rudiments" are squeezed into five pages. Then follow 117 pages of song. Davisson claims eleven of the songs as his own,[6] and he asserts a partnership interest in six other pieces. Three of these are by "White and Davisson." In the others he seems to have collaborated with Wyeth, Carrell, and Dare.

Joseph Funk's German "Choral-Music"

While the Davisson books were supplying the English-speaking people of the Shenandoah Valley, the very numerous Germans there used *Choral-Music,* published in 1816 and full of German songs. It was not a highly significant book, as such. But Joseph Funk, the man who made it, and the influences which he and his descendants have exerted in the field of music in the South for more than a hundred subsequent years have made his first book important far beyond its intrinsic worth.

John Funk, father of Joseph, was of that big band of German protestants of the Mennonite variety who in the early part of the eighteenth century found Pennsylvania more agreeable to them than the Rhine-Palatinate. But when, toward the end of that century, eastern Pennsylvania became pretty well filled up, John Funk and his wife, who had been Barbara Showalter, and their big family of children moved southwestward into the Shenandoah Valley and settled not far from Harrisonburg. Joseph was one of these children.

[6] They are Humble Penitent, Harrisonburg, Changeing [*sic*] Seasons, Imandra, Prodigal, Crucifixion, Davisson's Retirement, Emerald Gates, Haywood, Redemption, and Royal Proclamation.

And when he got big enough to shift for himself, he took to himself a wife (Elizabeth Rhodes, englished from "Roth"), cleared a small plot of land, and built a little log house by a clear spring in a hollow which was called afterwards Mountain Valley and still later, and with intentional musical significance, Singer's Glen.[7] Data as to Joseph Funk's formal education are lacking. But after a study of his manuscript and published writings the only conclusion I can make is that even if he did not go to school he did nevertheless acquire an excellent education. And it is astounding to realize that with all his manifest struggles in creating a home and farm out of the virgin forest and soil and in acquiring his mental equipment, he still found time to learn music and to teach it, so that at the age of thirty-eight he was able to carry his manuscript of *Choral-Music* to its printer, Laurentz Wartmann, in Harrisonburg, eight miles away.

Choral-Music is an oblong book, five by eight and three-fourths inches, of eighty-eight pages. A reproduction of its title-page (see Frontispiece) shows that it is in German. The date of its finishing, "in the month of July, 1816," appears on page 86. And my presumption is that it was published in that year. The book appears in Whitty under the heading "Entries Without Dates."[8] The Foreword "On Music, or the Tonal Art," written by Pastor Johannes Braun, is a long apology for the art and proof of its being biblically authorized and even required. But the poor singing up to that time distressed him. "It is to be regretted," he declared, and I translate, "that we Germans, especially in these parts, are so

[7] For most of the information as to Joseph Funk's life I am indebted to Dr. John W. Wayland of Harrisonburg, Virginia, and more especially to his monograph entitled "Joseph Funk, Father of song in Northern Virginia" appearing in the *Pennsylvania-German,* a monthly magazine published in Lititz, Pennsylvania, Vol. XII (October. 1911), No. 10.

[8] *Op. cit.,* p. 41.

backward in the practice of the vocal art. Nowhere is this more noticeable . . . than in public gatherings and, more or less, in all religious organizations. There are many, and with the scarcity of singing schools more and more, who do not open their mouths to sing at all; and there are others who cause, by unsuitable sounds, such discords that both the song service and the devotional service are disturbed if not entirely broken up." So Pastor Braun urges the establishment and support of singing schools, and he calls attention to *Choral-Music* as a book that will be, as its title suggests, "generally useful" in such environment for people of all sects and for young and old. After sixteen pages of this argument, eight pages of Rudiments follow before the fifty-six pages of songs start. Following the songs there is a five-page "conversation between a scholar and his teacher," which functions as a sort of review of the Rudiments. At the end is an Afterword by Joseph Funk, which is in reality a Preface.

The songs, in two parts only, bass and tenor, are taken, as Funk tells us on page 86, from among those "which are most widely used in the services of the different religious organizations, for example, many psalm tunes from the song book of the Reformed Church." He also indicates that the song books of the Mennonites and the Lutherans have been his sources. Two songs on page 48 of the Funk book are taken, as the compiler acknowledges, "von der Kentucky Harmonie." They are "Ihr junge Helden, aufgewacht!" and "Ach Gott, wie manches Herzeleid," which have the *Kentucky Harmony* titles, "Rockbridge" and "Supplication." Two other songs have been borrowed from the same source but without acknowledgment. They are "Was mich auf dieser Welt betrübt" (*Choral-Music,* p. 58; in *Kentucky Harmony,* p. 22, entitled "Salvation"), and "Auf, Seele, auf, und säume nicht"

(*Choral-Music,* p. 65; in *Kentucky Harmony,* p. 18, entitled "Primrose").

I have said above that this German book was not intrinsically of great significance. It seems never to have enjoyed even a second edition. But I do not wish to repeat the mistakes of some hymnologists and historians of music and carry on the error of supposing that such books as this, because of their not being in the English language, were of no influence in the general upbuilding of song. The people of the Shenandoah Valley were, when *Choral-Music* came out, predominatingly German. They were changing the spelling of their names to conform to the standard language of their adopted land. They were surprisingly quick to conform to their new environment in speech and customs.[9] But what must be realized is that they were Americans whose culture was most potent in those formative years in a broad rural territory, and it was from this territory, with these important cultural factors, that influence spread to unmeasured lengths. So the fact that this early indigenous song book is in German is of minor historical significance. Equally unimportant is the fact that most of the German songs disappeared (excepting in church environment) with the discontinuance of the language in which they were written. But the fact that the soon-to-become-American Germans were actively engaged in music propaganda is of more than passing import to the musical historian.

Carrell's Songs of Zion and Virginia Harmony

Two other books had their origin in Harrisonburg, Virginia. William E. Chute said that he had found a copy of

[9] Exceptions to this rule of quick adaptation to the new American environment are seen in the nonconformist branches of some religious denominations like the "old order Amish" branch of the Dunkers.

James P. Carrell's *Songs of Zion,* which was a sixty-four-page book printed by A. Davisson in Harrisonburg in 1821.[10] The copyright office in Washington adds to this information by fixing its copyright entry date as 1820 and its full title as "Songs of Zion, being a small collection of tunes, principally original, with appropriate lines, adapted to Divine Worship. By James P. Carrell." (Both "Carroll" and "Carrell" were used.) I have never seen a copy of this Carrell book. I picked up a copy of Carrell's other book in a Nashville old-book shop. Though its title-page is gone, I established its identity as the *Virginia Harmony* by the repeat of its title which is to be found on page 15 at the beginning of the songs themselves. Chute supplied further information by telling, in the article mentioned above, that Carrell and David S. Clayton published this book in 1831—where, he did not say, but the style and the excellent quality of its binding and printing point to the Shenandoah Valley, perhaps to the Wartmanns in Harrisonburg.

My copy of the *Virginia Harmony*—the only one of which I have any trace (it is not mentioned in Grove's *Dictionary*)—is of its second edition, which, the Preface tells, is forty pages of music bigger than the first edition. The book is five and a half by nine inches, with two hundred pages over all. There are seventeen songs composed by Carrell.[11]

These songs are uniformly dignified and decidedly above the average rural southern product in the matter of musical invention or, I might almost say, inspiration. The rest of the tunes conform to what the Preface promises, namely, that

[10] *Musical Million,* VI (1875), 71.

[11] They are Sussex, Anticipation, Dying Penitent, Majesty, Sharon, Evening Hymn, Complaint, Tribulation, Tender Thought, Lexington, Perseverance, Westbury, Staunton, The Pilgrim's Song, Intercession, Palestine, and New Year. The songs Lexington and Staunton are doubtless named after the composer's neighboring cities in the Valley.

"the compilers . . . have passed by many of the light airs to be found in several of the recent publications . . . and have confined themselves to the plain psalmody of the most eminent composers." This selectivity may be the reason for Carrell's using but two of the many songs made by his erstwhile collaborator, Ananias Davisson.

In the *Virginia Harmony's* "Rudiments," Carrell has explained unusually well the advantages of shape-notes. The four syllables, he tells us, must be learned if one is to sing by note. "It is therefore an irksome task, with most persons," he admits, "to acquire such a knowledge of the lines and spaces, through the various transpositions dependent on the signature, as to enable them to give each note its proper name. This difficulty has, however, been almost entirely obviated, by using four characteristic notes, whose shape at once determines their name, as well as their relative quantity: they are called *patent notes,* on account of their author's having obtained a patent for the invention. In these Rudiments Carrell also elucidates the fine art of beating time: In the first mood of common time," he explains, "we let the fingers of the right hand fall on the desk or table, or upon whatever you beat, while sounding the *first* note; for the *second,* bring down the wrist; for the *third,* raise the hand a little, at the same time moving it about three inches to the left; for the *fourth* bring the hand to its first position." For other types of even time he directs simply up and down with the hand. And for triple time, "omit the third motion used in the first mood of common time."

Songs by Carrell, appearing in many of the southern fasola books published during the decades following 1821, indicate a degree of recognition of the man in the rural musical field. In one of these subsequent books, Hauser's *Hesperian Harp*

JAMES P. CARRELL

Composer and song-book compiler of Lebanon, Virginia. From an oil painting in the Methodist Church in Lebanon.

(Georgia, 1848), I found a clue to Carrell's identity. Hauser included in his book a song entitled "Ebenezer" and gave as its composer "Rev. James P. Carrell of Lebanon, Va." A little searching in Lebanon yielded the following information.

Lebanon is a little quiet town about thirty miles to the northwest of Abingdon, Virginia, over the Clinch Mountain, and lying in one of those high Allegheny valleys of the "Mountain Empire." There "Uncle Jimmie" Carrell, as the oldest people there still remember him, was born February 13, 1787, and died October 28, 1854, according to court records and inscriptions on his gravestone in the "Old Cemetery" on a hilltop just outside the town.

According to dim oral tradition, as imparted to me by Mr. Walter Gray, who is a member of the far-flung Carrell connection, James Carrell's parents died when he was quite young, and he was adopted by a family named Gibson, in which there was (afterwards?) a young wife, Martha Gibson, who was only one year older than the adopted son, James. And it was this woman, James Carrell's foster-mother, whom, after she became a widow, young Carrell married. She died in 1872 and is buried at his side. There is no direct male-line descendant of this union. But Russell County, of which Lebanon is the county seat, is said to be full of his kinfolk, Grays, Gibsons, and others.

Carrell became a well-to-do and prominent man, if we may judge by the nature of the many court records pertaining to him. Those records (of bonds, deeds, and finally his will) begin in 1816 and end with his death. He was for a long time clerk of the county court. His will showed him to be, at the time of his death, a wealthy farmer and slaveholder. His attitude toward his slaves is indicated by the paragraph of his will which designated that his son Charles take "the control and management of my farm and slaves, treating the slaves with all the forbearance that circumstances may permit; and if any of them should become unmanageable, that they should be sold to some master that they may select, provided he will pay a fair price for them."

His ministerial activities seem to have come early, perhaps around the 1820's when his song books appeared. But that his enthusiasm for the Methodist cause was lifelong is indicated by a late-in-life gift of the land on which the Lebanon Methodist Church now stands and by the generous bequests, provided for in his will, to the Methodist Publishing House in Nashville and the Methodist Missionary Society.

I found no trace in Lebanon of Carrell's musical activities. They seem to have found no place along with the other Carrell traditions. Eight songs ascribed to him and appearing in subsequent books are "Solemn Thought" (*Hesperian Harp* and elsewhere), "Messiah" (*Sacred Harp* and elsewhere), "Melody" *(Supplement to The Kentucky Harmony),* "Mouldering Vine" (*Union Harmony* and elsewhere), "Patmos" (*Columbian Harmony* and elsewhere), "Sussex" *(Hesperian Harp),* "Ebenezer" *(Hesperian Harp),* and "Lebanon New" (*Sacred Harp* and elsewhere). The last named song may have been named for Carrell's home town.

CHAPTER IV

A MISSOURI BOOK, TWO IN KENTUCKY, ONE IN MIDDLE TENNESSEE

The Missouri Harmony

Before discussing still younger books from the Shenandoah Valley, I wish to speak of a few which sprang up in the meantime farther to the west and south.

Browsing through the private song-book collection of the late J. S. James of Atlanta, I came upon a copy of the *Missouri Harmony*. As to the nature and genesis of this book, Ernst Christopher Krohn gives us the information that, "Although Carden's *Missouri Harmony* was printed in Cincinnati, it was probably compiled in Missouri. The title reads: The Missouri Harmony, or a Choice Collection of Psalm Tunes, Hymns and Anthems, Selected from the Most Eminent Authors, and Well Adapted to all Christian Churches, Singing Schools, and Private Societies, Together with an Introduction to Grounds of Music and Plain Rules for Beginners. By Allen D. Carden, St. Louis. Published by the Compiler. Morgan, Lodge & Co., Cincinnati, 1820. [Boards, Oblong, 12mo., pp. 200].

"Carden may have prepared this work," Krohn goes on to say, "expressly for use in his 'School for teaching the theory and practice of Vocal Music' which he formally announced in the *Missouri Gazette* of May 31 and June 7, 1820. At any rate, the same issues of the *Missouri Gazette* contain an advertisement of 'Vocal Music Books. The Missouri Harmony, just published and for sale at the bookstore of Mr. Thomas (E)ssex.' This book must have been very useful, for editions are extant printed in 1827, 1835, 1838, and a revised one in 1850."[1]

The *American Supplement* of Grove's *Dictionary* gives merely the title, the compiler's name, and 1827 as its date, but on the following page of Grove there appears another *Missouri Harmony,* compiled by G. Warren and published in Cincinnati "probably before 1860."[2]

The copy I found in Georgia is very defective, but I was fortunate in finding subsequently a better one. Carl Sandburg put me on its track. He had made mention of the *Missouri Harmony* and had reproduced its title-page and four of its songs in his excellent *The American Songbag.*[3] The copy examined by Mr. Sandburg was, he told me, in the private library of Mr. Oliver R. Barrett of Chicago, and Mr. Barrett kindly lent it to me.

The Barrett book and the one I found in Georgia are evidently of the same edition. The first cover page shows "A Supplement" had been added to the book "containing a number of admired tunes of the various metres, and several choice pieces, selected from some of the most approved collections of sacred music. BY AN AMATEUR. Cincinnati, Printed and Published by Morgan and Sanxay. Stereotype Edition. 1836." It was copyrighted by Morgan and Sanxay in 1835. (See illustration opposite page 42.)

In his "Grounds of Music" Carden acknowledges that John Wyeth's *Repository* (1820) has furnished him with music-educational ideas. A perusal of the songs shows them to be much the same as those in Davisson's *Kentucky Harmony.* I find, indeed, five songs which Davisson claimed as his compositions, but there is no acknowledgment in the *Missouri*

[1] *A Century of Missouri Music* (Privately printed, St. Louis, 1924), p. 5.

[2] *American Supplement,* pp. 389, 390.

[3] Pp. 152 ff.

Harmony of the authorship of these songs, or of any others, for that matter. A few of the anthems are the only pieces which bear their composers' names. The *Missouri Harmony* was notated in the four shapes. Its songs are in three- and four-part harmony.

Krohn thinks that Carden's book was the very first song collection made in Missouri, and, according to Krohn's findings, the book seems to have functioned as one of the earliest documents in the musical life of the English-speaking elements in Missouri Territory. (The Territory became a state one year after Carden's book appeared.)

As to the popularity of the book I have the following scraps of information: J. S. James's *Brief History of the Sacred Harp* tells that the *Missouri Harmony* was used in Georgia in the 1830's and in the 1840's.[4] A correspondent to the *Musical Million* mentions that it was his only source of musical knowledge in Mississippi around 1840.[5] We read in Carl Sandburg's *The American Songbag* that "young Abraham Lincoln and his sweetheart, Ann Rutledge, sang from this book in the Rutledge tavern in New Salem according to old settlers there."[6] Sandburg's date of the *Missouri Harmony's* first edition, 1808, is apparently erroneous.

That Carden's personal musical activities were subsequently not confined to St. Louis is indicated by the *Western Harmony,* in the compilation of which, at Nashville, he seems to have had a leading part. An old-book store yielded me a copy of this otherwise unrecorded song book. Its title-page reads, "The Western Harmony, or the Learner's Task Made Easy: Containing a Plain and Easy Introduction to the Grounds of Music, and a Choice Collection of Tunes for Church

[4] (Douglasville, Ga., 1904), pp. 101, 133.
[5] Vol. XI (1880), p. 135.
[6] P. 152.

Service, Some of Them Entirely New, Suited to the Various Metres in Watts' Hymns and Psalms, & The Methodist & Baptist Hymn Books, to which is Added a Few of the Most Approved Anthems. Selected by A. D. Carden, S. J. Rogers, and J. Green.—Nashville: Published and Sold by Allen D. Carden and Samuel J. Rogers, and for sale at the Bookstores of Robertson and Elliott and Dr. Hayes, and in the Principal Towns in Tennessee, Kentucky and Alabama. Republican Office—Carey A. Harris, Printer, College Street, Nashville, 1824." (See illustration facing page 42.)

The book has twenty-four pages of "Rudiments" and one hundred and twenty-seven pages of song followed by a tune index. The songs are not especially noteworthy. About half of them were in the earlier *Missouri Harmony*. All are stock selections. Carden did not claim one of them. The straw-board cover stock, rough paper, printing and composition are what one might expect of a newspaper printshop in the then small town of Nashville. Was Carden at that time—four years after his St. Louis, Missouri, début—teaching singing schools in the Middle Tennessee district?

The Kentucky Harmonist

Samuel Lytler Metcalf, compiler of the *Kentucky Harmonist,* cannot be looked on as entirely separate from the Shenandoah Valley music teachers, song makers, and book publishers, for he was born near Winchester in that historic vale, September 21, 1798. "While he was yet young," Frank J. Metcalf tells us, "his parents moved to Shelby County, Kentucky, and he began his education in Shelbyville."[7] He was musical and he began teaching singing schools when a mere boy. When only nineteen years old he compiled the *Kentucky Harmonist* and had it printed in Cincinnati. From Frank J.

[7] *Op. cit.,* pp. 227 ff.

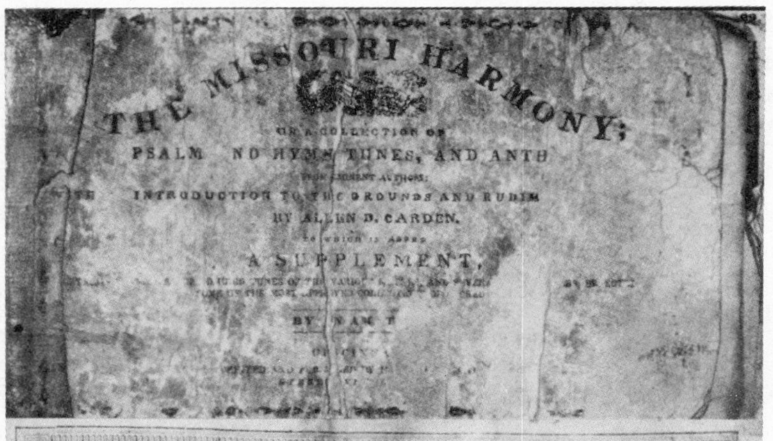

THE MISSOURI HARMONY;

OR A COLLECTION OF

PSALM AND HYMN TUNES, AND ANTH

INTRODUCTION TO THE GROUNDS AND RUDIM

BY ALLEN D. CARDEN.

TO WHICH IS ADDED

A SUPPLEMENT,

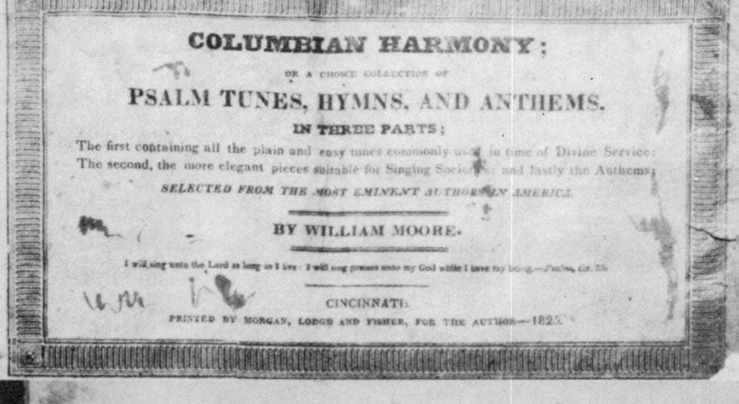

COLUMBIAN HARMONY;

OR A CHOICE COLLECTION OF

PSALM TUNES, HYMNS, AND ANTHEMS.

IN THREE PARTS;

The first containing all the plain and easy tunes commonly used in time of Divine Service: The second, the more elegant pieces suitable for Singing Societies: and lastly the Anthems;

SELECTED FROM THE MOST EMINENT AUTHORS IN AMERICA.

BY WILLIAM MOORE.

I will sing unto the Lord as long as I live: I will sing praises unto my God while I have my being.—Psalms, civ. 33.

CINCINNATI:

PRINTED BY MORGAN, LODGE AND FISHER, FOR THE AUTHOR—1825.

THE

WESTERN HARMONY,

OR,

THE LEARNER'S TASK MADE EASY:

CONTAINING

A PLAIN AND EASY INTRODUCTION TO THE GROUNDS OF MUSIC,

AND

A CHOICE COLLECTION OF TUNES FOR CHURCH SERVICE,

SOME OF THEM ENTIRELY NEW,

SUITED TO THE VARIOUS METRES IN WATTS' HYMNS & PSALMS, & THE METHODIST & BAPTIST HYMN BOOKS,

TO WHICH IS ADDED

A few of the most approved Anthems.

SELECTED BY

A. D. CARDEN, S. J. ROGERS, F. MOORE, AND J. GREEN.

NASHVILLE:

PUBLISHED AND SOLD BY ALLEN D. CARDEN AND SAMUEL J. ROGERS, AND FOR SALE AT THE BOOKSTORES OF ROBERTSON & ELLIOT AND DR. HAYES, AND IN THE PRINCIPAL TOWNS IN TENNESSEE, KENTUCKY AND ALABAMA.

REPUBLICAN OFFICE—CAREY A. HARRIS, PRINTER, COLLEGE STREET, NASHVILLE.

1824.

TWO TITLE-PAGES AND A COVER PAGE

Top: *Cover page of an undetermined edition of the* Missouri Harmony *by Allen D. Carden, St. Louis. Printed in Cincinnati.* Middle: *Title-page of William Moore's* Columbian Harmony, *Wilson County, Tennessee, 1820. Printed in Cincinnati.* Bottom: *Title-page of the* Western Harmony.

Metcalf's description of the boy's book, it was, from title to index, much the same in form and content as all the other books that we have described. It was "for the use of Christian churches, . . . singing schools and private societies," it had the usual Rudiments of Music, and it was a "choice selection of sacred music," etc.

A second edition is dated 1819, the year in which Samuel entered Transylvania University in Lexington; and when the fourth edition came out in 1826,[8] his name appeared in it with an M.D. following. Dr. Metcalf became quite prominent, published a number of worth-while books, pursued advanced work in medicine in London, and died at Cape May in 1856. And it was the humble work of teaching singing school and selling singing books that boosted him on his way to his accomplishments.

The Western Harmonic Companion

As to the *Western Harmonic Companion,* Chute records that it was compiled by James W. Palmer of Lexington, Kentucky, printed in Cincinnati in 1826, and had fifty-six pages.[9] In Grove's *Dictionary* it is called *Western Harmonia Companion* and the date of publication is placed as 1832.[10] Which is right?

The Columbian Harmony

Just as this book, *White Spirituals,* was about to go to the printer, a copy of the *Columbian Harmony* was laid in my hands by Miss Lucile Wilkin, of the Juilliard Foundation, who was then residing in Nashville. Grove does not include it, I have ascertained, in his list of American tune books. It is

[8] William E. Chute tells us in the *Musical Million,* VI (1875), 71, that this edition has 128 pages.

[9] *Ibid.*

[10] *American Supplement,* p. 389.

not mentioned in any of the hymnological articles in the *Musical Million*. And the Library of Congress has not heard of it. So all I can tell is what I get from my own yellowed but otherwise fairly well preserved 106-year-old copy.

The *Columbian Harmony* was compiled by William Moore, registered in the District of West Tennessee on April 2, 1825, and printed in Cincinnati by Morgan, Lodge and Fisher. A reproduction of its title-page will be found opposite page 42. It is a book five and a half by nine inches in size, containing seventeen pages of Introduction, Rudiments, etc., and one hundred and eighty pages of song.

The Introduction shows that Moore leaned heavily on Ananias Davisson. In it the Tennesseean declared that he had followed the Shenandoah musician "in laying aside several [musical] characters as useless, viz., the accidental sharp and flat, the natural, the hold, the staccato, the direct,[11] and the counter cleff." And, as to stating reasons for his exclusions, "Mr. Davisson has done it before me, and my own experience proves to me their inutility."

But Moore makes other Davisson adoptions, largely rhetorical ones, without acknowledgment. He insists, as did Davisson, on "the purity of my intentions" as a source of consolation if the public might not like his book. Both compilers "cherish a fond hope" that their books "will merit and obtain the approbation of an enlightened publick." Both strike a personal note to the effect that they are "gliding down the stream of time to the shades of night and although the path seems to be tinctured with the robes of mortality, yet I must confess it is full of pleasantness and peace." And when each

[11] The "direct" was a little wavy line, somewhat like an "m," placed at the end of a staff of music on the line or in the space where the first note of the *following* staff appears. It was intended to help the singer by "directing" his voice in the pitch direction of the coming note, even before his eye had time to jump to the following staff.

reflects "on the many delightful assemblies with whom I have been permitted to mingle my voice in singing the praises of the most high," he "cannot be sufficiently thankful." Moore also reproduces Davisson's directions for constructing a practical metronome.

Moore's "Rudiments of Music," eight pages of them, are practically identical with those of all other rural song books of his time. Following these Rudiments are four pages of "General Observations," which, again, are largely cribbed from his compiling compeers. They have to do with proper accent in singing, a genteel pronunciation, a becoming seriousness, a graceful manner of beating time, and a long list of don'ts. "Too sudden and nimble motions," should be avoided. "Nothing is more disgusting in singers than affected quirks and ostentatious parade, endeavoring to overpower other voices by the strength of their own, or officiously assisting other parts while theirs is silent. . . . Teachers should inculcate soft singing. . . . There should be no noise in the time of singing except the music alone. All whispering, laughing, talking, or strutting about the floor in time of school is ridiculous and should not be suffered. . . . Teachers should sing but a few tunes at a time, and continue to sing them until they are well understood. The parts should be exercised separately until each part could perform their own, before they should be permitted to join in concert. . . . In fuging music the part that leads should be sung soft, gently increasing as the rest of the parts fall in." And after two pages of proof of the divine source of sacred music and of its high mission in bettering the world, he subscribes himself, "William Moore, West Tennessee, Wilson County, March, 1825."

The songs of the *Columbian Harmony* are largely the same ones that we have found in the Carden and the Davisson collections. And they are arranged in the usual three sections, songs for "divine worship," for "concert or singing societies," and "anthems and odes of first eminence." With his anthems he gives "a few pieces never before published in patent [four-shape] notes."

Davisson, among southern tune makers, has been drawn on most often. Thirteen of the Virginian's songs are used. Carrell, also a Virginian, has furnished three. Moore himself claims authorship of eighteen songs in the collection.[12] His songs are of varying worth. Three of them, "Holy Manna," "Sweet Rivers," and "Converted Thief," received the indorsement of being rather widely adopted by subsequent compilers in the South. The *Sacred Harp,* for example, has all three of them. But while our William Moore suffered, in the editions of the 1830's and 1840's by being called "More," he was entirely ignored in the 1911 edition of the *Sacred Harp,* where his songs were attributed to one J. W. Moore, of Vermont. His songs, "Wilson" and "Lebanon," seem to have been named respectively for his home county and its county seat.

I have learned nothing further as to William Moore, the man.

[12] They are Solemnity (p. 37), The Sufferings of Christ (39), Jubal's Trump (109), Heavenly Prospect (108), Royal Proclamation (110), Evening Meditation (111), Harewell (113), Jackson (112), Salem (121), Lebanon (122), Holy Manna (122), Wilson (124), Wesley (130), Sweet Rivers (135), Converted Thief (147), Bethlehem (148), The Christian Soldier (149), and Montgomery (150).

CHAPTER V

VIRGINIA AGAIN; EAST TENNESSEE

A Later Compilation in the Valley of Virginia

For the next important book we shall have to go back to the Shenandoah Valley and to the village, Mountain Valley (near Harrisonburg), the home of Joseph Funk. Sixteen years after the appearance of the modest little German song book, *Choral-Music,* Funk brought out *Genuine Church Music,* a far different and infinitely better book, one which shows that its compiler had grown in mental and musical stature and that he now took the English language for granted as the medium of communication and of song, even in the Valley.

The size of the book is six by nine inches. The first twenty-four pages include the Preface—the best written, most dignified, cogent, and concise one in any of the southern books; "an elucidation of the science of vocal music," a novel part of which is a double-spread "table showing the nature and the use of transposition," that is, the construction of the scales in the different keys, with a page devoted to an explanation of the table; a page in defense of shape-notes, which Funk called "patent" or "character" notes; and a metrical index. The tunes cover one hundred and eighty pages and they are composed in three-part harmony, with two songs on each page, an arrangement which gave room for the insertion of a number of additional stanzas of text. So that, instead of the single stanzas found in the collections spoken of above, we have here usually four or five. The composers of the tunes are not given. But the book from which each is taken and the number of the particular tune in the source book are carefully given. These sources are given as Watts, Rippon, *Village Hymns, Assem. Coll., Christian Lyre,* John Newton, *Gems of Sacred Poetry,* and "H. M." As to the meaning of the abbreviated and initialed words, I have no information. I discuss some of the other sources on page 153, below.

The title gives the best description of the general character of the songs. They are really "genuine church music" of the old school. They are, as Funk declares in his Preface, those "which have stood the test of time and survived the changes of fashion," and practically nothing else. And while my examination of the book has not been thorough, still it would surprise me if a thorough examination revealed many tunes made on these American shores. Moreover, I should judge the collection as over the heads of the largely rural and untutored people to whom it was expected to appeal. And that is why its big sale, in many editions, is hard to explain.

By 1847 four editions had appeared. The first two were printed in Winchester, the third in Harrisonburg, and the fourth in Joseph Funk's own shop (see opposite page) in Mountain Valley. Solomon and Benjamin, two of Joseph's sons, did the printing, and Benjamin and Timothy, another son, bound the books.

The popularity of the book may be judged from the fact that the first four editions totaled 28,000 copies.[1] They were sold principally in the near-by territory of Virginia and what is now West Virginia,[2] but they found buyers to some

[1] I take these figures and much other information as to *Genuine Church Music* from Dr. John W. Wayland's monograph, "Joseph Funk, Father of Song of Northern Virginia," *loc. cit.*

[2] Wayland lists the following counties as sales territory of this book: Greenbriar, Randolph, Monroe, Preston, Boone, Bath, Upshur, Floyd, Mercer, King George, Harrison, Barbour, Lewis, Buckingham, Washington, Raleigh, Frederick, Fairfax, Botetourt, Appomatox, Louisa, and Pocahontas.

TWO MEMORABLE SPOTS IN THE SHENANDOAH VALLEY

LEFT: *The log loom-house, Singer's Glen, Rockingham County, Virginia, which became Joseph Funk's print shop and book bindery. Tens of thousands of* Genuine Church Music *books left this hut for singers in a dozen states.* RIGHT: *The clear, cold spring just around the corner of the loom-house. Its waters drew "the father of music in the Valley of Virginia" to this spot over a hundred years ago. Joe K. Ruebush, great-grandson of Joseph Funk, is sitting at the spring.*

UNION HARMONY

OR FAMILY MUSICIAN.

BEING

A CHOICE SELECTION OF TUNES;

SELECTED FROM THE WORKS OF THE MOST EMINENT AUTHORS,

ANCIENT AND MODERN

TOGETHER WITH A LARGE NUMBER OF ORIGINAL TUNES.

COMPOSED AND HARMONIZED BY THE AUTHOR, TO WHICH IS PREFIXED A COMPREHENSIVE VIEW OF

THE RUDIMENTS OF MUSIC,

ABRIDGED AND ADAPTED TO THE CAPACITY OF THE YOUNG.

BY WILLIAM CALDWELL.

PRINTED BY F. A. [illegible]

MARYVILLE, TEN.

1837.

THE KNOXVILLE HARMONY

OF MUSIC MADE EASY

WHICH IS AN INTERESTING SELECTION OF

HYMNS AND PSALMS,

USUALLY SUNG IN CHURCHES;

SELECTED FROM THE BEST AUTHORS NOW IN GENERAL USE.

ALSO

A VARIETY OF ANTHEMS,

TO WHICH IS ADDED

A NUMBER OF ORIGINAL TUNES,

BEING ENTIRELY NEW, AND WELL ADAPTED FOR THE USE OF SCHOOLS AND CHURCHES

COMPOSED BY JOHN B. JACKSON.

TOGETHER WITH A COMPLETE INTRODUCTION TO THE PROPER GROUNDS OF MUSIC,

AND RULES WELL EXPLAINED TO BEGINNERS.

D. & M. SHIELDS & CO. AND JOHN B. JACKSON, PROPRIETORS.

PRINTING & BOOKBINDING.

JOHNSTON & EDWARDS,

Respectfully informs the public, that they have removed their establishment from Madisonville, to Pumpkintown, on the head waters of Eastanallee, Monroe County, E. TEN.—Where they can execute BOOK & JOB PRINTING, neatly and with despatch.

THREE COVER PAGES

TOP: *William Caldwell's* Union Harmony, *Mayville, Tennessee, 1837.* MIDDLE: *John B. Jackson's* Knoxville Harmony, *Madisonville, Tennessee, 1838.* BOTTOM: *Fourth (back) cover page of the* Knoxville Harmony.

extent also in Georgia, Illinois, Ohio, Maryland, North Carolina, Indiana, Pennsylvania, Iowa, Missouri, and Canada. The states to the southwest (Tennessee, Kentucky, Alabama, Mississippi, etc.), did not use the Funk book to any extent, and there is no record of any substantial sales in Georgia. One might conclude from this that the influence of *Genuine Church Music* on those parts of the country that will have our special attention in the following pages, was negligible.

I shall discuss the subsequent editions of *Genuine Church Music,* which appeared under the changed title, *Harmonia Sacra,* in connection with the seven-shape books, on page 330, below, for with the new name came the new notation.

Caldwell's Union Harmony

The tendency to make homespun song books in the four-shape notation traveled down the mountain valleys fast. And the subsequent compilers leaned heavily on their predecessors. A shining example of this book-to-book relationship is found in William Caldwell's *Union Harmony,* printed by A. Parham in Maryville, Tennessee, in 1837, though registered in the district of East Tennessee in 1834. Maryville is a little town lying in the basin of the Tennessee River in the eastern part of the state and near the foothills of the Smoky Mountains, some four hundred and fifty miles to the southwest of the Shenandoah region whence the musical influences had flowed.

Of William Caldwell, the man, little is now known. In his Preface we find that he had been "a teacher [of singing schools] for fifteen years" when the *Union Harmony* came out. All my attempts to dig up further information in and around the town of Maryville have been fruitless.

I have two copies of the *Union Harmony or Family Musician.* One of these, somewhat defective, was obtained from Creed F. Casteel, an octogenarian singer in Knoxville. The other, a perfectly preserved copy, was lent me by W. S. Bandy, an aged Methodist circuit rider and singing-school teacher of Greeneville, Tennessee. It is six by nine inches and contains one hundred and fifty-one pages, of which the first twelve are given over to Preface, Rudiments, and General Observations on the art of singing. The Preface shows Caldwell's purpose in putting the book on the market. It was to supply "the different branches of the church of Christ in the Southern and Western country" with a book that would suit them all. Hence the name, *"Union" Harmony.*

His Rudiments show the orthography usual in those times. He speaks of the "stave" (still usual in England), the "trebble" part, the "cliff," and "treble" (triple) time. Among his note lengths are the "minum," "quiver," "semiquiver," and "demesiquiver." The "crochet rest" is shown by the symbol of a "santed stroke with a dash" called a "suttlon," also a "sutton."

One of the most significant aspects of the *Union Harmony* is its close relationship to Davisson's books and more especially to his *Kentucky Harmony.* This relationship is shown in a number of ways. In Caldwell's Rudiments he makes a direct reference to Davisson's views in the matter of harmony. And an examination of the tunes shows that sixty-three out of a total of one hundred and forty-five are lifted bodily from the *Kentucky Harmony.* This practically clinches the assumption of Caldwell's heavy leaning on the Harrisonburg musician. I said "practically," because the mere appearance of the same tunes in different books did not, in those "borrowing" times, prove anything conclusively. But here the *Kentucky Harmony* tunes amount—after we deduct the forty-two pieces claimed by Caldwell as his own compositions—to more than 60 per cent of the songs. And there is further internal evidence of direct wholesale borrowing from Davisson. Caldwell has named the composers of but eighty tunes besides his own, and out of these eighty, sixty-one are just those composers' names which Davisson's *Kentucky Harmony* Index shows affixed to just those tunes which Caldwell adopted. And in copying the composers' names Caldwell made two curious mistakes. He gave Morgan as the composer of the tune "America," where Davisson had this man as the composer of "Amanda," on the line above "America," in his *Kentucky Harmony* Index; and Caldwell gave Wyeth as the composer of "Liberty Hall," whereas Davisson gave Wyeth as the composer of "Liberty." That Caldwell had also the *Supplement to the Kentucky Harmony* at his elbow is indicated by his inclusion of "Emerald Gates" (Davisson) and "Morality" (White and Davisson) from that volume.

Considering the forty-two tunes to which Caldwell has affixed his own name as composer,[3] it would seem, offhand, that he was a prolific maker of tunes. But a statement of the compiler in his Preface modifies this assumption. He states there that "many of the tunes over which the name of the Subscriber [the undersigned, namely, Caldwell], is set are not entirely original, but he has harmonized, and therefore claims them." He states further that "many of the airs which the author has reduced to system and harmonized, have been selected from the unwritten music in general use in the Methodist Church, others from the Baptist and many more from the Presbyterian taste."

Students of folk-lore may therefore thank Caldwell for renouncing the task of tune making and for taking up that

[3] They are Amazing Grace, Bethesda, Canton, Concord, Erie, Fortitude, Frugality, Funeral Thought (on the death of an infant), Family Bible, Hopewell, Humility, Iantha, Imandra, Immensity, Intercession, Joyful Sound, Loving Kindness, Majesty, Malinda, Merit, Mount Carmel, New Hope, New Port, New Market, Redemption, Redeeming Love, Sharon, Solemn Thought, Star in the East, Sweet Prospect, Saint Paul, The Good Shepherd, The Pilgrim's Lot, The Shepherd's Joy, The Mariner, The Mouldering Vine, Tranquility, Union, Wakefield, Westford, Zion's Call.

of tune collecting. He probably recorded some tunes that had been notated, but of whose notated form he was ignorant. In fact, I have found four of the songs which he seems to have looked upon as "unwritten music" in older books and claimed by others. They are "Imandra" (by A. Davisson), "Redemption" (by R. Boyd), "Solemn Thought" (by Carrell and Davisson), and "The Mouldering Vine" (by Carrell); and all four are to be found in the *Supplement to the Kentucky Harmony*. But it is likely that many of the Caldwell tunes *were* "unwritten music" as he said, and that they represent his notion of how they actually sounded when sung by religious gatherings of those times without help or hindrance of notes. We may therefore look upon him as a recorder of religious folk-tunes from oral tradition, long before folk-tunes as such were identified in America as a specific musical form. And the folkish character of many of these recorded tunes is perfectly evident in their primitive five-tone modes and their melodic trend.

Names of Eastern Tennessee towns are found as the titles of Caldwell's songs: "Canton," "Newport," "New Hope," "Concord," "New Market," and "Erie."

The first cover page of the *Union Harmony* appears opposite page 49.

Jackson's Knoxville Harmony

A year later and not far from the home of the *Union Harmony* another book sprang up. It was the *Knoxville Harmony,* compiled (and in part composed) by John B. Jackson of Madisonville, Tennessee, printed by A. W. Elder of Madisonville, and copyrighted in 1838. The full title[4] is *The Knoxville Harmony of Music Made Easy,"* and the cover and the title-page show that to the hymns, psalms, anthems, etc.,

[4] According to a copy which I have borrowed from Joe R. James of Atlanta.

"are added a number of original tunes . . . composed by John B. Jackson." A second edition[5] came out two years later (1840) printed in Pumpkintown, "on the head waters of Eastanallee, Monroe County, E. Ten.," by Johnston and Edwards. (See cover pages reproduced opposite page 49.)

The book is five and a half by nine inches, pasteboard bound with cloth back. It has in all two hundred pages, seventeen of which are devoted to the regular Preface, with its apology for the shape-notes, and to the Rudiments. The rest is song.

Nothing is now known of Jackson, and perhaps that is as well, for he has added nothing new to the story of shape-note songs. There are, to be sure, a few songs that bear his name as composer, but they are uniformly worthless. In the first edition he claimed a dozen or more. But in the second printing this claim was wisely renounced, except in half a dozen cases. To songs other than his own he has added no composers' names. But I have found that he has leaned heavily on Caldwell and on Caldwell's main source, the *Kentucky Harmony*. Indeed, there are in the *Knoxville Harmony* seventy-five songs that are also in Caldwell's *Union Harmony,* including eight of Caldwell's own compositions. Jackson has not acknowledged his neighbor's authorship to any of these. One of them, "Star in the East," he actually claimed (in the first edition, but not in the second) as his own work. Fifty-four of the songs are identical with those which are found in Davisson's *Kentucky Harmony,* and forty-two *Knoxville Harmony* songs are in both the *Kentucky Harmony* and the *Union Harmony.* Thus the inter-relationship of the three books seems clear.

Even though Jackson, as man and composer, is negligible,

[5] A copy is to be seen in the Lawson McGhee Public Library in Knoxville, Tenn.

the collection of songs he has given us has a number of interesting features which shed additional light on the musical taste in East Tennessee a hundred years ago. One thing the people of that section seem to have liked was tunes of the five-tone-scale sort. I have found thirty-three tunes of this primitive melodic material in Jackson's book.[6] A favorite musical form that seems to have been in high favor there and then—even though it had been long since under the ban of the musical purists in the urban East—was the fuguing tune, for I find twenty-eight of them in the *Knoxville Harmony;* and I find them repeated in either the Davisson or the Caldwell book and usually in both. A third phase of popular taste is illustrated by Jackson's considerable number of popular secular tunes which appear with sacred words. At least a dozen of such melodies—from "Home, Sweet Home" to "Turkey in the Straw"—appear in the *Knoxville Harmony.* These popular tunes were evidently too good and too well known to remain the exclusive property of the sinful and to contribute solely to what these good books called "carnal mirth."[7]

[6] I have made further study of the five-tone tunes, as such, on pp. 160 ff below.

[7] More on the subject of secular tunes in the fasola books will be found on pp. 160 and 164 ff below.

CHAPTER VI

"SINGIN' BILLY" WALKER AND HIS "SOUTHERN HARMONY"

"Singin' Billy"

While the main path of the pioneers and pioneer music led down the valleys and through the gaps to the west of the Blue Ridge and Smoky Mountains, another trail led these Germans, English, and Celts (Irish, Scotch-Irish, Scotch, and Welsh) down along the eastern slopes of these ranges, into the mountains themselves and into the hilly out-runners of the Appalachians to the south. The pioneers settled all along the routes, anywhere where they could be to themselves on their little farms and apart from the Negro-employing big-plantation type of civilization. It is significant, perhaps, that the first rural shape-note singing and song-book-making activity which we hear of in those parts emanated from a Welshman who was born in South Carolina almost within sight of the Blue Ridge.

During the early decades of the nineteenth century there were three William Walkers in the little town of Spartanburg, South Carolina. One of them had a sort of porcine way-station behind his house, where droves of swine, on their way from the hinterland to the coast market, were over-nighted and fed. So he got the distinction, "Hog Billy Walker." Another William Walker was the son of this stockyard man, and he naturally received from his townsmen the sobriquet, "Pig Billy." The third was "Singin' Billy" Walker, in whom we are interested.

From the *History of Spartanburg County*[1] I quote the following:

"Professor William Walker, A. S. H., was born May 6th, 1809, on Tyger River and near the village of Cross Keys in Union County. He was of Welsh descent, his father emigrating from Wales in the eighteenth century. His mother was a Miss Jackson, granddaughter of Ralph Jackson, Esq., who was elected by the state legislature a justice of the quorum in Union District, S. C., only a few years after the close of the Revolution. It is said that she was a relative of General Stonewall Jackson, with whom Mr. [William] Walker during the Civil War became quite familiar. During his service as hospital nurse he visited the general quite frequently, from whom he learned his mother's kinship to the illustrious general.

"When [young William Walker was] about eighteen years of age, his parents, who were in straitened circumstances, migrated to Spartanburg district and settled in the neighborhood of Cedar Spring.

"The scholastic education of the son, the subject of this sketch, was of an elementary kind. He made good use of the advantages afforded him and in course of time gratified a large ambition which he had worthily imbibed to advance the psalmody of his church. He joined the Baptist church at a very early age, and amid the ebullitions of his early Christian piety and religious fervor he conceived the idea that to praise the Lord on string instruments, the psaltery and harp, as well as with the human voice, was not only a requisite, but a grand concomitant of religious worship.

[1] By J. B. O. Landrum, Atlanta, Ga., Franklin Printing and Publishing Co., 1900, pp. 491-95. An article that quotes largely from a story by T. O. P. Vernon, published shortly after William Walker's death in the *Musical Million* (Dayton, Va.), VII (1876), 1 ff.

"To perfect the vocal modes of praise became the leading ambition of his long, laborious and useful life. Determined, *at once* he resorted to pen and paper. From the deep minstrels of his own bosom he gathered and arranged into meter and melody a wonderful book suitably adapted to the praise and glory of God.

"He soon published a musical work entitled The Southern Harmony. This popular book comprised the shaped notes of that peculiar style of musical notation which contradistinguishes the same from the more current literature of the present age.

"Notwithstanding some depreciation by the press, he adhered to his original system, and his reputation for attainments in his science soon spread all through the South and Southwest. Everywhere his popularity as a music teacher went and his work received a most popular indorsement.

"To distinguish him from others of the same name he was known as William Walker, A. S. H., author Southern Harmony.

"Scarcely a hamlet, scarcely a church in the wooded coverts of those several sections, have not been made to reverberate the praises of God in accordance with the metrical spirit of that system which he originated. [Walker originated, as a matter of fact, none of the note shapes used in *Southern Harmony* and but three of the seven used in his post-Civil-War books. See samples of notation forms on page 337.] The Southern Harmony and his name, the name of the distinguished author, are as familiar as household duties in the habitations of the South.

"Mr. Walker, not content with his first publication, determined to prepare and publish a more elaborate and thoroughly revised musical work, which he did under the title of the

'Christian Harmony.' This book has met with a like popular currency, and the two conjointly have given him a most enviable reputation as author, vocalist and teacher. Everywhere within the limitations of the South and West he organized 'singing schools,' as they were popularly denominated, and in each prepared, qualified and commissioned *in persona* many of the brightest of his pupils as instructors in the department of music.

"He was author and co-publisher with the Miller Publishing House of Philadelphia, Pa., in publishing his musical works, and he realized a large sum from the sale of his books throughout the country.

"Mr. Walker was devoted to the service of a religious and pious life from early youth, and steadfastly held to it during his sojourn here on earth. . . . He possessed in an eminent degree a happy disposition, an elastic feeling that all would be well in the end, and would never suffer his buoyancy of mind and heart to yield to any gloomy foreboding whatever might befall him. He quoted his great Psalmist: 'That the righteous would never be forsaken nor his seed begging bread.' He was possessed of a mind of a literary turn, and had a large and valuable library, and having been engaged for some years in the introduction and sale of books in the town of Spartanburg, he became possessed of many rare and valuable books of general interest.

"He was a man of quite liberal views, and was every ready with his means and influence to advance the cause of any enterprise which seemed to be a public benefit.

"At the age of about twenty-four years Mr. Walker married Miss Amy Golightly[2] and settled near Spartanburg. His

[2] That the Walkers, Golightlys, and Whites (see my chapter on B. F. White's *Sacred Harp,* p. 81 below) were early comers into the Spartanburg section is testified by the court records of Spartanburg County beginning 1785 and by the U. S.

WILLIAM WALKER, "A. S. H."

The initials mean "Author of Southern Harmony." "Singin' Billy's" tuning fork, after over a hundred years of "keying" tunes, is still in use in rural singing schools and conventions.

marriage was a happy one, their tastes being congenial and their dispositions naturally equable and uniform. By this marriage ten children were born, five sons and five daughters, nine of whom survived him."[3]

The stories of William Walker's deathbed are various. "It is said," Landrum declares, "that Mr. Walker died, as it were, 'with melodies on his tongue for the goodness and tender mercies of God.'" But his granddaughter, Gaetana (Mrs. T. W.) Jackson, told me that her grandfather could not even speak for some time before his death. She declared that about half an hour before the end came, he wrote with his finger on the palm of his other hand "R-e-a-d-y." A Mr. Brown, an old resident of Spartanburg, told me that he was at the deathbed of William Walker, saw him look at the clock and heard him say, "At three o'clock I'll be in heaven." And Mr. Brown assured me that the old singer died at that time to the minute.

The stories of Walker's funeral are also interesting because tinged with that variability which attends progressive traditional accretion. Mrs. W. B. Montgomery of Spartanburg was at Walker's funeral, of which she told me the following incident: "Directly the body was brought in, a bird, pure white, perhaps a pigeon, lighted on the floor near the coffin. It was driven into a little room and the door was shut. After the prayer when heads were raised, the bird was back again, on the pulpit by the Bible." Mrs. Gaetana Jack-

Census of 1790. See J. B. O. Landrum, *Colonial and Revolutionary History of Upper South Carolina,* Greenville, S. C., Shannon & Co., 1897. The Spartanburg telephone directory of 1930 testifies that these families have remained prolific.

[3] These nine children were, according to Landrum, Joseph D., Absalom, Miles T., Franklin Boyd, Mrs. J. B. Davies, Mrs. Emma Logan, Mrs. Lou Lynch, Mrs. Flora Justice, and Miss Mary Walker. All are now (1930) dead. Absalom died quite recently in Arlington, Texas, I was told by Mrs. Gaetana Jackson, daughter of Mrs. Emma Logan, living in Forest City, N. C. Miles and Joseph taught music and all the girls sang, Mrs. Jackson told me.

son, the then sixteen-year-old granddaughter of the deceased, was at the funeral and saw nothing of the bird incident, as she recently told me.

The significance of William's Walker's personality is indicated by the I-used-to-know-him pride of many. L. P. Epton (Spartanburg) heard Walker say "I would rather have A. S. H. after my name than P-R-E-S." Epton's father and Walker were "near friends." E. W. Miller, the Philadelphia publisher of *Southern Harmony,* has handed down to his grandson, William C. Wetherill, the information that he "used to travel with him [Walker] to open classes in singing, visiting many southern towns," and told of "the tremendous energy of William Walker in leading classes, these classes being left in charge of local leaders whom he taught, all with the idea of selling *Southern Harmony* and later the *Christian Harmony.*" James G. Douthit, a contemporary of Walker and a singing teacher of prominence, tells of Walker's being "a large and corpulent man of fine physique" right after the Civil War when Douthit, Walker, and J. G. McCurry worked together in Franklin County, Georgia. When Douthit last saw Walker he was thin and bent and Walker's wife later told Douthit that her husband had died of consumption.[4] W. S. Bandy, a venerable singing-school teacher and "Old Harp Singer" of Greeneville, Tennessee, writes me: "My father (H. Q. Bandy, Catawba County, N. C.), was a student and assistant of William Walker."

The proud possessor of William Walker's tuning fork is A. B. Pearson, a song leader living near Woodruff, South Carolina. Mr. Pearson told me that Walker, when he was finishing his career in music, gave the fork to one of his favorite pupils, Mr. Calvin Wall, who used it in leading singing schools. At the death of Mr. Wall the fork fell into the

[4] *Musical Million,* XXIV (1893), 53.

hands of Mrs. A. P. Golden of Spartanburg who, having no use for it, gave it to "Professor" A. M. Golden, her husband's brother, who used it for many years in his professional singing-school work over a large territory. In 1926 when Mr. Golden —who was then living in Kentucky—visited Woodruff, South Carolina, he presented it to Mr. Pearson, an active teacher of rural singing schools; and the latter intends, at the end of his musical activity to pass it on into still other hands who will continue its usefulness. The fork, pictured opposite page 58, has already been used by four generations of active teachers throughout probably more than a hundred years and has helped to "key" the sacred tunes for uncounted thousands of country singers.

THE SOUTHERN HARMONY

The full title of Walker's notable book, the *Southern Harmony,* may be read from the illustration facing page 90, which shows the book's first cover page. The editions came out, as far as I have been able to learn, as follows:

1835: xxxii and 216 pages, c. 1835 in the district court of the Connecticut district, printed by Nathan Whiting, New Haven. A copy is in the Kennedy Free Library, Spartanburg, South Carolina. It was presented to the library in 1885 by Mrs. William Walker.

——: xxxii and 232 pages. I have the last hundred pages of this edition. Judged by its number of pages, 264 in all, it must have been issued sometime between the 1835 (248-page) and the 1847 (304-page) editions. On the fourth cover page is "Edward W. Miller, Principal Agent, 11 George St., Philadelphia, Pa."

1847: xxxii and 232 pages, may be another printing which is essentially identical with the above edition. I have a very defective copy of it. It is printed by Thomas Cowperthwaite & Co., Philadelphia, Pennsylvania.

1849: xxxii and 304 pages; Preface, dated 1847, tells of its enlargement over the previous edition by "about forty pages." When then did the "previous edition of around three hundred pages appear? I have a very defective copy of this edition. Printed by Thomas Cowperthwaite & Co., Philadelphia.

1854: xxxii and 236 pages, "new edition, thoroughly revised and much enlarged." Published by E. W. Miller, 1102 and 1104 Sansom St., Philadelphia. A good copy is in the Kennedy Library, Spartanburg, South Carolina. It was presented to the library by Mrs. William Walker.

Of the two hundred and nine pieces of music in the first edition, Walker's name (a few times in conjunction with that of some other) stands at the right upper corner as the composer of twenty-five. By the time of the 1854 edition he had eliminated two of those earlier songs of his and added seventeen more, making a total in this edition of forty bearing his name. Of the remaining pieces, the texts of many were borrowed from *Mercer's Cluster* (a book of hymn poems without music), *Baptist Harmony, Dover Selection, Methodist Hymn Book,* and from individual composers where no tune book is mentioned; a large number bear no indications as to source.

Writers of words are mentioned in but few cases. In the first edition the influence of other southern song books is not felt in the way of song borrowings. Ananias Davisson's *Kentucky Harmony* is an exception. In the 1854 edition, however, we find the *Sacred Harp* compilers, B. F. White and E. J. King, represented by one song each; and Leonard P. Breedlove, a Georgia contributor to the *Sacred Harp,* has three songs in this edition. That Walker was on good terms with the Georgian, William Hauser, author of the *Hesperian Harp*

(1848), is shown by his using, in this 1854 edition, two songs composed by Hauser, one arranged by him, and four to which Hauser had added a treble. The larger number of the *Southern Harmony* songs are in three-part harmony.

Walker claimed, in the Preface to his *Christian Harmony,* a song book that came out shortly after the Civil War,[5] to have sold up to that time 600,000 copies of the *Southern Harmony.* But despite this indication of its great popularity for a third of a century, it would be reasonable to suppose—in view of Walker's having then transferred his enthusiasm to the subsequent *Christian Harmony* and bearing in mind the blighting effect of the conflict between North and South on the pre-war sort of song and the fact that no edition of the *Southern Harmony* came out after 1854—that the venerable book had gradually fallen into disuse and had disappeared long since. This was at least my assumption up to the spring of 1931 when the present volume was about to go to the publishers. But at that time my information as to the fate of the *Southern Harmony* was increased as the result of a singular accident.

Intending to show the readers of this book what the *Southern Harmony* looked like, even though they might never hope to see a copy of it or to hear its songs sung, I took the Spartanburg Library's copy to a Nashville photographer, George Douglas. As I was explaining to him the rarity and importance of the old book and the kind of photographic reproduction I wanted, it became evident to me that the cameraman's thoughts were far away, that they were occupied with something he was about to reveal.

"Do you know," he at length asked me, "that that book is

[5] The *Christian Harmony,* being a seven-shape book, will be spoken of in its appropriate place on pp. 331 ff below.

not dead? I can lead you to a *Southern Harmony* singing this spring." And he did.

A Southern Harmony Singing

Armed with a camera and all my William Walker impedimenta, Mr. Douglas and I set out a few weeks later for Benton, a small county seat in western Kentucky where my companion had grown up and where, he told me, the yearly *Southern Harmony* singing had been going on, the fourth Sunday in every May, since long before he was born.

As we approached the place by motor, early on Sunday morning, everybody in the countryside seemed to be going our way, in autos, buggies, springless farm wagons, and on foot. The town was already crowded with visitors when we arrived at ten o'clock. Ropes kept the entire courthouse square free from vehicles and reserved it for the thousands of men, women, young folk, and children who covered the shady spaces under the trees surrounding the county building and the streets and sidewalks adjoining. A half dozen barrels of drinking water were placed here and there. An itinerant preacher was shouting at and entertaining highly one section of the crowd grouped around him, as he darted about in the manner of the Italian bandmaster of the one-time popular "athletic" type. Another group of a hundred or more was being entertained by a blind man singing religious ballads, strumming his own accompaniment on a guitar and playing interludes between stanzas on a mouth-harp that was held in playing position by a wire contraption around his neck, leaving his hands free for the guitar playing. The country girls in their gayest colors, shortest skirts, and tightest shoes were strolling around in twos and threes to the natural delectation of the sun-tanned swains. Old men and women were indulging in impromptu reunions and discussions of old times and new crops. The strains of choral singing came down faintly from the open court-room windows on the second floor. It was a big day in Benton.

Wedging our way into the court-room we found ourselves in the presence of thirty to forty singers occupying the space behind the chancel rail and as many listeners as could find seats or standing space in the court-room proper. The singers were old and very old men and women, and the tattered books from which they sang were, I saw at once, the old *Southern Harmony* that I had thought dead and gone. Some sang without books.

In talking with the listeners I found that a few of them were interested, as I was, in the event as a unique survival in cultural tradition, in listening to musical "antiques" as one of them called the songs. Most of the people, however, listened with a rapt expression which told me they were not thinking at all of any historical significance. To them it was just sweet music, "old-time singing" for which they had the same reverence and love as for its close kin, the "old-time religion," and for which the more recent makers of religious songs had brought them no satisfying substitute. It was this serious significance of the occasion, as it seemed, however much the out-door part of it might have reminded one of circus day, which put it beyond the criticism of the Lord's Day observationists and into the class of religious celebrations.

An elderly man with handle-bar moustache was leading in the most approved manner, holding his book in the left hand and beating time, down, left, right, up, with his right. And when the page of music called for a pause in the singing, he filled it out dutifully with his beats, calling them out audibly, "down, left." The singers first went through the song singing the notes, that is, the syllables *fa, sol, la,* and *mi.* If the leader was familiar with more stanzas than appeared in the book, he lined them out.

The response of the singers seemed to me pathetically weak, as I contrasted it to the vocal volume I had heard many times at *Sacred Harp* conventions and seven-shape gatherings farther south. (These will be described in appropriate environment below.) And they took the songs at a slow, draggy pace which reminded one strikingly of the primitive singing in some of the country churches of the Afro-Americans. The voices of the old singers were thin. Leaders were few. The memory of those singers who had no books was noticeably waning. The man, younger than the average, who shared my book and sang lustily, had lost his *Southern Harmony* when his house burned some time before. Some of the favorite songs were, "How tedious and tasteless the hours," "Salvation, Oh the joyful sound," "Oh, when shall I see Jesus and reign with Him above."

Because of the crowd which had come for the big holiday, the ancient institution of a general picnic "dinner on the grounds" to which all were to contribute and of which all were to partake, was out of the question. So at twelve the great throng left the court-room, gathered in little and larger groups in public eating places, in private homes, and on the grass under the trees, and opened their baskets.

It was during this period that I met Mr. George W. Lemon, who, with his brother, James Roberts Lemon, had started these Benton singings in 1884, and I heard from him about those early times. The Lemon brothers were little children in 1852 when their parents made the six-hundred-mile trek by covered wagon all the way from Guilford County, North Carolina, across the Blue Ridge, the Smoky, and the Cumberland Mountains to Marshall County in the western wedge of Kentucky. A copy of the *Southern Harmony,* widely

SOUTHERN HARMONY SINGING AT BENTON, KENTUCKY

The author of this book keys "Bound for Canaan" with William Walker's tuning fork and then leads the singing from a Southern Harmony *that was once Walker's private copy.*

VIEWS AT THE BENTON, KENTUCKY, SOUTHERN HARMONY SINGING

Top: *People assemble for the singing, May 24, 1931.* **Middle:** *In the courthouse square.* **Bottom:** *A blind singer of ballads, perpetuating a hoary tradition in folklore, draws his share of the crowds outside the singing hall.*

used at that time in the Old North State, must have been tucked away somewhere in that prairie schooner. Anyway, young James Lemon used the Walker book later in "literary" schools and in singing schools which he taught, and when he and his brother George started the Benton singings it became the official song collection. The meager dozen copies of the William Walker book which the singers found at the start grew to a score as interest increased and as the singers inquired for further copies in the adjoining counties; until now the number of the precious volumes (last printed in 1854) in use at the Benton singings is about thirty, Mr. Lemon told me. Every year since 1884 the *Southern Harmony* singings have been held on the same day, the fourth Sunday in May, and always, excepting for a few times in the earlier decades, in the courthouse at Benton. James Lemon died about ten years ago. George W. Lemon, James K. Fields, and "Uncle Bud" Hunt are now the leading spirits in the continuation of the musical tradition.

The singers and listeners showed deep interest when I told them the story of William Walker's life and activities, and they responded with their best efforts when I led "Bound for Canaan," singing from a book that had been Walker's own copy and keying the song with Walker's own tuning fork, which its owner had lent me for the occasion. Afterwards a number of them wanted to examine the fork and listen to the clear "C" which had keyed unnumbered songs during the past century.

"Now I can say that I have held William Walker's tuning fork in my hand!" one old man exclaimed exultingly.

The Passing of Southern Harmony Singings

The *Southern Harmony* singings at Benton are probably the last of their kind anywhere and dissolution stares them in the face. The only thing that can lengthen their life is a new supply of the song books with which the tradition is inseparably bound up. Will some worshiper at the shrine of "old-time songs" provide that supply? I heard rumors in Benton that one of the faithful was about to undertake that labor of love.

A still more advanced stage of *Southern Harmony* disintegration is seen across the Ohio River from Benton. In answer to my inquiry Rev. T. Leo Dodd, "Old-Baptist" preacher of Eldorado, Illinois, wrote: "There is no church to my knowledge in southern Illinois which now uses the *Southern Harmony* book. However, there are singing conventions held irregularly in which that book is used. Twenty years ago these conventions were more common than now. They were held at two churches, Wolf Creek and Friendship, near Eldorado, and at Cottonwood near Ridgewood, Ill. The old singers are about all gone now." But W. F. Pinnell, one of those old singers, pathetically hopeful, wrote me: "They are Crying for New Southern Harmoneys to be adopted and Teachers apointed to teach in Each [Old-Baptist] Church throughout the United States. It can Be done."

A. D. Hancock of Eldorado wrote me: "I learn that it [*Southern Harmony*] was compiled by the Methodist of the South and later our people [Old-Baptist] adopted it that is the regular Predestinarian Baptist on the account that we consider that there is more Christ in the Hymns of that Book than there is in all others together and then the music appeals to our feelings more than any other . . . maby we could find anywhere from 16 to 20 books in our community and up to three years ago we would have an all day singing and basket dinner but that has played out . . . my father bought a Southern Harmony Book when I was a verry small Boy and he attend a singing school at Farmersville in Posey County . . . but of course I did not pay any attention to the book until I was about twenty years of age when I joined the Church and they started me off as a Leader of the singing then I began to realize the need of the knowledge of music so I began to study Southern Harmony music . . . there is a lot of miner music in the Southern Harmony and it suits my voice the best but I can sing either major or minor . . . now I lead the singing at nearly all of our Associations or big gatherings that I can attend . . . as to the use of the Southern Harmony in conventions . . . it has been three or four years since we had a singing and I do not know whether we will ever have another one or not we talk about it but we neglect it we have talked of getting up a class and singing over radio but we neglect that but I know it would be the most new thing on the air and the most interesting thing that could go over the air by man."

William S. Nash, of Poseyville, Indiana, tells me that the *Southern Harmony's* "are pretty near a thing of the past in Southern Indiana. I use to sing in them when I was a boy but not for a long time. We have a lot of the [*Southern Harmony*] songs in our [Old-Baptist] church books." I shall speak of these songs surviving among the Old Baptists on page 312 below.

CHAPTER VII

TWO GEORGIANS AND THEIR WORK

If we were to proceed in the discussion of the fasola song books strictly according to the years of their first appearance, the story of the unique *Sacred Harp* would be our concern at this juncture. But since that story will stretch out to include activities of the present time, activities important out of all comparison with the present-day vestiges of *Southern Harmony* singing, the cause of chronological sequence will be better served if we speak first of two subsequent but shorter-lived collections, the *Hesperian Harp* and the *Social Harp*.

"Rev. William Hauser, M.D."

For versatility and education, William Hauser, author of the *Hesperian Harp* and the *Olive Leaf* song books, holds the record in shape-note circles. He was a doctor, preacher, editor, teacher, composer, and singer. From an article in the *Musical Million*[1] on the life of Hauser, written by William E. Chute, musicologist and co-laborer with Hauser, and published, a few months after the death of the *Hesperian Harp* author, I glean the following:

"Rev. William Hauser, M.D., son of Rev. Martin Hauser, second junior, was born near Bethania, Forsyth County, North Carolina, December 23, 1812, and was the youngest son of eleven children. His father died when he was but two years old, and his mother was able to give him only education enough to read, not 'read, write and cipher,' which was considered the acme of good education in those days. But his

[1] XII (1881), 65.

thirst for knowledge caused him to persevere in his studies, and by his own exertion he succeeded in acquiring a thorough knowledge of the English, Latin, and Greek languages and not a little of the German. Dr. Hauser joined the Methodist church in 1827. In 1834 he was licensed to preach, and traveled a circuit for two years. Subsequently and up to the time of his death, he was a local preacher in the Methodist church, preaching, praying, and singing wherever he went."[2]

William Hauser's wife was Eliza M. Renshaw of Rowan County, North Carolina. They were married in 1837, and in October, 1839, they moved to Emory and Henry College, Virginia, where he was to study Greek and Latin. In 1841 Dr. Hauser, with his wife and one child, moved from Marion, Virginia, to Richmond County, Georgia, where he taught school. "That year he began the study of medicine under Dr. Samuel B. Clark, began its practice in Burke County, Georgia, in 1843, and took rank, ultimately, among the foremost in the medical profession in his state. In 1859-1860 he was professor of physiology and pathology in the Oglethorpe Medical College, Savannah, Georgia.

"For several years he was assistant editor of the Georgia "Blister and Critic" and the Oglethorpe Medical Journal. In addition to his medical profession he was a musician. In

[2] Of his ancestry, Chute has the following to say: "Dr. Hauser was of Moravian stock." (Forsyth County, North Carolina, of which Winston-Salem is the county seat, was and is still a notable center for the Moravians, a sect, incidentally, that is unusually zealous in fostering music.) "His great-grandfather, Martin Hauser, was born in Momplegard, Switzerland [now Montbeliard, France], in the year 1695, and emigrated to North Carolina under the leadership of Count Zinzendorf, about the year 1750, and settled near Bethania, North Carolina. Martin had seven sons and three daughters. . . . The sons were combatants in the Revolutionary War. . . . Of the seven, one was Martin, Jr., whose son, Martin, second Jr., was the father of William, the subject of this sketch." William's father was a Methodist minister. "His mother was the daughter of an English Quaker, Edward Billiter. She was born on the eastern shore of Maryland, and her father emigrated to North Carolina during the Revolutionary War to escape the troubles and trials incident to that struggle. There she married Martin Hauser and became the mother of the subject of this sketch."—*Ibid.*

1848 he published in Philadelphia the Hesperian Harp, a patent-note [four-shape] song book that had an immense sale. Thirty years after, in 1878, he published his second work, The Olive Leaf, in Aikin's seven-shaped notes. It contains many of the old tunes of fifty years ago as well as a great many new ones.

"In February, 1846, he removed to Wadley, Jefferson County, Georgia, where he continued to reside until his death.

"He was a man of earnest zeal in everything he undertook. When in active medical practice he made it a rule, no matter how sick the patient was, to kneel by the bedside and ask God's blessing on the sick one before administering a dose of medicine. For several years prior to his death he practiced medicine very little, devoting his time principally to music teaching, in which he was eminently successful. Overwork of brain and body, coupled with declining years, prostrated him in July, 1880, and after an illness of over two months he died Sep. 15, 1880. Before he breathed his last he said to his family, 'I feel that my work on earth is done, and there is not a cloud between me and God.' His body sleeps in the family burying ground near his residence not far from Wadley. He left a widow, a daughter and two sons."[3]

The Hesperian Harp

William Hauser's book, the *Hesperian Harp,* came out in 1848 and it had the name of being the largest and most comprehensive song collection that had, up to that time, appeared in America. The copy in my hands has no covers and the title-page and Preface are gone. So I am unable to give the name of its Philadelphia printer. Its size is six and one-fourth by ten inches, and an inch and a quarter thick.

It opens with the conventional Rudiments, twenty-nine

[3] *Ibid.*

pages of them, and one page of explanations of musical terms. Then follow 552 (!) pages of music with texts that are predominatingly sacred, though a goodly number of dignified secular pieces, like the "Last Rose of Summer," and patriotic songs are mixed in.

Thirty-six of the songs are composed by Hauser himself.[4] And he arranged, "rearranged," and wrote parts for numerous others, and "southernized" one. The standard northern and foreign tune makers of earlier times contributed probably the majority of the pieces in this book. But Hauser found scores of his songs among the compositions of his contemporary and earlier southern colleagues. He has, for example, fourteen songs that are attributed to Ananias Davisson,[5] nine by William Walker,[6] and four by William Caldwell.[7] E. J. King, co-author of the *Sacred Harp,* has furnished Hauser with three of his compositions.[8] E. K. Davis, Cedar Bluff, Alabama, has

[4] Carvosso (p. 31), Haines (34), Third Creek (39), Calhoun (68), Markham (70), Wilson (79), Gaines (122), Thorn (123), Alton (144), Sweet Home (149), Masonic Dirge (155), Burdened Pilgrim (162), Golgotha (164), Holly Springs (174), Floyd (176), Alabama (181), Campbell (181), Concordia (186), Mocksville (208), Backslider's Sorrow (209), Wheeling (210), Texas (216), Rock of Salvation (239), Young Ladies' Farewell (261), The Gospel Among the Indians (281), Isles of the South (284), Indiana (304), Sweet Gliding Kedron (305), The Wanderer (308), Collins (323), The Landscape (348), Gethsemane (351), Hope Hull (363), Flower of Calvary (369), Break of Day (427), and Afflicted Zion (546).

[5] Those which are found also in the *Kentucky Harmony* are: Solemnity (p. 6), Tender Thought (11), Glasgow (17), Immensity (32), Solitude in the Grove (166), Tribulation (55), Golden Hill (211), and Zion's Hill (228). Those from the *Supplement to the Kentucky Harmony* are Davisson's Retirement (13), The Humble Penitent (16), Concert (by Weyth and Davisson (198), Solemn Thought (by Carrell and Davisson, 225), Imandra (316) and Emerald Gates (338).

[6] They are Watchman's Call (38), Parting Hand (47), Mutual Love (50), Hallelujah (102), Heavenly March (192), Saints Bound for Heaven (by J. King and Wm. Walker, 219), Thorny Desert (235), Harrison (by Walker and Hauser, 301), and Christian's Hope (354).

[7] They are Newport (115), Iantha (227), Zion's Call (321) and Caldwell's Funeral Thought (372). All are found in Caldwell's *Union Harmony* (see p. 49, above).

[8] Pp. 256, 362, and 517. It is probable that E. J. King's brother, Rev. Jonas (Joel?) King is the father of the tunes on pp. 48, 219, and 220.

three songs[9] and his brother, B. F. Davis, has one. Ten of the *Hesperian Harp* song texts were taken from *Mercer's Cluster*.[10]

One of Hauser's greatest services to music resulted from his habit of catching up melodies from the singing of individuals and recording them. Examples of folk melodies rescued thus are on pages 70 and 94, and there are a number of others. Hauser's own tunes, those which he recorded from others' singing and many of those which he adopted from others' books are, to a surprising extent, of the five-tone-scale sort. I have found thirty-three melodies of this type,[11] and I am sure that there are others.

John G. McCurry

Aldine Kieffer wrote and published, in his Dayton, Virginia, *Musical Million* of 1883,[12] an editorial about the *Social Harp,* a four-shape song book compiled and in part composed by John G. McCurry of Hart County, Georgia, and published in 1859. The copy of the song book which had just fallen into the shape-note champion's hands led him to tell the *Million* readers something of the interesting old compilation of camp-meeting and revival songs and of its maker. For Kieffer had visited McCurry in the latter's northeastern Georgia home but a few months before. The information given in this editorial was all I had as to the *Social Harp* until Will H. Ruebush of the Ruebush-Kieffer musical publishing firm of Dayton, Virginia, lent me a copy of the book—the only one, incidentally, that I have been able to locate; and it was

[9] Pp. 51, 94, and 182. B. F. Davis's song is 258.

[10] They are Williams (143), Washington (156), Christian Travellers (185), Evening Shade (199), Wondrous Love (234), Mixture (240), Blairsville (243), War Department (277), Be Gone, Unbelief (303), and Miss Hataway's Experience (421).

[11] Pp. 8, 29, 39, 40, 41, 42, 44, 47, 70, 79, 82, 84, 94, 101, 102, 111, 123, 128, 143, 144, 152, 153, 160, 181, 216, 217, 262, 301, 310, 323, 357, 362, and 441.

[12] XIV, 70.

WILLIAM HAUSER OF GEORGIA

Doctor, preacher, editor, teacher, composer, singer, and compiler of the Hesperian Harp, *the rural South's biggest and best song book.*

JOHN GORDON McCURRY

The author of the Social Harp *and his home at Bio, Hart County, Georgia.*

all I knew of McCurry until I made a visit to Hart County, Georgia, in the spring of 1931.

Hart County is on the eastern edge of the state and on the Savannah River about a hundred miles northeast of Atlanta. It is a stretch of hilly cotton fields tilled largely by whites. Hartwell, the county seat, has about two thousand souls. It is reached now by one good highway and is the terminus of one very primitive spur track of the Seaboard Air Line.

The search for McCurrys was not hard. I learned, immediately upon my arrival, that the name was well known and highly esteemed in those parts and that nearly everybody was "some sort of kin" to the old family. So it was easy, after a day or so of inquiry among these relatives, and in conference with J. W. Baker, Hart County's historian, to piece together the following story:

In the latter part of the eighteenth century a group of Scotch-Irishmen and their families—Johnsons, Gordons, McDonalds, and McCurrys—came from North Carolina to what is now Hart County. They camped together, in the present McCurry district to the south of Hartwell, for mutual protection against the very hostile Indians, while the menfolk built their houses. Among these pioneers was Angus McCurry. It was in 1799 that his son, John McCurry, married Susan McCurry (a relative it seems). John became a soldier of the War of 1812. The seventh child of John and Susan, born April 26, 1821, was John Gordon McCurry, the *Social Harp* man. John Gordon married Rachel S. Brown in 1842, but they had no children. I met many who had known McCurry personally, and all of them agreed that he was a most unusual man. As a farmer he tilled several hundred acres. He could walk around a piece of land and then tell with great accuracy how many acres it contained. He took one of the first censuses in Hartwell. As president (judge) of the inferior court during Civil War times he signed script that was used as currency in that county. He was a Royal Arch Mason. Although his father had been, for traditional reasons we may presume, a member of the Associated Reformed Presbyterian Church, John G. went the more popular Missionary Baptist way. He could nod, as he usually did, throughout the sermon and could still tell the rest of the churchgoers more than they knew of the preacher's words. He was the "mud sill" of the Baptist church at Bio in the McCurry district and is buried in its churchyard.

McCurry's esthetic bent is well shown by the "dream quilt" story. He dreamed one night, Mrs. T. R. Estes, his grandniece, told me, of a beautiful "piece quilt" design. In the morning he took a stick and drew the design in the sand of the yard beside the house, and from this he cut a pattern. Two-color quilts made from this pattern soon became very popular, and today the "dream quilt" may be found in numerous homes.

Mrs. Estes told me that her great-uncle was also a tailor to whom the people from miles around would bring their homespun cloth to be cut. And she maintains that the dozen dressmakers (including herself) among the grandnieces now living ascribe their inspiration to their "Uncle Gordon."

As a man who had the reputation for knowing everything, McCurry was consulted on all imaginable subjects from song composition to horse trading. And once, at least, this fame got on his nerves. It seems, according to Dr. George S. Clark, who knew McCurry well, that a distant farmer who had the business of a horse trade on his mind, drove up to McCurry's house at eleven o'clock one black night, long after everybody had gone to bed, and rapped. After a time he succeeded in arousing the head of the family who came to the door in his night clothes.

"Good evenin', Mac!" greeted the farmer out of the darkness. "I want you to tell me how old my horse is." McCurry, irritated at being pulled out of bed on so trivial a matter, answered curtly, "He's seventy-seven," and went back to bed.

Aldine Kieffer tells, in the editorial of 1883 referred to above, that he, Kieffer, was one of a group who spent an evening in the McCurry home singing with the venerable musician and discussing musical matters. Dr. Clark told me, however, that McCurry had some voice affection which almost completely prevented his singing during the last forty years of his life. McCurry died Dec. 4, 1886. His grave is shown facing page 308. His wife survived him thirteen years.

The Social Harp

A representation of the first cover page of McCurry's *Social Harp* appears opposite page 91. That page reads, "The Social Harp, a Collection of Tunes, Odes, Anthems, and Set Pieces, Selected from Various Authors: Together with Much New Music Never Before Published; Suited to all Metres and Well Adapted to all Denominations, Singing-Schools, and Private Societies. With a Full Exposition of the Rudiments of Music. And the Art of Musical Composition so Simplified that the Most Unlearned Person Can Comprehend it with the Utmost Facility. By John G. McCurry. Philadelphia: Published by S. C. Collins, N. E. Cor. Sixth and Minor Sts. For the Proprietor, John G. McCurry, 1859."

Its back cover page shows that it was for sale, wholesale and retail, by John B. Watson, Anderson C(ourt) H(ouse), S. C.; H. S. and J. P. Rees, Columbus, Ga.; and W. N. White, Athens, Ga.; and that its "travelling agents" were R. W. Waldrup, G. W. Bo . . . . (unreadable), Wm. C. Davis, J. H. Moss,

A. N. Benton, and Joseph Lawrence. These were probably singing-school teachers.

Although the date 1859 appears on the front cover of this book as on the copy which Kieffer saw, still it is probable that this is a later printing of the book and that its first appearance was in 1855. The only information we have as to this first printing is given by J. S. James in his 1911 edition of the *Original Sacred Harp,* page 507. Referring there to the *Social Harp,* he states that its Preface was signed by McCurry in Andersonville, Hart County, Georgia, March 16, 1855. I cannot verify James's statement from my copy, since its first six pages, including Preface, are gone. But a little internal evidence points to the correctness of James's observation. I refer to the fact that dozens of the songs are dated. These composition dates run from the 1840's down to 1855. But not one song has a date later than that year.

The word "Social" in the title meant what is now understood by "congregational." The 237 pages of song in this book form one of the richest storehouses of southern indigenous music and text in all the fasola literature. McCurry, himself a facile composer or recorder, or both, of sprightly tunes, was successful in obtaining for his *Social Harp* also the songs of a number of his composer-friends in that remarkably pregnant northeastern Georgia and northwestern South Carolina field.

Songs in the *Social Harp* claimed by McCurry as his own compositions number forty-nine.[13]

[13] They are Glorious News (p. 18), The Cross (18), Mandaville (19), River of Jordan (21), Substantial Joys (28), Martin (29), Happy Children (33), To the Land (34), Hallelujah, Third (35), The Traveller (37), Better Day (47), (Here four pages are torn out of my book. Enough of them remains to show that McCurry composed at least two tunes on the missing pages). Heavenly Meeting (60), Kay (61), Maxwell (62), A Home in Heaven (68), Hermon (70), Dove of Peace (71), Old Tory (75), Bower's, or Happy Souls (82), Raymond (83), Weeping Mary (98), Hail, Ye Sons (100), Parting Friends (101), Teasley (102), Mosley

That he was in close touch with the *Sacred Harp* group is indicated by his using eleven songs by B. F. White, ten of which were in the *Sacred Harp,* which had made its appearance eleven years before; four songs by the *Sacred Harp's* co-author, E. J. King; one song by J. Tom White, B. F. White's nephew; and four and three respectively by the *Sacred Harp* contributors, Leonard P. Breedlove and T. W. Carter.

Through inquiry in Hart County, I have been able to identify a number of the *Social Harp* song producers as relatives and other neighbors of the compiler. A(lec) W. McCurry (two songs) was the compiler's brother. William C. Davis (eleven songs), Henry F. Chandler (seven), and E. R. White (four), were Hart Countians, as were in all probability J. F. and J. A. Wade (nine songs between them), Silas W. Kay (two), and Thomas Maxwell (one).

McCurry's songs bearing local family names are "Teasley," "Derrett," and "Vanderver." Those having local place names as their titles are "Hartwell," "Bowman," and "Eagle Grove." His song "John Adkins' Farewell" bears the name and tells the sad story of a man who murdered his wife and was hanged for it in Clarksville, Georgia, so I was told in Hartwell. The song thus fits nicely into the frame of indigenous balladry which is carrying on the immigrant folk traditions.

Mixed in here and there are songs that are designated as "set pieces."[14] Seven out of the eleven "set pieces" are the melodic product of McCurry's pen. That McCurry considered especially the metrical form when he called a song a "set piece," seems clear from his statement on page 11 of his "Rudi-

(103), Burges (106), Memphis (107), Derrett (108), The Harvest Field (134), Zion's Walls (137), Morning Star (138), Crumbly (139), Sweet Canaan (140), Slabtown (141), Bowman (143), Roll Jordan (145), Wake Up (155), Navigation (165), Wilkes (183), Hartwell (193), Birth of Christ (199), John Adkin's Farewell (200), Vanderver (201), Few Days (209), The Beggar (212), Eagle Grove (227), Marion (228), and Good By (253).

[14] They are on pages 18, 29, 37, 68, 80, 137, 142, 194, 201, 209, and 212.

ments" that "set pieces have no general rule of measurement." And we come nearer to understanding the fasola concept of "set pieces" when we note Carden's remark in the Introduction to his *Missouri Harmony* of 1820 (page 11). Carden advised singers to apply different text poems to one and the same piece of music, this as a good exercise in learning to sing. "And likewise applying different tunes to the same words," he went on to suggest, "will have a great tendency to remove the embarrassment created by considering every short tune as a 'set piece.' " It seems, then, that a short tune which could be used with only its one original text was a "set piece."

The extraordinarily large number of indigenous tunes in this book are, naturally, predominatingly of the five-tone-scale type. I say "naturally" because I am thinking of the important Scotch-Irish element in the Hart County folk.

Perhaps it was Civil War conditions, coming on so short a time after the *Social Harp* appeared, that cut the book's life short. A more considerable reason, however, for there being no post-Civil-War printings was probably McCurry's important civic duties and his voice affection, both of which must have effectively prevented his pushing the sale of his book at singing schools and conventions as his competitors—Hauser, Walker, and White, for example—were able to push the sale of theirs. Certainly the book's short life was not due to any intrinsic defects. For if ever a book grew out of its native soil, that book was McCurry's *Social Harp.*

CHAPTER VIII

BENJAMIN FRANKLIN WHITE OF GEORGIA AND HIS ASSOCIATES

WHILE William Walker's *Southern Harmony* was the first far-southern-made song book of the four-shape brand to gain long and wide recognition in its rural home territory, there was another book, born a few years after the *Southern Harmony,* which from the start rivaled it in popularity, far surpassed it in longevity, and eventually won the distinction of being the only four-shape book which has stemmed the seven-shape tide and all the other adverse currents, decade after decade, and has remained a widely used collection of fasola song down to the present time. This book was and is the *Sacred Harp.* B. F. White, William Walker's brother-in-law and whilom co-worker in preparing the *Southern Harmony* was its chief compiler.

THE AUTHOR OF THE SACRED HARP

I have the following data as to White's life and activities, largely from a ten-page account appearing in James's *A Brief History of the Sacred Harp.*[1] These facts have been verified and supplemented by Joe S. James personally, by White's daughter, Mrs. M. A. Clarke, and by his granddaughters, Mrs. Mary White Lloyd and Mrs. Burgin Fortune. The last three named live in Atlanta.

James was a lawyer of the old-time rural type. What education he had was self-acquired. For at least three generations back his family has been enthusiastically musical, and

[1] Pp. 27-37.

many members of it have been teachers and singers. His father, Stephen James, was a friend of B. F. White. James's *Brief History of the Sacred Harp* is poorly organized, its language is often hard to understand, and in the few instances where I have been able to check up on his data, I have found a quite considerable number of errors. But, until further investigations are made in this field, we shall have to take James's findings for what they are, namely, the only attempt at a history of the *Sacred Harp* in existence, indeed the only historical attempt that has ever been made in any angle of the shape-note song field. And we shall have to be grateful for this as the work of one who was on the inside, one who was boundlessly enthusiastic over the "beautiful and delightful science," and one of the many who looked upon their beloved book as almost coördinate with the Holy Bible, regarding those who had a hand in its making as apostles of light, and those who taught the singing of its songs as near-saints. When James died in the winter of 1931, a chorus of several hundred "Sacred Harpers" sang his favorite songs at a memorial service in Atlanta.

The quotations on the pages immediately following are from the James *History*. I have made few references as to just where, on his 156 badly mixed-up pages, the particular citations have been found, and I have not attempted in all cases to correct his English.

Benjamin Franklin White was born September 20, 1800, near Spartanburg, South Carolina, and near the homestead of William Walker. He was the youngest of the fourteen children of Robert White who lived to 104 years of age and died in Augusta, Georgia. "His [B. F. White's] brother, Robert White, Jr., took him when he was an infant and reared him to manhood." His education was meager. "We are informed that he only attended a literary school for about three months," that is, he attended "three sessions of the school held after laying by crops."[2] "These were the only schools that were anywhere taught in the country at that time. His father was inclined to music and the son fell into line. . . . His talent for this great science was astonishing and amazing, when all the surroundings and circumstances are considered. . . . He took up the science of music without a preceptor, and while it was hard to get hold of sufficient treaties [*sic*] on the subject, he started out with a determination to master the science. It is said of him that he would sit for hours at a time and look at the different freaks [aspects?] of nature, and note the regularity and harmony with which it did all its work." He would also "listen to birds, and learned as much or more from these observations than he did from other men's works." He was a deeply religious man and a member of the Missionary Baptist Church. "When he started to compose a tune it was his habit to invoke the blessings of his Maker. And if he felt that he did not have it [the divine blessing] on the particular work he was engaged in, he would abandon and lay aside the piece of music." B. F. White's daughter, Mrs. Mattie America Clarke, told me that her father was a fifer in the War of 1812, hence at twelve years of age.

He married December 30, 1825, Thurza Golightly (b. Oct. 13, 1805; d. Sept. 2, 1878), sister of Amy Golightly, who married William Walker, in Spartanburg, South Carolina. James tells his version of White's collaboration with the nine-years-

[2] "Laying by crops" is an expression used in the South for leaving the fields to themselves, around the middle of the summer, after the last cultivating of corn, cotton, etc., is done. The intervening period of some weeks before harvesting begins, is a time of comparative leisure for the farmer and his family. It is therefore the accepted season for a term of school, family reunions, revivals, baptizings, primary elections, and, above all, singings.

younger Walker as follows: "Major White[3] and his brother-in-law wrote a book known by the older people as the Southern Harmony, in four-shape notes, the same as those used in the Sacred Harp. . . . An arrangement was made between them for Walker to go north and have the book published, there being no publishing houses in the South with a plant suitable to print the book. Walker took the manuscript, and he and his publishers changed the same without the knowledge or consent of Major White and brought it out under the name of Walker, giving Major White no credit whatever for its composition. Walker also entered into a combination with the publishers and in this way managed to deprive Major White of any interest in the Southern Harmony, although all the work, or most of it, was done by Major White. On account of this transaction and treatment the two men never spoke to each other again." And Major White "soon after moved to Harris County, Georgia [Mrs. Clarke told me this was in either 1840 or 1841], and engaged in composing and writing the songs in the Sacred Harp.

"Before he began the writing of the Sacred Harp he was running a newspaper called The Organ—the official paper published in Harris County at Hamilton. . . . A large number of the compositions that were first printed in this paper are now embodied in the Sacred Harp. For several years he was clerk of the superior court of Harris County and was a very popular man in that section of the state."

A Lifelong Teacher of Singing

It seems that White was a lifelong teacher of singing. But "he never used his talent as a musician to make money. He

[3] He got the title "from being a major of the malitia [*sic*] before the Civil War. . . . He went into the malitia as private and soon rose to the rank of major." He organized several Civil War companies but was then too old (sixty-one) for active service, Mrs. Clarke told me.

BENJAMIN FRANKLIN WHITE AND THURZA GOLIGHTLY WHITE

The author of the Sacred Harp *and his wife.*

had a higher, greater, and more glorious intention in view, and was untiring in his energy and efforts to bring simplicity to the singing of music and to furnish to beginners and to the poor a form of music . . . that would find lodgment in the hearts and quicken the inner recesses of the soul; to look farther than to the mere rendering of the song, and to bring them to a higher and intimate relation to the Author of all music and in harmony with the fountain from whence blends [*sic*] all the charms and concords in music, and to teach them to sing such songs as would bring them in sacred nearness to their Maker.

"It is said of him that if he found in his travels in teaching a person with a musical voice, and they were unable to pay their tuition for instruction, he invariably gave them their instruction free. He never turned one away on account of poverty, or inability to pay. He carried to his home in his early days many poor girls and boys and learned [*sic*] them music. It was a habit of his never to allow any one to pay board or lodging who stayed at his house, it made no difference whether the visit was long or short. It is claimed that he has taught more people to sing than any other man who ever lived in the South; not that he taught all of them himself but has been instrumental in putting the ball into motion by which the people had the opportunity to learn music. Some of the most noted teachers in the state were under his instruction. We mention a few of them: J. P. Reese, H. S. Reese, R. F. M. Mann, E. T. Pound, Elder E. Dumas, E. J. King, A. Ogletree and, in fact, most of the composers whose names are given in the *Sacred Harp*."

James has much to say of the personal attractiveness of B. F. White. "He was gentle in his nature, lovable in disposition and treated everyone with universal kindness. . . . He had sufficient resentment, however, for his own protection, but he would not allow his wrath or unkind feelings to go any farther than to protect his own reputation and his dignity as a gentleman." And while he was a Missionary Baptist, "he was liberal in his views" and "worshipped in the various churches: the Primitive Baptist, Presbyterian, Lutheran, Methodist, Christian," etc.

Despite his limited and almost self-gained musical education, "White gave to the world some of the sweetest and most melodious music that is printed in any of the song books." And yet, his professional generosity made him hospitable to other contributors to the *Sacred Harp*. "And numbers of tunes in this book which were composed and arranged by him" have been credited to others. I shall have more to say of his compositions in the following chapter.

Gift for Organization

It seems that one of White's valuable gifts was that of organization. This "keen sense . . . and his quickness of observation" led him to see, in the then sparsely settled condition of the country, that it was necessary to have some kind of musical organization in Georgia, and the result of his efforts was the formation of the Southern Musical Convention in 1847 in Upson County. White was president of this convention from the time of its organization up to 1862, in 1867, "and perhaps in other years."

In the last eight days of Major White's life, while he was suffering from injuries resulting from a fall on the streets of Atlanta, "he recounted all the mistakes as well as the good that had followed him throughout his life. He summed it all up in the words, 'The end has come and I am ready.'" A short time before he died he sang "Sounding Joy," a tune of his (words by Watts) in the *Sacred Harp*, "plainly and distinctly." The song begins, "Behold, the morning sun begins its glorious way." He died December 5, 1879, and is buried in Oakland Cemetery in Atlanta near the Decatur Street entrance in the northeast corner. In 1927, forty-eight years after his death, his surviving descendants and the *Sacred Harp* singing organization erected the memorial tombstone which is shown in the illustration facing page 308.

White's Descendants

Fourteen children were born to the B. F. White family and nine lived to be men and women. These were William Decatur, David Patillo, Robert H., Mrs. Carrie Adair, Mrs. Nancy White Byrd, Mrs. W. B. Mann, B. F., Jr., James Landrum, and Mrs. Mattie America Clarke. Mrs. Mann and Mrs. Clarke were the only survivors in 1929.

James L. White, son of B. F. White (b. 1847 at Hamilton, Georgia, d. 1925 in Atlanta), sang with his father's family and studied music at an early age. At eighteen he began attending musical gatherings and studied music under his father. At twenty-eight years of age (1875) he began teaching. According to James, "He teaches his scholars to read and compose from the beginning. . . . He has composed a great deal of music. Prof. White was . . . perhaps the leading spirit in the organization of the Stone Mountain Convention (originally the Fulton and DeKalb Singing Convention). He is [ca. 1904] the musical director of the convention and keys all the music when called on to do so. Everybody loves Jim White and he numbers his friends by the thousand." In the notice of his death which appeared in the Atlanta papers I read, "He was for many years a soloist in various churches of this city."

D. P. White, son of B. F. White, married Celeste Brown in Alabama and moved to Texas, where he died in 1903. He taught music in Alabama and Texas for many years. He was "extremely fond of music and sang from the old Sacred Harp as long as he lived."

William Decatur White, son of B. F. White, died in 1903. He was the father of seven children. "He was educated in music the same as the other White children and was a dear lover of sacred songs." One of his sons, Harry D. White, was president of the Stone Mountain Singing Convention. Another son, Joe White, who is now a captain on the Atlanta police force, told me "If I was singing for a railroad [as a prize], I wouldn't get a cross tie."

Lola, a daughter of William Decatur White, "performed well on the piano and organ and was thoroughly posted in music. She was in the choir of one of the leading churches [in Atlanta] and led the music for several years before the time of her death. . . . She had a sweet voice, pleasant manners and led music to perfection. One of the quarterlies of the Stone Mountain Singing Convention has been converted into a memorial singing in memory of Miss Lola."

Robert H. White, son of B. F. White, "was a fine singer and loved music as well as any of the family."

Of B. F. ("Frank") White, Jr., James says: "He is a fine musician and can compose music and does so readily. . . . It is said that he is one of the finest bass singers in all the country."

Mrs. Carrie Adair, daughter of B. F. White, "was well versed in music . . . took lessons from her father, was a fine singer, and taught instrumental music."

Mrs. W. B. Mann, a daughter of B. F. White who was still living in 1929, "loves the old Sacred Harp . . . and believes in music."

Mrs. Nancy White Byrd, daughter of B. F. White, was "born with the faculty of music, was educated in music by her father and is a great admirer of the old Sacred Harp, but loves all good music. . . . She was one of the leaders in the Sacred Harp when she was a young woman. And all her children are musicians. Mrs. John Cooper, one of her daughters, is the leader of the First Presbyterian church choir in Atlanta."

Mrs. E. H. Clarke, youngest child of B. F. White, is still living. Of her James says: "Mrs. Clarke is a fine singer, has a splendid voice, and is well remembered by all the people who attended the singings during the lifetime of her father." She used to travel around with him, she told me. "Her children are all inclined to music."

Fasola Patriarchs of Georgia Associated with White

"James R. Turner," James tells us, "was born in Hancock County, Ga., Nov. 8, 1807, and died at his home, Oct. 14, 1874, about three and one half miles north of Villa Rica, Carroll County, Georgia. He was buried at Wesley Chapel Methodist church near where he died." In 1866 he was engaged "in teaching singing schools all over the country and had ten schools at this time. . . . Many times if a stranger had dropped into [one of] his schools he would have found himself in the midst of a revival. . . . In leading music he never took his book or opened it. Every page and tune was perfectly familiar to him and he rendered the music by notes as well as by words, called the pages, names of songs and sang them, keeping correct time without reference to the book.

"He managed all his singing schools on the same plan as a school master. He opened his schools with prayer and never failed to ask the blessings of God on all the members of his class. He dismissed with the benediction. . . . He believed that God would have a place for him, when his mission on earth was over, and allow him first to sing the songs in heaven he sung on earth. . . . All of his [seven] children were fine vocalists of exceptionally good voices. . . . He composed "Confidence" in the *Sacred Harp.*

"In 1866 he was president of the largest singing convention held in all the country, at Pleasant Hill Church, Paulding County, Georgia. It convened on Thursday and ended on Monday following. There were vocalists in attendance from several states. It was the second annual meeting of the Chattahoochee Musical Convention after the Civil War. The crowd on Sunday was immense,—estimated at 8,000 people. The weather was very warm. There were three wells close by, from which the water to furnish the crowd was drawn. Before one o'clock they were drawn dry and it was almost impossible to get water."

Turner's prominence in *Sacred Harp* circles is shown by the fact that he "helped organize the Chattahoochee convention in 1852 and was its president in the years 1865-1869 and again in 1873."

Of E. J. King, whose name appeared on the *Sacred Harp* with White's as its author, James was able to find little information. The reason seems to be that he died so far back, for I find a note in the 1866 edition of *Christian Harmony* (page 330) reading, "This old tune (Fulfilment) was set to music by E. J. King, junior author of the 'Sacred Harp,' who died in a few weeks after its publication in 1844." Absalom Ogletree, an octogenarian singer and pupil of B. F. White, told James that he met King at Hamilton, Georgia, in 1850 (six years after Walker supposed him dead) and that he was a fine singer.

Elder Edmund Dumas, Primitive Baptist preacher and notable contributor of songs to the old *Sacred Harp,* "died at Forsyth, Georgia, . . . we have not been able to ascertain the time of his death." He was "one of the shining lights

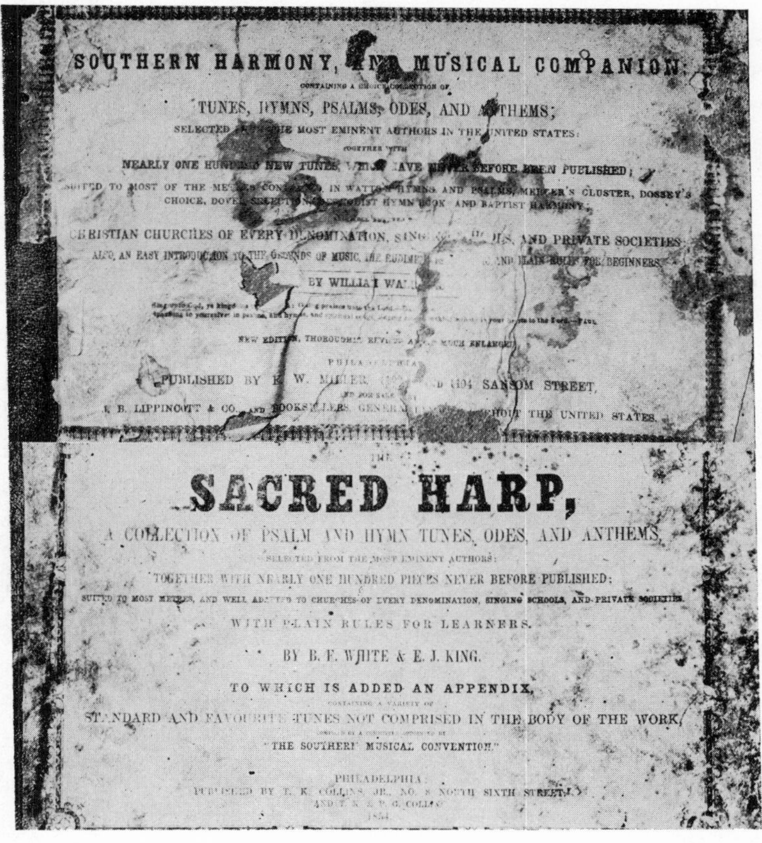

SOUTHERN HARMONY, [illegible] MUSICAL COMPANION:

CONTAINING A CHOICE COLLECTION OF

TUNES, HYMNS, PSALMS, ODES, AND [illegible]THEMS;

SELECTED [illegible] MOST EMINENT AUTHORS IN THE [illegible]NITED STATES:

TOGETHER WITH

NEARLY ONE HU[illegible] NEW TUNES, [illegible] HAVE [illegible] BEFORE BEEN PUBLISHED;

SUITED TO MOST OF THE ME[illegible] IN WATTS'S HYMNS AND PSALMS, MERCER'S CLUSTER, DOSSEY'S CHOICE, DOVE[illegible] HYMN BOOK AND BAPTIST HARMONY;

CHRISTIAN CHURCHES OF EVERY DENOMINATION, SING[illegible] AND PRIVATE SOCIETIES.

ALSO, AN EASY INTRODUCTION TO THE GROUNDS OF MUSIC, [illegible] PLAIN RULES FOR BEGINNERS.

BY WILLIAM WA[illegible]

NEW EDITION, THOROUGHLY REVISED A[illegible] MUCH ENLARGED.

PHILADELPHIA:

PUBLISHED BY E. W. MILLER, [illegible] 1104 SANSOM STREET,

[illegible] B. LIPPINCOTT & CO., AND BOOKSELLERS GENERA[illegible] THE UNITED STATES.

THE

SACRED HARP,

A COLLECTION OF PSALM AND HYMN TUNES, ODES, AND ANTHEMS,

SELECTED FROM THE MOST EMINENT AUTHORS:

TOGETHER WITH NEARLY ONE HUNDRED PIECES NEVER BEFORE PUBLISHED;

SUITED TO MOST METRES, AND WELL ADAPTED TO CHURCHES OF EVERY DENOMINATION, SINGING SCHOOLS, AND PRIVATE SOCIETIES.

WITH PLAIN RULES FOR LEARNERS.

BY B. F. WHITE & E. J. KING.

TO WHICH IS ADDED AN APPENDIX,

CONTAINING A VARIETY OF

STANDARD AND FAVOURITE TUNES NOT COMPRISED IN THE BODY OF THE WORK,

"THE SOUTHERN MUSICAL CONVENTION."

PHILADELPHIA:

PUBLISHED BY T. K. COLLINS, JR., NO. 8 NORTH SIXTH STREET,

AND T. K. & P. G. COLLINS.

1854.

COVER PAGES

TOP: *William Walker's* Southern Harmony and Musical Companion, *edition of 1854. Compiled in Spartanburg, South Carolina and printed in Philadelphia.* BOTTOM: *Cover-page of B. F. White's and E. J. King's* Sacred Harp, *edition of 1854. Compiled in Hamilton, Georgia, and printed in Philadelphia.*

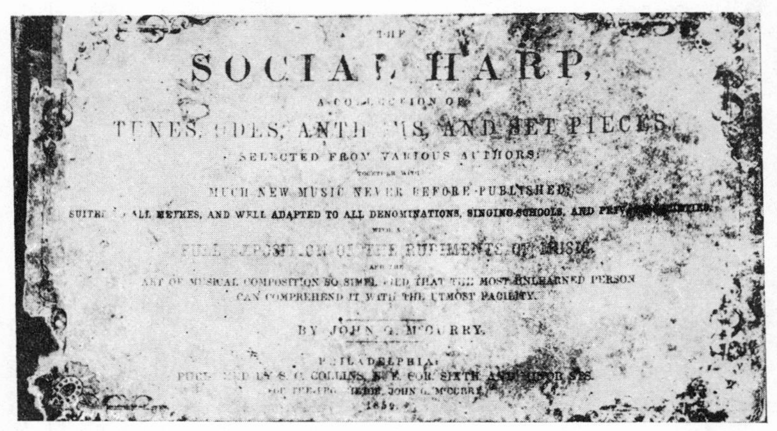

THE

SOCIAL HARP,

A COLLECTION OF

TUNES, ODES, ANTHEMS, AND SET PIECES,

SELECTED FROM VARIOUS AUTHORS:

TOGETHER WITH

MUCH NEW MUSIC NEVER BEFORE PUBLISHED;

SUITED TO ALL METRES, AND WELL ADAPTED TO ALL DENOMINATIONS, SINGING-SCHOOLS, AND PRIV[illegible]

WITH A

FULL EXPOSITION OF THE RUDIMENTS OF MUSIC,

AND THE

ART OF MUSICAL COMPOSITION SO SIMPLIFIED THAT THE MOST UNLEARNED PERSON CAN COMPREHEND IT WITH THE UTMOST FACILITY.

BY JOHN G. McCURRY.

PHILADELPHIA:

PUBLISHED BY S. C. COLLINS, N. E. COR. SIXTH AND MINOR STS.

[illegible] JOHN G. McCURRY.

1859.

COVER PAGE

Cover-page of John G. McCurry's Social Harp, *edition of 1859. Compiled in Hart County, Georgia, and printed in Philadelphia.*

of the Southern Musical Convention, was present at its organization and attended its meetings as long as he lived. He was also a member of the Chattahoochee Convention. He was an admirer of B. F. White, J. P. Reese and J. T. Edmonds and named a tune of his [in the *Sacred Harp*] in honor of each of them." Dumas was "ordinary" (probate judge) of Monroe County at the time of his death.

If Absalom Ogletree, patriarchal singer and composer, was eighty-five (according to James) in 1904, then he must have been around twenty-five years old when the first *Sacred Harp* came out. "He helped in the organization of the Southern Musical Convention, in Upson County, in 1845. He was also appointed on a committee to revise the Sacred Harp in 1850, in 1859 and in 1869." He had a strong voice, was a favorite among the teachers. "He received musical instructions from B. F. White and James R. Turner." He could sing "Claremont" (a famous five-page anthem) without looking into the book. The tune "Ogletree" in the *Sacred Harp* is named after him.

Professor Ivy M. Shell, patriarch of the *Sacred Harp* group, was born in South Carolina in 1826 and died at Senoia, Georgia, in 1908, according to James. When he was a babe in arms his father moved to Georgia. Young Shell "never had an opportunity to attend school but seventeen days up to his majority, and has attended but little since. He studied music without a preceptor. He first studied the Missouri Harmony, next the Southern Harmony and then the Sacred Harp in 1844. He began teaching music in 1847 and taught regularly until 1879. His schools were in Merriwether, Henry, Paulding, Fayette, Carroll, Harralson, Douglas, Harris and Heard counties in Georgia, and in Randolph and many other counties in Alabama. He composed the tune, Warnerville, in the Sacred Harp and he has composed a number of other tunes in other works."

"Prof. Shell is at present [1904] chairman of the B. F. White and J. P. Reese Memorial Singing Society and also president of the Chattahoochee Musical Convention."

Rev. H. S. Reese (also written Rees) was born in 1827 in Jasper County, Georgia, and was reared in Muscogee County. He was a preacher in the Missionary Baptist Church and a member of the Southern Musical Convention and the Chattahoochee Singing Convention. He died in 1922 at Turin, Georgia, at the age of ninety-five.

"John P. Reese, brother of H. S., was born in 1828 in Jasper County [Georgia] and died at his home two miles north of Newnan, Georgia, in 1900. . . . He began to teach music when he was a little over twenty years of age and quit teaching in 1885. He taught schools all over middle and north Georgia and eastern Alabama. He began writing music when about twenty years of age and continued from that time up to 1885 or near that time. . . . He was for many years president and vice president of the Chattahoochee Musical Convention" and a "member of the Southern Musical Convention."

"R. F. N. Mann composed a number of songs in the Sacred Harp. . . . He was a good singer, had a strong voice, and was a teacher of music. He lived somewhere near Griffin, Georgia, and died several years ago, but we have not been able to learn the particulars further than that he became diseased in body and mind and died at Milledgeville." He was a Methodist and belonged to the Southern and Chattahoochee conventions.

Leonard P. Breedlove evaded James's search for vital statistics. "We have conflicting reports about him. One says that he died in southern Georgia over twenty-five years ago [hence around 1879]. . . . He was a member of the Southern and Chattahoochee conventions, helped revise the Sacred Harp in 1850 and took an active part with Major White . . . in introducing the Sacred Harp in Georgia and adjoining states."

Thomas W. Carter, contributor of seven songs; W. L. Williams, five songs, and Henry G. Mann, four songs, have not been written up by James.

Songs in the *Sacred Harp* attributed to B. F. White and his relatives and descendants total sixty-three. To this number the other old-school patriarchs added compositions of their own to a total of one hundred and fifty-four.

CHAPTER IX

THE SACRED HARP

From 1844 to 1879

B. F. White and E. J. King produced the first edition of the *Sacred Harp* in Hamilton, Harris County, Georgia, in 1844. The first cover page of an 1854 printing is reproduced opposite page 90. This shows it to have been printed by T. K. Collins, Jr., No. 8, North Sixth Street, Philadelphia. Its title was a favorite. The number of song books appearing in the first half of the nineteenth century with the word "Harp" in their titles is amazing, and there were several "Sacred Harps" among them. The first edition of White's book comprised 262 pages, twenty-six of which were devoted to Preface, "Rudiments of Music," and "Dictionary of Musical Terms."

In 1850 a revised and enlarged edition came out with 104 additional pages of music as an appendix, making the size 366 pages. This revision was undertaken at the behest of the Southern Musical Convention by a committee which, as we see by their report on page 263 of the 1850 *Sacred Harp,* was composed of B. F. White, Joel King, Leonard P. Breedlove, A. Ogletree, S. R. Pennick, J. R. Turner, R. F. M. Mann, and E. L. King.

In 1859 a second revision and enlargement, authorized by the same convention, brought the size up to 430 pages. The committee this time was B. F. White, E. T. Pound, J. P. Reese, R. F. Ball, A. Ogletree, J. T. Edmonds, and A. S. Webster.

In 1869 a third revision and enlargement, under the same auspices, "introduced a large number of new compositions from the pens of the most eminent teachers and composers of vocal music" and did away with some less popular tunes in the former editions. The result was a book of 480 pages. At this time when the new *Christian Harmony* and other seven-shape books were commencing to make their way into the *Sacred Harp* precincts, the question as to whether or not this book should follow suit came up in the committee. In his 1869 Preface, B. F. White, the venerable and intransigent chairman of the committee, settled the dispute as follows: "During the last 27 years . . . we have been especially vigilant in seeking musical terms more appropriate to the purpose than the four note-names used in this book. But candor compels us to acknowledge that our search has been unavailing. The [four-note] scheme . . . has had the sanction of the musical world for more than four hundred [!] years; and we scarcely think that we can do better than to abide by the advice. . . . 'Ask for the old paths and walk therein.' "

The *Sacred Harp* seems to have been hard pressed after 1870. Its use, according to James, "began to wane and it was not so extensively taught in the singing schools as before."[1] The reason for this was, apparently, that same notational conservatism which seems to have split the big Southern Musical Convention, to have brought into that Convention other books with other notations (Pound's, for example), and to have driven the stand-patting Sacred Harpers over to the Chattahoochee and other conventions.

In 1879 a committee was ready to make a fourth revision of the *Sacred Harp*,[2] but its activities were terminated by the death of its chairman, B. F. White.

Two Editions in 1911

In 1911 two editions of the *Sacred Harp* appeared. One was made under the leadership of James Landrum White, son

[1] *Op. cit.*, p. 20.

[2] James, *op. cit.*, p. 103.

of B. F. White, with a revision committee of thirty "from the states of Ga., Ala., and Fla." It was printed in Atlanta, Georgia. It contained 550 pages plus a supplemental "Singing School Department" of twenty-six pages at the end including a simplified "Musical Notation and Rudiments." This edition is still on the market. The other edition was made under the leadership of Joe S. James, chairman, and a committee which had been appointed by the United Sacred Harp Musical Association in 1906 for this purpose. The James revision was called the *Original Sacred Harp*. The book's back (fourth) cover page tells that the music and words in the book "ARE IN ACCORD AND KEEPING WITH THE SACRED MUSIC IN THE BIBLE, FROM JUBAL 160 A. M., 1500 YEARS BEFORE THE DELUGE, FROM ABRAHAM, MOSES, THE CHILDREN OF ISRAEL, THE PROPHETS, LEVITES, DAVID, SOLOMON DOWN TO JESUS CHRIST, HIS DISCIPLES AND THE FOUNDING OF HIS CHURCH AND TO THE PRESENT." The whole revision committee of twenty-three members selected a sub-committee of five to do the work. This sub-committee consisted of S. W. Everett, S. M. Denson, G. B. Daniel, and M. D. Farris, with Joe S. James as chairman. (See illustration on the opposite page.)

The Original Sacred Harp

The *Original Sacred Harp,* being the version that contains practically all the songs that were in former editions, and a book that is most widely used among the four-shape fraternity today, deserves a few paragraphs of description.

A "Summary Statement" opens the book and tells the singer that there are 609 tunes awaiting his voice, that S. M. Denson composed and added 327 altos which have made almost all the old three-part tunes over into those of four-parts

The foregoing photographs contain the committee appointed by the United Sacred Harp Musical Association in September 1906, who have just completed the revision and compilation and present "Original Sacred Harp" as revised by them A perusal of its pages will show the work done. Further statements of the corrections in music, additions made, in this valuable song book will be found in the Introductorv, by the chairman of the committee, on following pages.

SACRED HARPERS OF GEORGIA AND ALABAMA

This group picture appears in the Original Sacred Harp, *which these men produced in 1911. Absalom Ogletree, bottom row, center, began his life's devotion to the* Sacred Harp *in 1849 as a member of the first revision committee.*

From the best information we can get, this tune was named in honor of the celebrated poet, William Cowper. The words were undoubtedly composed by him. They are so much in accord with the trend of the hymns composed by this great man, we give him credit for same. We, however, have not been able to find this poem in any of the Hymnologies, but have added another verse to it. See full history of him under tune Bethel, page 27.

"FUGUING TUNE"

An eighteenth-century "fugue piece" from the Sacred Harp.

and have added two inches to the latitude of the book (it is eight by ten and one-fourth inches). We are informed further that there are 10,643 "lines of poetry in these hymns," 563 Scripture citations under the song titles, 4,295 sharps, 2,241 flats, 183,240 words, etc., etc.

Somewhat more important is the "Summary" fact that there are within the covers 1,226 names of authors of music and composers of words, showing that James and his committee worked hard to find out who was who. And even more valuable is his statistical information that out of these 1,226 words and tune contributors 461 are Georgians and 360 are Alabamians, with a total for all the southern states of 861 or about two-thirds of the entire number.

The Preface expresses the gratification of the editors that "the music writers of the South have kept before the singing public more of the standard . . . hymns and melodies than [those] in any other part of America." It deplores the fact, however, that many sacred song books in this section are "badly tainted with operatic, secular and rag-time strains of music," and expresses satisfaction that there are in the *Sacred Harp* "but few of the twisted rills and frills of the unnatural snaking of the voice . . . which have in the last decade so demoralized the church music . . . in this section, but in other sections to an alarming extent." Here the editors were making a veiled indictment of the seven-shapers whose livelier and newer songs were competing keenly for the rurals' interest and allegiance.

On the "Introductory" pages the committee's chairman tells of how his workers have proceeded. They left the edition of 1869 intact. Altos have been supplied everywhere excepting in tunes "which could not be improved" thereby. "Dispersed harmony" (one part to each staff) has been adhered to. Additional stanzas of "words" have been inserted. And at the bottom of each tune the committee sought to give a condensed story of the lives of poet and composer.

The twenty-six pages of "Rudiments of Music" need take little of our attention. They are much the same as those in all the song books of rural appeal for nearly two hundred years back in America.

The 1869 edition of the *Sacred Harp* has a few "General Observations" that do not appear in the 1911 version. These are in reality a rather interesting set of don'ts. One of them warns that "a cold or cough, all kinds of spirituous liquors, violent exercise, too much bile on the stomach, long fasting, the veins overcharged with impure blood etc. etc., are destructive to the voice of one who is much in the habit of singing." These warnings had appeared in practically the same words in one fasola book after another for a hundred years previous. In another paragraph we find that "there should not be any noise indulged while singing, except the music, as it destroys entirely the beauty of harmony and renders the performance very difficult, especially to new beginners; and if it [the noise presumably] is designedly promoted, it is nothing less than a proof of disrespect in the singers to the exercise, to themselves who occasion it, and to the Author of our existence." And "all affectation should be banished, for it is disgusting in the performance of sacred music, and contrary to that solemnity which should accompany an exercise so near akin to that which will, through all eternity, engage the attention of those who walk in climes of bliss."

Seventy-one songs were added to the 1911 edition of the *Sacred Harp*. Of these by far the larger number were songs that had been included in the earliest editions but discarded in the edition of 1869. Among these reinstated tunes were a number by William Walker, Leonard P. Breedlove, T. W. Carter, and John G. McCurry, and one each by William Hauser and Andrew Johnson. All these were Georgians and South Carolinians excepting Johnson, who was of Tennessee.

From a perusal of the more recently composed songs in this new part of the *Original Sacred Harp* (pages 478-550), it is easy to see that the eyes of the active revisers were turned mainly to the west and that S. M. Denson, the Alabamian who was the most active individual on their committee, was largely responsible for it. Alabamians living at that time composed twenty-eight of the newly added tunes and living Georgians composed but six.

CHAPTER X
THE SACRED HARPERS

Georgia Singing Organizations Devoted to the Sacred Harp

We have seen that the territory in which a book is used is determined primarily by the range of its author's personal activities in singing schools and conventions, and secondarily by the conventions themselves in which the particular book gets a hold. Thus the Funk books were most popular in the Virginias, the Walker books, at first, in the territory that had Spartanburg, South Carolina, as its center. It is natural, therefore, that the early *Sacred Harp* sphere of influence should be Georgia and parts of eastern Alabama.

Our best pointers as to those parts of Georgia where the *Sacred Harp* was most popular before the Civil War may be gained from the records of the two singing conventions that were the center of the activities of the *Sacred Harp* authors and singers. These were the Southern Musical Convention and the Chattahoochee Musical Convention.

The Southern Musical Convention[1] was organized in Upson County in 1845 with B. F. White as president. Its subsequent meetings up to 1867 were held in Lamar, Randolph, Merriwether, Henry, Crawford, Fayette, Pike, and Troup counties. One might reasonably gather from this that the *Sacred Harp* was used in those years largely in that part of western central Georgia which is within a hundred-mile radius of Hamilton, Harris County, the home of B. F. White and the *Sacred Harp*.

The Chattahoochee Musical Convention was organized in

[1] See James, *op. cit.*, pp. 55 ff.

Coweta County in 1852. The list of the counties in which, according to James,[2] its annual meetings were held—Coweta, Douglas, Paulding, Carroll, Campbell, and Fayette—shows its sphere of influence to have been the valley of the Chattahoochee River and west to the state line, that is, simply a farther west sector in that hundred-mile circle which had Hamilton, Georgia, as its center. Its territory did not overlap that of the Southern Convention to any great extent.

In 1867 the tendency toward separatism which was inevitable among such individualists as these appeared in the ranks of the Southern Convention singers. It was all started, as it seems from James's account,[3] by E. T. Pound of Barnesville. Being himself author of a number of song books he saw in this big convention a fine sales opportunity. So he and his friends got the convention to give up its *Sacred Harp* "closed shop" policy and to allow the use of "other books" as well. Pound was elected president. The intransigent Sacred Harpers, "after wrangling for some time," deserted the Southern, and went over to the Chattahoochee Convention.

For the subsequent history of the Southern Musical Convention we shall have to consult other authorities than James, the dyed-in-the-wool Sacred Harper. He does tell us, however, that it has kept up its meetings "to the present time [1904]."

James looked on this Southern Musical Convention as the "greatest organization of vocal musicians that ever met in Georgia." Its meistersinger-like activities included the granting of licenses to singing teachers, the supervision (by a special committee) of singing (not allowing any leader "to vary in rendering music from the way it was written"), and the preservation of order at the meetings. "On several occasions charges were brought against members, and oftentimes they were expelled." What the charges were, we are not told.

[2] *Op. cit.*, pp. 63 ff.

[3] *Ibid.*, pp. 59 ff.

While the Southern Convention, according to James, went down, the Chattahoochee group has held its own and increased even. In 1904 it had "by far the largest membership of any singing convention in the state." In the Chattahoochee region "you can shake a bush anywhere in its bounds and a leader will walk out at once who can sing any tune that you may present to him."

While the Chattahoochee Musical Convention was still in existence as late as 1921, it had by that time lost its primacy in Georgia in favor of the United Sacred Harp Musical Association, of which I shall speak presently.

Other *Sacred Harp* conventions in Georgia in 1904 and mentioned by James were the Stone Mountain Musical Convention, Douglasville Sacred Harp Convention, Tallapoosa Singing Convention, Heard County Sacred Harp Convention and others in Chattooga, Milton, Haralson, and Gwinnett counties and the Hayne Creek and Centerville conventions.[4]

Further light on the geographic spread of the *Sacred Harp* singing in Georgia around the beginning of the present century is shed by the list of "Leaders in the Sacred Harp" given by counties in James.[5] The counties represented were DeKalb, Fulton, Gwinnett, Cobb, Campbell, Douglas, Clayton, Coweta, Fayette, Carroll, Chattooga, Paulding, and Haralson. All these counties are around Atlanta and reaching out to the west. James's list has the names of 278 leaders. Carroll County tops the list with fifty-seven.

It was in 1904 that the United Sacred Harp Musical Association was formed with its permanent headquarters in Atlanta and with the hope that it might become the central organization of all local conventions, singings, teachers, and leaders that use the *Sacred Harp*. J. S. James became its president

[4] *Ibid.*, pp. 73 ff.
[5] *Ibid.*, pp. 145 ff.

BERNARD AWTREY

President of United Sacred Harp Musical Association, of Georgia.

and remained at the helm until a mental disorder made his retirement necessary in 1928. Bernard Awtrey of Marietta, Georgia, is its present president.

Interesting insights into the character of the Association may be gained by a look into its by-laws. These ban all sectarianism and all politics from its considerations. Teachers of singing may obtain the Association's license to teach for $1.00. "All singing shall be soft, smooth and sung according to the time laid down in the music." "All sessions . . . shall be opened and closed with prayer," and the official title of members "should be 'sister' or 'brother.'" The four-shape note system is compulsory in its singings. Almost all business matters are given to committees "to keep from having the time of rendering music interfered with by wrangles in the open convention." In singing "all should keep the same time so as to prevent confusion." "A correct calling of the notes when they are sung, as they are spelled, me, faw, sol, law," is urged.

From a perusal of the minutes of the conventions of the United Sacred Harp Musical Association between 1914 and 1924 it would seem that their hopes of bringing all the *Sacred Harp* organizations under their wing had been only partially successful. In their list of delegates to the 1922 convention, for example, there were several hundred from Georgia, but only ten from Alabama and but one from Florida. That none was in attendance from the local conventions in South Carolina, Mississippi, Arkansas, Louisiana, and Texas may be laid partly to their distance from Atlanta.

The Atlanta convention gets a group of about a thousand singers together on the Friday before the second Sunday in September of each year in the smaller assembly hall of the civic auditorium in Atlanta for a three-day session of song from the old *Sacred Harp.* I attended the 1929 convention and saw about a thousand, predominatingly old men and old women but with youthfulness in their hearts if not in their voices. These men pointed with pride to the fact that Atlanta's then mayor, I. N. Ragsdale, was an enthusiastic *Sacred Harp* singer and leader.

At the present day there are around 156 annual singings in nineteen Georgia counties, in which the *Sacred Harp* is the official song book.

Alabama Sacred Harpers

Alabama's rural white settlers came in from the east (Georgia and the Carolinas) and from the northeast through the Appalachian valleys. And when they came, they brought their song books along. The probabilities are that there was little organized music of the singing convention type until after the Civil War. M. L. Swan of eastern Tennessee taught schools in the 1860's in the valley of the Tennessee River in Jackson County, Alabama, using his seven-shape *Harp of Columbia;* and there must have been others plying their musical trade in this northeast section. But all signs point to the predominance of song influence from the east.

The oldest annual Alabama singing of which we have any record is the Ryan's Creek Sacred Harp Singing Convention in Jasper County. It was organized in 1873 and held its fifty-sixth annual meet in 1929. In Winston County the "Clear Creek Mountain Home Singing Association" was organized in 1874[6] and in 1880 the annual Helicon singings were started and have been kept up to the present time. Greer Ward, of Cobb County, Georgia, brought the Albertville (Marshall County) Sacred Harp Convention into existence in the nineties. And the annual conventions in Edwardsville (Cleburne County)

[6] See *Musical Million,* XXVI (1895), 166.

had in 1904 been meeting for years.[7] In the *Musical Million* of 1886 I find the "Alabama State Singing Convention" mentioned.[8] Its third annual meeting convened that year in Four-Mile Church, Shelby County. As to whether this was a *Sacred Harp* or a *Christian Harmony* organization I have no information. In 1896 three conventions that are still carrying on, came into existence. They are the Bear Creek Sacred Harp Memorial Singings (Winston County), the Boiling Springs Sacred Harp Singing Convention (Clay County), and the Rock Creek Mountain Home Sacred Harp Convention in Cullman County.

In 1909 the Alabama State Sacred Harp Musical Association was organized and it has continued to the present time. The delegates to its three-day annual (July) conventions in Birmingham come from a score of counties, and records of its doings are to be found in the yearly pamphlets which it publishes as the "minutes" of the conventions. These minutes are also a rather detailed summary of all the local *Sacred Harp* annual singings held elsewhere in the state and affiliated with the central organization. In their 1929 minutes I find mention of one hundred and ten local *Sacred Harp* annual singings held elsewhere in the state and affiliated with the central organization. Nine of these are three-day affairs, eight last two days, and the rest are merely for one day. The present president of this big association is A. Marcus Cagle, of Birmingham.

Another state-wide singing organization known as the B. F. White Sacred Harp Musical Society of Alabama, Inc., was founded in 1915. J. C. Brown of Gadsden was its president in 1930. It meets in Birmingham every year for a three-day convention in the latter part of August. Its delegates assemble from somewhat the same territory as do those of the older state

[7] See James, *op. cit.*, pp. 77 ff.

[8] XVII, 172.

association. But the local singings which send the delegates are usually distinct, one local group sending its delegates to the B. F. White convention, and the other to the Alabama State gathering. Certain local groups, however, are represented in both conventions. In the 1929 minutes of the B. F. White society I find its affiliated local annual singings recorded to the total of forty. Add this to the one hundred and ten of the other state group and we have the grand total of one hundred and fifty *Sacred Harp* singing festivals held in what is, roughly speaking, the northern half of Alabama.

In southeastern Alabama the *Sacred Harp* singers have a distinct organization. Their separation from their brethren to the north is due partly to their geographical remoteness and partly to the edition of the *Sacred Harp,* by W. M. Cooper of Dothan, Alabama, which they use. Dothan lies in the extreme southeast corner of the state.

It was in the year 1902—a time when interest in the old *Sacred Harp,* which had seen no new edition for a third of a century, was lagging—that Cooper made what he called a a "revision." The reawakening of interest in the old book brought about by the Cooper revision is seen from the fact that it enjoyed subsequent reprintings in 1907 and 1909. It may have been the success of this Cooper activity that inspired the Atlantans to get out the *Original Sacred Harp* edition. Naturally the two books clashed. Cooper had recourse to the courts to help him defend what he conceived to be his exclusive right to title and songs, but his claim was not sustained.

To what extent and where the Cooper *Sacred Harp* is used today I cannot state, excepting that it is used in southern Alabama and in parts of Texas. Letters which I have addressed to its publishers have not been answered. The present owner

A SINGING OF THE ALABAMA STATE MUSICAL ASSOCIATION

Held in the Jefferson County Courthouse, Birmingham, Alabama, August, 1925.

of the Cooper *Sacred Harp* is Dr. R. D. Blackshear, of Panama City, Florida.

The Denson Singing Dynasty

One of the most interesting points of dissemination of the *Sacred Harp* four-shape singing and songs in Alabama is the Helicon district in Winston County, one of the remote districts of Alabama which railroads, highways, and schools have left comparatively undisturbed. Its sparse population was so predominatingly white during Civil War times that it sided very definitely with the Union in that conflict. Winston County is the long-time place of song fostering. The Densons have been and are the fosterers.

James M. Denson, a prominent singer of Walton County, Georgia, born over a hundred years ago, composed a comprehensive "Christmas Anthem," which appeared in the *Sacred Harp* of 1844 on page 225. Two of his nephews, the brothers Seaborn M. Denson and Tom J. Denson, who are now living in the Helicon district of Winston County, Alabama, are what might be called the deans of the fasola folk of the present generation.

I can best tell of S. M. Denson by reproducing the answers to a set of questions which I addressed to his wife a few years ago:

Dr. Jackson,

Kind Sir:

I have just received your letter of inquiry concerning my husband, S. M. Denson.

Question 1. When born? April 9, 1854.

Question 2. Where? Near a little village called Arbacoochee or the Denson Gold Mines. [Cleburne County, Alabama.]

Question 3. What Education? Webster's Blueback Speller

in [Civil] war times by a pine-knot fire. [Mr. Denson assured me recently that it was his wife, the writer of this letter, who taught him to read.]

Question 4. Where has he taught singing schools? Alabama, Georgia, and Mississippi.

Question 5. How many has he taught to sing? Every year, excepting four, since 1874. He has taught from 25 to 100 scholars a term, ten days and sometimes twenty [per term] and as high as 80 days in one year. You can estimate the vastness of his musical work for the past fifty-one years. [I have estimated, roughly, of course, that he taught fasola singing to between 8,000 and 12,000 young rurals.]

Question 6. How many songs has he composed? I can not say just how many. He has written 327 alto parts to the songs in the Old Sacred Harp. [Mr. Denson told me subsequently that there are ten of his compositions in the *Sacred Harp* and that fifteen others had appeared in the *Union Harp* and in *Sacred Hymns and Tunes*.]

My husband blows the fife and is a violinist. [Not a secular "old fiddler," I take it.] He has devoted his life to the musical cause and is the father of a large family—seven boys and two girls—seven of whom are living and are singers, most of them are teachers. Yours respectfully,

MRS. S. M. DENSON.

The two brothers, "Seab" and "Tom," as they are called, had the good sense to select as their wives two sisters from another musical family. The talent of Mrs. S. M. (born Sydney S. Burdette) is shown by a composition of hers in the *Original Sacred Harp,* page 523. In the same book are two pieces by her son, Whit Denson, one of which he named "Burdette" in honor of his mother's family. Whit is now, at the age of forty, an active singing-school teacher and the father of ten youthful musicians, two of whom, Owel and De-

A FOURTH OF JULY SACRED HARP SINGING IN HELICON, ALABAMA, 1926

UPPER LEFT: *Leaders.* UPPER RIGHT: *"Dinner on the Grounds."* LOWER LEFT: *Mule wagons were the singers' sole means of travel.* LOWER RIGHT: *The crowd at noon under the trees. At the right is the little school-church where they sang all day.*

lila, are teaching and composing—the fourth song-fostering generation of this remarkable fasola family.

Tom Denson, younger brother of S. M., has taught "more singing schools and more people to sing," so says a biographical sketch in the *Original Sacred Harp,* "than any [other] teacher in Georgia or Alabama." Be that as it may, he is still active. In the summer of 1930 he was teaching a big *Sacred Harp* class in Mineral Wells, Texas. Four of his songs are to be found in the *Original Sacred Harp.* His first wife, she who was Amanda Burdette, is represented in the venerable book by her song "Kelly." Among their many children who "are all up in music," teaching and composing, according to the *Original Sacred Harp* sketch of their father; one, Payne Denson, a prominent attorney in Birmingham, does not allow the demands of his profession to interfere with his song-leading activities in as many *Sacred Harp* conventions as are held thereabouts.

At the July convention, 1931, of the Alabama State Sacred Harp Musical Association, which packed the Ben Hur hall in Birmingham for three days running, I saw Payne and Evan Denson among the basses, Mrs. Maggie Denson Cagle and Owel Denson among the tenors, Robert Denson and Mrs. Annie Denson Aaron singing treble, and Delila Denson and Mrs. Reedie Denson Barnes active in the alto section. Uncle Seab Denson held a seat of honor in the arena and was granted extraordinary privileges as leader. Whit Denson played the piano. A. Marcus Cagle—Uncle Seab's brother-in-law and composer of two *Sacred Harp* songs—was elected president of the state organization for the music-year 1931-1932.

The Sacred Harp in Mississippi

I have not learned that there is in Mississippi any comprehensive state Sacred Harp organization. And the rarity of singers from that state attending the big conventions in other states as delegates indicates the low estate of Sacred Harp singing in that commonwealth. The hoary song book still has a foothold in the northeastern corner of the state where the Prentiss and Tishomingo Counties Sacred Harp Singing Convention, under the leadership of another Denson, T. C., holds its annual two-day convention "in one county or the other," and where, as they reported in the 1930 minutes of the Texas Interstate Sacred Harp Musical Association, "we have singing somewhere [in those counties] nearly every Sunday" (of the year). We get a glimpse of the sylvan surroundings in which this ancient art still lives without any particular nursing, from their announcement of the 1931 convention at Bay Springs, not on a Rand-McNally map, but noted for "its high rocks, clear spring water and beautiful scenery." It is "on the headwaters of the Tombigbee river, on a state highway, nine miles west of Belmont and twenty-one miles east of Booneville, Miss."

The Sacred Harp in Arkansas

It is quite a trip westward from the hill country of northeastern Mississippi before we again strike the trail of the Sacred Harpers. In the Mississippi River lowlands they seem never to have made a stand in their trek toward Texas, the Promised Land of uncounted thousands of rural southerners after the Civil War. Vestiges of what was once probably far more extensive four-shape singing are found in western Arkansas. And in northeastern Texas we again come into a *Sacred Harp* singing region that rivals anything we have seen in Georgia or Alabama.

The threshold organization is the "United Sacred Harp Musical Association of Arkansas, Texas, Louisiana and Oklahoma," according to its life secretary, E. D. Lingold, in a letter to me. "It was organized April 24, 1922, and now has a

THREE MEMBERS OF THE MUSICAL DENSON FAMILY

LEFT TO RIGHT: *Seaborn M. Denson, his son Whit, and his brother Tom. "Uncle Seab," musical reviser of the* Original Sacred Harp *in 1911, is "dean" of the* Sacred Harp *singing and lore. Whit Denson, composer and carrier-on of the hoary traditions, teaches both fasola and seven-shape singing. "Uncle Tom" is one of the few old-time* Sacred Harp *singing-school teachers still active. He teaches in Alabama and Texas.*

membership in the four above-named states of 2,502, with J. A. Burgess of Maud, Texas, as president, also elected for life, and with permanent headquarters at Texarkana." This town, it will be remembered, is on the line between Arkansas and Texas and is hardly an hour's motor trip from the corner of Oklahoma in one direction and the corner of Louisiana in the other. We may, therefore, see how the convention may enjoy some patronage from these four states and still not be as comprehensive as its name would indicate. Its annual conventions are held in Texarkana the fourth Sunday in July and the Friday and Saturday before. Its semi-annual singings come the fourth Sunday in October and the Saturday before. The James edition of the *Sacred Harp* is official with this convention, though the Cooper edition is also used to some extent in its territory.

The Sacred Harp in Texas

Of the surprisingly early introduction of the *Sacred Harp* into Texas we read in the *Musical Million* of 1880 that the East Texas Musical Convention, which met in that year "is the oldest musical body in the state. It was organized in 1855 and has held its annual sessions regularly except three or four years during the [Civil] war. Its organizers adopted the *Sacred Harp* . . . at the start and have held to it up to date."[9] The *Sacred Harp* popularity around "Kentucktown" (Kentucky Town, Grayson County, Texas?) in post-Civil-War times (1866) is asserted in *Musical Million,* as is also its wide use in Upshur County in the same year.[10]

The East Texas (Sacred Harp) Singing Convention was organized in 1914. R. J. Behannon, Lufkin, Texas, is its present president, elected for life. Its delegates come from thirteen counties. Among them are Angelina, Cherokee, Nacog-

[9] XI, 135.

[10] See *Musical Million,* XVII (1886), 42, 156.

doches, Shelby, San Augustine, Tyler, Polk, Trinity, and Jasper. It has four hundred and fifty registered members and meets annually for a two-day session in September. Mr. Behannon, a prominent wholesale merchant of his city, tells me the convention has been growing rapidly during the last few years. Besides, they have numerous smaller conventions meeting here and there in the district and on nearly every Sunday (often also on Saturday before) in the year.

In 1922 the name of the dominant organization of Texas was "State Sacred Harp Singers' Association," according to the minutes of the United Sacred Harp Musical Association, Atlanta, for that year.

In the territory tributary to Dallas, Fort Worth, and Mineral Wells the Midway Sacred Harp Convention of Texas was, from earlier years up to 1929, an influential group under the presidency of W. T. Coston of Dallas. The sphere of its influence extended over Dallas, Tarrant, Palo Pinto, Erath, Coleman, Brown, Hill, Ellis, Wood, Cass, Smith, Upshur, Hunt, Panola, Bell, Wise, Henderson, Taylor, McLennan, Harrison, Rusk, Stephens, Grayson, Angelina, Bowie, Van Zandt, Bosque, and Parker counties. At the present time (1931) it thrives, under its new name (adopted in 1929), The Texas Interstate Sacred Harp Musical Association, as the most representative group west of the Mississippi and has met for several years for its three-day annual August convention in Mineral Wells. I attended the 1930 convention at Mineral Wells and I know of no better way to close this story of the *Sacred Harp* singing guilds than to tell of the experience, in the hope that the story may bring my readers into a little closer mental touch with this old-time present-time singing guild and give them a little clearer idea of its significance.

CHAPTER XI

A SACRED HARP SINGING CONVENTION IN TEXAS

The Convention Calendar

The "little singings," one day long, sometimes two, come almost any Sunday with its Saturday or on any other holiday during the year. The Fourth of July, for example, is a popular date for all-day singings in the rural song belt, where the firecracker method of celebrating the nation's birth has never been customary. Perhaps the oldest Fourth-of-July singing is the one at Helicon, Winston County, Alabama, twenty-five miles from a railroad. It was established in 1891. In the Shenandoah Valley, New Year's Day is an equally popular date for "old folks' singings." But it is the six- or eight-week period between the first part of July and the first part of September when crops are "laid by," that furnishes the Sacred Harper his annual big-convention singing opportunities.

Despite the shortness of this musical "season," the competition for favorable dates is not unfriendly. The leaders of each convention have a fraternal consideration for the calendar rights of their neighboring singing groups. Thus it came about in 1930, for example, that the Alabama Sacred Harp Musical Association met in Birmingham late in July, that the Texas Interstate Sacred Harp Musical Association met at Mineral Wells on the second Sunday in August and the two days before, and that the B. F. White Sacred Harp Musical Society of Alabama, Inc., met in Birmingham and the United Sacred Harp Musical Association met in Atlanta respectively two and four weeks later, with less widely representative conventions taking place in different parts of that same territory on the intervening Sundays.

The Interstate Sacred Harp Convention

I arrived in Mineral Wells, Texas, toward the end of the Great Drouth of 1930. The clerk of the sky-scraping Baker Hotel in the Lone Star State's favorite spa could not direct me to the Interstate Sacred Harp Convention. He knew nothing of it. He was able, however, to direct me to the municipal convention hall. The Friday morning session was just starting with a song as I entered. After the song the chaplain read from the scriptures, offered a prayer, and then singing, nothing but singing, filled the forenoon from nine to twelve excepting for a short recess in the middle.

I observed the singers. There were about two hundred of them, men, women, and children. They were all country folk, of course, though some of them lived, as I learned, in Texas cities. They were the same type, precisely, that I had met in many other Sacred Harp conventions. This was evident from their work-browned faces and their absence of "style." Galluses were much in evidence.

The singers were what is commonly called "pure Anglo-Saxon stock," but what is in reality, as we have seen above, Celtic, Teutonic, and Anglo-Saxon, and hence Nordic. If they are to be dubbed "poor whites," the term should be used to signify those people who have not yet turned from their ancient attitudes toward life values and adopted the current commercially standardized ones. The singers at Mineral Wells had not, like the guests of the Baker Hotel, come to look on air-cooled dining rooms and tiled swimming pools or even on bathtubs, tooth-brushes, and lipstick as the great values of this life. They had, for example, not been willing to exchange their birthright of singing for the meager mess of "listening" pottage. They sang and sweated while the Baker Hotel folk lolled about, ate, smoked, gossiped, philandered, and tried to keep from listening to a jazz band.

The singers occupied the level floor space of the auditorium, leaving the tiers of seats, rising to both sides, for the sparsely assembled listeners. These listeners were also country people. The singers sat in folding chairs on four sides of a rectangular open space where the leader stood. The men and women "tenors" (sopranos) were in front of the leader, the men and women "trebles" (tenors) at his left, the women altos behind him, and the basses at his right. Each singer had a copy of the big *Sacred Harp* on his lap. Some of these were of the 1930 printing. But here and there I saw yellowed copies of an edition that had appeared two generations ago, heirlooms that were brought along, mayhap, when the singers' forebears moved into the new state of Texas. But this difference in edition brought no confusion, for the song on any given page was the same for all the printings of this 86-year-old survival in musical culture.

Each singer wore a ribbon badge which showed him to be an accredited delegate from some other singing convention or singing school. They had gathered, as I learned later, largely from Texas and the adjoining states to the north and east. Though Alabama organizations were represented by over twenty delegates, one hailed from Georgia and one from Tennessee.

The president, W. H. Coston of Dallas, announced the "brother" who was to "sing." (In Alabama he "led" a lesson." And in the *Harmonia Sacra* singings of the Shenandoah Valley he "entertained us.") His time on the floor was three songs long. He called the page of his first song and then "keyed" the tune by singing its tonic and other opening tones without the help of even a tuning fork. "Faw, law, sol!" The singers of all four parts got their pitch instantly and, after the one deliberate chord with which all the *Sacred Harp* songs begin, the whole chorus was on its way singing the song once through by "notes" (solmization syllables) only, a practice which is unique today with these four-shapers and is clearly recognizable as the survival of a custom started two hundred years ago in the first American singing schools. Then came the words, one to three stanzas. Some leaders stood still. But most of them walked around the open space giving the entrance cues—in the often-sung "fuguing" songs—successively to the different sections. The leader's beat was with both arms, for he was seldom encumbered with a book; and his arm movements were simply down and up. The songs seldom demanded anything else, and if they did it made no difference. The response of the singers was usually vigorous and rhythmically precise, for they, making little use of the book, kept their eyes on the leader and beat time also, always with one arm or merely the hand. And if that hand held a fan, it was given a little twist, half a revolution, each time it came up. The reading ability of these singers was nothing short of astounding. There are 550 pages of four-part music in the *Sacred Harp,* and they tackled and mastered, by solmization as well as by text, anything that any leader put up. This meant either that they had, by long years of singing, learned the entire book practically by heart, or that they were sight readers of what we could call "professional" stature. I came to the conclusion that both memorization and sight-reading ability were responsible for this remarkable accomplishment.

The women were not declassed in this *Sacred Harp* convention. While male singers were perhaps more numerous,

A TEXAS SACRED HARP SINGING CONVENTION

The Texas Inter-State Sacred Harp Musical Association's Convention at Mineral Wells, Texas, August 9, 1930.

still the womenfolk were an important element in the ranks and as leaders. Owing to the lack of volume in their voices, it was customary for some man to "key" the tune for them. But otherwise their conductorial work was on a par with that of the males.

This singing went on busily for over two hours. And one session was much like all the others, but for the choice of leaders and songs. The program committee strove to make it possible for each delegate who was a leader—and most of them were—to have his or her turn on the floor. The patriarchs like the Alabama Densons and C. J. Griggs, delegate from the United Sacred Harp Convention of Georgia, were accorded special leadership privileges. Thus during the seven sessions at least fifty delegates led one or more "lessons." I have no record of the number of songs sung on this occasion. But the figures for similar meets held in Birmingham in 1924 and 1925 show an average of forty songs sung each session, or two hundred and eighty during the seven sessions of three days. The most industrious singing seems to have been done at the 1925 convention of the B. F. White organization in Birmingham, where one session showed as many as fifty-three songs sung, one full day of three sessions, one hundred and forty-one songs, and for the entire three-day meet three hundred and twenty.

The Contest of Child Leaders

A feature of the Saturday forenoon session at Mineral Wells was the contest of child leaders. They called it a "singing contest." It seems that the older fasola singers, concerned as to the persistence of their art, have seen that it will endure only to the extent to which they succeed in interesting the children. This first prize contest, made possible by the generosity of President W. T. Coston, was the logical result, and similar efforts are now being made in the states farther east.

One after another these children—there were some fifteen contestants—entered the arena and led one or two songs each. The three judges marked them on *time* (tempo of the song, and their keeping step with the music while walking around the open space), *accent, pronunciation* (of the "notes." They should pronounce sol "sole," not "saul," they were told. And was that why they and their singers sang "abroad" as if it were "abrode" in forcing it to rime with "rode"?), *expression* (pertaining to the "message" of the song words), and *rendition,* meaning bodily gracefulness and looking up and out while leading.

The ability of these children, from six years old to those in their early teens, provided another surprise. A number of them had but one or two brief singing schools' instruction behind them, but they led without using the book and like veterans. An interesting example was that of Carl Miller, about ten years old, pupil for twenty-five days, of the veteran four-shape master, Tom Denson, leading the difficult fuguing song "Logan" which his master had composed. That aged Harper now sat in front of his pupil and keyed the song for him as he had been keying for five decades. Carl sang, first time through, every fa-sol-la syllable of his own part and gave the cue faultlessly, with syllable, pitch, and gesture to each singing section as it was to come in on the fugue. Loraine Miles, six years old, did apparently the same task. At any rate her "class" responded with fine enthusiasm. "She has never been to school, doesn't even know her abc's, but she can read notes like fun," the tot's father, John W. Miles of Mineral Wells, assured me. More a matter of promise than of realization was the leading done by the tiny Evelyn Krause, three years old. But her going through the motions was one of the delights of the occasion.

This contest was in reality a test of ability in conducting, solmization, and music memory. Vocal quality was not mentioned by the chairman as a point to be considered. Two girls, Lola Jones and Melba Head, each with a grade of one hundred per cent, won the $30 cash prizes of the contest. But lesser prizes in amounts down to $7.50 were awarded to all who had participated.

Following the awarding of the prizes by their donors, Mr. and Mrs. Coston, a little ceremony took place which gave me an inkling as to the powerful grip which this singing holds on the souls of its devotees and the depths of emotion it touches. The president invited all the young contestants to stand in a row and all the singers to shake hands with them. A song was started:

> If a mother wants to go,
> Why don't she come along?
> I belong to this band
> Hallelujah!

One of those exhortational folk-spirituals of infectious tune, compelling march movement, and a never-ending series of verses (made by substituting "father," "brother," "sister," etc., for "mother") known to all. At first the happy children received merely a warm hand-shake and pat on the shoulder from the men and a kiss from the women. But by degrees the wave of emotion rose, swept on by this song and then by another one spliced on, and by the really parental joy in those children who had so beautifully proved that they could carry on their fathers' and mothers' beloved art—until the warm congratulatory reception became a veritable and ardent "love feast." The little ones were smothered with kisses and hugs. Tears streamed down the cheeks of young and old. And one patriarchal fat man, looking on, crying, laughing, sweating, and fanning, shouted intermittently.

The Effect Upon the Singers

I look upon the whole demonstration, and especially upon the shouting, as something significant. In itself the "shout" was nothing more nor less than the short staccato whoop or yell or yip that is still heard widely in uncowed environments. But here it told me that emotion, raised to the highest pitch, was venting itself. The group as a whole got its catharsis in songs and tears. The old man, who filled up like the rest but had ceased singing, blew off in shouts. And if we are to agree with the psychologists as to the "immorality" resulting from the excitation and non-satisfaction of the emotions, then those *Sacred Harp* singers were engaged in one of the most purely moral pursuits. Their emotional catharsis was one hundred per cent. On the one hand, inhibition, the necessary evil of civilization; on the other, complete release, the blessing of this music-making and the prime reason, perhaps, for its longevity; a blessing which obviously cannot descend upon those ominously great masses of mere hearers of music.

If these people were not happy, in the best and fullest meaning of the word, then I have never seen human happiness. The contrast presented here to those many other gatherings of different sorts, where "whoopee" is conventionally conjured by artificial methods and dispensed in Room 256, inevitably came to my mind.

May I stress the importance of the emotional element in this singing by quoting from a declaration made to me by Charles Martin, an inveterate Sacred Harper of Atlanta:

"Every time I go to one of these singings I feel that I am attending a memorial to my mother. Twenty years ago she floated out into the harbor of eternal rest. Today she is taking part in the Royal Band. This singing takes me back to the dearest spot known to humanity, that of a mother's knee. It never fails, on such occasions, that some song or some voice amongst the singers reminds me of my dear old mother. And then it just seems as if the purest joys nearest heaven were bidding clouds give way to sun and light and as if heaven itself hovered over the place.

"You'll have to put up a mighty high fence," the old singer declared convincingly after a little pause, to keep me out of a Sacred Harp Singing."

A similar ecstasy was reported thirty years ago in the *Musical Million* by A. G. Holloway, an old-time Alabama singer. He was versed in the lighter "gospel song." But "whenever I begin singing these older songs of my childhood, I get up, as it were, into the elysian fields and seem for a time almost transported to the regions of perfect love and joy."

This musical-religious ecstasy sometimes takes its toll. William Walker *(Southern Harmony)* and John G. McCurry *(Social Harp)* are among the notable singing enthusiasts who are recorded as having suffered with a "throat affection" which made them voiceless for some time before their death. The recent case of J. C. Brown came to my observation. He was president of the Alabama State B. F. White Sacred Harp Singing Association. He could not sing or lead more than a few minutes before his tears were streaming. The greater emotion seemed to call forth the greater vocal exertion. He was known as the most zealous of all the Sacred Harpers. I have run across Brown at conventions in Georgia, Alabama, and Texas. Between singings he clerked in a furniture store in Gadsden, Alabama. An illness nearly ended his life in the winter of 1930; but he got up and into the round of singing conventions again. The following summer I saw him pressing into his beloved service of song his tired and diseased voice and body. Six months later he died of tuberculosis. I find cases like Brown's, Walker's and McCurry's reported in the rural musical periodicals, *Vaughan's Family Visitor* and the *Herald of Song*.

But even such victims are sure of their compensation. The Sacred Harpers' mental picture of heaven is, as it is expressed repeatedly in their songs and as one hears them declare in conversation, prayer, and convention speeches, that of a place where they will meet again those beloved singers who have gone before, and sing again with them, endlessly.

Songs for the Singers, Not for the Listeners

The effect of this singing on the singers is one thing, the most important thing indeed. But the impression made on the mere listener is quite another matter.

The person of standardized urban-musical background who hears casually his first *Sacred Harp* music is apt to judge it harshly. He will be impressed unfavorably by the shrill voices of some of the women, by the trotting movement of the songs, which will strike him as being at variance with their religious aspects, by the harmonic effects (he will call them "discords") that are strangely different from those to which his ear has been accustomed, by what seems to be an absence of melody or tune, and by the fact that all songs sound much alike to him.

As to the shrill voices, the Sacred Harpers will readily admit that a minimum of attention is paid to individual voice quality by the leaders. The song is the thing—the mass effect. And who is going to tell Sister So-and-so not to step on it quite so hard, or that she should place her tone differently, anyway? And why, in the name of good sense, should she bear the audience in mind when there is none? This is democratic music making. All singers are peers. And the moment selection and exclusion enter, at that moment this singing of, for, and by the people loses its chief characteristic.

The reason why some high female voices stand out with undue prominence is not, after all, primarily a matter of individual vocal quality. We are accustomed to hearing female voices predominate when they sing the melody part in mixed choruses. But here they sing, according to hoary tradition, a middle part corresponding roughly to the urban tenor of today. They call it treble and pronounce it "trible." Even when this part is taken by men, it *seems* to be pitched higher than the soprano melody. But when it is sung by women it is *actually* higher. So we have, under the circumstances that obtain in *Sacred Harp* circles, a "middle part" in the harmony, sung very high and by the women, whose voices have normally greater carrying qualities than those of the men. And this female tenor part is exposed still more completely as the result of another ancient song custom of these singers, namely, the custom which gives the melody part into the keeping of the normal-voiced men, not exclusively but mainly. This means that the melody, while full, has not the carrying power that it would have if sung by female sopranos as we are accustomed to hearing it sung. And it is easy to see that with this partial submergence of the melody the prominence of the female tenor part becomes all the greater, a prominence which brings clearly to the ear of the listener all the vocal qualities, good or bad, of the singers of that part.

And it is, I am convinced, this same unique distribution of parts—men "sopranos" and women "tenors"—that is largely at the root of what strikes the novice-listener as "peculiar harmonic effects." There may be other reasons for the effects.

My attention has been called also to the "successive fifths" in *Sacred Harp* songs as a factor in their harmonic character. Whit Denson, a *Sacred Harp* composer, doubts the importance of the "successive fifths" feature and calls attention to the frugality in the use of different chords. He points out that the *Sacred Harp* songs tend to specialize on the tonic and dominant chords and to neglect the subdominant and practically all others. As still further contributions to the unique musical character of these songs, it may be mentioned that many of them show pentatonic melodies, that very many of the songs are in minor keys, and that the fuguing songs are structural puzzles which demand a number of hearings and some study before the hearer can understand "what it is all about."

In the above paragraphs I have called attention to characteristics which have been at the bottom of the "peculiar harmonic effects," and which have contributed to the submergence of the melody. There is, however, still another reason why it is hard for the listener to identify the tune in *Sacred Harp* singing. In urban music of the usual simpler sorts the tune is paramount and the other parts are comparatively modest and subservient in their trend. This is not true for the *Sacred Harp*. There the melody part (they call it "tenor") is of hardly any greater import than any other. For the custom of the rural composers has been, from time immemorial, to make the parts, as nearly as possible, equally interesting to the singers. This objective seems to have been justified by the necessity, in the utter absence of instruments, for each of the four parts to be well manned. So we see treble, alto, and bass indulging in about as much running around as does the tune-carrying tenor. They even snatch a bit of the tune away from the tenor, here and there, forcing it to put up with the

LEADING SACRED HARPERS FROM THREE STATES

LEFT TO RIGHT: *J. C. Brown, president of the B. F. White Sacred Harp Musical Society of Alabama; W. T. Coston, president of the Texas Inter-state Sacred Harp Musical Association; C. J. Riggs, patriarch of Georgia's fasola folk.*

notes of a "middle part" or observe a "rest." The result of all this poaching of one part on the preserves of the others is confusion on the part of the listener who tries to identify the parts—soprano, alto, and tenor, the bass being more easily recognizable—to which his urban ear has become accustomed in choral church music *comme il faut.*

A word as to the trotting movement of practically all the *Sacred Harp* songs, that characteristic which usually impresses the city-dwelling listener as being inappropriate to the religious character of the words. The movement of these songs is, to be sure, uniformly sprightly, about the tempo of the march. And this condition often imposes on the singers the task of negotiating some very fast note and word sequences. But, after all, who has decreed that all sacred music should be slow? The old chorale type of music was slow, to be sure. The early American colonists dragged their tunes along. And modern city congregations pull back, despite the efforts of organ and quartet to overcome their phlegm. But does all that establish any immutable law? Certainly the congregations have found no scriptural injunctions against sprightly, glad music. On the contrary.

Another estranging rhythmic feature in the *Sacred Harp* singing is their common custom of not tolerating any dead spaces or long rests, those pauses which are found in instrumentally influenced music and even to some extent in the *Sacred Harp* pages—"waits" which are felt as needed to make the rhythmic form mathematically correct or quadratic, holes that are filled, in other environments, by instrumental inserts. But here, with no instrument to fill the melodic-rhythmic vacuum, the leaders and singers deliberately disregard the rest-beat and proceed as though it did not exist. This procedure naturally throws the leader's regularly alternating beat out of joint with the tune, making him beat "up" on a down-beat and vice versa, until he comes to another discarded pause that sets him straight again. With all this, it will be seen, much of the variation in accent heft is lost by the singer and to the hearer, and the rhythmic flow becomes mechanized.

It would seem, then, that the *Sacred Harp* type of music is to be sung and not listened to, and that the critic who makes his judgments from the false observation point of the twentieth-century hearer is pretty sure to draw unhappy and impertinent conclusions. Incidentally, the paragraphs above may also indicate why the phonographic recordings of this strange choral singing have not sold to any considerable extent.

CHAPTER XII

THE SONGS THEMSELVES: EIGHTY MOST POPULAR TUNES

The Civil War as a Dividing Line Between Periods

We have been concerned thus far principally with the fasola or four-shape tune books, their compilers and teachers, their singing conventions and singers. Our consideration of the songs themselves, that body of musical and poetic material around which all this rural singing activity revolves, has been incidental. In the following pages we shall focus our attention on the pre-Civil-War fasola songs, as such.

My reason for inserting a study of the old songs themselves at this time, before having told of the post-Civil-War period in rural song development, is that this more recent span of years and its songs tell a quite different story. The last few chapters above have, to be sure, dealt with very recent happenings and editions and with singers now living, young even. But I hardly need remind the reader that those books, events, and individuals, though *in* the present age are not *of* it.

With the opening of the Civil War we are at the end of one distinct period of song development. The reasons why the end came at this particular time are not hard to see. One reason was that the period of that conflict brought an almost complete, though not long, interruption of southern singing schools, conventions, and song-book distribution. Singers and teachers had more exacting tasks. And even if they had been able to continue their musical practices, such practices would have been crippled by the complete cutting off of their song-book supply. For it will be remembered that practically all of the widely popular southern-compiled books had been printed either in Philadelphia or Cincinnati. And it so happened that the war came at just the time when the old four-shape notation was giving way to the seven-shape. The many years of interruption became, therefore, a sort of *coup de grâce* to the antiquating fasola notation, to the books which used it, and, in a large measure, to the songs in those books and to the manner in which the songs were made and sung.

I may add here parenthetically that the song conditions at the end of the period of hostilities were just what we might have expected. The first publications of the late sixties were mostly new books rather than new editions of old books. All these new books used the new do-re-mi notation, were quite hospitable to new songs, and showed the influence of younger song makers.

Bases of Selection of Eighty Most Popular Songs

I have found material for examination in fifteen of the song books, eleven of which are described in the foregoing, and four in subsequent chapters. They are the *Kentucky Harmony,* edition of 1821, hereinafter referred to as KYH, *Supplement to the Kentucky Harmony,* edition of 1820 (SKH), *Missouri Harmony,* edition which is probably of 1836 (MOH), *Genuine Church Music,* edition of 1832 (GCM), *Southern Harmony,* revised edition, 1854 (SOH), *Union Harmony,* edition of 1837 (UH), *Knoxville Harmony,* edition of 1838 (KNH), *Sacred Harp,* edition of 1854 (SAH), and its most recent edition of 1911 (OSH), *Hesperian Harp,* edition of 1848 (HH), *Social Harp,* edition of 1859 (SOCH), *Christian Minstrel,* edition of 1850 (CM), *Harp of Columbia,* edition of 1855 (HOC), *Western Psalmodist,* edition of 1853 (WP), and

Timbrel of Zion, edition of 1854 (TZ). I have also made some use of my most recent find, the *Columbian Harmony* of 1825.

These are all song collections that were more or less widely used in the southeastern rural song district during the forty-five years from 1815 to 1860. The selection of these particular books for closer study has been determined partly by their being most accessible to me, and partly by the accidental fact of their covering the period and the territory so well that the bringing of still other books into this consideration could hardly change the findings materially.

Even among the songs themselves I have naturally had to be selective. For intensive examination I have chosen from among the several thousand songs of the fifteen books those which show, by their reappearance in book after book, that they were among the most popular songs of the period and section under scrutiny. The reliability of this popularity yardstick is vouched for by the fact that the compilers took no orders, in the selection of the songs they should include, from anybody but the singers. They knew no such groups as "boards of publication" or church-appointed "song book committees." The inclusion of the popular and the exclusion, from edition to edition, of the less widely sung songs was, therefore, the compiler's first and last law. And from the workings of this law we can see what the rural liked and did not like.

Exotic and Indigenous Types of Song

The first conclusion I reached after making a list of around one hundred oftenest recurring songs, was that they fell naturally into two fairly distinct types which may be roughly designated as exotic and indigenous. The exotic songs were, as a rule, those inherited from earlier times and from sources that were more artistic and more specifically churchly. The indigenous songs were those whose tunes, and to some extent words also, either were made in the rural South or were of a nature that made them very much at home there. These latter songs were intended for social singing (singing schools), revivals, protracted or camp meetings—everything, indeed, but that authoritatively and traditionally "churchly" use and environment from which the rural singers were almost to a man fugitives. To a certain extent, therefore, the name "folk songs" would also be appropriate to these home products and "art songs" to the other sort.

Among the songs of the first or less domesticated type I have found fifteen which appear in from four to all fifteen of the rural books. They are "Albion," "Arlington," "Aylesbury," "Bethel," "Balerma," "China," "Duke Street," "Hebron," "Mear," "Ortonville," "Old Hundred," "Pleyel's Hymn 7's," "Saint Thomas," "Wells," and "Wyndham." These appear in an average of eight books each. The four songs most often found in the list are "Mear" (in all fifteen books), "Old Hundred" (in all fifteen), "Wells" (in ten), and "Wyndham" (in thirteen).

Many readers will recognize these as standard hymns, some of which are still to be found in church collections. Their tunes are dignified. Their harmony is correct. They are usually (thirteen out of the fifteen) in the major mode. They make use of the whole diatonic scale, that is, without any characteristic melodic "skips," and their words are based directly on the psalm texts as versified by Watts and others. These characteristics are largely at variance with those of the domestic songs which we shall now discuss. And the differences lead to the assumption that those standard hymns and tunes were quite a bit too good for the southern rural when his honest tastes were taken into consideration. They were relics from musical-culturally better times and places.

Songs Listed According to Melody

In listing the popular and largely homemade songs according to their melodies, rather than by their titles or texts, I have followed the more reliable course. For titles are borrowed, lent, duplicated, and altered almost at the will of the compiler, and the texts slither about from tune to tune. Also we find various texts mixed in one and the same song, and certain popular "errant" stanzas doing service here and there in many songs. Furthermore, a favorite tune is prone to be associated with widely liked text material. And again, the southern rural is primarily a singer, not a poet. His point of gravity is in the music and that is where his contributions have been most striking. So I shall be concerned in the subsequent paragraphs largely with tunes and shall be guilty perhaps of slighting the discussion of the texts as such.

As a result of my hunt for "most popular domestic tunes" I found eighty, not one of which occurred in less than three books and many in all fifteen, the average occurrence being about six books. I said there were eighty tunes. The figure is a bit arbitrary, for the differences between some of them are slight, so slight indeed that the tunes in question might be looked on as variants of the same tune instead of distinct melodies. But the point is not important.

My method of classifying the tunes, that is, of bringing likes together, may be worthy of description. I first transposed the song to be classified into B flat, selecting that key as one which would bring the notes of the average melody usually within the five lines of the staff. I then put down, in that key and in the usual round-note form, at the top of a regular library catalog card the first musical phrase of the tune with words of the first stanza beneath. On the line below the musical phrase and text I recorded the book and page where I had found it. As these tune cards piled up and further occurrences of the same tunes were found, a scheme of arrangement of cards had to be found—a scheme which would make it possible to find quickly if a melody to be recorded had already been found in another book and notated on a card. The method which suggested itself here was to place first in the stack of cards that melody which began on the *lowest note* below the tonic B flat. Then the tune beginning on one note above that of the first entry was placed right after it, and so on, the beginning notes taking the place of the initial letters in the usual alphabetical classification. When more than one tune began on the same note, the pitch of their second notes determined their respective positions in the card file, the card with the lowest second note preceding the one with the next lowest, just as "Aaron" precedes "Abbott" in an alphabetical list. It seldom became necessary to take into consideration more than the first three or four notes of any tune. For if two melodies were identical as far as that, they were usually found to correspond throughout. In case of such identity all that was necessary was to record the place of its new occurrence and the first lines of its text if these lines varied from those already recorded with the first occurrence of the tune. In the classification of these eighty tunes—around five hundred occurrences—this method has worked out satisfactorily.[1]

It has been for the sake of brevity that I have reproduced only the beginning phrase of the melodies. Each tune, without regard to its original key, has been presented in the key of B flat major or in G minor. The absolute pitch of the tunes will have

[1] Tune indexing is still an infant endeavor. That my scheme is somewhat in line with other successful attempts may be verified by consulting Gustave Otto Arlt, "Status of Research in Folk Melodies," Master's Dissertation, University of Chicago, 1929. An even more recent work dealing with melody classification is Hans Mersmann, *Grundlagen einer musikalischen Volksliedforschung,* Leipzig, 1930.

to be judged by the singer or player of these melodic passages. The clef is the treble or G clef. The time designations are as they have been found in the books excepting when the book notation was manifestly erroneus. A typical error found consisted in giving the time of many songs as $\frac{2}{2}$, when it is in reality $\frac{3}{2}$.

Eighty Most Popular Tunes[2]

No. 1. Supplication, Bourbon, Consolation (Watts, Dean, Chapin)

Shew pi- ty, Lord, o Lord, for-give, let a re - pent-ing reb- el live.
or 'Twas on that dark that doleful night when pow'rs of earth and hell arose.
or From deep distress and troubled thoughts to thee, my God, I raised my cries.
or Once more, my soul, the rising day salutes thy waking eyes.
or O Thou who hear'st when sinners cry, tho' all my crimes before thee lie.
or (*Choral-Music*)
Ach Gott, wie manches Herzeleid, begegnet mir zu dieser Zeit.

Found in KYH 20, SKH 61, MOH 60, GCM 159, HH 8, KYH 28 variant, MOH 25, 26, GCM 110, SOH 5, UH 14, KNH 31, SAH 45, HH 5, SOCH 55, and Choral-Music 48.

No. 2. Liberty Hall (Watts, Wyeth, Chapin)

Death, what a sol - emn word to all! What mor - tal things are men!
or Alas, and did my Savior bleed, and did my sov'reign die?

MOH 32, GCM 127, UH 22, KNH 99, KYH 27.

No. 3. Leander (Austin)

My soul for-sakes her vain de-light, and bids the world fare - well.
or Jesus, the vision of thy face hath overpow'ring charms.
or Am I a soldier of the cross, a follower of the lamb?

SOH 128, UH 66, SAH 71, CM 310, HOC 61, WP 52, TZ 100.

[2] We shall refer to this series of song beginnings as the "MPT" list. For other abbreviations see p. 128 above and the alphabetical list on p. 437 below.

No. 4. Dismission

I can-not bear thine ab-sence, Lord, my life ex-pires if thou de-part.

MOH 143, UH 17, and HH 8.

No. 5. Primrose (Watts, Chapin)

Sal - va - tion, oh the joy-ful sound, 'tis pleas-ure to our ears.
or Hosanna to the Prince of Light that cloth'd himself in clay.
or (*Choral-Music*)
Auf, Seele, auf, und säume nicht, es bricht das Licht herfür.

KYH 18, MOH 21, GCM 86, SOH 3, UH 21, KNH 19, SAH 47, HH 3, SOCH 24, WP 15, and Choral-Music 65.

No. 6. New Britain, Symphony, Solon, Redemption (A. W. Johnson, *Village Hymns, Baptist Harmony*)

A - maz-ing grace! (How sweet the sound!) That saved a wretch like me!
or Alas and did my Savior bleed and did my sov'reign die?
or There is a fountain fill'd with blood drawn from Immanuel's veins.
or When languor and disease invade this trembling house of clay.

SOH 8, WP 27, GCM 105, SAH 45, HH 104, SOCH 190, and TZ 90.

No. 7. Deep Spring (Douglass)

As on the cross the Sav - ior hung, and wept and bled and dy'd.

UH 89, KNH 90, SOCH 249, and HOC 93.

No. 8. Detroit (Bradshaw)

Do not I love thee, O my Lord? Be - hold my heart and see.
or Behold the Savior of mankind nail'd to the shameful tree!
or This is the day the Lord hath made; he calls the hours his own.

SKH 85, SOH 40, UH 33, KNH 23, SAH 39, HH 158, SOCH 175.

No. 9. Solemnity (Davisson)

'Twas on that dark, that dole-ful night, when pow'rs of earth and hell arose.
or **How happy every child of grace, who knows his sins forgiven!**

KYH 40, MOH 40, GCM 97, UH 38, KNH 74, HH 6.

No. 10. Salem (Bovelle, *Methodist Hymn Book*)

He dies, the friend of sin-ners dies! Lo Sa-lem's daugh-ters weep around.

KYH 45, MOH 47, SOH 53, UH 22, KNH 26, SAH 68, HH 17, and HOC 23.

No. 11. Idumea (Watts, Davisson)

My God, my life, my love; to thee, to thee I call.

KYH 33, GCM 36, SOH 31, UH 19, KNH 36, SAH 47, HH 224, SOCH 55, HOC 44, TZ 122, and MOH 38.

No. 12. Dublin (Watts, Kirby)

Lord, what is man, poor fee - ble man, born of the earth at first.
or Out of the deeps of long distress, the borders of despair.

KYH 22, MOH 27, GCM 55, SOH 13, UH 29, SAH 46, HOC 129, and WP 31.

No. 13. Restoration

Mer - cy, o thou Son of Dav - id! Thus blind Bar-ti - me - us pray'd.
or **Jordan's stream shall ne'er o'erflow me while my Savior's by my side.**

SOH 5, HH 217, and WP 25.

No. 14. Star in the East (Caldwell, Jackson, *Baptist Harmony*)

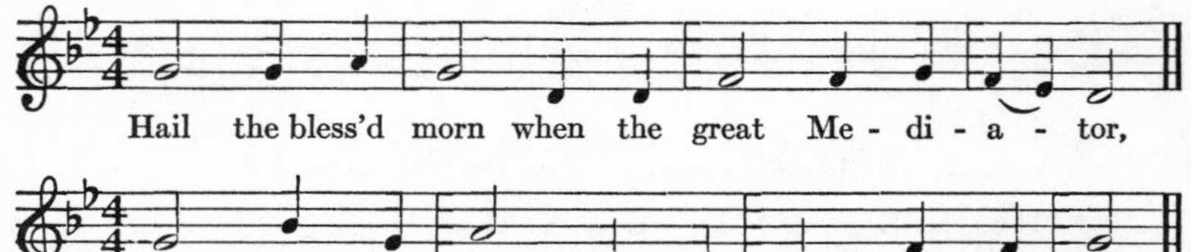

SOH 16, UH 36, KNH 40, HH 306, HOC 108, and WP 76.

No. 15. Fiducia (Watts, Robertson, Robison, J. Robertson)

or Hark, from the tombs a doleful sound! Mine ears, attend the cry.

KYH 39, MOH 43, GCM 186, SOH 92, KNH 97, TZ 101.

No. 16. Tender Thought (Rippon, Davisson)

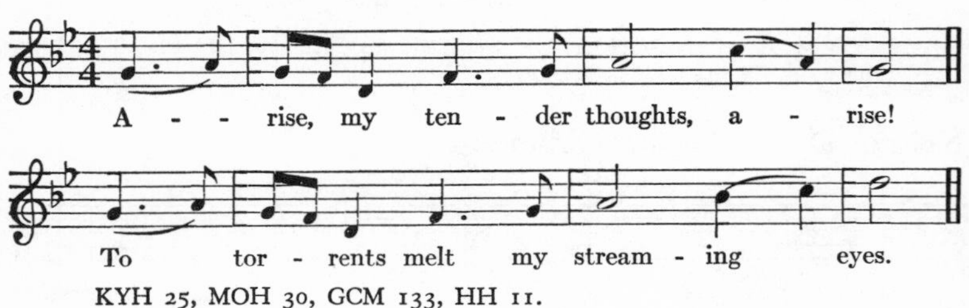

KYH 25, MOH 30, GCM 133, HH 11.

No. 17. King of Peace (F. Price, B. F. White)

or Lord, I can not let thee go till a blessing thou bestow.

SOH 6, KNH 60, SAH 74, SOCH 59.

No. 18. Fairfield (Watts, Hitchcock)

With rev'r-ence let the saints ap - pear and bow be- fore the Lord.
or Come, humble sinner, in whose breast a thousand thoughts revolve.
or Alas, and did my Savior bleed? And did my Sovereign die?
or Come, let us lift our voices high, high as our joys arise.

KYH 39, MOH 43, GCM 186, SOH 48, KNH 24, SAH 29, HH 64, SOCH 54, HOC 20, WP 18, TZ 91.

No. 19. Solemn Thought (F. Price, Caldwell, Carrell, and Davisson)

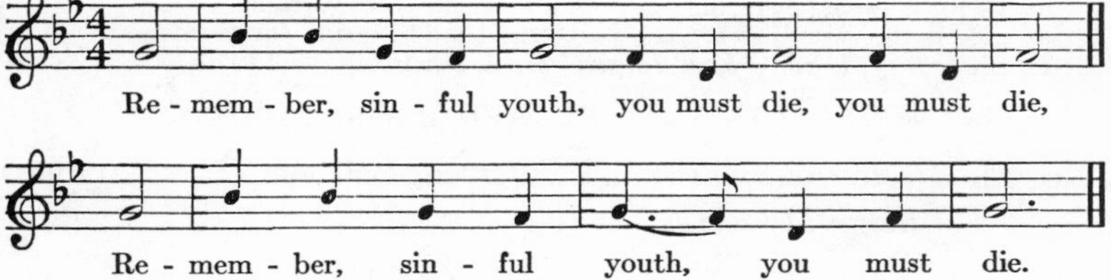

Re - mem - ber, sin - ful youth, you must die, you must die,

Re - mem - ber, sin - ful youth, you must die.

SKH 66, SOH 29, UH 56, KNH 108, HH 225.

No. 20. Promised Land, Heavenly Armor (Miss M. Durham, John A. Cooper, A. M. Scott, Walker)

On Jor - dan's storm-y banks I stand and cast a wish - ful eye.
or Come, let us join our friends above that have obtain'd the prize.
or And if you meet with trou-bles and trials on the way.

SOH 51, SAH 128, HH 154, SOCH 114, HOC 47, WP 53, HOC 56.

No. 21.[3] Bound for Canaan, Converted Thief, The Pilgrim's Lot, Contemplation (Mercer's, E. J. King, More, A. Gramblin, Caldwell)

Oh when shall I see Je - sus and reign with him a - bove?
or As on the cross the Savior hung and wept and bled and died.

SOH 193, SAH 82, SAH 44, SOH 9, SOH 138, UH 28, HH 152, SAH 156, HOC 104, HOC 48.

[3] Closely related to No. 30.

No. 22. Holy Manna (More, Moore, *Baptist Harmony*)

Breth-ren, we have met to wor-ship and a - dore the Lord our God.

SOH 103, KNH 88, SAH 59, HH 244, SOCH 191, HOC 107, WP 89, TZ 301.

No. 23. Devotion (Rippon)

Sweet is the day of sa-cred rest, no mor-tal cares shall seize my breast.
or O, for a sweet, inspiring ray to animate our feeble strains.
or Life is the time to serve the Lord, the time to insure the great reward.
or Show pity, Lord, O Lord forgive! Let a repenting rebel live!

SKH 9, MOH 34, GCM 91, SOH 13, UH 48, SAH 48, WP 17.

No. 24. Protection, Christian's Farewell, Bellevue (C. Chambless, *Village Hymns*)

How firm a foun-da - tion, ye saints of the Lord.
or Farewell, my dear brethren, the time is at hand.

GCM 196, SOH 334, UH 58, KNH 72, SOH 204, HOC 57, SAH 72.

No. 25. Ninety-third (Watts, Chapin, *Baptist Harmony*)

My Sav - ior and my King, thy beau - ties are di - vine.
or Grace, 'tis a charming sound: harmonious to the ear.
or We lift our hearts to thee, O Day-Star from on high.
or Jesus invites his saints to meet around his board.

KYH 26, MOH 31, GCM 125, SOH 7, UH 39, KNH 35, SAH 31, HH 422, SOCH 187, HOC 25, WP 21.

No. 26. Reflection (Davisson)

No sleep nor slum-ber to his eyes, good Dav- id would af - ford.
or Blest be the dear uniting love that will not let us part.
or And let this feeble body fail and let it faint or die.

KYH 42, MOH 44, UH 31, KNH 22, HH 63, HOC 13, WP 36.

No. 27. Prospect (Graham)

Why should we start or fear to die? What tim'r-ous worms we mor-tals are.

SOH 92, SAH 30, HH 33, HOC 15.

No. 28. Pisgah (Watts, Lowry)

And let this fee - ble bod - y fail and let it faint or die.
or When I can read my title clear to mansions in the skies.
or Jesus, thou art the sinner's friend, as such I look to thee.
or On Jordan's stormy banks I stand and cast a wishful eye.

SKH 25, MOH 59, GCM 104, SOH 80, UH 23, KNH 56, SAH 58, HH 112, SOCH 205, WP 83, TZ 92.

No. 29. Rockingham (Watts, B. F. White, Chapin)

Thus saith the mer - cy of the Lord, I'll be a God to thee.
or Come, happy souls, approach your God with new melodious songs.
or Salvation! let the echo fly the spacious earth around.

KYH 35, MOH 39, GCM 31, SOH 300, SAH 284, HH 55, CM 61 variant, WP 56 variant.

No. 30. Hallelujah, Way to Zion, Heavenly Armor, Sweet Prospect (Walker, Caldwell, *Dover Selection, Baptist Harmony*)

And let this fee - ble bod - y fail and let it faint or die.
or Amazing grace, (how sweet the sound!) that saved a wretch like me.
or And if you meet with troubles and trials on the way.
or O when shall I see Jesus and reign with him above.

SOH 107, SAH 146, HH 102, SOCH 207, HH 242 variant, SOH 93 variant, SAH 129 variant, HOC 56 variant, UH 97 variant. This tune is closely related to No. 21.

No. 31. Kingwood (Humphreys, *Village Hymns*)

My days, my weeks, my months, my years fly rap-id as the whirl-ing spheres.
or When with my mind devoutly press'd, dear Savior, my revolving breast.
or Come on, my partners in distress, my comrades through the wilderness.

SKH 44, GCM 36, SOH 98, UH 71, KNH 162, SAH 66, HH 371, HOC 83, TZ 300.

No. 32. Plenary (A. Clark, A. C. Clark)

Hark, from the tombs a dole-ful sound, mine ears, at-tend the cry.
or There is a land of pure delight where saints in glory reign.

SOH 262, SAH 162, SOCH 123, WP 74.

No. 33. Concord (Caldwell)

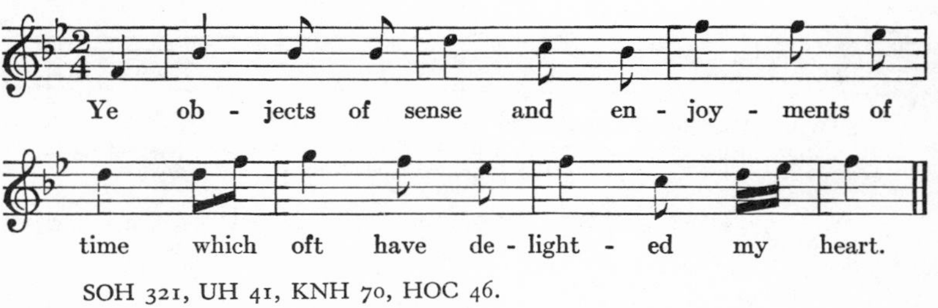

SOH 321, UH 41, KNH 70, HOC 46.

No. 34. Animation (Mercer's)

And let this fee - ble bod - y fail and let it faint or die.

SAH 103, HH 192, SOCH 125.

No. 35. Complainer (Walker)

I am a great com - plain - er that bears the name of Christ.

SOH 18, KNH 77, SAH 141, HH 416, WP 51.

No. 36. Washington (Munday, Monday)

Dis-miss us with thy bless-ing, Lord; help us to feed up - on thy word.

SKH 27, SOH 67, UH 74, KNH 103, SAH 147, HH 444, WP 109.

No. 37. The Romish Lady, Star in the East (R. Herron)

There was a Rom - ish La - dy brought up in po - per - y.

HH 257, KNH 188, SOH 82. A variant melody is GCM 104, SAH 175.

No. 38. Rockbridge (Watts, Chapin)

Sweet is the work, my God, my King, to praise thy name, give thanks and sing.
or Life is the time to serve the Lord, the time t'ensure the great reward.
or There is a God who reigns above, Lord of the heav'n and earth and seas.
or (*Choral-Music*)
Ihr jungen Helden, aufgewacht! Die ganze Welt muss seyn verdacht.

KYH 16, MOH 22, GCM 93, SOH 288, UH 16, KNH 28, HH 4, TZ 42. Choral-Music 48.

No. 39. Bower of Prayer (Richerson and Walker, E. J. King)

To leave my dear friends and with neigh - bors to part.
or To go from my home and from kin-dred to part.

SOH 70, HH 327, SOCH 26, TZ 296.

No. 40. Olney (Dr. Rippon, Chapin, Boyd)

Come, thou fount of ev'-ry bless-ing, tune my heart to sing thy grace.
or Hail, thou once despised Jesus! Hail, thou Galilean King!

SKH 65, MOH 33, GCM 90, SOH 64, UH 30, SAH 135, HH 378, SOCH 127, TZ 185.

No. 41. Liverpool (M. C. H. Davis, Bradshaw)

Young peo-ple all, at - ten-tion give and hear what I shall say.
or Behold the man three score and ten upon a dying bed.
or My Savior, my almighty Friend, when I begin thy praise.

SOH 1, UH 27, SAH 36, HH 83, HOC 113, WP 36, SOCH 76.

No. 42. New Port, New-Port, Newport (Caldwell)

As on the cross the Sa - vior hung and wept and bled and died.

HOC 17, HH 115, KNH 71, UH 24.

No. 43. Tribulation (Davisson, Chapin)

Death, 'tis a mel - an-chol - y day to those who have no God.
or (*Choral-Music*, variant)
Seelen-weide, meine Freude, Jesu lass mich fest an dir.

KYH 43, MOH 46, SOH 119, UH 37, KNH 38, SAH 29, HH 55, Choral-Music 64 variant.

No. 44. Abbeville, Golden Hill (E. J. King, Davisson)

Come, Ho - ly Spir - it, come with e - ner - gy di - vine.
or With joy the people stand on Zion's chosen hill.
or To God in whom I trust I lift my heart and voice.

SAH 33, SOCH 120, KYH 42, MOH 42, HH 211, CM 141, TZ 107.

No. 45. Parting Hand, Departing Saint (*Baptist Harmony,* William Walker)

My Chris-tian friends in bonds of love whose hearts in sweet-est u-nion join.
or Hark, hark, she bids her friends adieu, some angel calls her to the spheres.

SOH 113, KNH 102, SAH 62, HH 46 two variant tunes, SOCH 122, HOC 95, WP 33, TZ 46.

No. 46. Webster (*Psalmist*)

Come, we that love the Lord, and let our joys be known.
or And can I yet delay my little all to give.

SKH 60, SOH 10, KNH 74, SAH 31, SOCH 119, TZ 123.

No. 47. Sweet Rivers (*Baptist Harmony,* More)

Sweet ri - vers of re - deem - ing love lie just be - fore mine eyes.

SOH 166, SAH 61, HH 163, SOCH 66, HOC 41.

No. 48. Minister's Farewell

Dear friends, fare-well, I do you tell, since you and I must part.

SOH 14, KNH 75, SAH 69, HH 106, SOCH 124, WP 27.

No. 49. Vernon (Chapin)

Come, o thou tra - vel - ler un-known, whom still I hold but can-not see.

SKH 77, MOH 35, SOH 34, HH 352, SAH 55.

No. 50. Antioch, Immortality, Columbus, Hopewell, The Old Ship of Zion (Mercer's, F. C. Wood, Thos. W. Carter, Swan, Caldwell, Wm. C. Davis)

I know that my Re-deem - er lives, glo - ry, hal - le - lu - jah!
or O, once I had a glorious view of my redeeming Lord.
or There is a land of pure delight where saints immortal reign.
or What ship is this that will take us all home. Oh glory, hallelujah!
or Come along, come along and let us go home, Oh, glory, hallelujah!
or I have my trials here below, Oh, glory, hallelujah!
or Come, tell me of your ship and what is her name, O, tell me happy sailor.
or When rising from the bed of death, o'erwhelm'd with guilt and fear.

SAH 277, SOH 55, SAH 67, HH 128, UH 57, KNH 42, HOC 37, SOCH 109, SOCH 158. Closely related tunes are SAH 79, HH 355, SOCH 203, HOC 64.

No. 51. Albion (Rippon, Boyd, R. Boyd)

Come, ye who love the Lord, and let your joys be known.
or My soul, with joy attend, while Jesus silence breaks.
or And am I born to die? to lay this body down?

MOH 49, KYH 18, GCM 171, SOH 23, UH 21, KNH 51, SAH 52, HH 201, HOC 12.

No. 52. Dunlap's Creek (Watts, F. Lewis)

Sing to the Lord, ye heav'n-ly hosts, and thou, o earth, a - dore.
or My God, my portion and my love, my everlasting all.
or When languor and disease invade this trembling house of clay.

SKH 83, GCM 63, SOH 276, SOCH 238, WP 44, TZ 77.

No. 53. Resignation (M. H.)

And let this fee - ble bo - dy fail and let it faint or die.
or My Shepherd will supply my need; Jehovah is his name.

GCM 144, SOH 38, KNH 137.

No. 54. Royal Proclamation *(Dover Selection)*

Hear the roy - al pro - cla - ma-tion, The glad tid-ings of sal - va - tion.

SKH 107, SOH 146, UH 91, KNH 91, HH 468.

No. 55. Mear (Watts, Brown)

In God's own house pro-nounce his praise, His grace he there re - veals.
or Sing to the Lord, ye distant lands, ye tribes of every tongue.
or Will God forever cast us off, his wrath forever smoke.

KYH 26, MOH 24, GCM 34, SOH 24, UH 46, KNH 29, SAH 49, HH 4, SOCH 129, GM 80, HOC 14, WP 65, TZ 67.

No. 56. Glasgow (Davisson, Dare)

KYH 45, MOH 47, SOH 295, HH 17.

No. 57. Communion, Tennessee, The Christian's Comfort, Come and Taste (Watts, Chapin, J. Robertson, L. P. Breedlove, Wm. C. Davis, Walker)

How sweet and aw - ful is the place with Christ with-in the doors.
or Afflictions, though they seem severe, are oft in mercy sent.
or Shepherds, rejoice, lift up your heads and send your fears away.
or And let this feeble body fail and let it faint or die.
or Come and taste, along with me, consolation running free.

SKH 23, GCM 134, SOH 28, SAH 51, HH 140, HOC 114, WP 96, TZ 94, SOCH 78, SOCH 81, SOH 105.

No. 58. Clamanda, Clamandra (Chapin)

Say now, ye love-ly so-cial band, who walk the way to Ca-naan's land.

SKH 47, UH 63, KNH 109, SAH 42, SOCH 168, HH 28.

No. 59. Salvation (Boyd, Rippon)

Come, hum-ble sin - ner, in whose breast a thou-sand thoughts re-volve.
or (*Choral-Music*)
Was mich auf dieser Welt betrübt, das währet kurze Zeit.

KYH 22, GCM 136, SOH 84, UH 34, KNH 32, HH 71, HOC 24, TZ 101, Choral-Music 65.

No. 60. Pilgrim

Come, all ye mourn-ing pil-grims dear, who're bound for Ca-naan's land.

MOH 147, SOH 150, KNH 57, SAH 201, HH 392, SOCH 117, WP 46.

No. 61. China (Swan)

Why do we mourn de-part - ing friends or shake at death's a-larms?

KYH 29, MOH 32, SOH 276, SAH 37, HH 57, CM 111, HOC 39, TZ 74.

No. 62. Saints Bound for Heaven (J. King and W. Walker)

SOH 258, SAH 224, HH 219, TZ 297.

No. 63. Family Bible

How pain - ful - ly pleas - ing the fond re - col - lec - tions.

SOH 20, KNH 133, HH 310. Same words but different tune attributed to William Caldwell, UH 110, SAH 165, SOCH 58.

No. 64. Imandra (A. Davisson, W. Caldwell)

I love thee, my Sa - vior, I love thee, my Lord.
or Oh, how I have longed for the coming of God!
or O Jesus, my Savior, I know thou art mine.

SKH 21, MOH 146, SOH 134, UH 15, HH 316.

No. 65. Pleyel's Hymn, 2d (Pleyel, M. H.)

While thee I seek, pro-tect-ing pow'r, be my vain wish - es still'd.
or O joyful sound of gospel grace, Christ shall in me appear.

MOH 76, GCM 114, KNH 152, SAH 143, HH 105, SOCH 93, HOC 151, TZ 95.

No. 66. Vernon (E. Heritage)

Let the cares of the week all be ban - ish'd far hence: To de - vo - tion now let us be giv'n.

or O how happy are they who their Savior obey and have laid up their treasures above.

SOCH 210, CM 219, WP 38, TZ 267.

No. 67. Never Part, Never Part Again (John Carwell)

Je - ru - sa-lem, my hap - py home, O how I long for thee!

or Come, humble sinner in whose breast a thousand thoughts revolve.

SOH 198, SAH 294, HH 80, SOCH 94, CM 302, TZ 284.

No. 68. Spiritual Sailor (I. Neighbors)

The peo - ple call - ed Chris - tians have ma - ny things to tell.

SOH 41, KNH 135, SAH 150, HH 198.

No. 69. Solitude in the Grove (Davisson)

My God, my Ref - uge, hear my cries, be - hold my flow - ing tears.

or O were I like a feather dove and innocence had wings.

KYH 41, MOH 45, UH 73, KNH 127, SAH 138, HH 166, HOC 154.

No. 70. The Morning Trumpet (B. F. White)

O when shall I see Je - sus and reign with him a - bove?

SOH 195, SAH 85, SOCH 111, HOC 99.

No. 71. Kedron (Dare, Dr. Rippon)

Ye that pass by, be-hold the man, the man of grief con-demn'd for you.
or Thou man of grief, remember me, thou never canst thyself forget.
or Here in thy name, eternal God, we build this earthly house for thee.

GCM 165, SAH 48, SOCH 175, HOC 45, WP 16, SOH 3.

No. 72. Greenfields (Edson, *Methodist Harmony, Baptist Harmony*)

How te-dious and taste-less the hours when Je-sus no long-er I see.

SKH 18, MOH 52, GCM 144, SOH 71, UR 112, KNH 80, SAH 127, HH 345, SOCH 30, CM 24, HOC 16, WP 74, TZ 237.

No. 73. Home

Mid scenes of con - fu - sion and crea - ture com-plaints,
How sweet to my soul is com - mun - ion with saints!

GCM 196, SOH 251, UH 118, KNH 73, SAH 161, SOCH 84, HOC 55.

No. 74. Rhode Island (M. H. B.)

Thou great mys-terious God un-known, whose love hath gen-tly led me on.

SOH 145, SAH 70, HH 376, SOCH 198.

No. 75. Missionary Hymn (L. Mason, *Baptist Harmony*)

From Green-land's i - cy moun-tains, from In - dia's cor - al strand.

UH 40, KNH 69, SAH 133, CM 197, WP 50, TZ 215, SOH 111, HOC 88.

No. 76. Happy Land (L. P. Breedlove)

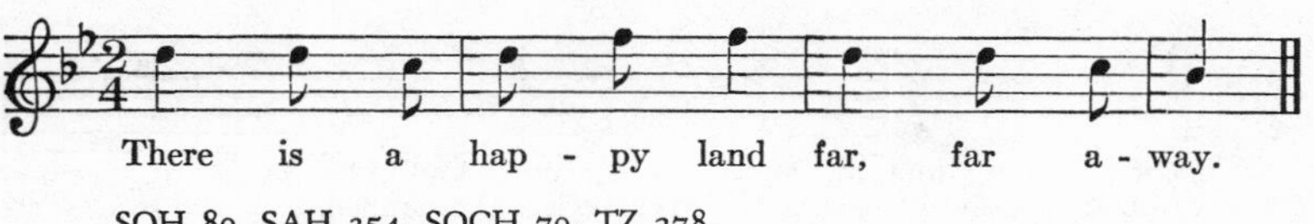

There is a hap - py land far, far a - way.

SOH 89, SAH 354, SOCH 79, TZ 278.

No. 77. Sweet Prospect (Wm. Walker)

On Jor-dan's storm-y banks I stand and cast a wish-ful eye.

SOH 137, SAH 65, HH 122, SOCH 166.

No. 78. Pilgrim's Farewell (Dover, French)

Fare - well, fare - well, fare - well, my friends.

GCM 164, SOH 158, UH 72, KNH 110, SAH 185, HH 358, TZ 282.

No. 79. Morality (White and Davisson)

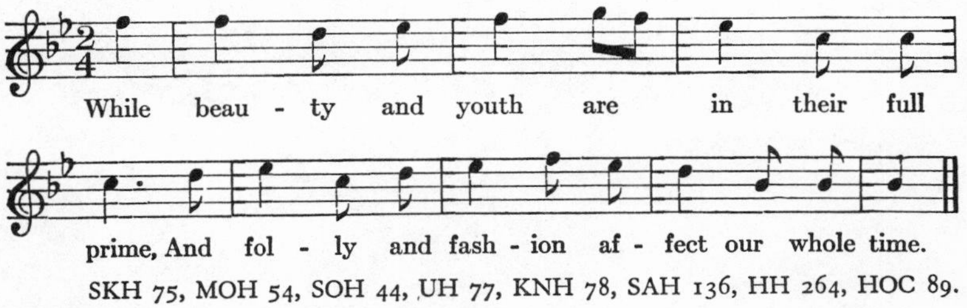

While beau - ty and youth are in their full prime, And fol - ly and fash - ion af - fect our whole time.

SKH 75, MOH 54, SOH 44, UH 77, KNH 78, SAH 136, HH 264, HOC 89.

No. 80[a]. Importunity, Sweet Affliction, Greenville (Rousseau, Rippon)

Sure - ly once thy gar-den flour-ish'd, ev - 'ry part look'd gay and green.
or Far from mortal cares retreating, sordid hopes and vain desires.
or Savior, visit thy plantation, grant us, Lord, a gracious rain.
or In the floods of tribulation, while the billows o'er me roll.

HH 255, CM 218, WP 33, TZ 179, HOC 60, KNH 66, UH 62, GCM 30, SOH 259, SAH 145.

No. 80b. Good Shepherd, Sinner's Call

Let thy king-dom, bless-ed Sa - vior, come and bid our jar-rings cease.
or Come, ye sinners, poor and needy; weak and wounded, sick and sore.

HH 207, KNH 58.

CHAPTER XIII

SONG TITLES, SOURCES, COLLOQUIALISMS

Relation of Titles to Tunes

The tunes in the preceding chapter have sometimes one, sometimes a number of titles. A single title found regularly from book to book, in Nos. 10, 11, 14, and 22, for example, indicates probably a strong individual tune coupled so firmly to a text of wide appeal that the combination has resisted the borrowing-and-lending process as well as the imitation tendency. The tune which is found under many titles indicates less individuality and more folk-typicality on the musical side. This typical sort of tune, being looked on somewhat as common property, is fitted to this and that text, from which it is likely to take its title. Or it is given a new title arbitrarily. Some good examples of this are Nos. 1, 6, 21, 30, 50, 57, 80[a], etc.

The fasola compilers seem to have used a free hand in naming their songs. In making this clear I shall go beyond the eighty songs in the MPT list. Some names bear direct reference to the text content. I refer to such as the experience, hallelujah, and farewell songs. But more often the titles indicate nothing as to the character of the text or tune, but shed, instead, some light on the geography of the singing and the personalities engaged in the activity.

The fasola songs bear the names of all the southeastern states, many counties (DeKalb, Cleburne, Cullman, etc.), towns (Nashville, Chattanooga, Spartanburg, Knoxville, Vicksburg, Hartwell, Milledgeville, Bowman, Jonesboro, Atlanta, Calhoun, Huntsville, La Grange, Blairsville, Greenville, Cornelia, Taladega, Carnsville, Griffin, Abbeville, Hamilton,

Augusta, Columbiana, Toccoa, Cusseta, Edneyville, Gainesville, Jasper, etc.), and numbers of little "places" like Arbacoochee, too small to be found on the map. The names of rivers (Pacolet, Holston, French Broad), creeks, springs, valleys (Blue Vale of Nacoochee), hills (Golden Hill, Cole's Hill, Pleasant Hill, Red Hill), and groves (Eagle Grove, Valley Grove, Harmony Grove, Mulberry Grove, Union Grove, Pleasant Grove, Shady Grove, etc.), may show where the song "came to" its composer, or they may tell merely of a favorite place for singings or singing schools. The song makers were wont also to name their productions for friends or relatives. Some musical people thus honored were Kay (Silas W.), Markham (Sarah Ann), Caldwell (William), Edney (Jas. M., through the title "Edneyville," his North Carolina home), Martyn (Rev. Henry A., missionary to India), Jester (N. D.), Ogletree (Absalom), Penick (Prof. S. R.), Sidney (given name of the composer's mother), and White (B. F.). The songs named "Rees" and "Dumas" memorialize a mutual friendship of two composers, Elder E. Dumas and J. P. Rees. William Hauser honored Charles Collins, the president of Emory and Henry College, Virginia, while the composer was studying there, by his song "Collins." The Alabama composer, M. F. McWhorter, showed his regard for the notable song-making dynasty of his state in the *Sacred Harp* song, "Denson." Caldwell's "Wakefield" was probably named after Samuel Wakefield, ancestor of Charles Wakefield Cadman, the composer. Samuel was an early shape-note musician in Pennsylvania. And "Fillmore" got its name from the popular Cincinnati tune maker of numeral notation fame. We now return to the discussion of the MPT in particular.

Sources of Tunes and Texts

The data as to sources of tunes and texts—in parentheses at the right of the titles—are given for what they are worth. In many instances, we suspect, they are worth little. Some of the tune books (MOH and WP, for example), give almost no sources. Joseph Funk, on the contrary, was punctilious about giving the books and pages (or numbers) from which he drew for GCM; but no composer's name is given in that collection. The Georgia and South Carolina books, SOH, SAH, HH, and SOCH, give a deal of source information which seems to be fairly reliable when that source is a southern collection or a composer, arranger, adder of parts, spiritualizer or moralizer (of a secular text) or "southernizer" who is personally known to the compiler. Especially careful were the compilers of these books to credit themselves with any small or big part they may have had in inventing, recording, or changing tunes and texts, and that part is often exaggerated. The name of Ananias Davisson appears oftener as composer among these eighty popular tunes than that of any other southerner. We leave it to others to determine the correctness of his claims and, with it, the inappropriateness of his given name. After Davisson, with his thirteen tunes, William Caldwell and William Walker come next in popularity with eight each.[1] William Moore of Tennessee is represented by three tunes.

Among the earlier books accredited as sources, the most

[1] Other names belonging to southern tune makers (words written among them are rare) are A. W. Johnson (Tenn.), John B. Jackson (Tenn.), F. Price and B. F. White (Ga.), James P. Carrell (Va.), E. J. King (Ga.), Joel King (Ga.), Wm. C. Davis, C. Chambliss, A. C. Clark, M. C. H. Davis, F. C. Wood, Thos. W. Carter (all of Georgia), W. H. Swan (Tenn.), F. Lewis, L. P. Breedlove (Ga.), J. C. Lowry (probably a "Valley" Virginian), and Miss M. Durham (Ga.). The well known names, Lowell Mason and Pleyel are found with one song each. Chapin is credited with eleven. But who was Chapin? There are twenty other names which I have not identified.

often recurring is "Watts," meaning probably some American reprint of the Calvinistic and revivalistic collections of Isaac Watts[2] (1674-1748). Thirteen texts (he was not a man of tunes) are attributed to him. "Rippon" means some American reprint of the *Selection* compiled by the English Baptist, John Rippon.[3] *Village Hymns* was another book of hymn texts compiled by the New Englander, Asahel Nettleton, 1824.[4] "Wyeth" probably has reference to the four-shape *Repository of Sacred Music* compiled by the Pennsylvanian, John Wyeth, and copyrighted 1810. "Dover" points to the *Dover Selection of Spiritual Songs* published by Andrew Broadus of Virginia in 1828. I have not identified the sources given as the *Baptist Harmony* and the *Methodist Hymn Book*. "Mercer" or "Mercer's" is *The Cluster of Spiritual Songs, Divine Hymns and Social Poems,* compiled by Jesse Mercer and published in Augusta, Georgia. According to Burrage[5] three editions appeared "before 1817." Subsequently the *Cluster* was printed in Philadelphia. The fifth edition, containing 676 hymns, some by Mercer himself, appeared in 1835. The book "has had a

[2] Such American reprints appeared often during the hundred years or more following 1729. They were published in Boston, New York and Philadelphia. The singing of Watts became general in New England after the Revolutionary War. That fact would seem to time the peak of his popularity in the rural South about as we find it, namely, during the first half of the nineteenth century.

[3] Rippon's *Selection of Hymns, Intended to be an Appendix to Dr. Watts' Psalms and Hymns,* London, 1787, began small but grew to 1,174 hymns and functioned as an early standard of Baptist hymnody. It was reprinted in America (first in New York) from 1792 on. The immediate source of the southern compilers may have been *Psalms and Hymns of Dr. Watts Arranged by Dr. Rippon, with Dr. Rippon's Selection in One Volume,* Philadelphia, 1820.

[4] Its full title was *Village Hymns for Social Worship. Selected and Original. Designed as a Supplement to the Psalms and Hymns of Dr. Watts.* It contained 600 hymns and no tunes. Benson calls it (Louis F., *The English Hymn,* Philadelphia, The Presbyterian Board of Publication, 1915, p. 376), "the brightest evangelical hymn book yet made in America." It enjoyed seven editions within three years. Its Preface states that it was compiled in answer to an "imperious and pressing" call from Presbyterians "in the West and South."

[5] Henry S. Burrage, *Baptist Hymn Writers and their Hymns,* Portland, Maine; Brown, Thurston & Co.

place in the service of song in some of the southern Baptist churches nearly if not quite to the present [1888] time."[6]

Another source, not mentioned, as it happens, in these eighty songs, but found here and there in the books under scrutiny, was "Dossey," meaning a collection of hymn poems called generally *Dossey's Choice,* made by Elder William Dossey,[7] a Baptist preacher of Virginia, North Carolina, South Carolina, and Alabama, successively.

By way of summarizing these book sources we would call attention to the fact that they were all religiously dissenting sources, that is, Methodist and Baptist; they were also books of the revivalistic or evangelistic stamp. It is well to note, too, that nearly all the source collections mentioned are those of words only. This fact becomes significant when we remember that these borrowings were incorporated by the fasola folk in what were primarily books of music. It reminds us of the divergence of interest between the church congregations and the singing schools, the former laying stress on the words of the songs, the latter on the music. It also points us to the almost complete dependence of the fasola book compilers and composers

[6] Rev. Jesse Mercer was born in Halifax County, North Carolina, in 1769, and died near Indian Springs, Ga., Sept. 6, 1841. He was but fourteen when his father took the family to Georgia, where he spent the rest of his life. At eighteen he began preaching and was ordained in 1789. He was an outstanding personality in Georgia's Baptist circles, serving eighteen successive years as president of the Georgia Baptist Convention. His prolific writings were mainly on religious subjects. His gifts to Mercer University, a Baptist institution which was named after him and is still thriving in Macon, Georgia, amounted to more than $40,000. In 1835 Brown University conferred the D.D. degree on Mr. Mercer. James, the fasola folk's only chronicler, tells us interestingly that "Mercer's Cluster—is a hymn book published by Jesse Cluster who has been dead many years. Others contend that it was John Cluster."—*Op. cit.,* p. 22.

[7] According to Burrage (*op. cit.,* pp. 257 ff.) Dossey was born in Virginia, became a preacher in Halifax County of that state in 1803, moved to North Carolina, where he married Mary Eliza Outlaw of Bertie, N. C., and served, 1813-1833, as a pastor of the Baptist church at Society Hill, South Carolina. From 1834 until his death in 1853 he lived on his plantation near Shiloh, Marengo County, Alabama, and preached thereabouts. He seems to have possessed an education far in advance of most of his colleagues.

on the churches' hymn writers for their supply of texts, and to the rurals' self-sufficiency in the matter of melodies. They could write tunes and harmonize them after a fashion. This was their business. But, for some reason, they did little in creating verse for those tunes. Walker, White, McCurry, Davisson, Caldwell, and Swan should be looked upon simply as purveyors of *music* to their own people. And they should be judged solely by their success or failure in this one activity.

Man-handling of Inherited Texts by Fasola Singers

The fasola folk, as we have shown above, did not make their own texts to any extent. But they did unmake some of them. Bad English, that is, the colloquialisms usual in their spoken language, often pressed in on their song verses. A few examples are:

"I'll never turn back no more."—SOCH52.
"I feel no ways like getting tired."—KNH52.
"Are there anybody here like Mary a-weeping."—SOCH98.
"And to make lament [amend] to him."—SOCH228.
"Streams of mercy never ceasing,
Calls for songs of loudest praise."—SOCH35.
"Through heats and colds I've ofttimes went."—SOH19.
"My God has me of late forsook."—SOH109.
". . . . When the faint heart bleeds,
By the spirit stroke for its evil deeds."—OSH411.

An interesting example of homespun verse is the following:

"Oh, that I had some secret place where I might hide from sorrow;
Where I might see my Savior's face, and thus be saved from terror.
O had I wings like Noah's dove, I'd leave this world and Satan;
And fly away to realms above, where angels stand inviting.

"My heart is often made to mourn, because I'm faint and feeble;
And when my Savior seems to frown, my soul is filled with trouble.
But when he doth again return and I repent my folly;
'Tis then I after glory run, and still my Jesus follow."—HH213.

In view of all these, one can only imagine those other gems of English "as she is spoke" which the Philadelphia and Cincinnati publishers of these books corrected before printing. I shall speak in a later chapter of further man-handling of their inherited texts by the rural singers and of the recording of such variants by the fasola song-book compilers.

CHAPTER XIV

CELTIC MELODIC IDIOM

Scotch-Irish Element in Fasola Folk

On the following pages, where we shall look at concrete melodies and discuss melodic idiom, the reader will notice a persistent secularity in the songs; and he will note that the secular song flavor is what we may call, for want of a better term, Scotch-Irish. As a sort of preface to the following discussion, I wish to say a few words as to the reasons for this particular ethnic flavor and its worldliness.

We have seen above that the fasola folk were Scotch-Irish and German, with a small ingredient of English. The German influence *should* have been considerable. The Teutons were and are, as is generally known, a musical race. Their body of folksong is among the richest of those found in Europe. Their composers of church song have made great contributions to the Christian world's store of that sort of music, and many of their religious songs had folk-song sources. The Germans who came to Pennsylvania were, in the main, rural and deeply religious. They poured from Pennsylvania and Maryland into the southern mountains and hills and valleys from the start. They were the very first families in the Valley of Virginia and soon filled up that great tract to the extent of becoming, in many counties, over seventy per cent of the population. They composed, even as early as 1775, over fifteen per cent of the white population of South Carolina and Georgia and probably a much larger percentage of the hill population of those sections.

But despite their numbers, their religious bent, their musical nature, and their close association from the earliest times with the other ethnic sorts of fasola folk, their direct national-musical influence was practically nullified by one important condition. This condition was that whatever songs, religious or secular, they may have brought from the fatherland to the new homeland were wedded to texts in a tongue that was strange to their new environment, a tongue that was doomed as a medium of communication. And this was a most effective reason for the quick and sure extinction of such songs, by and large, in this region, and for the destruction of the direct German-national musical influence as such.

We must not conclude, however, that the German-become-American ceased singing. No, we have much proof of the fact that he did the natural thing. He became a regular fasola-American. He took up with the dominant tendencies, and these tendencies were largely Scotch-Irish.

The Scotch-Irish were far less numerous in the Virginias than were the Germans, but they were far more numerous than the latter in the far southern fasola belt, more numerous indeed than any other group. Campbell gives figures[1] which show that these people formed, in 1775, twenty-three per cent of the white population of Virginia (West Virginia and Kentucky included), thirty-one per cent of those in North Carolina (Tennessee included), fifty per cent of South Carolina, and forty-five per cent of Georgia. He shows also that Scotch-Irish and Germans together bulked as high as thirty-one per cent in the Virginias, thirty-five per cent in North Carolina and Tennessee, sixty-seven per cent in South Carolina, and forty-five per cent in Georgia. Knowing as we do the desire of these people to get away from the established-church, slave-working lowlands and to live in the hills, mountains, and high valleys—the fasola region; knowing also that these ru-

[1] John C. Campbell, *The Southern Highlander and His Homeland,* p. 355.

rals increased at the normal high rural birth-rate and that later influxes followed the earlier ones, the estimate that the fasola folk were, in the early part of the nineteenth century, from fifty to eighty per cent Scotch-Irish, with its German component, would seem to be a conservative one.[2]

Secular Element in Fasola Songs

If we have now given reasons for any Scotch-Irish flavor which we may find in the fasola songs, we have also incidentally found reason for the secular element which we shall surely meet. For "Scotch-Irish flavor" means precisely the secular or secular-national smack. It means the same quality that has been found in great purity in the secular ballad survivals in the southern mountains. But why should we expect to find that same secular-national flavor also in the religious songs of the section?

In attempting an answer to this question, we shall have to remember that these people, like their German brothers, were dissenters, escapers—Calvinists primarily, Wesleyan Methodists and Baptists subsequently, ruralists all, making their doctrinal distinctions and interpretations anew, and that with the resultant denominational groupings came also new or made-over song texts and, more especially, new or made-over tunes. With this new tunemaking or making-over process, what influence could be more potent, more surely felt, than that of their universally sung and loved folk-tunes and the folk-musical idiom in which they were couched?

Proportion of Major and Minor Tunes

Post-Civil-War propagandists for a lighter, "happier" type of spiritual melody criticized the "old songs," as a whole,

[2] John W. Wayland, *A History of Rockingham County, Virginia,* pp. 236 ff, gives the population figures for these two groups together at the beginning of the twentieth century in broad stretches of the Shenandoah Valley as approximately 82 per cent.

for being cast in doleful minor modes. This criticism is only relatively correct. Among the eighty tunes there are, according to my findings, but thirty in minor as against forty-nine major, and one that is a combination of both. This proportion of five major to three minor would be found, I am sure, to hold without much variation for all the songs in the fifteen books. But while the minor ingredient is small, it looked big to those of more recent times when that mode was in the process of disappearing from rural and urban sacred music. Another important modal-melodic peculiarity of the old songs, one whose existence seems nevertheless to have been completely ignored by the fasola folk themselves, was the use of gapped scales, that is, melodic progressions which avoided or skipped regularly certain notes in the diatonic scale with which we are familiar, the one which is conveniently represented by the white keys on the piano. The simplest note avoidance in the major modes was that of the fourth, or E flat in the scale of B flat major. In skipping this note the fasola singers produced what are called six-tone or hexatonic melodies. Another skip was that of the seventh, or A natural in the scale of B flat major. When both four and seven are avoided we have a five-tone or pentatonic tune.

The simplest avoidance in the minor modes is that of the sixth. But those tunes where both the second and the sixth are lacking are more often met with.

Summing up the different modes as they are found in the Table on page 162, we find fifty-eight of the eighty tunes under consideration to be of the gapped sorts. And of these twenty are of the six-tone (one-gapped) variety and thirty-eight are of the five-tone (two-gapped) sort. Of the remaining twenty-two full-scaled tunes fourteen are major and eight are minor.

Scales Used in the Eighty Most Popular Tunes

Major Scales

Full Major Scale—Used in tunes Nos. 40, 42, 51, 55, 61, 65, 66, 67, 72, 73, 75, 78, 79, 80.

Six-Tone Scale, fourth lacking—Used in tunes Nos. 31, 47, 52, 57, 76.

Six-Tone Scale, seventh lacking—Used in tunes Nos. 5, 21, 26, 29, 33, 34.

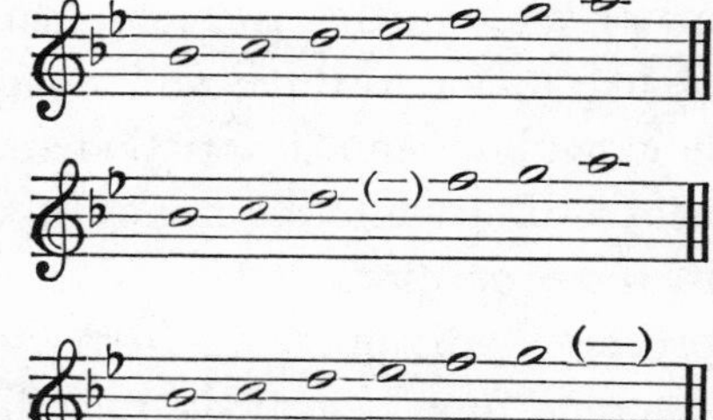

Five-Tone Scale, fourth and seventh lacking—Used in tunes Nos. 6, 7, 22, 23, 24, 25, 27, 28, 30, 32, 35, 37, 38, 39, 41, 44, 45, 46, 48, 53, 54, 56, 62, 63.

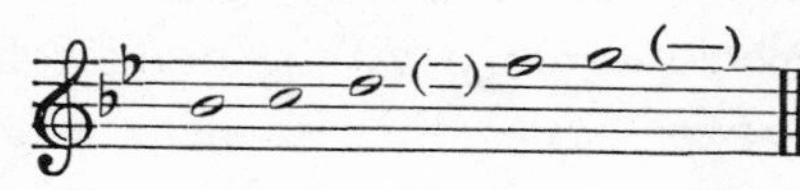

Minor Scales

Full Minor Scale—Used in tunes Nos. 1, 3, 9, 10, 36, 39, 69, 71.

Six-Tone Minor Scale, sixth lacking—Used in tunes Nos. 2, 12, 16, 17, 18, 20, 43, 68, 77.

Five-Tone Minor Scale, second and sixth lacking—Used in tunes Nos. 4, 8, 11, 13, 14, 15, 19, 49, 50, 58, 60, 64, 70.

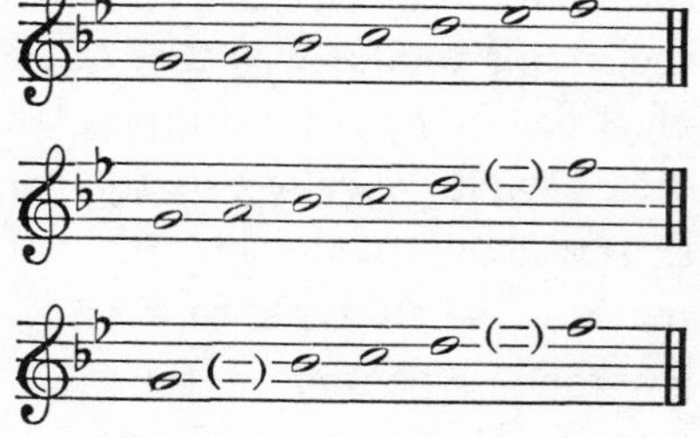

Song No. 73 has a hybrid mode.

I do not wish to enter into any considerable theorizing here as to the significance of these gapped scales. I shall simply state my opinion that their prevalence in this body of sacred songs indicates a degree of musical primitivity, on the part of tune makers and tune singers, which is comparable to—probably identical with—the musical status which has been recorded in the southern mountains in connection with the ballad melodies. Primitive singers, as is well known, do not conceive of music as built of diatonic scales. The two half-steps in that diatonic scale (those between 3 and 4 and between 7 and 1) were slow in becoming recognized, even in "art" music. And all students of musical history know how comparatively recent was the legitimatizing of the "leading tone" and its half-step to the tonic. In the songs under consideration precisely those tones have been avoided which would have brought half-steps into the tune. This avoidance leaves no melodic interval smaller than a whole step and it leaves the two gaps as intervals of one and a half steps each. According to their predominant preference, then, the rural singers of the South were, in the 1800-1860 period, at a stage of melodic development which was essentially centuries behind the calendar.

The twenty-two tunes with full major and minor scales do not weaken this assumption. They strengthen it. For with but few exceptions they are tunes which did not grow in the southern rural soil, but were taken over from "art" sources. That is, they were either written by some hymn-tune maker of outstanding ability, or they were borrowed from secular sources, vocal and instrumental. These full-scale tunes form the bulk of the MPT list from No. 63 to No. 80 inclusive. They are decidedly less "folkish" than the rest of the eighty songs.

CHAPTER XV

DANCE TUNES: OTHER SECULAR FEATURES

Fiddle Tunes with Sacred Words

It seems rather strange to find celtic dance tunes as the musical setting of spiritual texts, but it appears that the fasola folk had not yet thought of looking for personal devils in lively music. Fiddles and all that went with them were generally taboo with religious folk. But the fiddle tunes were too good to remain in the exclusive employ of the devil, and all it took to bring such tunes into books of "sacred" song was a set of religious words.

To understand what I mean by the celtic dance rhythm, the reader will simply have to recall such tunes as the "Fisher's Hornpipe," with its fast fiddle (or bagpipe) note successions in six-eight time. The "Fisher's Hornpipe," itself is used (SAH 342), as the melodic basis of "The Old-Fashioned Bible," which is, in turn, a text parody of "The Old Oaken Bucket":

And the chorus or second strain:

Another echo of this popular dance tune is in SOH 65; and in SOH 73 the same sprightly theme is hooked up, under the title

"Legacy," in a curious patchwork tune, with "Rubin, Rubin, I've Been Thinking."[1]

Another example of such jig tune is the following from SOCH 186:

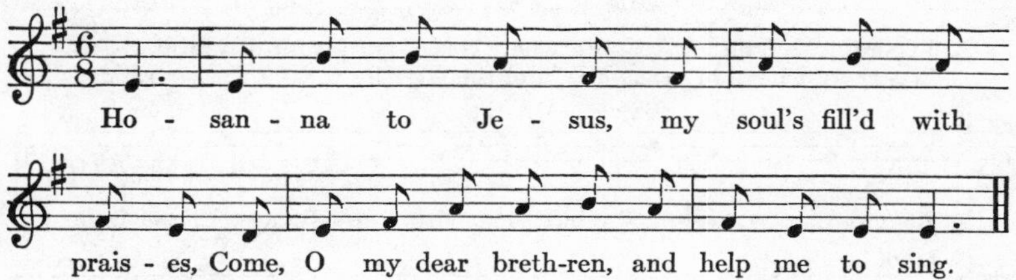

It seems to have been hard to find or to make poetry with enough syllables to the line. But the above example, and even better the following lines

Ho-san-na is ring-ing, I'm hap-py while sing-ing
A-shout-ing the prai-ses of Je-su-ses name.

show how the trick was turned and the text was stretched to make it fit the procrustean bed of the lively instrumental tune. Tunes in the same meter (called "12s and 11s" according to hymn-book practice) and others with similar Scotch or Irish flavor come thick and fast in HH,[2] SAH, and SOCH. They appear somewhat less often in the other books. And in the chaste GCM of the Valley of Virginia there is not a trace of them.

Secular Songs, Ballads, and Art Melodies Become Hymns

Secular songs, both those of merely current popularity and those of ancient ballad tradition, are echoed in fasola circles.

[1] Sandburg calls attention (*American Songbag,* p. 155), to the Irish ancestry of this song and to Thomas Moore as the author of its secular text.

[2] Nos. 38, 39, 40, 42, 44 ("When Johnny comes marching home," reminiscences), 213, 235, 256, 259, 265, 272, 273, 278, 294, 310, 336, 348, 377, 387, 408, 444, 454. See also in *Columbian Harmony* p. 140, "The Soldier's Return," and p. 113, a dance tune with an exhortational text.

In the *Knoxville Harmony* (165) is the following tune under the title, "The Rose Tree":

This tune is part and parcel with a popular song type which had a number of variants in the early part of the nineteenth century. "Turkey in the Straw," a good example of which may be found in Sandburg,[3] is one of these variants.

My mother, Mrs. Ann Jane Jackson of Birmingham, Alabama, heard the following related song sung by a hired girl in her mother's home in Monson, Maine, about 1859. I recorded it from my mother's singing on May 6, 1931, in Nashville, Tennessee.

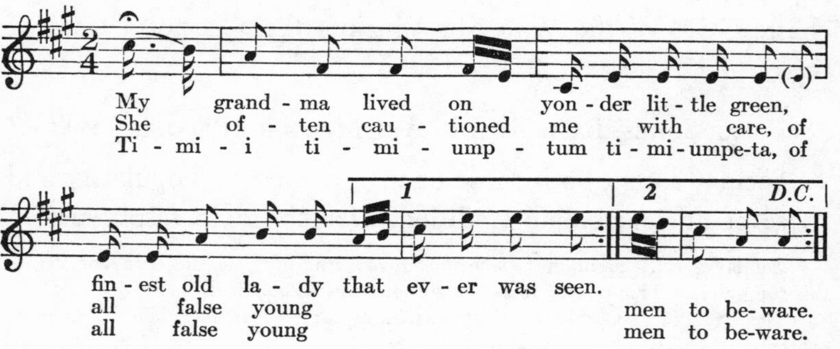

[3] *Op. cit.*, p. 94.

Another member of the same tune family is "Mecklenburg" (HH259):

And I heard its melodic mate (the name of which I have not learned) sung by a noisily intoxicated person in Cleveland, Ohio, in October, 1906:

"Sawyer's Exit" (SAH 338) is a religious parody on the tune called "Old Rosin the Bow":

A compiler's note below the song in the 1859 *Sacred Harp* tells that "these words were composed by Rev. S. B. Sawyer on the day of his death with request that this tune should be set to them." The reverend gentleman deserves commendation for preserving to the last an active sympathy with such profane ditties.

In picking this particular tune as the carrier of his verses, he was in line with the boosters of the presidential aspirants, Henry Clay, Abraham Lincoln, and Ulysses S. Grant, who, as Sandburg tells us,[4] used the same melody with improvised political texts.

William Hauser only thinly veiled the "Fisher's Hornpipe" when he "arranged" the melody of his "Methodist and Formalist" (HH 454):

[4] *Op. cit.*, p. 167.

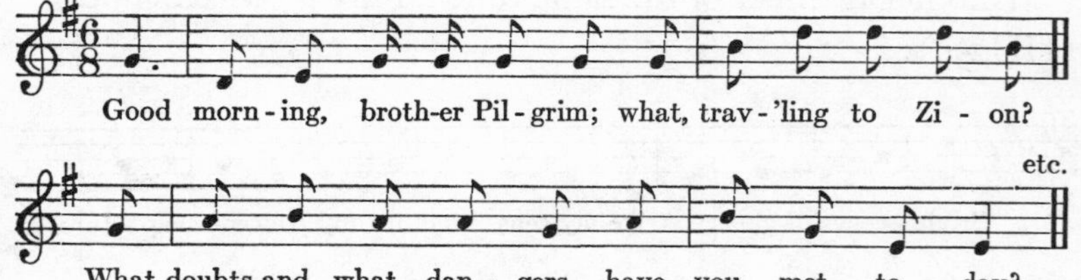

When we see that this unqiue song is for the express purpose of defending, throughout its eleven long stanzas, the institution, the stamping, jumping, and dancing of those in religious ecstasy, we must admit that the selection of the old Irish dance tune was not amiss.

Some sort of sailor's chantey must have been the father of the following tune, KNH 135, "The Spiritual Sailor":

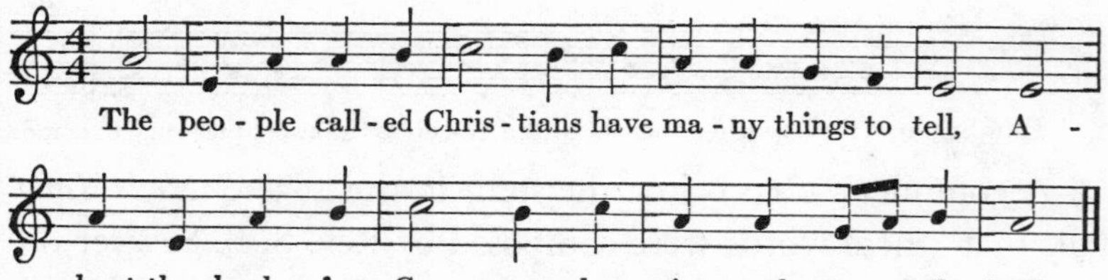

One can be almost sure that the secular text which was parodied in "The Spiritual Sailor," ran something like the following:

> I am a jolly sailor
> And have strange things to tell.

McCurry heard the tune "Goodby" (SCH 253), "played on the accordion by Mrs. Martha J. Hodges of Hartwell" (Georgia), and recorded it as follows:

In "Captain Kidd," SOH 50 (MOH 57 and elsewhere), we see clearly a parody of the song about the fabled pirate:

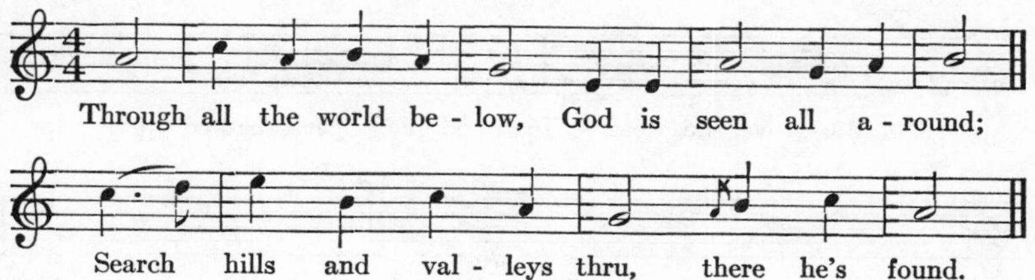

The song here parodied begins,

> My name is Captain Kidd, as I sailed, as I sailed,
> Most wickedly I did as I sailed.

In "Marion," SOCH 228, we seem to have an out-and-out secular ballad:

The stanza continues:

> I'll ramble and I'll rove
> And I'll call upon my God
> They may all say what they will,
> Resolved as I am
> So long as I live
> For to be a rover still.

The second stanza simply substitutes "mother" for "father" and is otherwise like stanza one. McCurry sets his name up as its composer.

To McCurry (SOCH 87) we are endebted for the ballad entitled "Musgrove":

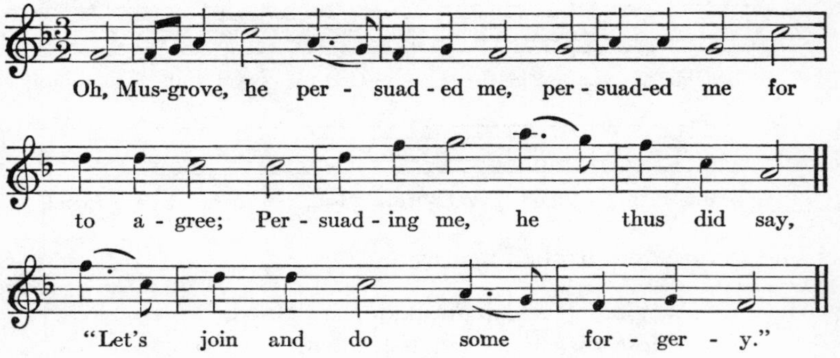

My greedy heart deceiv-ed me;
The pride of wealth and property
Led me a captive, now, you see,
All in the bonds of misery.

Oh, now, in jail, where I do lay,
In heavy irons, cold as clay,
I soon the day shall shortly see
That will land my soul in eternity.

Popular art melodies, intended presumably for piano, are HH 72 and 348. Another tune, "Blue-Eyed Mary," with a familiar ring even now, is called "The Singing Christian" (SOH 264) and "Wandering Sinner" (HH 249).

The beautiful tune "All Through the Night" is found in SOH 109 and HH 346, beginning

There's a friend above all others,
O, how he loves!

In SOH144 the long popular "O come, come away" or "Crambambuli" is fitted with a text that opens with

O come, come away, the Sabbath morn is passing.

Under the title "Soft Music," we find, SAH323, a musical and textual parody of the German love song, "Du, du liegst mir im Herzen," beginning

Soft, soft music is stealing,
Sweet, sweet lingers the strain.

The widely used tune, "Olney," MPT40, is, according to Lightwood,[5] Gounod's "There Is a Green Hill Far Away." Lightwood has also identified "Happy Land," SOH89, as a love song adapted by Alexander Young to Sunday school use; and "Sherburne" (Sherborne), SOH280, as a tune adapted from Mendelssohn's "The Vale of Rest," a four-part song.[6]

"Nellie Gray" is "Be Joyful in God," SAH348. "Believe me if all those Endearing Young Charms," is "Chariot of Mercy," HH290. "Home, Sweet Home" is often found with sacred words and the title "Home." "Blue Bells of Scotland" is "Celebration," HOC118. "Who'll Give me some more Peanuts when my Peanuts are Gone?" is "Joyful," HOC141. The German student song, "Was Kommt dort von der Höh," is "Marston," HOC131. "Drink It Down" is in "Minstrel" HOC166 and HH312. "Long, Long Ago" appears under its own title in HOC 183. "Hail to the King" is a temperance song called "Hail to the Cause," HH 534. "The Maltese Boatman's Song" also has a temperance text in HH 540. "The Old Oaken Bucket" is "The Inebriate's Lament," HH 148. "Hail Columbia" and "Yankee Doodle" are mixed in "Land of Pleasure," HH 153. "Joyful Spring," HH 385, fortunately not

[5] *Op. cit.*, p. 353.
[6] *Ibid.*, pp. 355 ff., 357.

altered in any way, looks very much like a seventeenth or early eighteenth-century love song.

In the same antique spirit is "Pastoral Elegy" (MOH 123, HH 452, SOH 147) sometimes called also "Corydon, or Caroline's Complaint." The poem has been attributed to the Reverend Nathaniel Dwight (1770-1831). Caroline bewails, for six stanzas, the death of her Corydon. This effusion closes with:

Since Corydon hears me no more,
In gloom let the woodlands appear,
Ye oceans be still of your roar,
Let autumn extend around the year;
I'll hie me through meadow and lawn,
There cull the bright flow'rets of May,
Then rise on the wings of the morn,
And waft my young spirit away.

"Robin Adair" is called "McAnally," HH315. "Drink to Me Only with Thine Eyes" is "Heavenly Wisdom," HH104. An instrumental (piano?) piece which I have not identified is the basis of "Murillo's Lesson," SAH358. "Bonnie Doon" has a sacred text in SOCH146. "Auld Lang Syne" is found variously parodied. Examples are KNH116 and HH537.

The Miss Lula Tune Type

Some of the songs in the MPT list seem to have been constructed on a plan so widely used in America that it should be looked on as a native melodic pattern or song type, one whose persistence of form (with only slight variations) and widespread use remind one of such folk patterns in language as proverbs. One example of this is what I have called the Miss Lula tune type. I have named it for a tune I heard sung by a Negro laborer in Birmingham, Alabama, thirty years ago. As he whacked with his pickaxe he drawled:

A glance at Nos. 44, 46, and 52 in the "Most Popular Tunes" list will show that the Negro's tune was not new, that its type had been in use as a formula in spiritual song at least eighty years before. Other old tunes in practically the same formula are "New Hope," UH 31, "Davis," SOH 15, "Mount Ephraim," GCM 65, "New Salem," GCM 65, "Charlestown," SAH 52, "Land of Rest," SAH 285, "Vicksburg," HH 153, "Edneyville," HH 193, "Zion's Hill," HH 228, "Mount Bether," HH 270, and "Newberry," SOCH 131.

"Amherst," SAH 314, a song of this type, was composed by William Billings in the eighteenth century.

"Go Tell Aunt Tabby"

Another favorite type is "Go Tell Aunt Tabby" (Aunt Nancy, etc.). Everybody in the South, singer and non-singer alike, seems to know this tune:

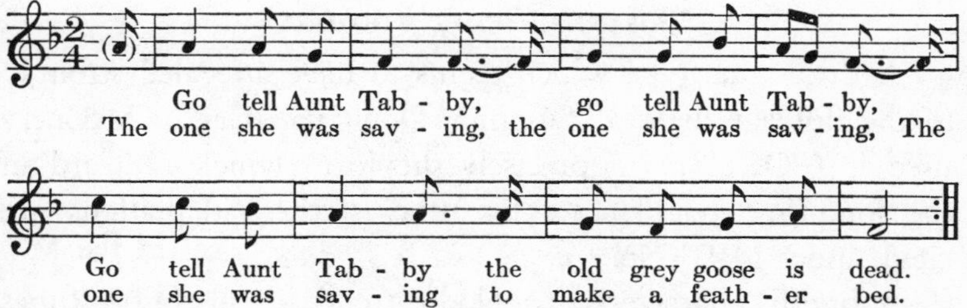

By referring to the MPT list we shall find in No. 80[a] its direct ancestor. Its composer is usually given as Rousseau, who was, according to the belief of the fasola compilers and singers, none other than the noted Jean Jacques. Indeed, William Hauser in his *Olive Leaf* (p. 223) calls it by its traditional name, "Rousseau's Dream." Lightwood corrects the popular notion as to its source by telling us that this tune was "got hold of" by one J. B. Cramer and published (in England presumably) as a piano solo, with variations, about 1818.[7] It would be interesting to know where Cramer "got hold of it."

A variant of the Tabby parody is also widely known. I have heard it in Maine as:

Tell Aunt Rho-dy, Tell Aunt Rho-dy, Tell Aunt Rho-dy the old goose's dead.

Its ancestor, a close relative of the "Rousseau's Dream" tune, is No. 80[b] in the MPT list. I have found the full tune in only two of the fasola books. Its middle part, however—that part known to composers as the "contrast" passage—is found incorporated in other tunes. Examples are "Scriptures Fulfilling," HH333 and "Return Again," SAH335. This tune, known to present-day church people as the popular setting of "Come, Thou Fount of Every Blessing," is thought by Metcalf to have been composed by Asahel Nettleton before 1813,[8] when it appeared in Wyeth's *Repository of Sacred Music* (p. 112).

"Susanna, Don't You Cry"

A third tune type which seems to have appealed strongly to the fasola folk was "Susanna, Don't you Cry." McCurry used it (SOCH81) in precisely the form which is heard in the long-time popular secular tune. Other adaptations are cited under MPT No. 57.

A highly characteristic melodic trend in the fasola tunes is illustrated by the first eight tunes in the MPT list. They are

[7] James T. Lightwood, *Hymn Tunes and Their Story,* p. 366.

[8] *Op. cit.,* p. 141.

largely of the minor mode and all but No. 3 are built up on the gapped-scale principle. No. 1 holds the popularity record. The eight related tunes occur sixty-two times in the books.

Among the songs whose wide popularity seems to rest on their individual worth rather than their folk-tune typicality are "Fairfield" (No. 18), "Ninety-Third" (No. 25), "Pisgah" (No. 28), and "Greenfields" (No. 72). They are found in eleven or more books each.

The following parody on some secular song which I have not identified appeared in SOCH 212, entitled "The Beggar." Its text shows it to be the good-bye song of a China-bound missionary. Is it some hunting song?—"And a-hunting I will go"?

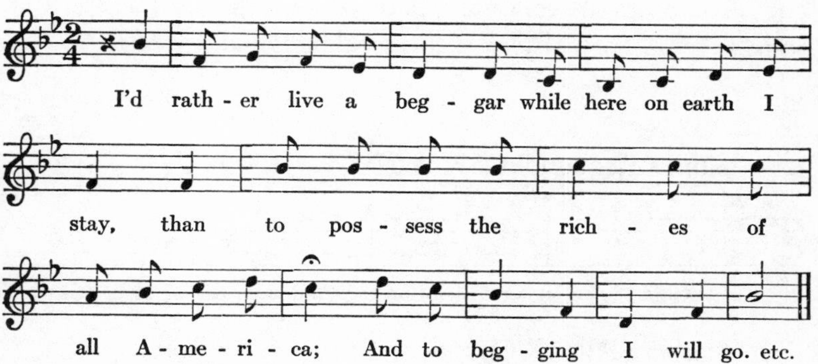

"The Blue Bird" (SOH, ed. of 1835, p. 153, and elsewhere), is a fife-and-drum piece which, according to Dolph, was played at the execution of Major André in 1780.[9] It is arranged with an impossibly precipitous part for each of the four voices but it lacks a text in all but the *Hesperian Harp* (page 249) occurrence.

[9] Edward Arthur Dolph, *"Sound Off!" Soldier Songs* (New York, Cosmopolitan Book Corporation, 1929), p. 490.

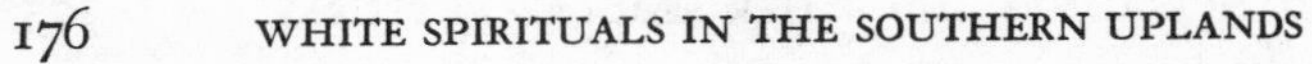

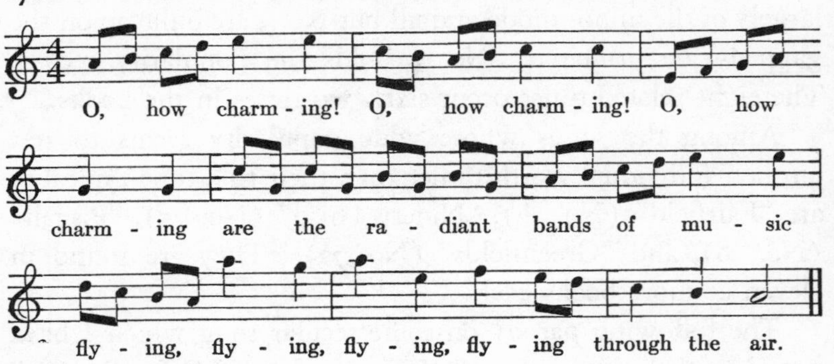

Spiritual Songs Based on Traditional Ballads

A number of the fasola spiritual songs show relationship, in tune or text, to the secular ballads of old-world origin. Compare as samples the following pairs of song parts. The spiritual song is represented by *(a)*; the secular ballad, by *(b)*.

I

(a) "Saint's Request," OSH 286.

(b) "Barbara Allen," Cox, *Folk Songs of the South,* p. 523.

The lower notes taken from the second half of the ballad show the tune resemblance better.

2

(*a*) "New Orleans," PB 255.

(*b*) "Greenwood Siding," Cox, p. 522.

3

(*a*) "Youngst," *Bible Songs,* p. 203.

(*b*) "Lord Lovel," Davis, *Traditional Ballads of Virginia,* p. 874.

4

(*a*) "Idumea," OSH 47.

(*b*) "Lord Thomas and Fair Elenor," Davis, p. 570.

"Idumea" was composed (recorded?) by Ananias Davisson of Rockingham County, Virginia, before 1816. The Lord Thomas and Fair Elenor tune was recorded in that same county a century later, May 19, 1916.

5

(*a*) "Restoration," SOH (edition of 1835), p. 5.

(*b*) "McAfee's Confession," Cox, p. 525.

This is evidently a poor recording. Folk singers do not sing as mechanically as this notation indicates.

6

(*a*) "To Die No More," OSH 111.

(*b*) "Three Crows," Davis, p. 562.

7

(*a*) "Look Out," OSH 90.

(*b*) "Three Crows," Davis, p. 562, and Cox, p. 522.

8

(*a*) "All is Well," OSH 122.

Farewell, my friends, adieu, adieu,
I can no longer stay with you,
My glittering crown appears in view,
All is well, all is well.

(*b*) "Lass of Roch Royal," Appendix, as heard by the author in Monson, Maine, in the early 1880's. See also Davis, *Traditional Ballads of Virginia.*

The tune of "All Is Well" is entirely independent of the above.

9

(a) "The Washington Badge," HH 536.

Fasola Songs Recall Historical Events

A number of song texts in the fasola books have to do with historical persons and events. One of these is the "Pilgrim Fathers" (HH551), the poem by Felicia Hemans:

The breaking waves dashed high
On a stern and rock-bound coast,
And the woods against the stormy sky
Their giant branches toss'd;
The heavy night hung dark
The hills and waters o'er,
As a band of exiles moor'd their bark
On the wild New England shore.

The Revolutionary War period appealed to the song makers. "Star of Columbia" (SAH198) reminds of the colonists' dependence on scientific development on these shores in winning their freedom from British domination. Its verses of lofty sentiments are ascribed to "Dr. Dwight" who is Dr. Timothy Dwight (1752-1817) one-time president of Yale University and a poet of mediocre attainments. The same patriotic theme runs through Sumner's "Ode on [or "to"] Science" (HH490 and elsewhere), a lengthy exultation over the broken "British yoke and Gallic chain."

The demise of the Father of His Country is bewailed in "Mount Vernon" (SOCH172 and OSH110):

What solemn sound the air invades?
What wraps the land in sorrow's shade?
From heaven the awful mandate flies:
The Father of his Country dies.

Among the songs which attached themselves, in retrospect, to George Washington and his period is "The Jolly Soldier" (SOCH194):

I once was a seaman stout and bold,
Ofttimes I've plow'd the ocean;
I've plow'd it all o'er and o'er again,
For honor and promotion.

Aboard a man-of-war and a merchantman,
Many be the battles I've been in;
It was all for the honor of George Washington,
And I'll still be the jolly, jolly soldier.

The SAH (340) brings further reminiscences of revolutionary heroes under the title "The American Star":

The spirits of Washington, Warren, Montgomery
Look down from the clouds with bright aspect serene,
Come, soldiers, a toast and a tear to their mem'ry,
Rejoicing they'll see us as once they have been [*sic*].

The fate of Napoleon is sung in "Buonaparte" (SOCH159):

Buonaparte is afar from his war and his fighting;
He has gone to a place he never can delight in.
He may list to the winds on the great Mount Diana,
While alone he remains on the Isle of Saint Helena.

Americans' concern with the Indian, his tomahawk and his soul, finds expression in song. Poor "Lo" himself is supposed to have been the author of "Indian Song" (SAH329 and elsewhere):[10]

In de dark woods, no Indian nigh,
Den me look heb'n, and send up cry
  Upon my knees so low;
Dat God on high, in shiny place
See me in night wid tearry [*sic*] face,
  My priest he tell me so.

[10] Metcalf tells us (*op. cit.*, pp. 335 ff) of its source and early popularity in camp-meetings.

One of the early breathing spells of the settlers after vanquishing the red men is memorialized in "War Department" (HH277 and often):

No more shall the sound of the war whoop be heard,
The ambush and slaughter no longer be fear'd,
The tomahawk, buried, shall rest in the ground,
And peace and good-will to the nations abound.

And the will to Christianize the subdued native crops out in such songs as "The Gospel Among the Indians" (HH281 and often):

All spirit of war to the gospel shall bow;
The bow lie unstrung at the foot of the plough;
To prune the young orchard the spear shall be bent,
And love greet the world with a smile of content.

Slight tinctures of skin shall no longer engage
The fervor of jealousy, murder and rage;
The white man and red shall in friendship be join'd,
Wide spreading benevolence over mankind.

In "Methodist and Formalist" (HH454) and in "Zion's Call" (HH321) we find a defense of the expressive "shouting Christian" or rural type of religionist against his more undemonstrative brother of the urban type, the "formalist":

The sweetest joys our pow'rs employ,
To see the cause advancing;
Tho' some go off and boldly scoff,
And say that we are dancing.

Some mournfully for mercy cry,
And stubborn hearts are bended;
But if we smile, some say we're wild
And so go off offended.

"The formalist" objects:

The preachers were stamping, the people were jumping,
And screaming so loud that I nothing could hear;
Either praying or preaching—Such horrible shrieking!
I was truly offended at all that was there.

* * * * * * *

The men they were bawling, the women were squalling,
I know not for my part how any could pray;
Such horrid confusion—if this be religion
I'm sure it is something that never was seen;
For the sacred pages . . .
Do nowhere declare that such ever has been.

But the Methodist meets the challenge and tells how David danced before the ark, how at the rebuilding of the temple and at Ezra's command "some wept and some praised, such a noise there was raised, 'twas heard afar off," and how Peter's preaching affected the people so deeply that Bible-time scoffers declared "they are fill'd with new wine. . . . They're drunkards or fools or in falsehood abound." In the end the formalist was won over to the Methodist's point of view. This argument represented a very real and important religio-cultural struggle during the first part of the nineteenth century.

The rush for California gold was doubtless the background of the following song called "The Dying Californian," OSAH 410:

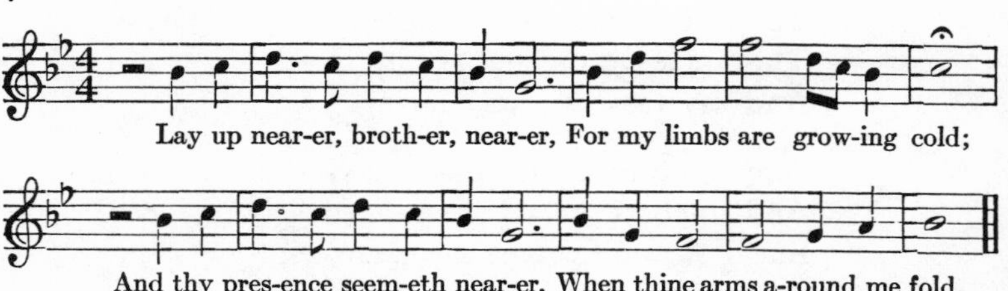

I am dying, brother, dying,
Soon you'll miss me in your birth [*sic!*]
For my form will soon be lying
'Neath the ocean's briny deep.

The dying man on shipboard sends messages, fifteen stanzas of them, to father, mother, sisters, wife, and children.

Tell them I never reached the haven
Where I sought the precious dust;
But I've gained a port called heaven,
Where the gold will never rust.

Then he dies. This tune is a good example of how the fasola folk notated in even time a melody that is clearly a three-part measure.

The most recent historical event to echo in the fasola books is the war with Mexico. McCurry's SOCH, page 254, brings a seven-stanza song about a dying soldier at the Battle of Buena Vista:

On Buena Vista's bloody field
A soldier, dying, lay, etc.

CHAPTER XVI

BALLADS OF RELIGIOUS EXPERIENCE, BAD WOMEN, BAD MEN, BIBLICAL EVENTS

Miss Hataway's Experience

The "experience" songs were a rather definite sort. They always began with the traditional "Come all ye" and went on to explain how the subject of the religious ballad, born in sin, experienced religion, was saved, and became a child of God. "Miss Hataway's Experience" (HH 421, text from *Mercer's Cluster,* p. 183), is a good example. Its wide popularity and the typical ballad-like elements in its make-up induce me to reproduce it in full:

No greater crimes did I commit
Than thousands do delight in yet;—
That heinous crime, called civil mirth,
God threatens with his dreadful wrath.
I oftentimes to church did go,
My beauty and fine clothes to show;
About my soul I took no thought,
Christ and his grace to me were nought.

Full eighteen years around did roll,
Before I thought of my poor soul;
Which makes me shudder when I think
How near I stood upon the brink!
At last I heard a Baptist preach,
His words into my heart did reach;
He said, "You must be born again,
Or heaven you never can obtain."

To keep the law I then was bent,
But found I fail'd in ev'ry point:
The law appear'd so just and true
Not one good duty could I do.
In silent watches of the night,
I went in secret, where I might
Upon my knees, pour out my grief,
And pray to God for some relief.

My uncle said, "Don't look so dull,
Come, go with me to yonder ball;
I'll dress you up in silk most fine,
And make you heir of all that's mine."
Dear Uncle, that will never do,
It only will augment my wo;
Nor can I think true bliss to win,
If I shall still add sin to sin.

"Well, if you are resolved to turn,
And after silly babblers run,
None of my portion you shall have,
I will it to some other leave."
I am resolved to seek the Lord,
Perhaps He may His help afford—
Oh! help me mourn my wretched case,
For I am lost without free grace.

Just in this last extremity,
As almost helpless I did lie,
I thought I heard a still small voice

Cry out, "Rise up, in me rejoice!"
Then to my mind did one appear
Wounded by whip, and nail, and spear,
Bearing my sin, a mighty load,
That I might be a child of God.

The experience songs were naturally bound up with an exhortational element which adjures the young folks to avoid "civil mirth practiced on earth" and warns especially the terpsichorean enthusiasts that "the coffin, earth and winding-sheet will soon your active limbs enclose."[1]

The Romish Lady

Miss Hataway gave up simply her inheritance for her religion. The Romish Lady gave her life:

There was a Romish lady, brought up in popery,
Her mother always taught her the priest she must obey.
"O pardon me, dear Mother, I humbly pray thee now,
But unto these false idols I can no longer bow.

Assisted by her handmaid, a bible she concealed,
And there she gained instruction, till God his love revealed.
No more she prostrates herself to pictures decked with gold;
But soon she was betrayed and her bible from her stole.

With grief and great vexation her mother straight did go
T'inform the Roman clergy the cause of all her wo.
The priests were soon assembled and for the maid did call,
And forced her in the dungeon to fright her soul withal.

The more they strove to fright her, the more she did endure;
Although her age was tender, her faith was strong and sure.
The chains of gold so costly they from this lady took,
And she, with all her spirit, the pride of life forsook.

Before the pope they brought her, in hopes of her return,
And there she was condemned in horrid flames to burn.

[1] Other experience songs are HH 40, 258, 441 and SOH 81.

Before the place of torment they brought her speedily;
With lifted hands to heaven she then agreed to die.

There being many ladies assembled at the place,
She raised her eyes to heaven and begged supplying grace:
"Weep not, ye tender ladies, shed not a tear for me,
While my poor body's burning, my soul the Lord shall see.

"Yourselves you need to pity, and Zion's deep decay;
Dear ladies, turn to Jesus, no longer make delay."
In comes her raving mother, her daughter to behold,
And in her hand she brought her the pictures decked with gold.

"O take from me these idols, remove them from my sight;
Restore to me my bible, wherein I take delight!—
Alas! My aged mother, why on my ruin bent?
Twas you that did betray me, but I am innocent.

"Tormentors, use your pleasure, and do as you think best;
I hope my blessed Jesus will take my soul to rest."
Soon as these words were spoken, up steps the man of death,
And kindled up the fire to stop her mortal breath.

Instead of golden bracelets, with chains they bound her fast;
She cried, "My God, give power, now must I die at last!
With Jesus and his angels forever I shall dwell;
God pardon priest and people, and so I bid farewell."

Is this a lyric from old-world sources and from those times when differences of religious opinion caused much suffering and martyrdom and drove the forefathers of many of these fasola singers to the continent of the West? The tune is MPT No. 36.[2]

Wicked Polly

It was Wicked Polly's moral irregularities, she and others were convinced, that caused her eternal damnation. The version which I recorded from the singing of Mrs. Elizabeth Showal-

[2] It is found KNH 188, SOH 82, HH 257, and elsewhere.

ter-Miller, Dayton, Virginia, December 22, 1929, follows. She learned it in her youth, about seventy-five years ago, in that same locality.

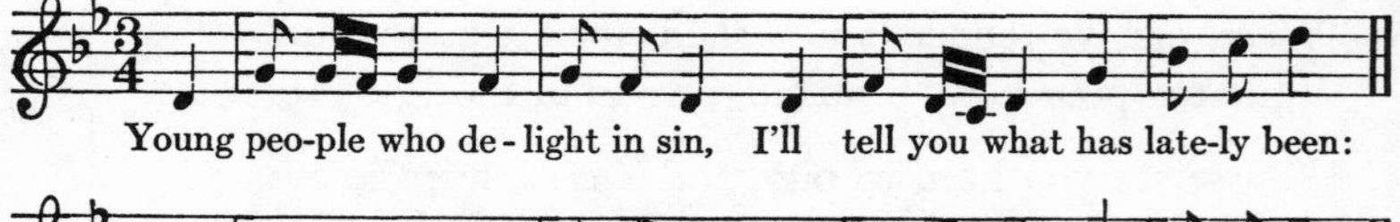

She went to frolics, dance and play, in spite of all her friends could say.
"I'll turn to God when I get old, and He will then receive my soul."

On Friday morning she took sick, her stubborn heart began to break.
She called her mother to her bed; her eyes were rolling in her head.

"O Mother, Mother, fare ye well; your wicked Polly's doomed to hell.
The tears air lost you shed for me; my soul is lost, I plainly see.

"My earthly father, fare ye well; your wicked Polly's doomed to hell.
The flaming wrath begins to roll; I am a lost and ruined soul."

She gnawed her tongue before she died; she rolled, she groaned, she screamed and cried:
"O must I burn forevermore till thousand, thousand years are o'er?"

It almost broke her mother's heart to see her child in hell depart:
"O is my daughter gone to hell? My grief so great no tongue can tell."

Young people, less this be your case, O turn to God and trust His grace.
Down on your knees fer mercies cry, less you in sin like Polly die.

The tune sung by Mrs. Miller will be recognized as the uniquely popular No. 1 in the MPT list. I have not found the text in any of the southern fasola books.

An interesting version of this lugubrious ballad, possibly its original form, is given by Edward S. Ninde on page 68 of his *The Story of the American Hymn:*

O young people, hark while I relate
The story of poor Polly's fate!
She was a lady young and fair,
And died a-groaning in despair.

She would go to balls and dance and play,
In spite of all her friends could say;
"I'll turn," said she, "when I am old,
And God will then receive my soul:"

One Sabbath morning she fell sick;
Her stubborn heart began to ache.
She cried, "Alas, my days are spent!
It is too late now to repent."

She called her mother to her bed,
Her eyes were rolling in her head;
A ghastly look she did assume;
She cries, "Alas, I am undone.

"My loving father, you I leave;
For wicked Polly do not grieve;
For I must burn forevermore,
When thousand thousand years are o'er.

"Your counsels I have slighted all,
My carnal appetite to fill.
When I am dead, remember well
Your wicked Polly groans in hell."

She [w]rung her hands and groaned and cried
And gnawed her tongue before she died;
Her nails turned black, her voice did fail,
She died and left this lower vale.

May this a warning be to those
That love the ways that Polly chose,

Turn from your sins, lest you, like her,
Shall leave this world in black despair.

As to its origin Ninde has the following story (undocumented): Gershum Palmer, an itinerant preacher, used to hold services once a month in the village church of Little Rest (now Kingston), Rhode Island. "When a young man, some years before the Revolution, he conducted the funeral of a girl by the name of Polly. She had scandalized the church people by her giddy behavior, and when she died, after a brief illness, there appeared some verses entitled 'Wicked Polly,'" which became popular in those parts. "One Sunday, at the age of ninety-two," Ninde goes on to tell, "Father Palmer himself sang it as a solo. The venerable man was assisted to the pulpit by two deacons, and as with quavering voice he uttered the words, the people listened with breathless attention."

Professor Chester Nathan Gould, of the University of Chicago, found a version of "Wicked Polly" among some old papers of his family in Edwards County, Illinois, and explained its arrival there as follows: It "was evidently written down by one of a group of young women at some time in the decade 1830-1840. They were members of a New England colony, which early in the century, had migrated from Charlemont, Massachusetts, to what is now West Virginia, and from there went to Edwards County, Illinois."[3]

It is evident that the oral tradition which brought the ballad from Rhode Island or Massachusetts to the Valley of Virginia has improved it. The crass realism is soft-pedaled somewhat. The expression is smoother, and the rhythm is better. Cox records this ballad for West Virginia, an early nineteenth-century version.[4]

[3] In the *Boston Transcript,* 1906, Notes and Queries, No. 3970.

[4] John Harrington Cox, *Folk-Songs of the South,* p. 411. For other variants see *Journal of American Folk-Lore,* XXIX, 192; XXXV, 430.

Negroes have taken "Wicked Polly," and made her into a male:[5]

Young people who delight in sin,
I tell you what I lately seen;
A po' godless sinner die,
An' he said: "In hell I soon'll lie."

* * * * *

He call his mother to his bed,
An' these is the dyin' words he said:
"Mother, Mother, a long farewell,
Your wicked son is damned in hell.

"He dance an' play hisself away,
An' still put off his dyin' day,
Until at las' ole death was sent,
An' it 'us too late fer him to repent."

A song recorded by a Georgian-Alabamian, John S. Terry, in the OSAH 437 and entitled "Ester" is interesting both for its text and its folk-tune:

This lesson she has left for you,
To teach the careless what to do;
To seek Jehovah while you live,
And everlasting honors give.

Her honored mother she addressed,
While tears were streaming down her breast;
She grasped her tender hands and said,
"Remember me when I am dead."

[5] Odum and Johnson, *The Negro and His Songs,* p. 73.

She called her father to her bed,
And thus in dying anguish said:
"My days on earth are at an end,
My soul is summoned to attend.

"Before Jehovah's awful bar,
To hear my awful sentence there;
And now, dear father, do repent,
And read the holy testament."

This theme is off the same piece with "Wicked Polly" and "Miss Hataway." The tune is very closely related to the secular melody used in North Carolina for the ballad "Geordie."[6]

The Female Convict

Another bad woman was "The Female Convict,"[7] who, as the title tells us, "after receiving pardon in the sight of God, thus addresst her infant":

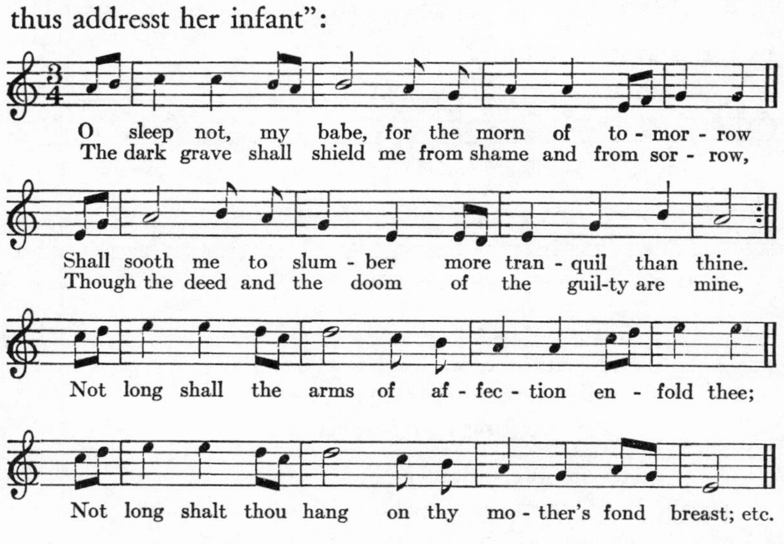

[6] See Campbell and Sharp, *op. cit.,* p. 118, tune C. *Cf.* also the same work, p. 98, tune 1.

[7] Found in SOH 160, UH 120, KNH 122 and elsewhere.

The first stanza concludes:

And who with the eye of delight shall behold thee,
And watch thee and guard thee when I am at rest.

The song continues:

And yet it doth grieve me to wake thee, my dearest,
The pangs of thy desolate mother to see;
Thou wilt weep when the clank of my cold chains thou hearest,
And none but the guilty should weep over me.
And yet I must wake thee, and whilst thou art weeping,
To calm thee I'll stifle my tears for a while.
Thou smil'st in thy dreams whilst thus placidly sleeping,
And O! how it wounds me to gaze on thy smiles.

Alas, my sweet babe, with what pride I had press'd thee
To the bosom that now throbs with terror and shame,
If the pure tie of virtue's affection had bless's thee
And hailed thee the heir of thy father's high name.
But now with remorse that avails not, I mourn thee,
Forsaken and friendless as soon thou wilt be,
In a world, if they can not betray, that will scorn thee,
Avenging the guilt of thy mother on thee.

And when the dark thought of my fate shall awaken
The deep blush of shame on thy innocent cheek;
When by all but the God of the orphan forsaken,
A home and a father in vain thou wilt seek;
I know that the base world will seek to deceive thee
With falsehood like that which thy mother beguiled,
Deserted and helpless, with whom can I leave thee?
O God of the fatherless, pity my child!

The Little Family

I wish to record another sacred ballad sung by Mrs. Miller.[8] She called it "The Little Family":

[8] See p. 189 above.

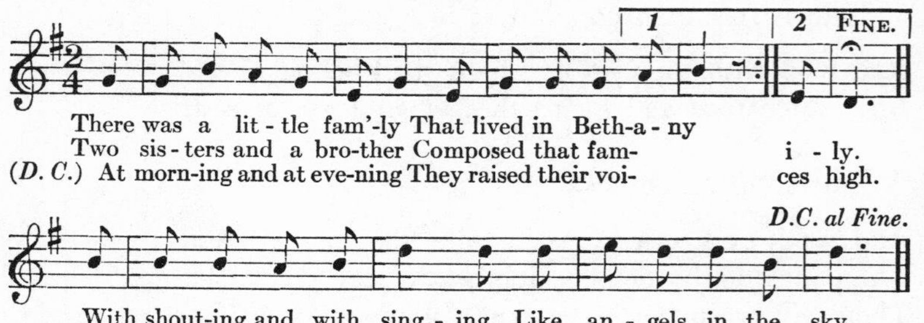

But while they lived so happy,
So poor, so kind and good,
Their brother was afflicted
And rudely thrown abed.
Poor Martha and her sister
Now wept aloud and cried;
But still he grew no better
And lingered on and died.

The Jews went to the sisters,
Put Lazarus in the tomb.
They wept their hearts to comfort
And drive away their gloom.
But Jesus heard their tidings
Fer in a distant land;
And swiftly did he travel
To join their lonely band.

When Martha saw him coming
She met him on the way.
She told him how her brother
Had died and passed away.
He cheered her and he blessed her,
He told her not to weep;
Fer in him was the power
To wake him from his sleep.

When Mary saw him coming
She ran to meet him, too,

And at his feet fell weeping,
Rehearsed the tale of woe.
When Jesus saw her weeping,
He fell to weeping too.
He wept until they showed him
Where Lazarus was entombed.

He rolled away the cover;
He looked upon the grave;
He prayed unto his Father
His loving friend to save.
And Lazarus in full power
Came from the gloomy mound,
And in full strength and vigor
He walked upon the ground.

So if we but love Jesus,
And do his holy will,
Like Martha and like Mary,
They always used him well.
In death he will redeem us
And take us to the skies,
And bid us live forever
Where pleasure never dies.

John C. Campbell records the first stanza of this song and a tune that is essentially identical with the one sung by Mrs. Miller.[9] He found it as No. 449 in "*A New and Choice Selection of Hymns and Spiritual Songs for the Use of the Regular Baptist Church,* by Elder E. D. Thomas, Catlettsburg, Ky., C. L. McConnell, 1871." This occurrence warrants its being looked on as belonging among the southern fasola spiritual ballads. It does not, however, occur in any of the fifteen books under immediate scrutiny.

[9] *Op. cit.*, p. 185.

Wedlock

In "Wedlock," SOCH 188 and SAH 115, we find a pretty complete set of biblically deduced rules of marital conduct for both man and wife:

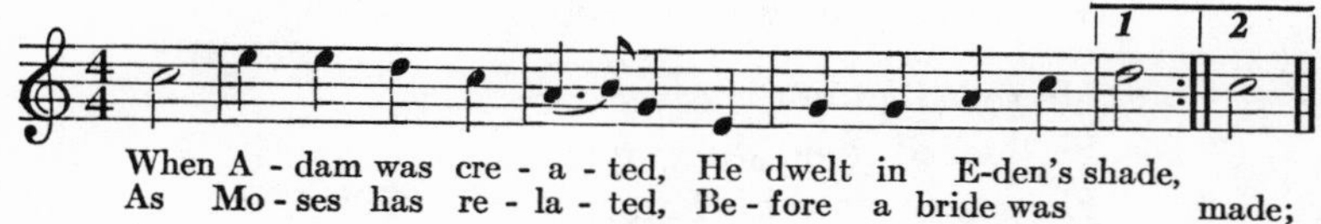

He had no consolation,
But seemed as one alone,
Till, to his admiration,
He found he'd lost a bone.

This woman was not taken
From Adam's head, we know;
And she must not rule o'er him,
It's evidently so.

This woman she was taken
From near to Adam's heart,
By which we are directed
That they should never part.

The book that's called the Bible,
Be sure you don't neglect;
For in every sense of duty,
It will you both direct.

The woman is commanded
To do her husband's will,
In every thing that's lawful,
Her duty to fulfill.

Great was his exultation,
To see her by his side;
Great was his elevation,
To have a loving bride.

This woman she was taken
From under Adam's arm;
And she must be protected
From injury and harm.

This woman was not taken
From Adam's feet, we see;
And she must not be abused,
The meaning seems to be.

The husband is commanded
To love his loving bride;
And live as does a Christian,
And for his house provide.

The woman is commanded
Her husband to obey,
In every thing that's lawful,
Until her dying day.

Avoiding all offenses,
Not sow the seed of strife,
These are the solemn duties
Of every man and wife.

The tune of "Wedlock" shows relationship to that of the "Happy Family" above and to a Cox recording of "Joe Bowers," a secular ballad.[10]

[10] *Op. cit.*, p. 527, No. 50.

Joyful Spring, Pastoral Elegy, and Solomon's Song

Eros had a hard time in fasola musical circles. It was, indeed, one of the chief purposes of these boosters for the attractions of another world to make mundane seductions seem undesirable. We have seen this in numbers of songs which decry these vanities in their obvious guises of feminine ornament, dancing, and "civil mirth" in general. But the spirit of earthly love slipped in among the sacred pages now and then in some sort of disguise or with a scriptural visa. This spirit was hardly recognized, for example, in the sylvan scene of "Joyful Spring," HH358:

> The voice of my beloved sounds
> While o'er the mountain top he bounds.

The same is true for the "absent love" song "Pastoral Elegy," HH452; where Caroline weeps for her lost Corydon in the bucolic-poetic style of a hundred years before. But the most unabashed and beautiful example of eroticism, with biblical sanction, ("The Song of Solomon, IV"), was introduced by the live wires, W. H. and M. L. Swan, into their *Harp of Columbia,* pages 187 ff:

Solomon's Song

Behold, thou art fair, my love;
Thou hast dove's eyes within thy locks;
Thy hair is as a flock of goats that appear from Mount Gilead.
Thy teeth are like a flock of sheep that are even shorn,
Which came up from the washing,
Whereof every one bear twins, and none is barren among them.
Thy lips are like a thread of scarlet, and thy speech is comely;
Thy temples are like a piece of pomegranate within thy locks.
Thy neck is like the tower of David builded for an armory
Whereon hang a thousand bucklers, all shields of mighty men.
Thy two breasts are like two young roes that are twins,
Which feed among the lilies.

. . . and so on to the end of the chapter.

A realistic contrast to this romantic scene is pictured in the often-met-with "Few Happy Matches" (SKH26), in which the sexually cynical poet—said to have been John Wesley himself—lists six sorts of marital mismating in so many stanzas.

Anti-Drink Songs

The temperance movement began in the South in the 1830's. William Hauser reminds us (HH536) that "the grand Washington Temperance movement was begun in Baltimore, Md., on Friday evening, April 2, 1840, by Wm. K. Mitchell, tailor; F. J. Hoss, carpenter; D. Anderson, blacksmith, George Steers, wheelwright; J. McCurley, coachmaker; and Arch Campbell, silver-plater. Mitchell wrote the grand teetotal Washington Pledge, and was the first president of their society." The subsequent fasola song books took up the cause by including a number of anti-drink songs. "The Drunkard's Burial," SOCH 154, will be recognized as a textual parody of Charles Wolfe's "The Burial of Sir John Moore," which begins "Not a drum was heard." And the tune is carved out of the student song "Drink it down." (Or was it the other way around?) I reproduce simply the beginning of the parody.

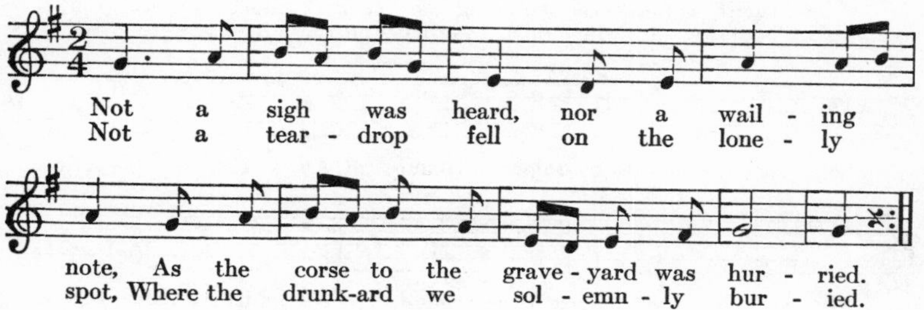

"John Adkins' Farewell," SOCH 200, was sung by the victim of excess alcohol who, having killed his wife, was in prison under a death sentence. In nine stanzas he pleaded that other

Poor drunkards, poor drunkards, take warning by me.
The fruits of transgression behold now I see.

His orphaned children were commended to the care of God and to "kind neighbors"; and his own guilty soul he cast at the feet of Him who "pardons poor drunkards and crowns them above."

Songs of Parting and Death

Not only the sinners, but the saints, too, were fond of their swan songs. Titles like "Parting Hand," "Pilgrim's Farewell," "Saint's Farewell," "Hicks' Farewell," etc., stand above songs which have been called forth by approaching death, departure for the mission field, or the close of an especially successful singing school. I shall reproduce "Hicks' Farewell" as being typical of the genre. I recorded it from the singing of Mrs. Elizabeth Showalter-Miller, Dayton, Virginia, December 22, 1929. She learned it from the singing of her father "about seventy-five years ago":

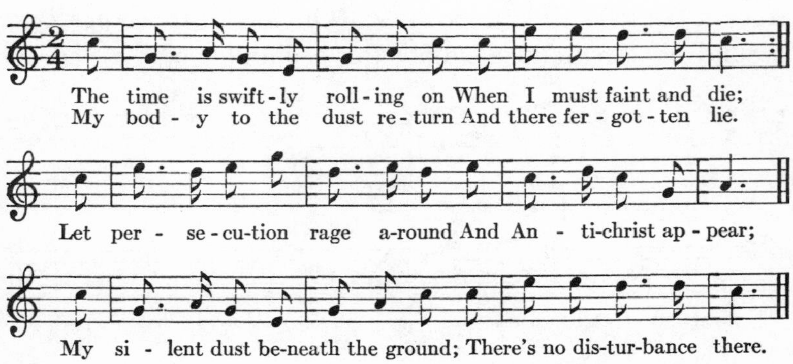

Through heats and cold I've ofttimes went, I've wandered in despair,

To call poor sinners to repent and seek their Savior dear.
My brother preachers, boldly speak and stand on Zion's wall.
Confirm the drunk, confirm the weak and after sinners call.

My loving wife, my bosom friend, the object of my love,
The time's been sweet I've spent with you, my sweet and harmless dove,
My little children near my heart my warm affections know.
From each the path will I attend. O from them can I go?!

O God, a father to them be and keep them from all harm,
That they may love and worship Thee and dwell upon Thy charm.
How often you have looked fer me and often seen me come.
But now I must depart from thee and nevermore return.

My loving wife, don't grieve fer me, neither lament nor mourn;
Fer I will with my Jesus be and dwell upon his charm.

The tune will be recognized as essentially identical with MPT36. The text is a fairly well preserved version of a song that appeared first on page 19 of William Walker's *Southern Harmony,* 1835. Walker claimed authorship of the tune he used. But I find it simply a slight revamping of the much older MPT2. As to the words, Walker appended the note, "The song [poem] was composed by the Rev. B. Hicks, a Baptist minister of South Carolina, and sent to his wife while he was confined in Tennessee by a fever of which he afterwards recovered." This started me on the trail of the Rev. B. Hicks.

Singing this song one day to a South Carolinian, Charles Madison Sarratt, a dean in Vanderbilt University, I was assured by him that B. Hicks was a real person and that his (Sarratt's) mother, born and reared in the South Carolina song belt, could give me the details. A letter to this lady, Mrs. Fannie Amos Sarratt, Gaffney, South Carolina, brought to me a yellowed copy of the *Southern Harmony,* an heirloom belonging to Theodore Hicks, and another book, *Sketches of the Broad River and King's Mountain Baptist Associations,* from 1800 to 1882, by Deacon John R. Logan, printed by Babington, Roberts & Co., Shelby, N. C., 1887. According to the *Sketches* (pp. 400 ff.), Elder Berryman Hicks was born in Spartanburg County (now Cherokee County) July 1, 1778. He "intermarried" with Elizabeth Durham in 1799 and "reared a large and interesting family." He joined the State Line Church in 1800 and was soon licensed to preach. "He was a great revivalist and went far and near with his great co-worker, Elder Drury Dobbins. The names of Hicks and Dobbins became household words, so great was their popularity as ministers. Hicks possessed poetical talent and composed numerous hymns and spiritual songs—adapted to revival occasions, which found wide use at that period. . . . In early life he became a good performer on the violin, the beautiful and melodious strains of which he suffered to be turned to a bad use in the service of sin. While thus perverting its use, and really abusing it, he acquired an ugly habit of twitching his head and keeping time to the music, which [habit] he afterwards carried with him into the pulpit, and from which it is said he never, during life, was entirely relieved. . . . He would often, after his conversion, amuse himself and family by playing on the violin as an accompaniment to the singing of the sweet songs of Zion."

It was doubtless his poetical and musical gifts as well as his "fine physique and attractive appearance generally" that won for him the distinction of being "the Appollos of the Broad River Association in his day." Later in life, however, Appollos "became financially embarrassed for a large amount whereby a brother, Deacon E. Jones, who was his bondsman, became a severe sufferer." So B. Hicks was dropped by his good Baptist brethren, and his demise, at Little Buck Creek, Spartanburg County, South Carolina, June 11, 1839, "is unnoticed in the minutes" of his Baptist association.

In his *Harp of Columbia* of 1848 (page 32), Swan gives four stanzas of the Hicks text and a different tune ascribed to W. Atchley. Campbell and Sharp recorded four very badly sung-to-pieces stanzas from the singing of Silas Shelton, Spillcorn, North Carolina, in 1916, in a melodic setting that points to the SOH tune.[11]

[11] *English Folk-Songs from the Southern Appalachians,* p. 227.

CHAPTER XVII

SONG CLASSIFICATION

Difficulty of Classifying the Songs

I MUST confess to a feeling of partial failure in my attempt to classify these songs as "folk" and "art" products. I have found elements of both types in profusion and in confusion. Some songs have been found to be clearly of the folk variety, others are pure art products, and many float in the limbo between the two. Also, the common distinctions, "sacred" and "secular," do not always apply. Religious elements are found in songs that are predominatingly worldly, and vice versa. Indeed, the songs of the fasola folk are like their talk, with religion tingeing one as the other.[1] They have not, like the urban folk, relegated their religion to one day or one hour in the week and to one place, the church.

The compilers of the books have made their own classifications of the songs. The first cover page announces "tunes, hymns, psalms, odes, spiritual songs, set pieces and anthems." But those same compilers would, I fear, have had as hard a time in explaining all the differences as would the average lawyer in distinguishing the individual infinitives in the series "to purloin, steal or carry away by theft." Inside the books the grouping is, as we have seen, *(a)* "Plain and Easy and Suitable to Divine Worship," *(b)* "More Lengthy Tunes Com-

[1] While we say "Goodby," the country singer often says, "Pray for me." One of my singer friends concludes his letters to me with "Thy friend." "Mister" and "Missis" are seldom heard in the rural singing circles, "Brother" and "Sister" taking their places. Campbell has an interesting chapter (*op. cit.,* pp. 176 ff.), making clear how religious thought pervades the southern mountaineer's whole sphere of mental activity. His conclusions are true also for the larger group of people under consideration here.

monly Used in Singing Schools and Private Societies," and *(c)* "Anthems." But there was no close fit of the songs to their rubrics excepting in the case of the anthems, pieces of considerable length and variety which included solo and duet passages for the different voices. These anthems were looked upon as the musical high points of the fasola folk, the masterpieces of their art. There were a dozen or so of these at the end of each book, and from book to book the group of anthems was much the same. Omnipresent compositions of this sort were "Easter Anthem" (Billings),[2] "Heavenly Vision" (French), "Judgment" ("Mr. Morgan"), "Funeral" (Billings), "Rose of Sharon" (Billings), "Clarement," "Ode on Science" (Sumner), and "Creation" (Shumway).

Fuguing Tunes

One song sort, found in all the books excepting GCM, is not segregated and specifically designated by the compilers; this despite their being a very distinct variety. I refer to the fugal or fuguing songs that were brought into American sacred music largely through the influence of the rural New England singing-school teacher and composer, William Billings (1746-1800). They enjoyed wide popularity throughout America for over half a century and then slowly went out of style. Their only place of survival today is among the Sacred Harpers, where they are as alive and as greatly enjoyed and as often sung apparently as when the *Sacred Harp* first appeared.

In the fuguing tune all the parts start together and proceed in rhythmic and harmonic unity usually for the space of four measures or one musical sentence. The end of this sentence marks a cessation, a complete melodic close. During the next four measures the four parts set in, one at a time and

[2] I have not verified the data in the books as to the anthems' composers.

one measure apart. First the basses take the lead for a phrase a measure long, and as they retire on the second measure to their own proper bass part, the higher-voiced men take the lead with a sequence that is imitative of, if not identical with, that just sung by the basses. The tenors in turn give way to the altos, and they to the trebles, all four parts doing that same passage (though at different pitches) in imitation of the lead singer of the preceding measure. The basses, and to some extent also the tenors, after they have done their one-measure leading stunt, often strike a single tone and stick to it with a peculiar droning effect for a number of measures or until the fuguing passage has been negotiated by each of the other voices. Following this fuguing passage comes a four-measure phrase, with all the parts rhythmically neck and neck, and this closes the piece; though the last eight measures are often repeated.

Billings himself was enthusiastically in favor of fuguing. "It has more than twenty times the power of the old slow tunes," he assures us in the Preface to his *The Continental Harmony* (Boston, 1794), "each part straining for mastery and victory. The audience is entertained and delighted, their minds surpassingly agitated and extremely fluctuated, sometimes declaring for one part and sometimes for another. Now the solemn bass demands their attention; next the manly tenor, now the volatile treble. Now here, now there, now here again. O ecstatis! Rush on, you sons of harmony." Others were less enraptured. Nathaniel D. Gould speaks of it as "a bewitching jingle which in a great measure covers the errors of the harmony."[3]

Father Joseph Funk had no "fondness for novelty" and "the changes of fashion" in sacred music. His GCM, therefore, contained not one fuguing piece. Ananias Davisson must have

[3] *Op. cit.*, p. 50.

had such people as his neighbor Funk in mind when he wrote (KYH, p. 14): "There are some of our superannuated old *Deacons,* who stand in opposition to fuging [*sic*] music; but it is an old maxim, and I think a very just one too, *that variety is always pleasing.*" Hence, we find many fuguing pieces in the popular *Kentucky Harmony* and its *Supplement.* All the Tennessee, South Carolina, and Georgia books, and the *Missouri Harmony,* have from twenty to seventy songs each, built on the fuguing plan, the number depending somewhat on the size of the book.

Southernizing of Songs

From what has been said above in connection with *Sacred Harp* singing in conventions, it may be inferred that vocal practice and the printed or notated page differ. This is true. It is also true that the fasola folk sing in a manner quite different from any present-day vocalism I have ever heard in any other section. I have already mentioned one of these differences—their more rapid tempo, or their penchant for singing more notes to the minute. I have also touched upon their unwillingness to tolerate, in any one of the four harmonic parts, long sequences of the same note repeated for successive text syllables and words. A third difference is their bent for melodic ornamentation.

When a song was made in the South, especially in the South Carolina-Georgia section, it was almost sure to show those earmarks. When it originated elsewhere—in the North or the East and was subsequently sung in the South and incorporated in southern song books—the local peculiarities were often grafted upon it, a practice which our Georgia musician, William Hauser, rightly called "southernizing." In Hauser's *Hesperian Harp,* page 347, is a song called "Prescott." And at the top right of this song we read, "Composed originally by Geo. Oates; but here *Southernized* by Wm. Hauser." I found the song which was subjected to the southernizing process in the *Christian Minstrel* (page 283), a song book which was made in Philadelphia (1846) by a Pennsylvanian and aimed at northern buyers and singers. The melody of this song has the same note sequence in both northern and southern versions. It is in the bass and the middle parts that the difference between the northern and southern arrangements appears, as the following samples will show:

It will be noticed that the servile and eventless northern alto has become southernized into a sequence that sounds like a fairly good independent tune. What violence such changes may have done to the harmony seems to have been looked upon as a secondary matter. The first rule was to make each part melodically interesting. And in this the fasola productions remind us strikingly of fifteenth-century polyphonic practice.

On the preceding pages we have given many illustrations of the fasola leaning toward the more-notes-to-the-minute style of delivery. Their fondness for dance tunes was one clear indication of this bent. I have found no such songs in northern-used books. When Pennsylvania's Jesse Aikin accepted the moderately lively and enormously popular "Greenfields" ("How tedious and tasteless the hours") for use in his *Christian Minstrel,* he was careful to preserve his professional dignity by explaining at the top right that the tune was "inserted by particular request." The southern fasola folk had no dignity to preserve, no draggy church traditions to uphold. Hence they all used "Greenfields" without apology. They hurried their borrowed songs as is seen in "Prescott," where the 3/2 tempo is changed to 3/4. And they made new tunes with perfect freedom to indulge their sectional tendency. E. J. King, the *Sacred Harp* co-author, made a tune, "Carnesville," which illustrates the point, for it is nothing, from beginning to end, but a many-note and hurried-up version of the familiar and dignified, "How Firm a Foundation" tune, which is called "Protection" in the fasola books.

(*a*) Traditional tune "Protection" (HOC 57)

(*b*) "Protection" southernized by E. J. King of Georgia and called "Carnesville" (SAH 109)

Ornamentation

The third feature of southern fasola singing, ornamentation, seldom gets into the notation. Watch closely a singer of *Sacred Harp* or *Southern Harmony* tunes and you will realize that the page before him shows only a fraction of what he sings. Like old-timey handwriting, his vocal production is full of stylistic flourishes. One of these flourishes, noticeable especially in closing cadences, is that in which the voice, usually a man's voice, flips up momentarily, on its transition from one long tone to another lower one, to a falsetto grace note much higher than either of the notes in the melody proper and then returns, equally momentarily, to the original note before proceeding to the closing one. Graphically it is something like *(a),* below. And when this flip or break in the male voice comes at the very end of the last note in the song, it sounds as indicated in *(b),* below.

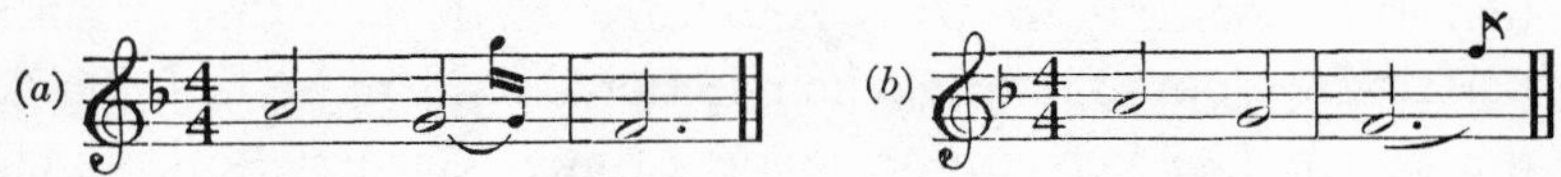

This particular type of ornament (it must be considered as ornament, for it is cultivated, even though perhaps unconsciously), seems to be related to what the Germans called the "Nachschlag" in eighteenth-century music, and what Emanuel Bach called "ugly, although extraordinarily in fashion." That William Walker seems to have tried to notate it in its *(a)* form is indicated by *(c)* below, which is found in SOH. And a somewhat similar "grace" taken from Walker's book is shown in *(d)*.

The scoop or slide, made use of in negotiating big or little intervals, and other tendencies toward livening up an otherwise bare melody are excellently shown in the Ninety-Third Psalm as it appears in a number of southern fasola books.

Ninety-Third Psalm (SAH 31)

The striking difference between the song tastes of northern and southern singers in the first half of the nineteenth century is emphasized by the 1840 edition of Timothy and Lowell

Mason's *Sacred Harp* (Cincinnati). I find in that comprehensive collection *only one* of the eighty tunes which are listed above as the most widely popular in the South. That one song was the "Go Tell Aunt Rhody" tune, called "Greenville," MPT 80[a]. But, after all, this difference may not be so much a matter of singers' tastes as a matter of compilers' tastes, the southern compilers allowing the singers to sing what they like; the northern compilers providing the public with what they *should* sing.

CHAPTER XVIII

SPIRITUAL SONGS BORN IN CAMP MEETINGS

The Revival or Camp-Meeting Song

While the fasola songs are of differing qualities and types and while they were intended to serve various social, musical, and religious purposes, still there is one song pattern that stands out clearly from all the tonal and poetic heterogeneity in these books. I refer to the revival or camp-meeting song, a sort which comes nearer to deserving the name of folk-song than does any other large group among the religious songs of the southern rurals. Before describing this type of song, I shall recall some of the factors which brought the type into existence, and in speaking of these factors I shall have to do first with the song texts.

Spiritual songs of recent Protestants, both in England and America, go back no further, for the great body of their poetic texts than to Isaac Watts (1674-1748). There are doubtless many reasons for this, but I would call attention to one that seems to me most important, namely, that Watts deliberately wrote down to "the level of vulgar capacities" and furnished hymns to "the meanest of Christians." This start from the ground, this hymnodic democracy, was doubtless the basis of the subsequent enormous popularity of the Watts manner of hymn; and John and Charles Wesley, whose life activity was in the middle decades of the eighteenth century, brought religious hymnody still nearer to the masses by endowing it with the elements of personal emotion, spiritual spontaneity, and evangelism.

Watts and the Wesleys and their associates furnished the

Americans of the latter part of the eighteenth century with the bulk of their church-song poetry. But when the apostles of these English movements tried to dictate to their American church groups the particular hymn books and hymns they should use, many of those groups, especially the rural ones, refused to be dictated to. Benson tells us, for example, how the song dictators fared among the Methodists, the most important of the evangelical groups and the one whose influence in song matters permeated many other denominations.

"The people were ignorant," Benson tells us, "the preachers were itinerant, the meetings as often as not in cabins or in the fields, and the singing largely without books, other than the one in the preacher's hand. The tunes [had to be] very familiar or very contagious, the words given out one or two lines at a time if not already known. Under these conditions the development of . . . a rude type of popular song, indifferent to anything in the way of authorized hymnody, seems to have been inevitable."[1] And it was equally inevitable, Benson goes on to declare, that "an illiterate and often vulgar Revival Hymnody" developed. One can see that Benson's viewpoint was not that of the folk-lorist. This whole development was, no doubt, "an incident of the choice of the revival method of church growth. It is of the very nature of revival enthusiasm to develop its own song."

At the beginning of the nineteenth century the revival institution took a new spurt and its songs broadened their conquests through the advent of the camp meeting. Camp meetings were born in the South. The very first one was held in Logan County, Kentucky, in July, 1800, and the evangelical novelty "spread like wild-fire," Benson tells us, first in the states of Kentucky and Tennessee, and then into the Carolinas and into the nation at large.

[1] *Op. cit.*, p. 284.

It would be hard to find a better story of the origin of folk-songs by the socalled communal method than Benson tells us in his account of how the camp-meeting spirituals were born:

Spontaneous song became a marked characteristic of the camp meetings. Rough and irregular couplets or stanzas were concocted out of scripture phrases and every-day speech, with liberal interspersing of hallelujahs and refrains. Such ejaculatory hymns were frequently started by an excited auditor during the preaching, and taken up by the throng, until the meeting dissolved into a "singing-ecstasy" culminating in a general hand-shaking. Sometimes they were given forth by a preacher, who had a sense of rhythm, under the excitement of his preaching and the aggitation of his audience. Hymns were also composed more deliberately out of meeting, and taught to the people or lined out from the pulpit.

Many of these rude songs perished in the using, some were written down, passing from hand to hand. The camp meeting song books which began to appear in the first decade of the nineteenth century doubtless contain such of these as proved effective and popular. . . .

A distinctive type is thus established, the Camp-Meeting Hymn. It is individualistic, and deals with the rescue of a sinner: sometimes in direct appeal to "sinners," "back-sliders," or "mourners;" sometimes by reciting the terms of salvation; sometimes as a narrative of personal experience for his warning or encouragement. The Camp-Meeting Hymn is not churchly, but the companionships of the rough journey to the camp reappear in songs of a common pilgrimage to Canaan, the meetings and partings on the ground typify the reunion of believers in Heaven, and the military suggestions of the encampment furnish many themes for songs of a militant host, brothers in arms in the battle of the Lord. . . . A longing for the heavenly rest and a vivid portrayal of the pains of hell were both characteristic; and a very special group of hymns was designed for the instruction and encouragement of the "seekers," who at the close of the sermon came forward to the stand, or "altar," and occupied the "anxious" bench.

The literary form of the Camp-Meeting Hymn is that of the popular ballad or song, in plainest every-day language and of careless or incapable technique. The refrain or chorus is perhaps the predominant feature, not always connected with the subject matter of the stanza, but rather ejaculatory. In some instances such a refrain was merely tacked on to a familiar hymn or an arrangement of one.

The ecclesiastical authorities, of course, combated this "off brand" of song with their own authentic hymn collections. But the masses of free rural Americans were not to be won away from a body of song that had grown up in their midst. In a few years, that is, during the first two decades of the nineteenth century, unauthorized song-book makers catered to the strong folk-song movement by furnishing collections of the texts of those songs "usually sung at camp meetings."

Before discussing the camp-meeting tunes as such, I shall give some illustrative samples of the texts as I have found them, largely in the *Original Sacred Harp.* First I shall reproduce the significant stanzas, with refrain or chorus where there is one, of twenty-five different songs which were built up from the four most popular "errant stanzas" of the orthodox hymnody of the eighteenth century.

O When Shall I See Jesus?

O when shall I see Jesus, and reign with Him above?
And from the flowing fountain, drink everlasting love?

When shall I be delivered from this vain world of sin,
And with my blessed Jesus, drink endless pleasures in?

Through grace I am determined to conquer though I die;
And then away to Jesus on wings of love I'll fly.

And if you meet with troubles and trials on your way,
Then cast your care on Jesus, and don't forget to pray.

Gird on the gospel armour of faith and hope and love,
And when the combat's ended, He'll carry you above.

[2] *Op. cit.,* pp. 292 ff.

O do not be discouraged, for Jesus is your friend;
And if you lack for knowledge, He'll not refuse to lend.

Neither will He upbraid you, though often you request;
He'll give you grace to conquer, and take you home to rest.
—OSH106.

James, the editor of the OSH (1911 edition of the *Sacred Harp*), attributes this hymn to the Baptist itinerant preacher, John Leland, a New Englander who preached in Virginia for about fifteen years, 1775-1790. The following choruses were either added or merely recorded by various southern rurals:

By T. W. Carter, of Georgia, OSH106:

O had I wings, I would fly away and be at rest,
And I'd praise God in his bright abode.

By an unnamed fasola tunester, OSH322:

Soon we shall land on Canaan's shore,
To live forever more.

By E. L. King, of Georgia, OSH320:

And to glory I will go.

By E. J. King, of Georgia, OSH82:

I'm on my way to Canaan
I'm on my way, etc.
I'm on my way, etc.
To the New Jerusalem.

B. F. White, of Georgia, interpolated, OSH85:

O when shall I see Jesus and reign with Him above,
  And shall hear the trumpet sound in that morning;
And from the flowing fountain, etc.
  And shall hear the trumpet sound in that morning.

Then White added the chorus:

Shout, O glory, for I shall mount above the skies,
When I hear the trumpet sound in that morning.

W. L. Williams, of Georgia, interpolated, OSH319:

O when shall I, etc.
Shout, glory halle hallelujah.

And he added the chorus:

Religion is a fortune and heaven is a home,
Shout, glory halle hallelujah.

William Walker, of South Carolina, parodied the fourth stanza of the Leland hymn, OSH141:

It is great pride and passion
Beset me on the way,
So I am filled with folly,
And so neglect to pray.

On Jordan's Stormy Bank I Stand

The famous hymn by Samuel Stennett (1727-1795),

On Jordan's stormy bank I stand and cast a wistful eye
To Canaan's fair and happy land where my possessions lie.

has been used by the camp-meeting and fasola folk in three variations. Miss M. Durham, of Georgia, seems to have added, or recorded, the following chorus, OSH128:

I'm bound for the promised land,
I'm bound for the promised land;
Oh, who will come and go with me?
I'm bound for the promised land.

Elder Edmund Dumas, a Primitive Baptist preacher of Georgia, added the chorus, OSH378:

We'll stem the storm, it won't be long;
The heav'nly port is nigh;

We'll stem the storm, it won't be long;
We'll anchor by and by.

J. T. White, of Georgia, interpolated, OSH486.

On Jordan's stormy banks I stand and cast a wishful eye,
On the other side of Jordan, hallelujah.

And he added a chorus made of the same ejaculatory phrases.

OH WHO WILL COME AND GO WITH ME?

Closely bound up with the above song group, though based on an older text that James attributed to Watts, is the song, OSH393, beginning,

Oh who will come and go with me?
I'm on my journey home;
I'm bound fair Canaan's land to see,
I'm on my journey home.

The above interpolation (second and fourth lines) was recorded by Miss Sarah Lancaster, of Georgia. She also added the chorus:

O come and go with me,
O come and go with me,
O come and go with me,
For I'm on my journey home.

R. F. M. Mann, also of Georgia, used the same interpolations, and added, OSH111, the chorus:

O come and go with me
For I'm on my journey home;
Home, sweet home, bless the Lord.

And a third Georgian, Oliver Bradfield, produced the version, OSH397:

O who will come and go with me?
We'll shout and sing hosanna;

I'm bound fair Canaan's land to see,
We'll shout and sing hosanna.

Farewell, Vain World, I'm Going Home

I have been unable to find the author of the hymn on which the following song texts are based. The first of the five variants was recorded by E. J. King, of Georgia, OSH80:

Farewell, vain world, I'm going home,
I'm bound to die in the army;
My Savior smiles and bids me come,
I'm bound to die in the army.
Chorus
I'm bound to die in the service of my Lord,
I am bound to die in the army.

Another version, OSH176, reads,

Farewell, vain world, I'm going home,
I belong to this band, hallelujah;
My Savior smiles, etc.
I belong, etc.

It has a chorus of the same material.

J. P. Rees, of Georgia, records, OSH274:

Farewell, vain world, I'm going home,
To play on the golden harp;
My Savior smiles, etc.
To play, etc.
Chorus
To play on the golden harp,
To play on the golden harp;
I want to be where Jesus is,
To play on the golden harp.

H. S. Rees, of Georgia, records, OSH278:

Farewell, vain world, I'm going home,
Where there's no more stormy clouds to rise;

My Savior smiles, etc.
  Where there's no more, etc.
    CHORUS
To the land, to the land, to the land I'm bound,
Where there's no more stormy clouds to rise.

L. P. Breedlove, of Georgia, records, OSH282:

Farewell, vain world, I'm going home,
My Savior smiles and bids me come,
  And I don't care to stay here long.
Sweet angels beckon me away,
To sing God's praise in endless day,
  And I don't care to stay here long.
    CHORUS
Right up yonder, Christians,
Away up yonder;
O yes, my Lord,
For I don't care to stay here long.

JESUS, MY ALL, TO HEAVEN IS GONE

John Cennick, the Englishman, provided the poetic base[3] of the following camp-meeting song. Its first version was recorded by the Georgians, J. A. and J. F. Wade, OSH70:

Jesus, my all, to Heaven is gone,
  Save, mighty Lord;
He whom I fix my hope upon,
  Save, mighty Lord.
    CHORUS
O save, save, mighty Lord,
And send converting power down,
Save, mighty Lord.

B. F. White, of Georgia, made an evident attempt, in his version, to soften the direct expression, "I don't care to stay here long," in his version, OSH88:

[3] Benson, *op. cit.*, p. 317.

Jesus, my all, to Heaven is gone,
And I don't expect to stay much longer here;
He whom I fix, etc.
And I don't expect, etc.

CHORUS

I am done with the world and I want to serve the Lord,
And I don't expect to stay much longer here.

Another unnamed Georgian interpolated, OSH324, the usual, "Glory Hallelujah," and added the chorus:

I want a seat in Paradise,
Glory hallelujah,
I love that union never dies (?)
Glory hallelujah.

John G. McCurry, of Georgia, recorded, OSH493:

Jesus, my all, to heaven is gone, happy, O happy,
He whom I fix my hope upon, happy in the Lord.
His tracks I see and I'll pursue, happy, O happy,
The narrow way till Him I view, happy in the Lord.

The way the holy prophets went, happy, etc.
The road that leads from banishment, happy in, etc.
I'll go, for all his paths are peace, happy, etc.,
The king's highway of holiness, happy in, etc.

Then will I tell to sinners round, happy, etc.,
What a dear Savior I have found, happy in, etc.
I'll point to thy redeeming blood, happy, etc.
And say "behold the way to God." happy in, etc.

CHORUS

We'll cross the river of Jordan, happy, O happy,
We'll cross the river of Jordan, happy in the Lord.

William Walker, of South Carolina, used this popular hymn as the basis of a fuguing tune, OSH53. He makes no interpolations in the stanza proper with which he begins the tune. But the fuguing part uses the favorite phrases,

I'm on my journey home to the new Jerusalem,
So fare you well, I am going home.

Other Camp-Meeting Songs Based on Well Known Hymn Texts

I shall now reproduce twenty-one other OSH camp-meeting songs, or the essential parts of them, which are based on seventeen different original hymn texts largely from the eighteenth century. The fact that these seventeen hymns were not forced to serve the camp-meeting folk as often, that is, with as many different interpolations, may be, in some instances, the result of their lesser spontaneity. Their listing is justified, however, by reason of the folk interpolations themselves.

1. OSH290, by Watts, recorded by Leonard P. Breedlove, of Georgia:

Alas, and did my Savior bleed
And did my Sov'reign die.

I have but one more river to cross
And then I'll be at rest.

2. OSH375, by Watts, recorded by J. P. Rees, of Georgia:

Alas, and did my Savior bleed
And did my Sov'reign die?
Would he devote that sacred head
For such a worm as I?

O who is like Jesus?
Hallelujah, praise the Lord.
There's none like Jesus,
Love and serve the Lord.

3. OSH438, by John Newton (?), recorded by R. F. M. Mann, of Georgia:

Amazing grace, how sweet the sound!
That saved a wretch like me;

I once was lost but now am found,
Was blind but now I see.

Shout, shout for glory,
Shout, shout aloud for glory;
Brother, sister, mourner,
All shout glory hallelujah.

4. OSH146, by Charles Wesley (?), recorded by William Walker, of South Carolina:

And let this feeble body fail,
And let it faint or die;
My soul shall quit this mournful vale
And soar to worlds on high.

And I'll sing hallelujah,
And you'll sing hallelujah,
And we'll all sing hallelujah
When we arrive at home.

5. OSH275, by Samuel Medley (1738-1799), recorded by J. P. and S. R. Penick, of Georgia:

Awake, my soul, to joyful lays,
Halle hallelujah!
And sing the great Redeemer's praise,
Halle hallelujah!

6. OSH424, by Samuel Medley (1738-1799), recorded by J. P. Rees, of Georgia:

Awake, my soul, to joyful lays,
O glory hallelujah!
And sing thy great Redeemer's praise,
Don't you love God?
Glory hallelujah!

CHORUS

There's union in heaven and there's union in my soul,
O glory hallelujah!
Sweet music in Zion's beginning to roll,
Don't you love God? Glory hallelujah!

7. OSH292, author unknown, recorded by R. F. M. Mann, of Georgia:

Blest is the man who shuns the place
Where sinners love to meet;
Who fears to tread their wicked ways
And hates the scoffers seat.

Yes, yes, yes, my Lord;
Glory hallelujah!

8. OSH294, by Edmund Jones (1722-1765), recorded by John Carroll, of Georgia:

Come, humble sinner, in whose breast
A thousand thoughts revolve,
Come, with your guilty fear oppres,
And make this last resolve.

CHORUS

We're marching through Immanuel's ground,
And soon shall hear the trumpet sound;
And then we shall with Jesus reign,
And never part again.

9. OSH145, Robert Robinson (1735-1790), and with camp-meeting chorus:

Come, thou fount of every blessing,
Tune my heart to sing thy grace;
Streams of mercy never ceasing,
Call for songs of loudest praise.

CHORUS

I'm bound for the kingdom,
Will you go to glory with me?
Hallelujah, praise the Lord!

10. OSH333, by Robert Robinson (1735-1790), recorded by R. E. Brown, of Alabama, and B. F. White, of Georgia:

Come, thou fount of every blessing,

Etc. (see above)
CHORUS
Bless the Lord, O my soul!
Praise the Lord, O my brother!
Shout and sing, O my sister!
Give Him glory, O my father!
And rejoice, O my mother!
And we'll travel on together
And we'll join heart and hands for Canaan.

11. OSH501, original hymn by Charles Wesley, recorded by John G. McCurry, of Georgia:

He comes, He comes, the judge severe,
Roll, Jordan, roll!
The seventh trumpet speaks Him near,
Roll, Jordan, roll!
CHORUS
I want to go to heaven, I do,
Hallelujah, Lord!
We'll praise the Lord in heaven above,
Roll, Jordan, roll!

12. OSH277, by Samuel Medley (1738-1799), recorded by U. C. Wood, of Georgia:

I know that my redeemer lives,
Glory hallelujah!
What comfort this sweet sentence gives!
Glory hallelujah!
CHORUS
Shout on, pray on, we're gaining ground,
Glory hallelujah!
The dead's alive and the lost is found,
Glory hallelujah!

13. OSH330, author unknown, recorded by R. F. M. Mann, of Georgia:

In the floods of tribulation,
While the billows o'er me roll;
Jesus whispers consolation,
And supports my fainting soul.
CHORUS
Hallelujah, praise the Lord!
(repeated)

14. OSH436, by Charlotte Elliott, recorded by H. S. Rees, of Georgia:

Just as I am, without one plea,
O pity me, my Savior!
Save that thy blood was shed for me,
O pity me, my Savior!
CHORUS
Is there any mercy here?
O pity me, my Lord!
And I'll sing halle hallelujah.

15. OSH170, author unknown, recorded by T. W. Carter, of Georgia:

O may I worthy prove to see
The saints in full prosperity,
Then my troubles will be over;
To see the bride, the glittering bride,
Close seated by my Savior's side,
Then my troubles will be over.
CHORUS
I never shall forget the day
When Jesus washed my sins away;
And then my troubles will be over;
Will be over, will be over, and rejoicing,
And then my troubles will be over.

16. OSH359, author unknown, recorded by Leonard P. Breedlove, of Georgia:

O may I worthy prove to see,
  Glory to Immanuel!
The saints in full prosperity,
  Glory to Immanuel!

17. OSH292, author unknown, recorded by Elder Edmund Dumas, of Georgia:

O 'tis a glorious mystery,
  'Tis a wonder;
That I should ever sav-ed be,
  'Tis a wonder.

18. OSH550, the last song in the book, and "the last tune that Rev. H. S. Rees has composed," James says:

A few more years shall roll,
A few more seasons come,
And we shall be with those at rest,
Asleep within the tomb,
Asleep within the tomb.
  Happy thought to die no more,
No, never, never more.

A few more struggles here,
A few more partings o'er,
A few more toils, a few more tears,
And we shall weep no more,
And we shall weep no more.
  Happy thought, etc.

19. OSH498, by Isaac Watts, recorded by F. Price, of Georgia:

When I can read my title clear
To mansions in the skies,
I'll bid farewell to every fear
And wipe my weeping eyes.
    Chorus
I feel like, I feel like

I'm on my journey home.
I feel like, I feel like
I'm on my journey home.

20. OSH381, author unknown, recorded by J. P. Rees, of Georgia:

When to that bless-ed world I rise,
I'll never turn back any more;
And join the anthems in the skies,
I'll never turn back any more.
CHORUS
Any more, any more, any more, my Lord,
I'll never turn back any more.

21. OSH275, author unknown, recorded by Miss Cynthia Bass, of Georgia:

Why should we start and fear to die?
What tim'rous worms we mortals are!
Death is the gate of endless joy,
And yet we dread to enter there.
CHORUS
Roll on, roll on, sweet moments, roll on,
And let the poor pilgrim go home, go home.

A LATER DEVELOPMENT IN CAMP-MEETING SONGS

It seems that the hybrid text—a happily suitable distich by a comparatively inspired poet, coupled to a camp-meeting cry or two—was the rule, the revivalistic song pattern, at least in the earlier stages of the religious campers' activities. The songs above would seem to prove this point. But a number of songs show no connection whatsoever with the traditional hymns. They seem to have been pieced together in toto in the camp-meeting atmosphere and made solely of the expressions and ejaculations of that environment. This type would seem to represent a later development of the rural song-crafters. The following 14 songs are of this sort.

1. OSH80, recorded (and claimed) by B. F. White, of Georgia:

> Jesus, grant us all a blessing,
> Shouting, singing send it down;
> Lord, above may we go praying,
> And rejoicing in Thy love.
> CHORUS
> Shout, O glory, sing glory hallelujah!
> I'm going where pleasure never dies.

2. OSH489, source unknown:

> Our bondage it shall end
> By and by, by and by,
> Our bondage it shall end
> By and by.
> From Egypt's yoke set free,
> Hail the glorious jubilee,
> And to Canaan we'll return
> By and by, by and by,
> And to Canaan we'll return
> By and by.
>
> Our deliv'rer he shall come
> By and by, etc.
> Our deliv'rer he shall come
> By and by.
> And our sorrows have an end,
> With our three score years and ten,
> And vast glory crown the day,
> By and by, etc.
>
> Tho' our enemies are strong,
> We'll go on, we'll go on,
> Tho' our enemies are strong,
> We'll go on.

Tho' our hearts dissolve with fear,
Lo, Sinai's God is near,
While the fiery pillar moves,
  We'll go on, we'll go on,
While the fiery pillar moves,
  We'll go on.

3. OSH401, recorded (and claimed) by H. S. Rees, of Georgia:

Go, preachers, and tell it to the world,
Go, preachers, and tell it to the world,
Go, preachers, and tell it to the world,
Poor mourner's found a home at last.
    CHORUS
Through grace and a dying lamb,
(repeated twice)
Poor mourner's found a home at last.

Go, fathers, tell it to the world, etc.
Go, mothers, tell it to the world, etc.
(with similar variations, indefinitely)

4. OSH481, by Peter Cartwright, Amherst, Virginia, who lived 1785 to 1872, according to James:

Where are the Hebrew children,
Where are the Hebrew children,
Where are the Hebrew children,
  Safe in the promised land.
Tho' the furnace flamed around them,
God, while in their troubles found them,
He with love and mercy bound them,
  Safe in the promised land.

Where are the twelve apostles
(repeated twice)
  Safe in the promised land.
They went up thro' pain and sighing,
Scoffing, scourging, crucifying,

Nobly for their Master dying,
Safe in the promised land.

Where are the holy Christians,
(repeated twice)
Safe in the promised land.
Those who've washed their robes and made them,
White and spotless pure and laid them
Where no earthly stain can fade them,
Safe in the promised land.

5. OSH114, source unknown:

When the midnight cry began,
O what lamentation!
Thousands sleeping in their sins,
Neglecting their salvation.
Lo, the Bridegroom is at hand,
Who will kindly treat him?
Surely all the waiting band
Will go forth to meet him.

Some indeed did wait a while,
Shone without a rival;
But they spent their seeming oil
Long since last revival.
Many souls who thought they'd [they had] light,
O when scene was clos-ed,
Now against the Bridegroom fight,
And so they stand oppos-ed.

Eight stanzas more in Walker's *Southern Harmony*.

6. OSH421, recorded (and "arrangement" claimed) by J. P. Rees, of Georgia:

The happy day will soon appear,
And we'll all shout together in that morning.
When Gabriel's trumpet you shall hear,
And we'll all shout together in that morning.
CHORUS
Sweet morning, sweet morning,
And we'll all shout together in that morning.

Behold the righteous marching home,
  And we'll all, etc.
And all the angels bid them come,
  And we'll all, etc.

7. OSH408, recorded or, according to James, words "arranged in their present shape" by J. P. Rees, of Georgia:

They crucified the Savior,
They crucified the Savior,
They crucified the Savior,
  And nailed Him to the cross.
He arose, He arose,
And ascended in a cloud.

See, Mary comes a-weeping,
See, Mary comes a-weeping,
See, Mary comes a-weeping,
  To see where He was laid.
He arose, He arose,
And ascended in a cloud.

8. OSH417, "words arranged by Prof. Rees," James said. He referred to J. P. Rees, of Georgia:

You may tell them, father, when you see them,
  I'm a poor mourning pilgrim,
  I'm bound for Canaan's land.
    CHORUS
I weep and I mourn and I move slowly on;
  I'm a poor mourning pilgrim,
  And I'm bound for Canaan's land.
You may tell them, mother, etc.
You may tell them, brother, etc.
You may tell them, sister, etc.

9. OSH400, "another of H. S. Rees' compositions, both words and music," according to James:

Our praying time will soon be o'er,
    Hallelujah!
We'll join with those who'er [*sic*] gone before,
    Hallelujah!
        CHORUS
Struggle on, struggle on,
    Hallelujah!
Struggle on, for the work's most done,
    Hallelujah!

10. OSH406, "Arranged by Miss M. L. A. Lancaster," of Georgia, according to James:

I want to live a Christian here,
I want to die a-shouting;
I want to feel my Savior near,
While soul and body's parting.
I want to see bright angels stand
And waiting to receive me,
To bear my soul to Canaan's land,
Where Christ is gone before me
(two more stanzas)

11. OSH79, author unknown, recorded by T. W. Carter, of Georgia:

What ship is this that will take us all home?
    Glory hallelujah!
And safely land us on Canaan's bright shore?
    Glory hallelujah!
        CHORUS
'Tis the old ship of Zion, hallelu, hallelu,
'Tis the old ship of Zion, hallelujah!

There are numerous verses to be found in the different song books. See page 00.

12. OSH506, by H. A. Parris, who still lives at Helicon, Alabama:

We have our troubles here below,
We're trav'ling through this world of woe
To that bright world where loved ones go,
Where all is peace and love.

We're fettered and chained up in clay,
While in this body here we stay;
By faith we know a world above,
Where all is peace and love.

I feel no way like getting tired,
I'm trusting in His holy word,
To guide my weary feet above,
Where all is peace and love.

This song is said to have such emotional effect on the *Sacred Harp* singers that the third stanza is seldom heard. The singers are in sobs and tears before they get to it.

13. OSH531, by S. M. Denson, of Arley, Alabama, who is still living:

If our fathers want to go,
Why don't they come along?
I belong to this band, hallelujah!
CHORUS
Hallelujah, Hallelujah!
I belong to this band, hallelujah!

If our mothers, etc.
If our brothers, etc.
If our sisters, etc.
(and so on)

14. OSH524, by S. M. Denson, of Arley, Alabama:

My father's gone to view that land,
My father's gone to view that land,
My father's gone to view that land,
To wear a starry crown.

CHORUS
Away over yonder, away over yonder,
Away over yonder, to wear a starry crown.

Subsequent stanzas deal with brother, sister, children, Savior, etc., and the last stanza reads, "I want to go to view that land," etc.

THE CAMP-MEETING TUNES

Listed into the cause of sin,
Why should a good be evil?
Music, alas! too long has been
Press'd to obey the devil.
—*Social and Camp-meeting Songs,* 1828.

The early camp-meeting folk themselves rarely if ever saw a notated form of any of the tunes which they made and sang so enthusiastically. These tunes were what William Caldwell called, even as late as 1837, the "unwritten music" of Methodists, Baptists, and Presbyterians. And if the matter of recording those tunes had been left solely to the camp-meeting people, that recording would probably never have been done. By the generally illiterate campers such musical records would have been even less needed than were the printed texts. One of the camp-meeting hymnsters expressed the viewpoint of his group as follows:

By rule I never learned to sing,
Artless my harmony I bring.
—*Zion's Songster,* p. 311.

But here is where the fasola singing-school folk came in. It was probably due to nothing more than a desire to strengthen their singing-school institution and to make their song books more widely sought, that the compilers of the fasola books began in the 1820's to include tunes of the camp-meeting flavor, tunes which were denoted on the title-pages of those books, as they had appeared in the titles of the earlier books of texts only, as "spiritual songs."

Perhaps the first southern compiler to espouse the camp-meeting tune was Davisson in his *Supplement to the Kentucky Harmony,* 1820. Indeed, the author's main purpose in putting out the *Supplement* was "that his Methodist friends may be furnished with a suitable and proper arrangement of such pieces as may . . . animate the zealous Christian in his acts of devotion." The half dozen songs of this sort in the Davisson collection increased to a full dozen in Moore's *Columbian Harmony,* which came out five years later in the camp-meeting belt of Tennessee. In Walker's *Southern Harmony* (South Carolina, 1835) we find a large number of this sort of tune. Caldwell's activity (eastern Tennessee, 1837) in recording the "unwritten music" and in claiming it as his own composition, has been mentioned. But the *Sacred Harp* (Georgia, 1844), as elaborated in its 1911 edition, contains perhaps the largest collection of this sort of music to be found in any of the southern books. An incident of my own recent observation may illustrate the fasola compilers' attitude toward this spiritual song type.

At the Birmingham convention of the Alabama State Sacred Harp Musical Association, July, 1931, S. M. Denson, whose name stands in the *Sacred Harp* as the composer of the words and music of the song quoted above, "My father's gone to view that land," led the Harpers in singing it. First, however, the aged singer explained: "This was an old camp-meeting song. I had heard it since I was a little boy. But I had never seen it in any book. I had always wanted to see it, for it was such a beautiful song. So when we were revising the *Sacred Harp* in 1908, I wrote it down and we put it into the book." And I must add that after half a dozen stanzas ("my mother's gone," "my sister's gone," etc.) had been sung, tears were streaming and voices were choking.

It seems to me that we could ask for no better illustration of how perhaps most of these old camp-meeting tunes, for a long time simply orally transmitted, appeared in time in the fasola books which have kept them from dying or even changing, along with the changing and dying religious institutions in which they were born and with which they were bound up. Now for a few considerations of the genesis and the nature of the tunes themselves.

The song stanza at the beginning of this discussion of tunes, taken from a popular camp-meeting song, incorporates an idea that has been attributed to John Wesley. That he was really hospitable to good tunes, wherever he might find them, is indicated by John Donald Wade's statement, in his excellent biography of John Wesley,[4] that the original Methodist's tunes were "adapted from salacious ballads" and that they were generally of a type "quickly got hold of." Dr. Wade also quotes the words of a person who had listened to some of that early Methodist singing in England and told of boys and girls who "sing hymns in parts to Scotch ballad tunes."

As to the music of the subsequent camp meetings, the many-denominational and wild progeny of Wesley's popular evangelical movement, Benson says: "Of the tunes to which the camp-meeting hymns were sung the leaders demanded nothing more than contagiousness and effectiveness. . . . Their resources were what might be expected of men in a situation almost apart from books. Words were adapted to the popular melodies then current and to remembered songs,

[4] *John Wesley* (New York, Coward-McCann, Inc., 1930), p. 168.

or to tunes that had been used on circuit; and simple melodies were composed on the spot."[5]

I am inclined to believe that the camp-meeting tunesters' musical debt to the slowly-dragged-out psalm tune of the colonial period before the revivals got under way was small. They probably did, however, draw some melodic bits from that source. The following songs may exemplify such borrowing. A widely used song of the old type was called "Albion." Its words have been attributed to Watts:

Some camp-meeting tune cobbler seems to have given this fearsome born-to-die text a far less doleful turn, and to have speeded up the tune and introduced the customary revival ejaculations. And these changes resulted in the song which was usually called "Burges":

[5] *Op. cit.*, pp. 293 f.

It will also be noted that the camp-meeting re-maker used the melodic trend of the older and more sedate song only as far as it would fit. Then he went over to his own, or the crowd's own, musical inspirations. He has also made the tune over from a full major to a five-tone minor one, the sort the camp-meeting folk liked far better.

We are sure, also, that the camp-meeting folk drew largely on secular music, both the popular tunes of the times and the traditional ones of earlier times, as Benson stated. Examples of such borrowing have been seen in preceding chapters of this work which have to do with the secular element in the fasola songs in general. Specifically camp-meeting or revival songs among the cited examples are "Hosanna to Jesus" (p. 165), "Good morning, Brother Pilgrim" (p. 168), "Young People all, attention give" (p. 176), "And am I born to die" (p. 177), and "To die no more" (p. 178). Those tunes in the MPT list above which are of the camp-meeting variety are Numbers 19, 20, 21, 28, 30, 50, 57, 62, 67, and 70.

Benson expressed the suspicion that "the negro 'spirituals' embody many reminiscences of the revival melodies of the South."[6] And his suspicion was well founded. It points us toward a rich survival of these very tunes. The discussion of that survival will be the subject matter of the next chapter. And the tunes which I shall present in that chapter, as sources of the Negro spiritual tunes, will supplement the examples already given and illustrate sufficiently, I think, the camp-meeting melodies.

[6] *Op. cit.*, p. 293.

CHAPTER XIX

TUNES OF THE WHITE MAN'S SPIRITUALS PRESERVED IN THE NEGRO'S RELIGIOUS SONGS

Come, parents, children, bond and free,
Come, will you go to heaven with me.—SKH52

The Sources of the Negro Spirituals

The question as to the sources of the Negro spirituals has been discussed rather widely and for a long time. In this discussion there have been two unfortunate elements. One element has been the romantic zeal of those who wish to believe that the Negro's songs are exclusively his own creations. The other element is the scarcity of evidence already presented in proof that the romancers are either correct or mistaken in their assumptions.

The belief in the purely African-American-Negro origins developed quite naturally. When the post-Civil-War workers in the Freedmen's Bureau took up the cause of the black man and heard him singing two apparently distinct sorts of song, the white man's gospel hymns and an older, more folkish type of song, the natural conclusion that the latter had sprung up independently of the whites was accepted uncritically. It was all the more quickly believed by the white workers in such centers as Fisk University and Hampton Institute, for the reason that they had little truck with the southern urban whites and even less with the whites in the rural stretches. In a short time slave-song collections and commentaries on them appeared. Inasmuch as they were published and found circulation largely in the North and the East, the belief that the slave had made his own religious songs became general in those parts.

This assumption stood unchallenged, or practically so, until Richard Wallaschek, in his *Primitive Music,* called the spirituals, "mere imitations of European compositions which the negroes have picked up and served up again with slight variations."[1] Henry E. Krehbiel, in his *Afro-American Folksongs,* attacked the Wallaschek declaration with the zeal which was characteristic of that excellent student of music. They are American folk-songs, he asserted, but made by the Negroes. "The white inhabitants of the continent have never been in the state of cultural ingenuousness which prompts spontaneous emotional utterance." Then he cites as specific types of life environments which are impossible as inspiration to folk-song creation, the mill life of New England and the segregated agricultural life of the western pioneers. "Those occupations lacked the romantic and emotional elements which existed in the slave life of the plantations in the South. . . . Nor were the people of the North possessed of the ingenuous native musical ability of the southern blacks."[2] But nowhere did Krehbiel consider the possibility of any considerable musical influences coming into the "slave life" of the Negroes from the whites of their own *southern rural milieu.*

Krehbiel's emphatic word remained law for around fifteen years. Then in 1928 came Newman I. White, insisting in his *American Negro Folk-Songs,* that Wallaschek and his school were on the right track, and that it was specifically that body

[1] I requote from Krehbiel, who does not give the page where he finds the Wallaschek citation.

[2] (New York, 1914), p. 23. The native musical ability of the white "of the North" has of course nothing to do with the case. It is that ability of the American whites in general, anywhere, that is pertinent. And this has been proved equal to that of the Negroes. I point to the psychological tests made by Carl E. Seashore for the whites and by Guy B. Johnson for the Negroes. After comparing the two sets of tests Mr. Johnson came to the conclusion that they "revealed no significant differences in the basic sensory musical capacities between whites and Negroes."—*The American Negro,* being Volume CXXXX of *The Annals,* published by the American Academy of Political and Social Science (Philadelphia, 1928), p. 188.

of "folksy" spiritual song, made by the whites and used in their revival and rural church environment during the first half of the nineteenth century, which became, broadly speaking, the basis of the spiritual song of the Negro, as that type has become known in the times since his emancipation.

White's most important contribution was the bringing of documentary evidence to support his contention, for he was practically the first scholar to sift any of the white man's antebellum rural song books for concrete sources and to cite them for comparison with specific songs of the Negro.

But valuable as White's source work was, it suffered, nevertheless, from two defects, namely, that the amount of his source material (rural song books) belonging precisely to the pertinent time (say 1820 to 1860) and section (the southeastern states) was comparatively limited; and that he failed to make use of the *tunes* in clinching the source nail. As far as I can find out, of the rural southern song books which we have examined in the present work, he drew on but one, William Walker's *Southern Harmony*. He did, however, consult Lemay's *Christian Companion,* a Greenville County, South Carolina, book of 1836 and presumably of the rural type, which I have failed to locate. The rest of his source song books seem to have been those not widely used in the southeast.

The musical side of the camp-meeting songs, the one not considered by Mr. White, was subsequently studied by Guy B. Johnson, and the results of his investigation are to be found in his *Folk Culture on St. Helena Island, South Carolina.*[3] Mr. Johnson agrees completely with White's belief as to the white man's camp-meeting source of the spiritual songs which were used and appropriated by the Negro, and he backs this

[3] (Chapel Hill, University of North Carolina Press, 1930), pp. 63-130. Mr. Johnson has condensed his findings in an article in the *American Anthropologist,* XXXIII (No. 2), 157-171.

conviction by a careful analysis of a large number of the white man's tunes and a summing-up of their melodic modes, pitch intervals, and melodic and rhythmic patterns. Then he compares his findings with those made by Krehbiel in his *Afro-American Folksongs.* Mr. Johnson also found a number of tunes in his camp-meeting books and established their source relationship to subsequently recorded Negro tunes. His song material was found in two camp-meeting tune books, the *Christian Lyre* (18th edition, New York, 1843), and the *Millennial Harp, Designed for Meetings on the Second Coming of Christ* (Improved edition, Boston, 1843). I am not acquainted with either of these books, but their titles and places of publication, as well as Mr. Johnson's findings in them, indicate that their songs may have been, in the main, not those which the southern Negroes heard and re-sang. Hence it is all the more remarkable that so many points of correspondence were found. Mr. Johnson points correctly to the "upper South, where the Scotch-Irish were the strongest" as the territory where the "camp-meeting movement reached its greatest heights." He also adds force to the white-to-Negro song-trend argument by reminding us that this hill country was the slave-breeding section, the area of small plantations and of the domestic type of slave economy." And he adds that "songs learned by the slaves here were quickly diffused through the South because of the movement of the domestic slave trade."

The four tunes which Mr. Johnson takes for granted as "undoubtedly borrowed" by the Negroes from the whites are (1) "Old Ship of Zion," (2) "Old-Time Religion," (3) "Out of the Wilderness," (4) "Safe in the Promised Land." Other tunes which he has traced "in whole or in part into the [Negro] spirituals" are: (1) "Christian Band" (*Millennial Harp,*

Part II, p. 30), traced into "Who'll Jine de Union" (Dett, p. 142); (2) "Judgment" (*Christian Lyre,* Part I, p. 90), traced into "I'm Rolling" (Dett. p. 186); (3) "Mariner's Hymn" (*Millennial Harp,* Part II, p. 39), traced into "I've Been Down into the Sea" (James W. Johnson, *Book of American Negro Spirituals,* p. 186); (4) "Angel, Roll the Rock Away" or "Hampton" (*Christian Lyre,* Part II, p. 20), traced into "De Angel Rolled de Stone Away" (Ballanta, *Saint Helena Island Spirituals,* 80); (5) "Lord, Remember Me," traced into the Negro spiritual of the same title; (6) "Judgment," traced into "I'm A-rollin'"; (7) "My Brother, I Wish you Well," traced into "There's a Meeting Here Tonight"; and (8) "Come to Jesus," traced into "Just Now."

Fasola Songs as Sources of Negro Tunes

On the following pages I shall augment, with material found in the fasola books—material which has never before been examined for Negro tune sources—the list of camp-meeting tunes which have gone over to the Afro-Americans. The books on which I shall draw primarily are *Columbian Harmony, Supplement to the Kentucky Harmony, Southern Harmony, Sacred Harp, Hesperian Harp, Social Harp,* and *Original Sacred Harp.* The fasola song will be designated by (*a*), and its Negro relative by (*b*).

I

(*a*) OS 524, "Resurrected," recorded by S. M. Denson.

(*b*) DT 92, "In the Kingdom."

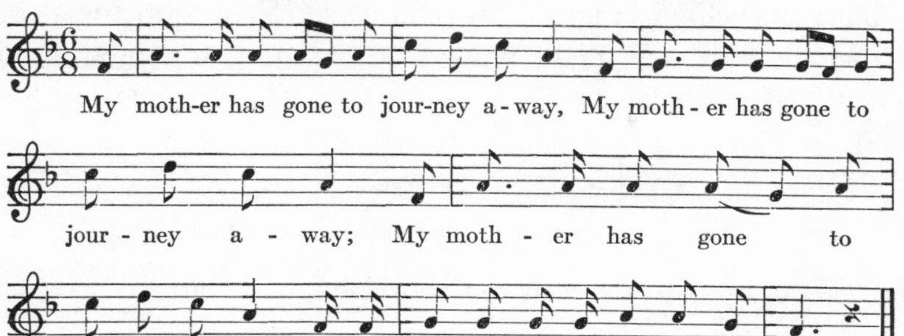

2

(*a*) OS 531, "Jester," recorded by S. M. Denson.

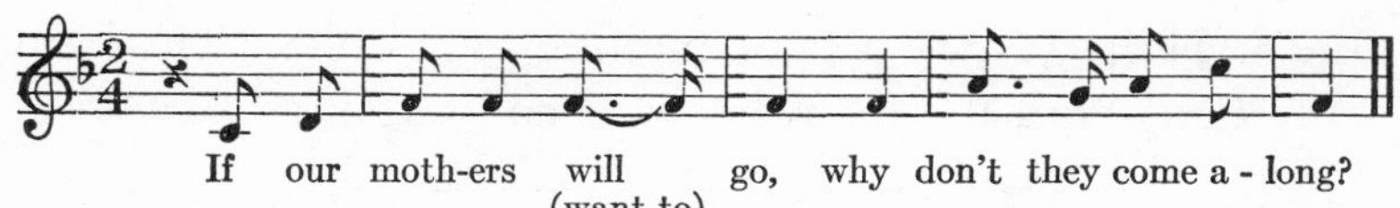

(*b*) DT 192, "Roll de Ole Chariot Along."

In the texts of all four of the above songs, the sequent stanzas go on to say the same of fathers, sisters, brothers, etc.

The text resemblances are obvious. The inorganic "Ef ye don't hang on behind" may be an echo of a refrain with the same melodic turn as William Walker's camp-meeting expression in SOH 18:

Tune resemblances in the above songs are largely between 1-*b* and 2-*b*.

3

(a) Elder Edmund Dumas, a Georgia Primitive Baptist minister and fasola musician, recorded for the 1859 edition of the SAH (page 378) a camp-meeting song called "The Heavenly Port" with the following tune and refrain:

(b) This reappears in Dett, page 189, under the title, "Oh, Stand the Storm":

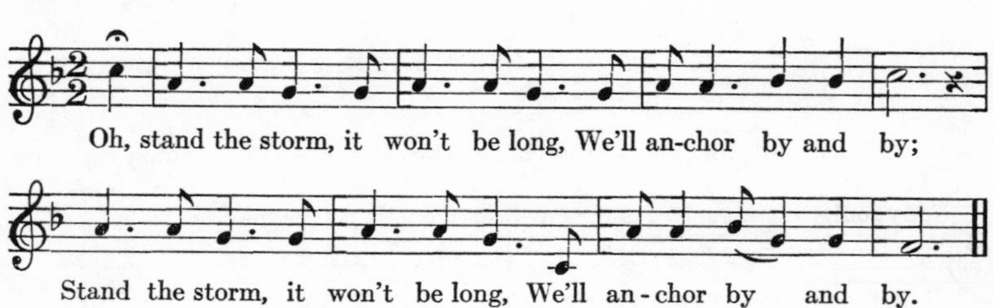

4

(*a*) "Something New" is the unusual title of an anonymous song in SOH, page 254:

(*b*) "My Soul Wants Something That's New" is the Negro version which I have found in Dett, page 105:

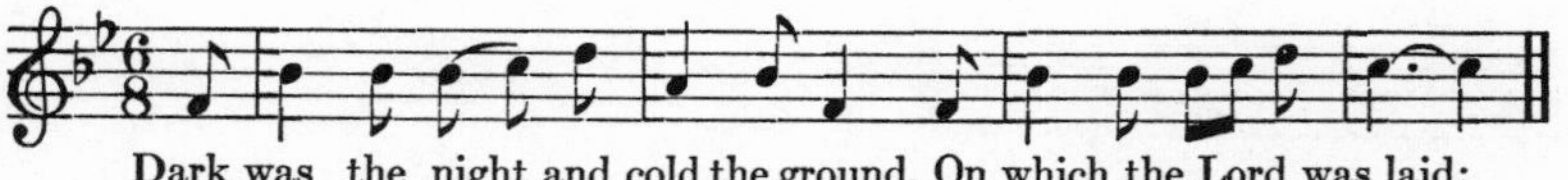

Dark was the night and cold the ground, On which the Lord was laid;
Was it for crimes that I had done, He groaned up-on the tree?

His sweat like drops of blood run down, In ag - o - ny He prayed.
A - maz - ing pi - ty, grace un-known, And love be-yond de - gree.

My soul wants some-thing that's new, that's new; My soul wants some-thing that's new.

My soul wants some-thing that's new, that's new, My soul wants some-thing that's new.

The Negro's first stanza was well liked by the fasola folk. Its author was Thomas Haweis, of England, who died in 1820 (see *Wesleyan Hymn and Tune Book,* Nashville, 1859, p. 118). The Negro's second stanza is borrowed from an Isaac Watts hymn (see *Methodist Hymn Book,* Nashville, 1889, No. 344). The two tunes will be seen to be almost identical.

5

(a-1) Under the title "Parting Friends," McCurry (SOC 101) gives the following song with the note: "The author, when eight years old, learned the air of this tune from Mrs. Catharine Penn." That was therefore in the year 1829. It will be seen that McCurry should have notated the song in 3/4 or 3/2 time.

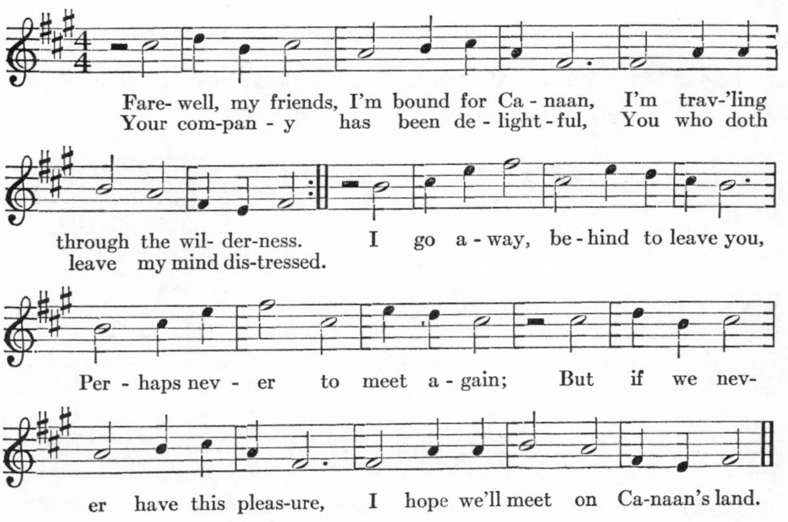

(a-2) "A Poor Wayfaring Stranger" is the title of the following variant of the above, found in GOS, No. 714. (A still further variant may be found in PB 254).

(*b*-1) A Negro version of this song, DT 191, is called "Pilgrim's Song."

The white man's song above, "A Poor Wayfaring Stranger," has three subsequent stanzas, with two of which the two subsequent stanzas of the Negro's song are practically identical.

(*b*-2) Let us examine also a Negro song which R. E. Kennedy gives in his *Mellows*.[4] Its words are a practically exact reproduction of William Williams' Welsh poem, four stanzas of it, as it was translated into English and composed by a num-

[4] (New York, A. and C. Boni, 1925), p. 111.

ber of American hymn-tune makers, including Lowell Mason, during the first part of the nineteenth century. Kennedy recognizes this text borrowing, but of the tune he declares that "there is no discoverable relationship between the Negro melody and any of the melodies given in any of the above books," that is, in any of the early hymnals which he had examined. He tells us that the song in question was sung for him by Emma Roussel, a Negress "who was a Baptist and had never attended a service at any church but her own. She said it was an old 'ballet' she learned from her mother, who had been a slave on the Destrehan plantation."

This "Baptist" clue and the hint of its "lonesome traveler" theme led me to compare it with the "Poor Wayfaring Stranger," found, as we will remember in GOS, the Primitive Baptist tune book. The two tunes are not identical. And I shall not try to make them appear so. I shall merely suggest their close relationship, with the GOS tune as a form which was nearer the original. All I shall do to make the recognition of this suggested relationship easier will be to change the time signature of the Kennedy tune to the 3/4 time of the GOS song and to alter some of the note lengths in accordance with the rhythmic pattern which is doubtless the prototype of the rhythmic procedure found in the Negro variant.

(*b*-3) William Arms Fisher, in his *Seventy Negro Spirituals,*[5] presents a song which belongs to this family. He entitles it "I'm Just A-goin' Over Jordan." It is, he tells us, "from the collection of Mrs. Stella May Hill." I have shifted Mr. Fisher's measure divisions, making the song more in accord with the other versions with which it is to be compared:

I'm just a - go - in' o - ver Jor -dan, I'm just a - go - in' o - ver home.

I'm just a - go - in' o - ver Jor-dan, I'm just a - go - in' o - ver home.

I'm go-in' there to meet my moth-er, I know she'll meet me when I come.
(fa-ther, etc.)

I'm just a - go - in' o-ver Jor-dan, I'm just a - go - in' o - ver home.

6

(*a*) I find the following song in the *Original Sacred Harp*, page 85, entitled "The Morning Trumpet":

[5] (Boston, Oliver Ditson Company), p. 88.

O when shall I see Je-sus and reign with Him a-bove, And shall
And from the flow-ing foun-tain drink ev - er-last-ing love, And shall

hear the trum-pet sound in that morning. Shout, O glo - ry! for I shall

mount a-bove the skies, When I hear the trum-pet sound in that morn-ing.

(b) In J. B. T. Marsh's *The Story of the* [*Fisk*] *Jubilee Singers,* page 136, is the following counterpart of the fasola song under the title, "I'll Hear the Trumpet Sound":

You may bu- ry me in the east, You may bu - ry me in the west,

But I'll hear the trump-et sound in that morn-ing. In that morn-ing, my Lord,

How I long to go, For to hear the trumpet sound in that morn-ing.

Of this melody, John W. Work says, "If there is in all the collections of folk song a pure melody, this is it. . . . It was born in Georgia, near Atlanta. A slave was sold from his wife and it seemed that he would really die of a broken heart, but as he was being led away he said with a wail: 'You may bury me,' " etc.[6] James Weldon Johnson calls the expression "I shall hear the trumpet sound," the Negro's "piercing lyrical cry."[7] And Krehbiel declares, "No one who heard Miss Jack-

[6] *Folk Songs of the American Negro* (Nashville, Fisk University Press, 1925), p. 82.

[7] *The Book of American Negro Spirituals* (New York, Viking Press, 1925), p. 41.

son, the contralto of the original Fisk Jubilee Choir, sing 'You May Bury Me in the East,' without accompaniment of any sort, is likely to have forgotten the clarion sound of her voice on the word 'trumpet.' "[8]

The only essential changes that the Negro singers have made in the earlier white camp-meeting melody are their raising the seventh and injecting a sharped sixth. We are not sure, however, that even these quaint features were not in the original tune. For "accidentals," while they seldom appeared in the fasola notation, were often approximated in the actual singing, if I may judge by my hearings of this very song as sung by the Sacred Harpers of the present day.

7

The "Weeping Mary" theme occurs first among the fasola folk in a stanza that is apparently of the "wandering" sort in SOH 103. This was in 1835. It runs as follows:

Is there here a trembling jailor
Seeking grace and filled with fears?
Is there a weeping Mary
Pouring forth a flood of tears?

(a) In the SOCH 98 of twenty years later I find the song entitled "Weeping Mary":

[8] *Op. cit.*, p. 84.

(*b*) Krehbiel gives a song by the same name which was, he says, recorded from the singing of the Negroes in Boyle County, Kentucky.[9] It follows:

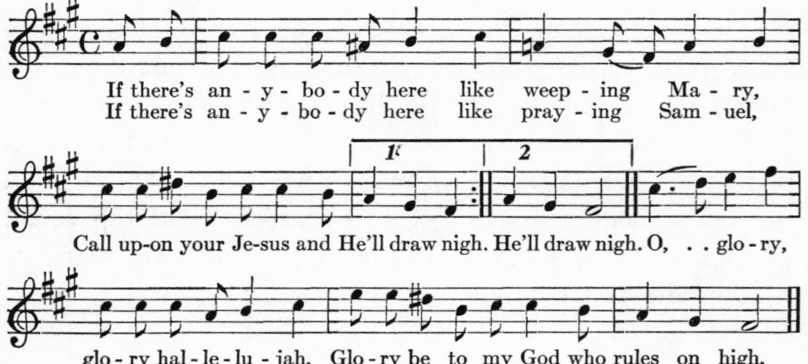

The SOCH song has but one stanza. The Negro version goes on one verse further by using "doubting Thomas."

The SOCH song was claimed by "John G. McCurry and Power," and Krehbiel acclaimed it as made by the Negroes. But both assertions have been nullified by Louise Pound, who tells us in an article in *Modern Language Notes*[10] that her grandmother had heard her servant sing it, between the years 1826 and 1830, in Hamilton, Madison County, New York. The servant had learned it at a Methodist protracted meeting thereabouts. She sang all the verses about "weeping Mary," "sinking Peter," "doubting Thomas," and other Biblical characters who had been in need of the divine blessing.

I reproduce here Miss Pound's text coupled with the tune (which does not appear in the *Modern Language Notes* article) as it was recorded for *White Spirituals* from the singing of Miss Pound's sister:

[9] *Op. cit.*, p. 157.
[10] XXXIII (1918), 442-44.

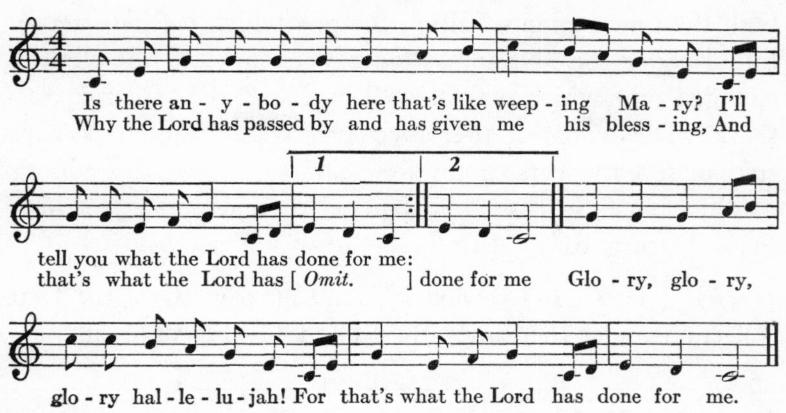

8

(a) The *Hesperian Harp,* a Georgia book of 1848, has, on page 355, a song with the familiar title, "The Old Ship of Zion":

A tune which is identical excepting for slight changes in the first four measures is on page 79 of the *Sacred Harp* (1844) and is ascribed to the Georgia song maker, Thomas W. Carter. The last word from a fasola authority as to the Old Ship's genesis was spoken by William Hauser, one of the most reliable of that school. In his *Olive Leaf* of 1874, page 355, he gives both the tune variants, calling the one which we have reproduced above the "North Carolina Version," and the slightly changed tune which was claimed by Carter the "Georgia version." The words of the latter song were "written perhaps sixty or seventy years ago by Rev. Samuel Hauser, this editor's paternal uncle, so I was told by an old contemporary of his," Hauser assures us.

(b) The Negro's version is found on page 81 of the Dett collection under the same title, "The Old Ship of Zion":

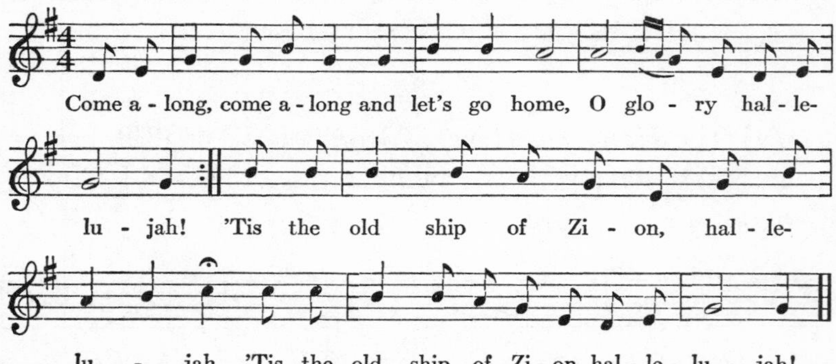

Another Negro song (Dett, p. 36) uses the chorus of the fasola "Ship of Zion" tune:

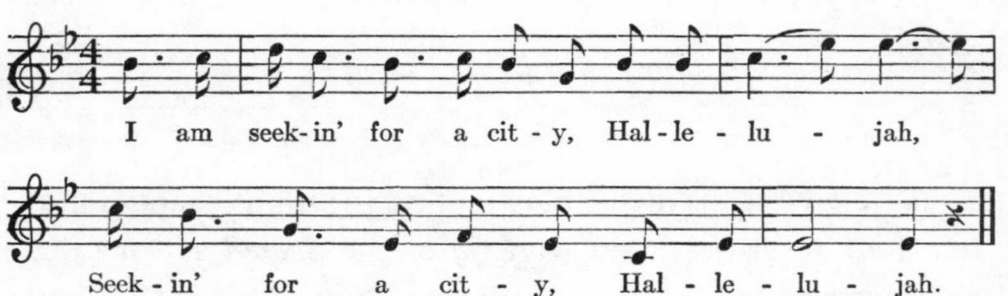

Subsequent stanzas in the fasola versions are compared to those in the Negro's (Dett) variants on page 296 of this work.

9

(a) In the *Sacred Harp,* page 277, is to be found the following song attributed to F. C. Wood and bearing the name, "Antioch":

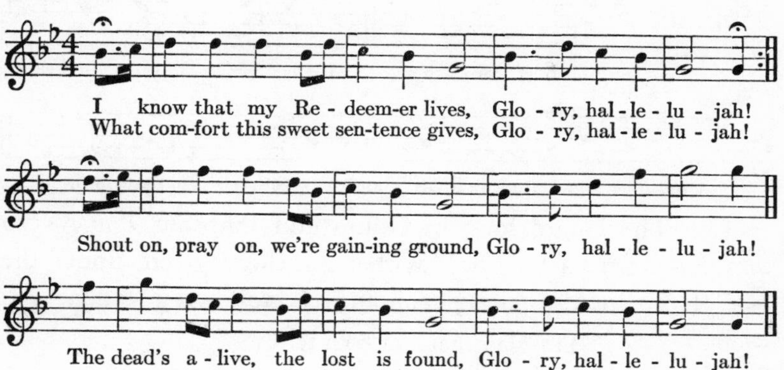

(b) I find the same tune in the Dett collection, page 195, under the name, "Let Us Praise Him":

10

(a) The following fasola song from the *Social Harp,* page 106, is closely related to the above pair, "Antioch" and "Let us praise Him." It is entitled "Burges":

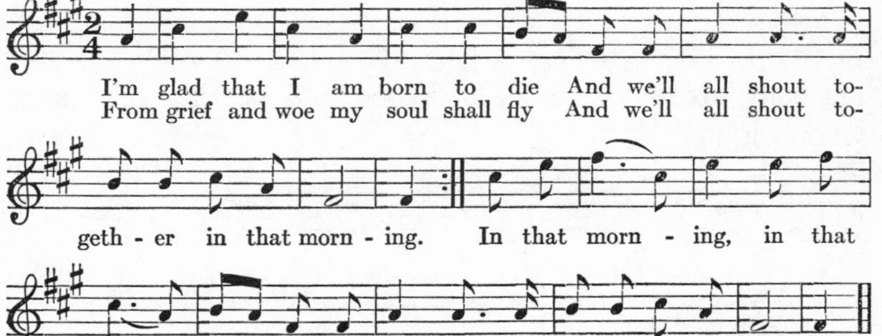

(b) The Negro song in Odum and Johnson, *The Negro and His Songs* (page 89), with no melody given, under the title "Keep Inchin' Along" contains the following stanza:

I'm glad that I'm bo'n ter die,
  Jesus'll come by an' by,
Frum trouble here my soul goin' fly,
  Jesus'll come by an' by.

II

(a) In the *Social Harp* (page 37) I find a song with the ascription "John G. McCurry and Wm. C. Davis, 1853" entitled "The Traveller":

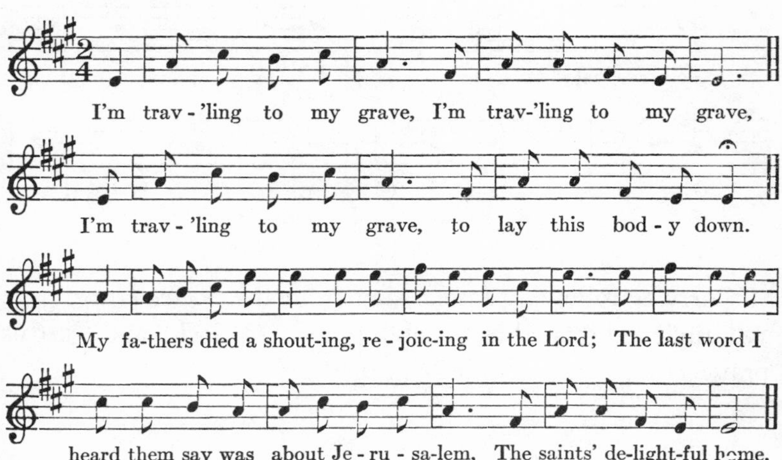

(*b*) A clear analogy in the Marsh collection is on page 146 under the title, "I'm Trav'ling to the Grave":

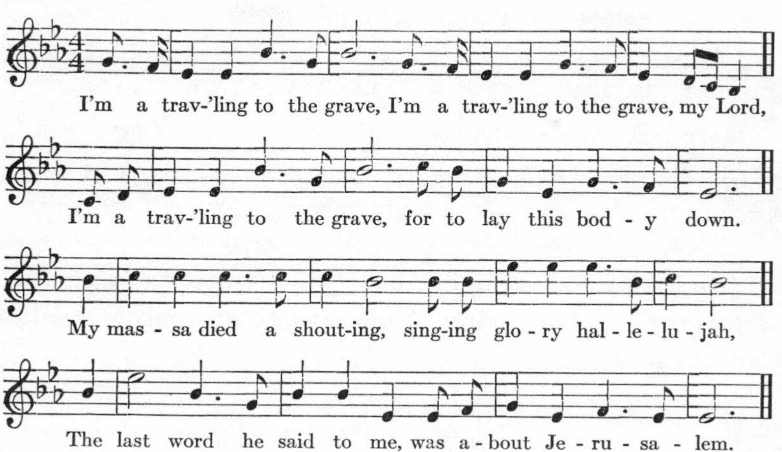

The SOCH song has but one stanza. The Negro variant goes on to further stanzas by changing "My Mas-sa," to "My Missis," "My brother," and "My sister."

The line, "The last word I heard him [her, them] say," seems to have stuck deep in the Negro's memory. It reappears in the following:

> I called to my father,
> And my father harkened to me.
> And the last word I heard him say
> Was save me, Lord, Save me.[11]

12

(*a*) A song in the *Social Harp* (p. 29) ascribed to "John G. McCurry & Wm. C. Davis" and dated 1854 is the following "Martin":

[11] In Reed Smith's *South Carolina Ballads* (Cambridge, Harvard University Press, 1928), p. 85.

(b) White cites a number of Negro versions (no melody) of this song and reproduces three stanzas of a recent North Carolina song, the first of which is

I'se got a mudder in the promised land,
I'se won't stop workin' till I'se shake huh han'.
I'm on muh way, I'm on muh way
To de promise' land.

The subsequent stanzas substituted "fatha" and "brotha" for "mudder."

13

(a) In the *Southern Harmony* (page 266) and the *Sacred Harp* (page 78) I find the following song under the name, "The Hebrew Children":

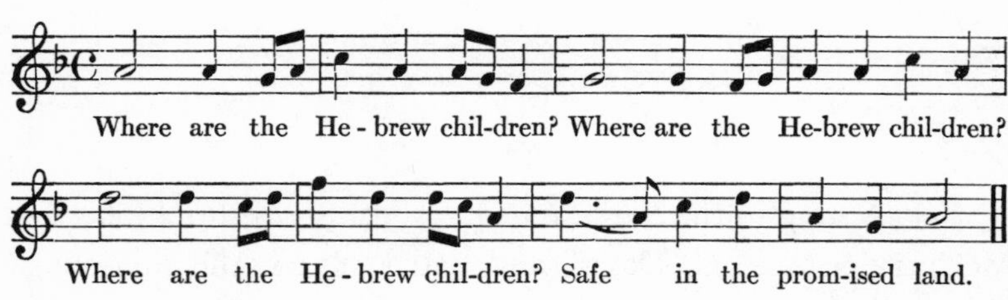

The verses go on to tell in succession of the twelve apostles, the holy martyrs, the holy Christians, God almighty, and blessed Savior. William Walker of the *Southern Harmony*

tells us, beneath the song, "This tune was set to music [harmonized?] by David Walker (William's brother) in 1841."

(b) The Negro's version is found in the Dett collection (page 73) under the title, "Wonder Where is Good Ole Daniel":

And the subsequent verses speak of the Hebrew children, twelve apostles, holy Christians, doubtin' Thomas, and sinkin' Peter. White quotes (page 46) an ante-bellum addition to the list of saints who are in the kingdom come:

> Where now is good old Dilsey, etc.
> Safely in the promised land.

14

(a) The first fasola appearance of "Roll Jordan" is in the *Supplement to the Kentucky Harmony* of 1820 (page 23), and the latest is in the *Social Harp* of 1855 (page 145), entitled "Roll Jordan":

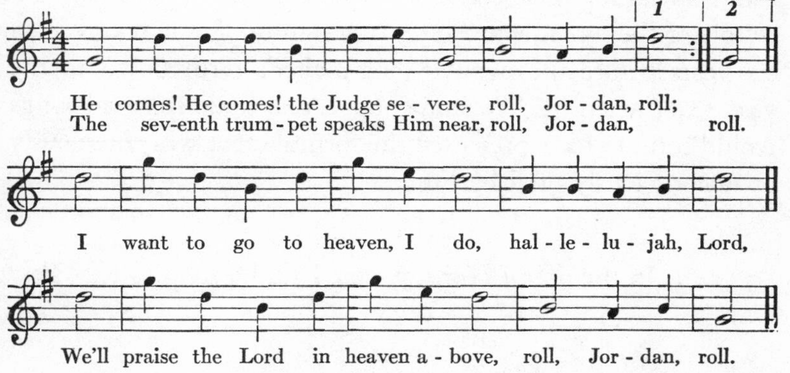

(b) In reproducing the Negro version of this very popular tune which I find in the Dett collection (page 52), I take the liberty of transposing the chorus with which the song begins (here and usually in the Negro songs) to the place where it is usually found in the white man's song, namely, *after* the verse. This in the interest of making its analogy to the Fasola tune more readily apparent. It is entitled, "Roll, Jordan, Roll":

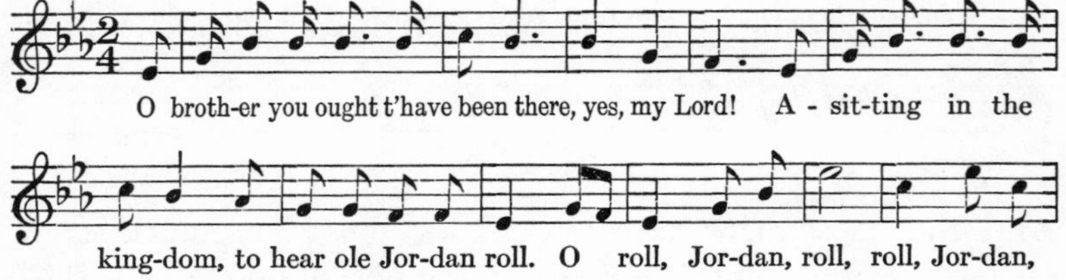

In this, more than in any other of the songs compared above, the Negro has taken liberties. That is, he has stuck merely to the melodic outline as a whole and to the text as it appears simply in the chorus.

Incidentally, we have stumbled here onto what is in all probability the source of Stephen Foster's "Oh, Suzanna" tune. Judging from the frequent appearance of this "Roll Jordan" tune and its variants—some of which are even more likely ancestors of the subsequent Foster tune—in the fasola books from six years before the popular-song-maker's birth down to the year 1848, when his "Suzanna" appeared, these spiritual songs would seem to have presented the formula that was consciously or unconsciously used by Foster.

15

(a-1) In the *Social Harp,* p. 209, I find a song called "Few Days":

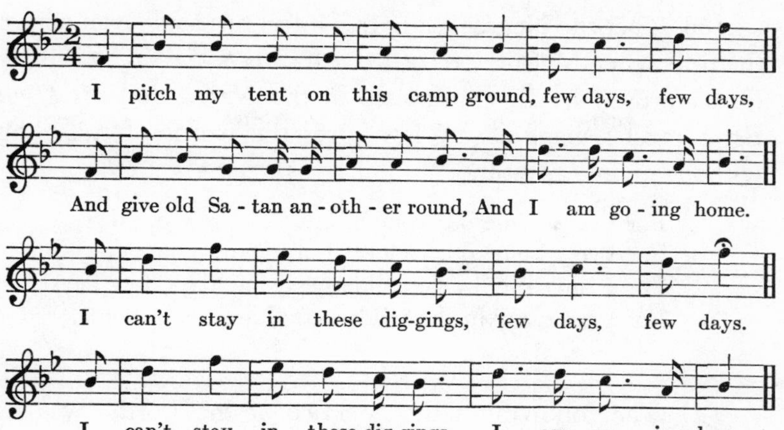

(*a*-2) Mrs. Ethel Park Richardson found a descendant of this song among the mountain whites. She does not say when or where she discovered it, but it was presumably in the 1920's and in eastern Tennessee. Its two verses will be seen to be intentionally comic, though Mrs. Richardson tells that Alvin York's mother "claims to have heard it in a church."[12] Its ancestor in the *Social Harp* of seventy years before was not, as we see, overburdened with dignity, either:

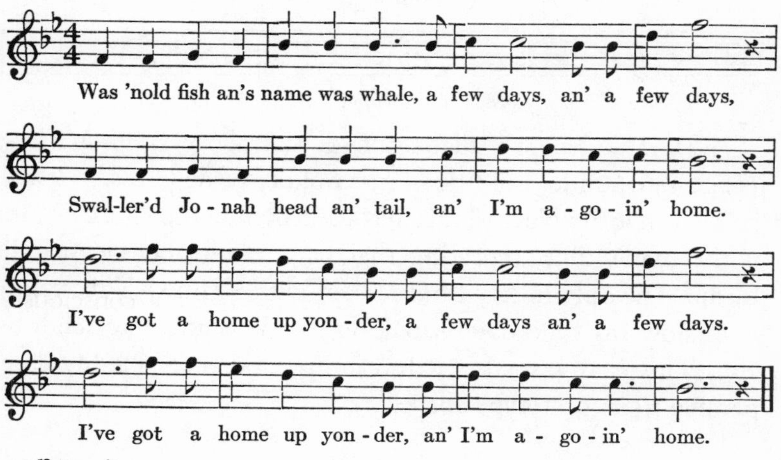

[12] *Op. cit.*, p. 72.

(b) That the Negroes sang this infectious song even before the time when McCurry recorded it for his *Social Harp* is practically proved by its appearance in the *Negro Singer's Own Book* (1846), page 96. White gives the words of this song without giving any tune:[13]

For I've a home out yonder, few days, few days!
For I've a home out yonder; I am going home.
For I can't stay in the wilderness; few days, few days!
For I can't stay in the wilderness, I am going home.

16

(a) The following song, "Service of the Lord," was recorded in 1844 by Georgia's E. L. King for the *Sacred Harp* (page 80):

(b) The Negro's adaptation of the above is in *Mellows* (page 146), under the title "I'm a Soldier of de Cross." It will be seen that the black singer has used merely the chorus of the white man's tune, repeating that part to fill out the melodic form. The only liberty I have taken with Kennedy's recording is to slow his tune down, making his sixteenth notes eighths, etc. This change makes it less jumpy and more readily comparable to its prototype above.

[13] *Op. cit.*, p. 53.

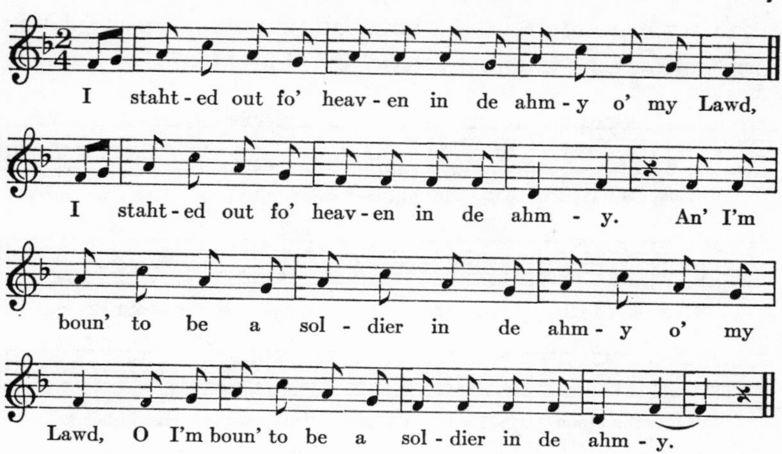

17

(a) In William Moore's 1825 *Columbian Harmony* (page 122), I find a song recorded by the compiler and entitled "Holy Manna." The song was often used by subsequent compilers, and they always gave Moore credit for its authorship.

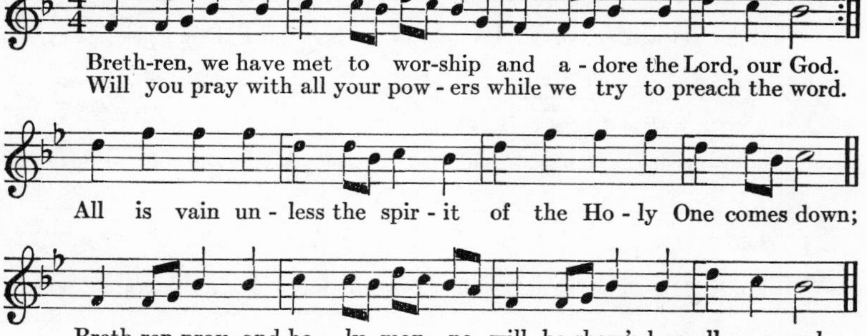

(b-1) Fisher gives a song, "Weepin' Mary," which he found in the collection of Mrs. Stella May Hill,[14] and although Mr. Fisher has made it over into a perfectly *konzertmässig* piece, I

[14] *Op. cit.*, p. 192.

shall try to restore (by the omission of repeated passages) its original melodic essentials, those of "Holy Manna":

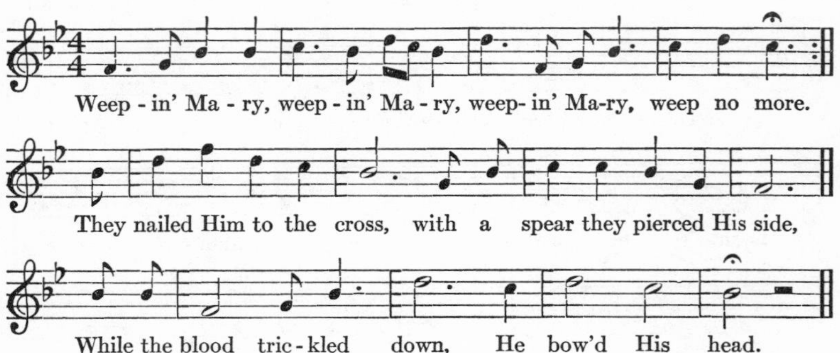

(b-2) The Negroes spliced the first part of the "Holy Manna" tune with the second part of "The Traveller" (No. 11-*a.*, above). Both tunes, we must remember, were widely popular in camp-meeting circles. The result was "Don't Get Weary," (DT 114):

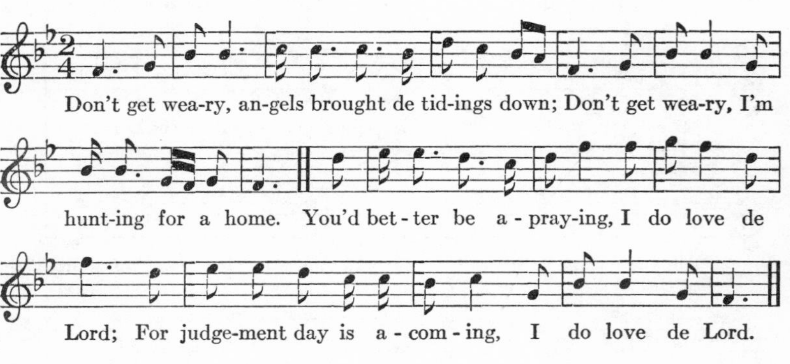

18

(a) The *Original Sacred Harp* contains (page 480) the following crucifixion song under the title "Weeping Mary" as recorded by J. P. Rees in 1859:

The musical selection today is a medley of old hymns:

Holy Manna from "Columbian Harmony"

The Lord Shall Bear My Spirit Home from "Southern Harmony"

and

Amazing Grace

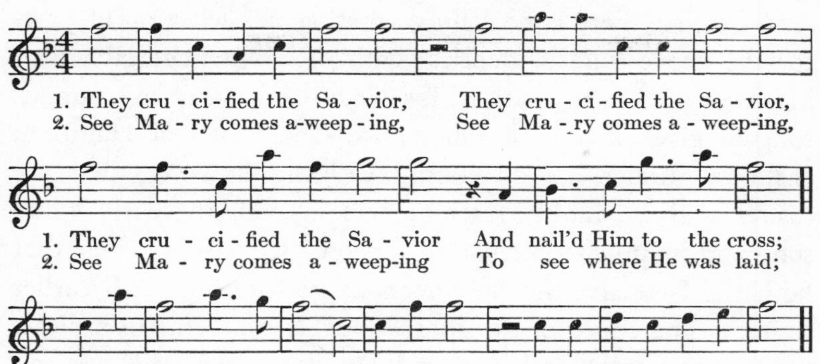

(b) Dett has a resurrection song (page 213), a sort of anthem called "Dust an' Ashes," from which I have been able to shell out the following:

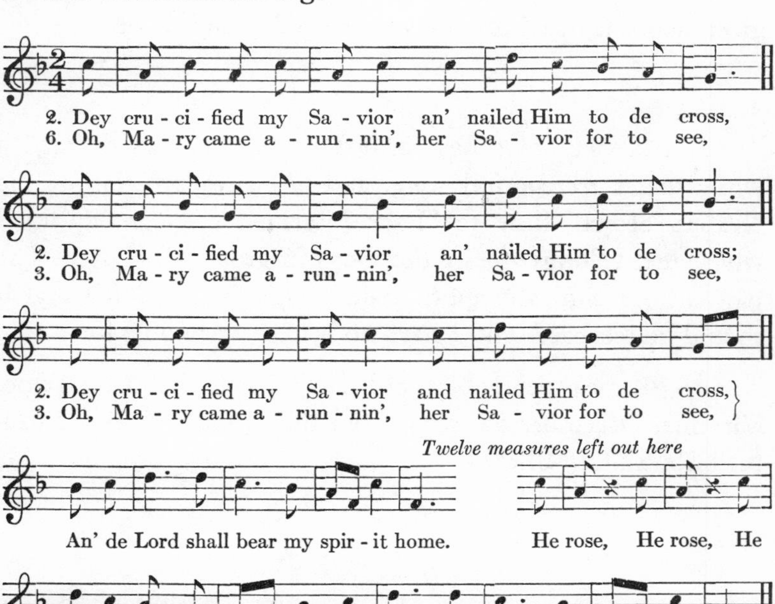

Of course there is no telling whether my selection of parts for the above tune is identical with the song material which Mr. Dett used as the basis of his "interpretation of this famous song as given at the church service each Easter at Hampton Institute" under his direction. I think, however, that the reader will see family resemblances in both the early white song and its much later Negro version. It is also possible that both the Dett and the Rees versions go back to a still earlier source. The editor of the 1911 *Sacred Harp* seems to indicate that the text went back farther than 1859, when Rees first put it into the *Sacred Harp,* by stating that "Rees arranged these words in their present shape when he wrote the music," and Rees's music was bungled. It is impossible to shell out a perfectly sure melody from among the four parts. The one I have given above is made of scraps of the treble and tenor.

19

My next pair of songs consists of *(a)* "Katie's Secret," a white man's *secular* folk-song, and *(b)* an adaptation of the "Katie's Secret" tune to "Poor Pilgrim," a Negro spiritual whose text belongs among the songs in group 16, above. The pair is not technically appropriate in this list, but I felt that it should be recorded, and I have no better pigeonhole for it.

(a) "Katie's Secret," recorded by the author in Dayton, Virginia, December 22, 1929, from the singing of Mrs. Elizabeth Showalter-Miller:

1. Last night I was weep-ing, dear Moth-er, Last night I was
2. Last night I was weep-ing, dear Moth-er, And Wil - lie came
3. And now I will gath - er my ros - es, And twine in my
weep-ing a - lone. The world seem'd so dark and so drear - y; My
down by the gate, He whis-per'd, "Come out in the moon-light, I've
long braid-ed hair; For Wil - lie will come in the eve-ning, And
heart had grown heav-y as stone. I thought of the lone - ly and
some-thing to say to you, Kate." O Moth - er, to him I am
smile when he sees me so fair. Then out in the moon-light we'll
love-less, How lone - ly and love-less was I. I scarce - ly know
dear - er, Than all else this wide world be-side; He told me so
wan - der, Way down by the old haw-thorn tree. O Moth - er, I
1
2
why it was, Moth-er; But oh I was wish-ing to die. -ing to die.
out in the moon-light; He call'd me his dar-ling, his bride. -ling, his bride.
won-der if an - y Were ev-er so hap - py as we. -py as we.
(b) "Poor Pilgrim" (DT 169):
1. I am a poor way - far - ing stran-ger, I some-times know
2. Some-times I'm both toss-ed and driv - en, I some-times know
3. My friends and re - la-tions for - sake me, And trou - bles roll
not where to roam; I heard of a cit - y called
not where to roam; I heard of a cit - y called
round me so high; I thought of the kind voice of
heav - en, I'm striv - ing to make it my home.
heav - en, I'm striv - ing to make it my home.
Je - sus, Say-ing "Poor pil - grim, I'm al - ways nigh."

Dett recorded his song from the singing of Mrs. Eva Evans, and although he does not state when or where, we may presume that it was in Virginia and comparatively recently. It seems, then, thinkable that the white people's folk-tune of love-lonesomeness went over easily to the Negro's song-story of *spiritual* forlornness; and the thought seems more reasonable when we notice that the two songs have the same rhythmic-stanzaic form and when we remember that both were recorded in the same state.

20

(a) I found "The Heavenly Mansion" in the *Temple Star*[15] and although it is a post-Civil-War finding, it has the old-time ring:

(b) I have heard this same tune sung by a Fisk University chorus conducted by the late John W. Work. Its chorus was:

Good news, the chariot's come (3 times)
And we'll be gathered home.

[15] (Dayton, Virginia, Ruebush-Kieffer Company), p. 100.

Extent of Negro Modification of Tunes

In view of the above lists of white camp-meeting songs and their Negro counterparts—Mr. Johnson's list and mine—the question as to the principal source of the Negro's spiritual tunes would seem to be definitely answered. I agree completely with Mr. Johnson's conclusion that "they are selections from white music, selections influenced by the Negro's African musical heritage." But my contributions to the list of the Negro's "selections," when compared with their prototypes, will help to show, I am confident, that the Negroes have never been content to use the white man's tunes without various and quite radical changes. A closer examination of the borrowings than I am warranted in making here would doubtless show that those changes were, as a whole, brought about by the Negro's traditional (African, if you please) feeling as to what song should be and by his unconscious approach, with the given material, to his own manner in song. Such an examination would probably show that the Negro has simplified the tunes in matters of pitch compass, loosened up the exactions of their scale intervals, and complicated their simple rhythmic trend.

For those who have been interested in the tendency of the Negro to sing in gapped scales and who have attributed that tendency to his African background it may be worth stating that among those nineteen songs which he took over from the camp-meeting stock fifteen were pentatonic, or essentially so. Of these fifteen, those in major amount to nine and those in minor six. It certainly looks, therefore, as if, whatever tonality tendencies the African may have brought to this land, he must have found the prevailing modes of the rural white spiritual singers quite pleasing to his ear.

CHAPTER XX

WHITE MAN'S AND NEGRO'S SPIRITUAL TEXTS COMPARED

. . . let the Negro,
Let the rude barbarian see
That divine and glorious conquest
Once obtained on Calvary.

IN COLLECTING the songs in the preceding chapter and in comparing them, I have had, first of all, the tune resemblances in mind. The accompanying one or two stanzas of the text have also often shown correspondence. Sometimes the Negro has preserved the identical words of the earlier white man's camp-meeting songs, but we have seen that in other instances the texts of similar tunes diverged widely, and were, in some cases, unrelated. Hence the above picture—as full a one as possible of the camp-meeting *tune ancestry* and the Negro spiritual *tune progeny*—must be looked upon as a far-from-complete portrayal of textual influences, white to black. I shall therefore try to finish the picture now by taking what seems to have been the most widely used of the camp-meeting song lines, distichs, and stanzas, and by associating them, for comparison, with similar or identical textual units found among the Negro spirituals. The occasional duplication in the following pages of the material used in Chapter XVIII is unfortunate but unavoidable.

My principle of arrangement is a topical one. The excerpts will occur in their natural sequence as portraying the events and psycho-religious conditions from the viewpoint of the rural fundamental religionist. That is, we shall begin with the efforts expended in converting the sinner and close with the "saints" basking—by wish and faith withal—in the endless joys of their home above. The white man's song excerpts will be found in the column at the left; those of the Negro, at the right. I have italicized those passages which were so well liked that they were adopted in song after song and deserve, therefore, the name of "wandering" stanzas and shorter units.

Songs of Exhortation

Religious experience begins with exhortation. The preachers and saints use their powers of seduction, through the vehicle of song, toward the conversion of sinful youth, backsliders, and the ungodly in general.[1]

Come along, and go with me.—HH355.

Come along, ef you want to get to
hebben. —DT134.

Oh, who will come and go with me?
—OS397, 111, 87; HH44.

O come and go with me,
I'm bound fair Canaan's land to see
For I'm on my journey home.—OS393.

Come all ye mourning pilgrims dear
Who're bound for Canaan's land.
—OS201.

Oh, pore mourner, won't you come and
go wid me? —SC17.

Are there anybody here like Mary
a-weeping?
Call to my Jesus and he'll draw night.
SOC98.

If there's anybody here like weeping
Mary
Call upon your Jesus and he'll draw
nigh. —KRE157.

O could I hear some sinner say,
I will go, I will go. —OS97.

Poor sinners, come to Jesus. —OS176.

The new way of life was to be no lonesome affair. Many were taking part. That is made clear in numerous songs.

[1] For explanation of abbreviated titles of tune books and hymn books see p. 437 below.

I belong to this band, hallelujah! —OS176, 531.

Hope I'll jine de band. —SC16.
I want to jine de band. —SS95.
I'll jine dat heavenly band. —SC198.

To jine de social band. —SS105.

Come join our happy pilgrim band. —HH172.

Do you belong to de union ban'? —DT166.

If our mothers want to go,
Why don't they come along.
I belong to this band, hallelujah. —OS531.

Ef my mudder will go,
She shall wear a starry crown.—DT193.

If my sister won't go,
I'll journey on. —WH118.

You need not be left behind,
For God hath bidden all mankind. —HH45.

Don't want to leave you behin'. —MEL41.

I am so weak and stumble,
And so I'm left behind. —SO18.

We'll all be left behind. —SC225.

I can't stay behind'. —SS6; DIT49.

One of the most effective means of inducing the sinner to repent was to sing of how Christ died for him on the cross.

Dark was the night and cold the ground
On which the Lord was laid;
His sweat like drops of blood ran down,
In agony he prayed. —WES118.

(the same entire stanza, DT105)

His sweat was as great drops of blood.

* * *

The Savior was hailed with a kiss.

* * *

The cords wrapped around his sweet hands.

O they bound him with a purple cord. —MEL127.

* * *

To Pilate's stone pillar was led.—SO85.

O they led him to Pilate's bar. —MEL127.

They made him a crown out of thorns,
They smote him and did him abuse. —SO85.

They plaited him a crown o' thorn. —MEL127.
An' they whipped him up the hill. —MEL127.

They rushed (pushed?) the nails through his hands. —SO85.

An' they nailed him to the cross. —MEL127.

Not a word he spoke. —SO268.

He gave his soul up to the stroke Without a murmuring word. —SO312; HH63.	An' he never said a mumblin' word. —MEL127.
He groaned his last and he died. The sun it refused to shine. They rushed the spear in his side. —SO85.	Were you there when they pierced him in the side? —DT106.
Saw ye my Savior, saw ye my Savior, Saw ye my Savior and God? Oh, he died on Calvary, to atone for you and me, And to purchase our pardon with blood. —SK39.	Were you there when they crucified my Lord? —DT106. Did you hear how dey crucified my Lord? —DT104.
He was extended, painfully nailed to the cross. Then he bowed his head and died. —SK39. He bows his head and dies. —SK60.	Did you heard how he hung on de cross? —DT104. He bowed his head to die no more. —FIS192. Did you hear how he groaned and bled and died? —DT104.
While the sun refused to shine. —SK39.	*Were you there when the sun refused to shine?* —DT106.
And was in a new sepulchre laid.	Were you there when they laid him in the tomb? —DT106. Did you hear how dey laid him in de tomb? —DT106.
They crucified my Savior and nailed him to the cross. See, Mary comes a-weeping to see where he was laid. He arose and ascended in a cloud. —OS408.	Dey crucified my Savior and nailed him to de cross. Oh, Mary came a-runnin' her Savior for to see. He rose, he rose from de dead. —DT214.
He dies, the friend of sinners dies, Lo, Salem's daughters weep around. A sudden trembling shakes the ground. —OS 472; CO45.	
Mary to her Savior's tomb Hasted at the early dawn. * * * But the Lord she loved was gone. —OS451.	Mary weep and Martha mourn.—DIT12.

The blessed Mary went to seek
The Lord entombed in stone.
The napkin and the sheet she found
Together in the tomb.
The angel said he is not here,
He's risen from the dead. —CO142.

De angel say he is not here,
He's gone to Galilee. —DT214.

Go tell his disciples,
He has risen from the dead. —OS473.

Aunty, did you hear when Jesus rose?
He rose and he 'scend on high.—SS70.

Jesus, my all, to heaven is gone.
He whom I fix my hopes upon.
His tracks I'll see and I'll pursue
The narrow way till him I view.
—SOC34, 47, 79, 99, 105, 108, 139; CO144; OS493.

Jesus, my all, to heaven is gone,
And I want to go there too. —SOC28.

My Savior's gone to glory
I want to go there too. —DT42.

Songs of Judgment Day

But an even more effective means of turning sinners from the evil of their ways in those hell-fire days was to keep the direful picture of the judgment day before them.

You must be a lover of the Lord
Or you can't go to heaven when you die.
—OS475.

In fiery chariots we shall rise
And leave the world on fire. —CO149.

You'll see the world on fire. —DT114.
Den you'll see de world on fire.
—DT156.

To see the earth in burning flames
The trumpet louder here proclaims.
—SO289.

Gabriel, blow your trumpet. —DT156.

His sounding chariot shakes the sky
He makes the clouds his home
There all his stores of lightning lie
Till vengeance darts them down.
—HH100.

Swing low, sweet chariot.—DT38, etc.
Chariot's a-comin', Oh, my Lord.
—DT184.
Swing low, chariot in de east.—DIT17.

We'll wait for his chariot. —SK67.

Sun darkened, moon turned to blood,
mountains melt, red lightnings blaze
thunders roar. —HH241.

He comes, he comes, the judge severe,
The seventh trumpet speaks him near;
His lightnings flash, his thunders roll,
How welcome to the faithful soul.
—SOC111; HOC99; SO195; OS85; HH359.

Yonder comes my Lord, bible in his hand,
A crown upon his head, He's come to
Judge the world, the livin' an' the dead,
Looks like Judgment day. —SC259.

He's comin' this away, with his sword in his han', he's gwine t'hew dem sinners down. —DT219.

Moon goes down in blood. —SOC46.

And the moon drips away into blood. —DT162

I've a long time heard there'll be a judgment day, O sinner where will you stand in that day?

Where shall I be when de firs' trumpet soun'? —DT173.

That the sun will be darkened,
That the moon bleeding
That the stars will be falling
That the earth will be burning.—SS70.

What a morning when de stars begin to fall. —DT157.

While the trumpet is sounding there is still time to turn. For the ransomed it is the year of Jubilee, for the sinners it is just hell.

Blow ye the trumpet, blow,

* * *

The year of jubilee is come,
Return, ye ransomed sinners, home.
—CO23.

This is the year of Jubilee. —DT231.

The trumpets are sounding
For the year of Jubilee. —SOC105.
The gospel sounds the jubilee
And I can not tarry here [a refrain].
—SOC183.
Hail, the gospel jubilee
Jesus comes to set us free. —CO85.
The fiftieth year is now roll'd round
The great Sabbatic year. —SK36.
Let the last loud trumpet sound.—CO34.
And when the last trumpet
shall sound through the skies
And the dead from the dust
of the earth shall arise. —SO60.

Arise an' shine, and give God de glory
For de year of Juberlee. —DT198.

Oh when shall I see Jesus
And reign with him above?
And shall hear the trumpet sound
In that morning.
And then away to Jesus
On wings of love I'll fly.
—SOC111; HOC99; SO195; OS85

But I'll hear the trumpet sound
In-a that morning. —WK82.
Good ole Christians in dat day dey'll
Take wings an' fly away. —JH(1)182.

In dat dreadful Judgment day I'll
take wings an' fly away. —FIS83.

In that morning, in that morning
And we'll all shout together
in that morning.
—SO194; SOC106; RES183.

Sweet morning, sweet morning,
And we'll all shout together
In the morning. —OS421.

What will the Christian do
When his lamp burns out? —OS531

What you gwine 't do
When de lamp burn down? —DT141.

What you goin' to do
When the world's on fire? —WH33.

What you goin' to do
When de crawfish gone? —MEL42.

Wonder where was Moses
When de church burn down?—DIT43.

Death is coming, hell is moving
Can you bear to let them [the sinners] go?
See our fathers—see our mothers,
And our children sinking down;
Brethren, pray and holy manna
Will be shower's all around. —SO103.

Your sparkling eyes will then roll round
While death will bring you to the ground;
The coffin, grave and winding-sheet
Will be shower'd all around. —SO103.
—HH39.

The coffin, earth and winding-sheet
Will soon your active limbs enclose.
—HH41.

Death, 'tis a melancholy day
To those who have no God.—HH55.

Hark! from the tombs a doleful sound
Mine ears attend the cry. —HH59.

Then, sinners, you'll be driven
Down to the lake of fire and pain
To scream in flaming sulphur.
—HH399.

Remember, sinful youth,
You must die, you must die. —HH225.

Ah, poor sinner, you run from the rock
When the moon goes down in blood
To hide yourself in the mountain top
To hide yourself from God. —SOC45.

O de rocks and de mountains
Will all flee away, an' you shall have
a new hidin' place dat day.—WH81.

Went down to the rocks to hide my face,
The rocks cried out no hiding place.
—WH121.

The Conversion Experience

After all this effort is expended by the redeemed, the revival gets under way. Sinners become mourners, and mourners "come through."

O save, save, mighty Lord
And send converting power down.
—OS70.

The news of his mercy
Is spreading abroad
And sinners come crying
And weeping to God.
Their mourning and praying
Is heard very loud
And many find favor
In Jesus'-es blood. —SOC75.

The glory of King Jesus
Triumphant doth arise;
And sinners crowd around it
With bitter groans and cries.—SOC126.

See our fathers, see our mothers
And our children sinking down.
Brethren pray, and holy manna
Will be shower'd all around.
Is there here a trembling jailor,
Seeking grace and filled with fears:
Is there here a weeping Mary,

Pouring forth a flood of tears?
—SOC191.

O, for soul-converting power
And a sanctifying shower. —SOC139.

I never shall forget the day
When Jesus washed my sins away.
—SOC85; SO54; OS170.

I never shall forget that day
When Jesus washed my sins away.
—DT49, 232, 195; JH(2)164.

Wasn't that a happy day
When Jesus washed my sins away?
—DT207

'Twas just about the break of day
King Jesus stole my heart away.
—KR85.

Ye who have fled from Sodom's plain
Say, do you wish to turn again?
—HH28.

I'll never turn back any more.—OS381.

Songs of Pilgrimage

From this time on, the convert is a pilgrim on his way to the promised land. And this fact is found as the burden of numerous refrains.

I'm bound for the kingdom
Will you go to glory with me?
—SO94; OS145; HH443.

We're bound to heaven
But you to hell. —SO263.

To the land I am bound. —SO313.

I'm on my way to Cannan. —CO108.

To the new Jerusalem. —OS82.

Sweet Canaan, sweet Canaan,
I'm bound for the land of Canaan.
—OS87.

I'm bound for sweet Canaan's happy land. —DT188.
I'm bound for Canaan's happy land.
—DT65.

Arise, we're going home
To the new Jerusalem. —OS336.

I'll march to Canaan's land
I'll land on Canaan's shore.
—SO158; OS185.

Hasten on in the good old way.—HH39.

And to Glory I will go. —OS320.

I'm on my way to Zion. —HH242.

Yes, I feel like going home. —OS51.

I feel like I'm on my journey home.
—OS198.

Lead me to the Rock
That is higher than I.—HH312; SO60.

If you get there before I do
You may tell them I am coming.
(or variants) —HH355.

If you get there before I do
Tell all my friends I'm coming too.
DT3, 102; DIT15; SC12, 25;
SS59; WH72, 111

Happiness of the Redeemed

For varying lengths of time the redeemed are very happy. They praise the Lord and bless his name. This praise is usually found in the refrains of choruses where all can take part in them, and do.

Hallalujah, praise the Lord! —OS330.

O who is like Jesus, hallalujah,
There's none like Jesus,
Love and serve the Lord. —OS375.

We'll shout and praise the
Lamb in glory. —OS377.

And give to Jesus glory. —CO97.

Glory to Emmanuel! —OS359.

And I will give him glory. —SO105.

And I'll sing hallelujah
And glory be to God on high
And I'll sing hallelujah
There's glory beaming from the sky.
—SO156.

And I'll sing hallelujah
And you'll sing hallelujah
And we'll all sing hallelujah.
—HH102.

Hosanna to the Lamb of God!—OS412.

How I love my Savior
Glory, yes I do. —SOC36.

I love my blessed Savior
I feel I'm in his favor. —SOC26.

Don't you love God? —OS497.

I'll sing and shout
I'll shout and sing. —CO51.

I know that my Redeemer lives,
What joy this blest assurance gives.
(or)
What comfort this sweet sentence gives!
—OS277; SOC158.

I know that my Redeemer lives
And by his death sweet blessings gives.
—DT146.

I feel, I feel,
I feel like shouting home. —CO144.

Happy, O happy
Happy in the Lord. —OS493.

Troubles on the Journey

But the journey is not all sunshine:

I have my bitters and my sweets
As through this world I travel;
I sometimes shout and sometimes weep
Which makes my foes to marvel.
—CO140.

Sometimes I'm up, sometimes I'm down
Sometimes I'm almost to de groun'.
—KR75.

This world's a wilderness of wo
—OS390.
We're traveling through this land of woe.
—OS506.

This world is a wilderness of woe,
Then let us all to heaven go. —FI64.

I have my trials here below.—SOC132.

I has my trials yer below. —SS78.

We have our troubles here below
—SO323.

I've had my crosses and trials here below. —SS59.

I'm a long time traveling here below
To lay this body down. —OS288.

I'm traveling to my grave
To lay this body down. —SOC37.

And am I born to die
To lay this body down. —SO31.

You may tell them father when you see them,
I'm a poor mourning pilgrim
I'm bound for Canaan's land
I weep and I mourn and I move slowly on. —OS417.

A pilgrim here below
While in this vale of woe

* * *

Though few my days have been
Much sorrow I have seen.—SO(35)99.

We have our troubles here below
We're traveling through this world of woe
To that bright world where loved ones go
Where all is peace and love.

* * *

We're fettered and chained up in clay
While in this body here we stay. —OS506.

My heart is often made to mourn
Because I'm faint and feeble;
And when my Savior seems to frown
My soul is filled with trouble.—HH213.

While traveling through this vale of tears
Amidst temptations, doubts and fears. —OS466.

Ye weary heavy laden souls
Who are oppressed sore,
Ye travelers through the wilderness
To Canaan's peaceful shore
Through chilling winds and beating rains
The waters deep and cold
And enemies surrounding you,
Take courage and be bold. —CO58.

I'm a-traveling to the grave
To lay this body down. —FK146.

I'm walkin' troo de grave yard
Lay dis body down. . . . . —KR110.

O heaven, sweet heaven, when shall I
see?
O when shall I get there? —OS278.

Sweet home! Oh, when shall I get
there? —OS500.

Satan's army rages
And all his hosts combine. —CO108.

I'm a long time traveling here below
I'm a long time traveling away from
home —OS288.

The Christian Soldier

Often the heaven-bound road is a real fight. Hence the ease with which the songs drop into the figures of warfare against the world, flesh and devil.

O when shall I see Jesus
And dwell with him above;
And drink the flowing fountain
Of everlasting love.
When shall I be delivered
From this vain world of sin
And with my blessed Jesus
Drink endless pleasure in.

* * *

But now I am a soldier,
My Captain's gone before;
He's given me my orders
And tells me not to fear.

* * *

Through grace I am determined
To conquer though I die;
And then away to Jesus
On wings of love I'll fly. —CO124.

And if you meet with troubles
And trials on your way,
Cast all your care on Jesus
And don't forget to pray.
Gird on the heavenly armour
Of faith and hope and love,
And when your race is ended
You'll reign with him above.
—CO124; SO18, 93 122; HO48, 56;
OS85, 129; HH317; GOS No. 420.

If you meet with trials
And troubles on de way,
Jis' put yo' trus' in Jesus,
An' don't forget to pray.
—DT30; SC12; GRIS81.

O do not be discouraged
For Jesus is your friend;
And if you lack for knowledge
He'll not refuse to lend. —CO124.

'Don't ever be discouraged,
For Jesus is your friend;
And if you lack for knowledge,
He'll ne'er refuse to lend. —WK43

And gird the gospel armour on,
March to the gates of endless joy
Where thy great Captain, Savior's gone.

—HH15.

Oh! Have you ventured to the field
Well armed with helmet, sword and shield?
And shall the world with dread alarms
Compel you now to ground your arms?
—HH28; SOC168; OS42.

Come, all ye mourning pilgrims dear
Who're bound for Canaan's land;
Take courage and fight valiantly
Stand fast with sword in hand.
Our Captain's gone before us,
Our Father's only son;
Then, pilgrims dear, pray do not fear,
But let us follow on.
—OS201; SO150; HH392; SOC117.

Am I a soldier of the cross
A follower of the lamb,
And shall I fear to own his cause
Or blush to speak his name? —SO45.

Am I a soldier of the cross
A follower of the Lamb? —WH47.

I'm a soldier of de cross
In de army o' my Lawd. —MEL146.

They want no cowards in their band,
(They will their colors fly,)
But call for valiant-hearted men,
Who're not afraid to die. —SO301.

We want no cowards in our band,
That from their colors fly;
We call for valiant-hearted men,
That are not afraid to die. —DT107.

God don't want no coward soldiers,
Some o' these days;
He wants valiant hearted soldiers,
Some o' these days.
—Sandburg, *The American Songbag.* p. 479.

We want no cowards in our day,
You shall gain the victory,
We call for valiant-hearted men,
You shall gain the day. —WK71.

I've listed in the holy war
Till the warfare is over, hallelujah
Content to suffer soldier's fare
Till the warfare, etc.

Till the war is ended [a refrain]
—WK71, 127.

Cho.
Crying amen, shout on,
Till the warfare, etc.
—SO314 (same chorus; OS76; SOC196).

I've fought through many a battle sore,
And I must fight through many more.

I take my breast-plate, sword and shield
And boldly march into the field.

Gwine take my breas'-plate sword in han'
An' march out boldly ina de fiel'.
—JH (2)56.

Our General he is gone before,
And you may draw on grace's store.

I'm bound to live in the service of my Lord
I'm bound to die in the army. [a refrain]
—OS80.

I'm boun' to be a soldier in the ahmy of my Lawd
I'm boun' to be a soldier in de ahmy.
—HEL146.

Companionship of Jesus

But for all the pilgrim's troubles there are compensations. The presence of Jesus and the hope of ultimate relief and reward help him to bear his burden, to rejoice even, as he wanders homeward.

Jesus has been with us
And he is still with us
And He's promised to be with us to the end. —SOC73.

Come life, come death, come then what will,
Jesus is my friend [*refrain*] —OS345.

How sweet the name of Jesus sounds
In a believer's ear;
It sooths his sorrows, heals his wounds
And drives away his fear.
—OS56; SOC190; CO121.

And since we have a Savior dear
Let's drive dull care away. —OS98.

Jesus says he will be with us to the end.
—OS429.

We have our trials here below
* * *
A few more beating winds and rains
* * *
A few more rising and setting suns
* * *
I feel no ways like getting tired
* * *
I hope to get there by and by
* * *
I have some friends before me gone
* * *
I'll meet them round our father's throne
* * *
O how it lifts my soul to think
* * *
Our God will wipe all tears away.
—OS506; KN52; SO323.

I don't feel noways tired. —DT37.
I don't feel noways tired in my heart.
—DT168.
I don't feel weary and noways tired.
—SS70.
Don't you get weary. —SS95; SC110.

Never get tired a-serving of the Lord
Come along and shout along,
Ye heaven-born [bound] **soldiers,**
Come along and shout along
And pray by the way.
—(reference is lost).

Travel on, heaven-bound soldier.—SS31.
Pray on, pray on,
Pray on, dem light us over. —SS97.
Pray on, prayin' sister
Light shine roun' de worl'. —DT23.

Shout on, pray on, we're gaining ground
The dead's alive, the lost is found.
—SOC158; OS277.

I feel like shouting home.
—CO144; HH36.

As we journey sweetly sing. —OS405.
Come, all you weary travelers
Come let us join and sing.
—SK91; CO82; SO79.

Children of the heavenly King
As we journey let us sing.
—SK77; SO6.

I'll sing my Savior's grace
And his dear name will praise
While in this land of sorrow I remain;
My sorrow soon shall end.

And then my soul ascend
Far off from trouble, sin and pain.
—SO (edition of 1935) 99.

Come, all you pilgrim travelers
Fresh courage take by me;
* * *
Through faith, the glorious telescope
I viewed the worlds above;
And God, the Father, reconciled
Which fills my heart with love.—SO150.

We're marching to Immanuel's ground
We soon shall hear the welcome trumpet sound. —HH80; SO198.

Roll on, roll on, sweet moments roll on
And let the poor pilgrim go home, go home. —OS275.

I'm glad that I am born to die
From grief and woe my soul shall fly,
—SOC104, 106.

I'm glad that I'm bo'n ter die
Frum trouble here my soul goin' fly.
—OD89.

Bless de Lawd, I'm born to die
I'm gwine to jedgment bye and bye.
—SC13.

And let this feeble body fail
Or let it faint or die;
My soul shall quit this mournful vale
And soar to worlds on high. —SK22.

Want to go to heaven when I die,
Good-bye, goin' to leave you behind,
Shout salvation as I fly,
Good-bye, goin' to leave you behind.
—WH102.

There's a better day a-coming, hallelujah [*a refrain*]. —SOC47, SO323.

Dere's a better day a-comin'
Don't you get weary. —DT27.
Dere's a better day a-coming'
Hallelujah. DT37.
Dere's a better day a-comin'.—DT156.

I want to live a Christian here,
I want to die a-shouting;
I want to feel my Savior near
When soul and body's parting.—OS406.

I want to go to view that land
* * *
Away over yonder to wear a starry crown. —OS524.

I want to go to heaven when I die,
view de land, view de land,
* * *
'Way over Jordan, go view de heavenly land. —DT138.

Our bondage it shall end by and by,
From Egypt's yoke set free.

* * *

Our deliverer he shall come by and by,
And our sorrows have an end.

* * *

Though our enemies are strong, we'll
go on,
Though our hearts dissolve with fear,
Lo, Sinai's God is near;
While the fiery pillar moves, we'll go on.
—OS489; HH219.

My fathers died a-shouting. —SOC37.

My massa died a-shouting. —FK146.

We hope to die shouting,
The Lord will provide. —SO33.

Chlidren of the heavenly King
As ye journey let us sing.

Cho.
I want to get as happy as I well can be,
Lord send salvation down. —SOC33.

I want to go to heaven, I do,
Hallelujah, Lord;
We'll praise the Lord in heaven above,
Roll, Jordan, Roll. —SOC145.

I want to go to heaven when I die
To hear ole Jordan roll. —DT52, 53.

I want to go where Jesus is,
I want to go there too [*refrain*]
—HH143.

I'm happy, I'm happy,
May the Lord continue with me,
I'm happy now and hope to be,
Come all my friends and go with me.
—SOC62.

Good morning, Brother Pilgrim,
What, bound for Canaan's coast?

* * *

Pray, wherefore are you smiling,
While tears run down your face?
We soon shall cease from toiling
And reach that heavenly place.
—CO54; SO143; SOC216.

Let nothing cause you to delay,
But hasten on the good old way.
—SO156.

Farewell Songs

The longed-for and hoped-for farewell from the earth is vividly imagined. It functioned as just another psychological "escape" while the traveler was still "fettered and bound up in clay." It will be noted also that the "end of all things earthly" falls often into the frame of the "end of all earthly things" or the conversion, and into the pattern of earthly farewells which sometimes did prove to be final ones. Hence the plenty of the time-is-short, and farewell songs.

I can't stay in these diggings,
Few days, few days,
I can't stay in these diggings,
I am going home. —SOC209.

For I've got a home out yonder,
Few days, few days
For I've got a home out yonder,
I am going home.
—*Negro Singer's Own Book* (1841), p. 96

A few more days of pain and woe,
A few more suffering scenes below.
—SK52.

A few more beating winds and rains,
And the winter will be over.
—OS323; OL355

A few more rising and setting suns,
And we'll cross over Jordan.
—SO323.

A few more days on earth to spend,
And all my toils and cares shall end.
—SO74; OS134.

A few more days of sorrow,
And the Lord will call us home.
—SOC80.

A few more rolling years at most,
Will land my soul on Canaan's coast.
—HH44.

A few more days or years at most,
My troubles will be over. —HH163.

I pitch my tent on this camp ground,
Few days, few days!
And give old Satan another round,
And I am going home. —SOC209.

He pitched his tent in Canaan's ground
And broke the Roman kingdom down.
—DT146.

Pull ol' Satan's kingdom down.—DT37.

Farewell, old soldiers of the cross,
[*refrain*] I can not tarry here.—SOC183.
Fare you well, my old companions,
I will not go with you to hell.

—BH124.

Farewell, my brethren in the Lord,
* * *
I hope that I shall meet you there.
—SK37.

The time is swiftly rolling on
When I must faint and die.
(A farewell to family)—SO19; OS124.

Dear friends, farewell, I do you tell,
Since you and I must part. —SO14.

Our cheerful voices let us raise
And sing a parting song.—SO30, SOC67.

Farewell, my lovely friends, farewell,
We must be separated. —SO35.

To leave my dear friends, and with neighbors to part,
And go from my home, it afflicts not my heart. —SO70

My Christian friends, in bonds of love,
Whose hearts in sweetest union join,
Your friendship's like a drawing band,
Yet we must take the parting hand.
—SO113.

Farewell, farewell, farewell, my friends,
I must be gone, I have no home or stay with you.—SO158; HH358; SOC138.

Farewell, my dear brethren,
The time is at hand,
When we must be parted
From this social band. —SO34, 334.

Farewell, farewell, to all below,
My Savior calls and I must go.—OS271.

Farewell, brethren, farewell, sisters,
Till we all shall meet again. —OS323.

The time must come when we must part,
When we must say farewell. —OS377.

And now, my friends, both old and young,

I hope in Christ you'll still go on;

* * *

An interest in your prayers I crave,
That we may meet beyond the grave.
—OS398.

Farewell, dear brothers, fare you well,
Pray do not weep for me.
[Then a message to sister, father,
mother]. —OS505.

I'm done with the world, and I want to
serve the Lord,
And I don't expect to stay much longer
here. —OS88.

Farewell, vain world, I'm going home.
Where there's no more stormy clouds to
rise. —OS278.

Vain world, adieu [*a refrain*].—OS329.

I'll bid farewell to every fear,
And wipe my weeping eyes.
—CO24; OS43; SOC24; Davis,
Traditional Ballads of Virginia, 269.

Farewell, vain world, I'm going home,
My Savior smiles and bids me come,
And I don't care to stay here long.

Right up yonder, Christians,
Away up yonder, O yes, my Lord,
For I don't care to stay here long.
—OS282; SOC165.

I don't expect to stay much longer here.
—DT15.

I don't want to stay here no longer.
—DT39.

Fare ye well, my ladies,
I'll jine dat heavenly band,
Where dere ain't any weepin' any mo'.
—SC198.

Most done lingerin' here. —SC25.

Crossing Jordan

Now the wayworn pilgrim stands on Jordan's banks. The passage is to be made variously. The wings of the eagle, of the morning, or of love may be his vehicle. The waters may be parted for his passage. He may travel by air as the prophet did, in a chariot. But the usual means of transportation is the boat or ship. The way is stormy. And here is where the trip merges figuratively with the whole Christian life-experience, the journey *through life* with that *after death.* And the goal of both is the same, Canaan's shore.

I have but one more river to cross, And then I'll be at rest. —OS290.	One wide river to cross. —WH32. Let us cross over the river and rest. —SC209.
I'd cross bold Jordan's stormy main, And leave this world behind.—SO135.	
On Jordan's stormy banks I stand, And cast a wishful eye.—SK50; CO94.	We're almost down to the shore. —DT84.
My home is over Jordan. —SO323.	*Deep river, my home is over Jordan.* —DT167.
Sometimes like mountains to the sky Black Jordan's billows roar. —SK36.	
I want to go to heaven, I do, * * * *Roll, Jordan, roll.* —SOC145; OS501.	*I want to go to heaven when I die* *To hear old Jordan roll.* —DT52. (See also SS1; WH87; DIT51; SS8.)
On the other side of Jordan, hallelujah! —SO318; OS486.	
I'm traveling over Jordan. —SOC164.	
The vale of tears surrounds me, And Jordan's current rolls before; Oh how I stand and tremble, To hear the dismal waters roar!	 Oh, how it makes me tremble.—DT104.
This stream shall not afright me, Although it takes me to the grave; If Jesus stand beside me, I'll safely ride on Jordan's wave. —SO63.	 I'm a-goin' to wade cross Jordan's river. —DIT22.
And when to Jordan's flood we're come, Jehovah rules the tide, And the waters he'll divide. (See II Kings 2:8). —HH219.	
When freed from this dull, crazy, cumbrous clay,	

On eagle's wings of love,
I then shall mount above,
And find a passage to eternal day.
—SO (edition of 1835)99.

I wish I have had the eagle's wing
I would fly all the way to paradise.
—DIT7.

But may I rise on wings of love,
And soar to the blest world above.
—SO265.

Oh! had I wings, I would fly away,
and be at rest. —SOC112.

Oh! had I the wings of the morning,
I'd fly away to Canaan's shore;
Bright angels should convey me home,
To the new Jerusalem.
—BH213.

I'll launch my bark on Eden's shore,
For Eden is my home. —OS154.

I'll launch my boat upon the sea,
This world is not the world for me.
—OS271.

The chariot method of transportation, owing to its being bound up scripturally with the fire motif, was usually brought into the end-of-the-world songs rather than into those which had to do merely with the end of the individual pilgrim. We showed, in that connection, its reflection in song. The Ship of Zion was the popular mode of travel across the Jordan, a body of water with very elastic boundaries. And even though the railroads entered the fasola consciousness in the 1820's, they did not get into his songs, it seems, nor into the Negro's spirituals, before the Civil War.

Come tell me of your ship
And what is her name. —SOC203.

O what ship is this that will
take us all home? —HH355.

(The same, DT81)

'Tis the old ship of Zion,
hallelujah! —HH355.

(The same, DT81)

Do you think she'll be able
To take us all home? —HH355.

I think she'll be able,
hallelujah! —HH355.

She has landed many thousands
And can land as many more.—HH355.

And will she have other comrades on
board? —OS388.

The winds may blow
And the billows may foam,
But she is able
To land us all home. —OS79.

She will land us safe
On Canaan's bright shore. —OS388.

Come, tell me of your captain.
—SOC203.

Jesus is our Captain and Friend.—OS79.

With Jesus in the vessel
The billows rise in vain. —SO332.

While we ride on the tide
With our Captain and his Mate.
—HH299; SO41.

She's waiting now for a heavenward gale,
Methinks I see her now hoisting her sail.
—OS79.

Behold the sails expanded,
Along the towering mast. —HH299.

We're now on the wide ocean.—HH299.

(The same, DT81)

O yes, she will be able
For to take us all home. —DT81.

(The same, DT81).
There's room for many a more.
—SCA255.

She's loaded with bright angels.
—DT221.
It's loaded with many a thousand.
—OD118.

King Jesus is our Captain. —DT189.

King Jesus is conductor [of Gospel
Train]. —SCA253.

King Jesus is the Captain.
The Holy Ghost is the pilot. —SS103.
O Jesus go de hellum. —SS51.

O de ship is at the landin'. —MEL41.

My ship is on the ocean. —DT189.
Don't you view dat ship a-sailin'?
—DT221.
Way out yonder in de ocean.—MEL40.

We'll stem the storm, it won't be long,
The heavenly port is nigh.
We'll stem, etc.
We'll anchor by and by. —OS378.

We'll stand the storm
It won't be long.
We'll anchor by and by. —DT189.

I'm making for the harbor.
—SO323; HO65.

She's making for the kingdom.
—DT189.

The Promised Land

At last the end is come. The heavenly port is reached. No words are too extravagant to describe its perfections. Everything hoped for on earth is found in heaven. These pictures are used with two purposes, to cheer the faithful and to turn the sinner to paths of righteousness.

Bright angels, strike your loudest strings —SK12.

I want to see bright angels stand
And waiting to receive me.
—CO140; OS406.

Look up yonder! What I see?
Bright angels coming after me.—DIT15.

Bright angels whispering me away.
—SK37.

Sweet angels beckon me away.—OS282.

And the angels stand inviting
To welcome travelers home. —HH483.

Then friends shall meet again.
—HH219.

I expect to join the army [the heavenly hosts] by and by. —SOC104.

For to jine de holy number. —DT37.

. . . Canaan's land
Where Christ has gone before me.
—HH213.

Gwine see my Massa Jesus.
—DT121, 201.

We have fathers [mothers, etc.] in the promised land. —SOC29.

I's got a father in the promised land.
—WH115.

I have some friends before me gone.
—SO323.

I've got a brother in the snowwhite fields. —WH119.

My father's gone to view that land.
—OS524.

. . . to see my friends again, and
hear them sweetly say: come weary dove.
—OS418.

That bright land where loved ones go
Where all is peace and love. —OS506.

[Hebrew children, twelve apostles,
holy martyrs, holy Christians, etc. are]
Safe in the promised land. —OS481.

I soon shall get to heaven
To sing redeeming love. —SO26.

When we all get to heaven
We will shout aloud and sing.
—SOC42; OS319.

I'll join with those who're gone before
Who sing and shout their sufferings o'er.
—SO74.
We'll sing and shout hosanna.—OS397.

There we shall sing praises
When we all shall meet above.
—HH298.

And shout with God eternally.—SK52

I'm going where pleasure never dies,
And troubles come no more.
—SOC110; SO158; OS185.

Where pleasure never dies.
—HH153; OS80.

Then my troubles will be over.—SOC85

Never-ceasing pleasures roll.
—CO95; SK51.

There'll be no more sorrow
When we all shall meet above.
—HH298

No sin there. —OS382.

I've got a mother in the Kingdom.
—DT189.

My mother's in de kingdom. —DT135.
I've got a brother 'way in de glory.
—WH76

That promised land where all is peace.
—FIS22.

(The same, DT73 and elsewhere).

I want to sing in heaven with the angels. —DIT2.

O when I get to heaven
Goin' to sing and shout. —DT125.

Gwine to shout an' nebber tire
—DT27.
Tell God 'bout my crosses. —DT37.
Talk de trouble over. —DT37.

Gwine sing around the throne.—DT121.

There'll be no trouble there. —DIT23.
All-a-my troubles will soon be over with. —WK57.

There'll be no more sinning.—HH298.
Pain is felt no more. —OS387.

There's union in heaven
There's union in my soul. —OS424.

This [heaven] is no world of trouble,
The God of peace is there;
He wipes away their sorrows,
And banishes their care. —SK88.

And there's no weeping there.—OS382.

Ain't any weepin' any more. —SC198.

God will wipe away my tears.—KN52.

When we get to heaven we will part no
more. —SOC20.

There we shall with Jesus dwell
and never part again. —HH80.

Never part no more. —DT9.

Where parting is no more. —CO115.

Saints arrayed in white. —SK88.

Gwine to wear a white robe.
—DT122, 193, 210; SS29.

My father's gone . . .
To wear a starry crown. —OS524.

I'm goin' to wear a starry crown over
there. —WH80.
Gwine to wear a starry crown.—DT121.

. . . I'm going home
To play on the golden harp.
—OS274; HH163.

All God's chill'n got a harp. —DT126.

The meanest child of glory
Outshines the radiant sun.
—HH374; SK88.

We'll outshine the sun. —DT123.

I'll outline, when rising,
The sun at mid-day. —HH241.

Outshine the glittering sun. —WH107.

My soul shall shine
Like the morning star,
In the new Jerusalem. —SOC138.

My little soul gwine shine. —DT122.

To range the new Jerusalem. —OS497.

Walk all over God's heaven. —DT126.
Walk about Zion. —DT201.

And flit all o'er this spacious mound.
—OS441.

I'm a-going to fly all around in heaven.
—DIT22.

I want a seat in Paradise. —OS324.
The saints' delightful home. —SOC37.

Gwine to sit down in de kingdom. —DT201.

For heaven's my home.—OS119; SO293.

Heaven shall be my home. —SS7; DT201.

Go, preachers, and tell it to the world,
Poor mourner's found a home at last. —OS401.

Po' mourner's got a home at last. —WK22

Religion is a fortune
And heaven is a home. —SOC42.

Religion is a fortune,
I really do believe. —WK48; DT201.

. . . mansions in the skies.—SK25.

In bright mansions above. —DT42.

Oh, walk and talk with Jesus.—SOC45.

Gwine to talk-a wid de angels,
Gwine to tell God 'bout my crosses. —DT37.

At his table we'll sit down.
Christ will gird himself and serve us
With sweet manna all around.—SO103.

Gwine to sit down at the welcome table,
Gwine to feast off milk and honey. —DT123.

. . . *walk the golden streets.* —SOC80; OS380; CO60.

We'll walk about dem-a golden streets. —DT9.

The mountains paved with gold. —SO150.

Where there's no more stormy
clouds arising. —SO313; SOC35.

To live forever more. —OS322.

Gwine to live for evermore. —DT121.

To die no more. —OS111.

Gwine to live wid God forever.—DT27.

There is perhaps no better way to close this chapter on the text comparison of white and Negro spirituals and to show, at the same time, the nature of their common textual inheritance from earlier and more artistic sources, than to give text samples of three eighteenth-century songs which have undergone the two changes; the first one being that imposed by the camp-meeting practices, and the second being the result of the Negro's subsequent transforming of the camp-meeting song:

Eighteenth-Century Hymn	Its Camp-Meeting Version	Its Negro Spiritual Remnant
Poem by John Leland (CO124) Through grace I feel determined to conquer, though I die; *And then away to Jesus* *On wings of love I'll fly.* (four more lines)	1 (SAH85) Through grace I feel determined To conquer, though I die; *And then away to Jesus* *On wings of love I'll fly.* Chorus Shout, O glory, *For I shall mount above the skies,* *When I hear the trumpet sound* *In that morning.*	(Johnson, I, 182) Good ol' Christians in dat day, *Dey'll take wings and fly away,* *For to hear de trumpet soun'* *In dat mornin'.*
Poem by Charles Wesley He comes, He comes, the Judge severe! The seventh trumpet speaks Him near; His lightnings flash, *His thunders roll.* How welcome to the faithful soul!	2 (SOC145) He comes, He comes, the Judge severe, *Roll, Jordan, roll!* The seventh trumpet speaks Him near, *Roll, Jordan, roll!* Chorus *I want to go to Heaven, I do,* *Halleluja, Lord!* We'll praise the Lord in heaven above, *Roll, Jordan, roll!*	(DT52) O roll, Jordan, roll, Roll, Jordan, roll; *I want to go to heaven when I die* *To hear ole Jordan roll.*
Author unknown. *Dover Selection* *A few more days* on earth to spend, *And all my toils and cares shall end,* And I shall see my God and friend And praise His name on high.	3 (Recorded, 1848, in Georgia) *A few more days or years at most,* *My troubles will be o'er.* (Recorded, 1857, in Georgia) I pitch my tent on this camp ground, *Few days, few days!* And give old Satan another round, *And I am going home.* *I can't stay in these diggings,* *Few days, few days!* *I can't stay in these diggings,* *I am going home.*	(*The Negro Singer's Own Book*, 1846) For I've a home out yonder, *Few days, few days,* For I've a home out yonder, *I am going home.* *For I can't stay in the wilderness,* *Few days, few days,* *For I can't stay in the wilderness,* *I am going home.*

CHAPTER XXI

CITY CHURCH FOLK SLOWLY ABANDON THE SOUTH'S INDIGENOUS SONGS

So music past is obsolete,
And yet 'twas sweet, 'twas passing sweet.[1]

The Attitude of Urban Hymn-Book Makers

It might well be expected that the fasola sorts of song, the product of primitive environment and suited perfectly to the tastes of the rural whites and only a little less so to the song concepts of the Negroes, would find a cool welcome, if any, in the culturally further advanced urban environments of the South, those environments whence emanated the big hymnals and, later, the big hymn-and-tune books. I have examined some of these books and have found precisely this inhospitality.

Methodist Hymn Books

The Southern Methodists' first official hymn book with tunes came out, if my information is correct, in 1859, and a radical revision of this book was made in 1889. In 1911 the northern and southern branches of the Methodist Episcopal church joined in a revision which resulted in producing a book used in both sections, and a joint committee is now (1931) at work on the revision of the 1911 book.

One might expect the oldest of these tune books, the one issued in 1859, to show the least antipathy toward the indigenous rural song of the fasola folk. But such is not the case. And the reason for the offishness seems to have been attributable largely to the book's editor (the man to whom,

[1] *Church Harmony* (Chambersburg, Pennsylvania, 1841), p. 300.

along with the "Book Agent" of the church, the production of the first "Tune-Hymn Book" was delegated), rather than to any general hymnodic snobbishness. This editor was L. C. Everett, an able composer and musical organizer of Virginia.[2] Indeed, Everett seems to have been far too good a musician for the South at that time and for his editorial task, for he provided the southern Methodists with a song book that broke, all but completely, with their own musical traditions.

As for the hymns, the Everett compilation contained over a thousand, only thirty-five of which were those poems which had been, and still were, popular in fasola singing circles. And of the three hundred and fifty-seven tunes in the Everett book I found but seventeen which had attained to any degree of fasola popularity.

The editor did not indicate the sources of any of his hymns, but they seem to be predominatingly those of the imported variety—Charles Wesley, I. Watts, Philip Doddridge, etc. He was careful, however, to credit the tune makers, as far as he knew who they were, with their products. Prominent among these composers were the Everetts themselves. The editor furnished sixteen, A. B. Everett, thirteen, and B. H. and E. G.

[2] L. C. Everett (1818-1867) was, according to the *Musical Million,* VII (1876), 9, a native of Rockingham County, Virginia, that Shenandoah district from which so much of musical import has sprung. Both he and his younger brother, A. B. Everett (1828-1875), received the best of musical education, in this country and in Europe. The natural result was that they were estranged from the rural fasola sort of music propagation of their early environment and threw their whole strength into the task of "advancing" the musically backward South. With headquarters in Richmond these brothers taught singing, and their pupils taught, using the "Everett Method" over wide stretches of the South.

Later they came into Tennessee. When A. B. Everett committed suicide in Tullahoma, Tennessee, the postmaster of that town wrote the following to the editor of the *Musical Million* (article cited above): "The Dr. Asa Brooks Everett, whom you reported as having committed suicide in Crockett County (W. Tenn.) a few days ago, was a native of Virginia. . . . He and three brothers (L. C., B. H., and N. E.), taught Music in Middle Tennessee in 1857 and 1858, and were all well known to most of the country towns in Tennessee, Georgia, Alabama, and Mississippi." Further information as to the Everetts may be found in Hall, *op. cit.,* pp. 97 ff.

Everett, three each. Numerous tunes were credited to the *Thesaurus Musicus,* and many others had merely the cryptic notice that it was "composed expressly for this work."

But the most significant feature of the book from which southern Methodists sang during the thirty years following 1859 was the complete absence of the domestic camp-meeting songs, both tunes and words. The book agent, Thomas O. Summers, in his own Preface to the book, regretted "the absence of certain favorite pieces." But the editor, in his particular Preface, defended his eliminations against such opinions as those of the agent and against the "formidable opposition" which he expected the book to meet "in certain localities, by a few, who, from a superstitious reverence for 'the good old tunes,'" might object to their being put on the shelf. And he reminded such old-tune enthusiasts of the biblical injunction to "sing unto the Lord with a *new* song." Everett's rôle of musical reformer is seen also in his earnest recommendation of "congregational singing classes" under a "regular teacher of vocal music," so that the new tunes might be learned by all.

If any southern Methodists regretted the absence of indigenous tunes and words from the Everett edition, they must have been somewhat consoled when the revision of 1889 came to their pews. This revision was in the hands, not of one man, but of a committee of eleven. As a result of the activities of these men the thirty-five fasola-loved hymns of the earlier book grew to forty-six, and the seventeen "good old" fasola tunes increased to thirty-two. At the same time the tunes made by the Everetts decreased from thirty-five to seventeen. Numerous other tunes disappeared—those from the *Thesaurus Musicus* and the "expressly composed" ones—their places being filled largely by such nineteenth-century composers as Woodbury, Hastings, Bradbury, Main, Gould, and, above all, Lowell Mason. R. M. McIntosh, an eminent southern tune composer of the urban stamp and an apostle of the Everetts, must be mentioned here as a contributor.[3] Three of his tunes had appeared in the Everett edition. In this 1889 book they increased to ten.

But the most significant innovation in the book under consideration is that it included six of the old camp-meeting tunes and their words. They were No. 881, O when shall I see Jesus; No. 883, We're Trav'ling home to Heaven above; No. 885, Together let us sweetly live; No. 899, Say, brothers, will you meet us; No. 907, The chariot, the chariot; and No. 914, The old ship of Zion.

There was, however, in some cases, a definite attempt to clean up the crude songs before introducing them to their prospective singers in the nicer places. Number 885 is a good example of this process. John Newland Maffit had made the words respectable some years before. R. M. McIntosh gave the tune a good scrubbing. The transformation will be seen by comparing the two following excerpts:

The camp-meeting version, SAH 87.

I have some friends be-fore me gone, I am bound for the land of Ca-naan;
And I'm re-solved to fol - low on, I am bound for the land of Ca-naan.

The Maffit-McIntosh version, M. H. & T. Book, No. 885.

Part of my friends the prize have won, I am bound for the land of Ca-naan;
And I'm re-solved to fol - low on, I am bound for the land of Ca-naan.

[3]Rigdon McCoy McIntosh was born in Maury County, Tennessee, in 1836 and died in Oxford, Georgia, in 1899. His important activities in composing church music, teaching singing, leading choruses, and compiling books of songs are outlined by Hall, *op. cit.*, pp. 103 ff.

But even though the unkempt songs were slicked up, their presentation by the editors was a bit apologetic. In the "Annotated Edition" of the hymns, which came out somewhat later than the tune book, nothing was said about these folk-tunes, or about any other tunes, for that matter, but Dr. Wilbur F. Tillett, the able editor of that edition, confessed that the hymn cited above had, despite Maffit's attempts at improvement, "not much claim to poetry." And "The Old Ship of Zion" was presented with the qualification that it was "anything else but good poetry, but" (and this is important) "it is one of the old-time hymns that has not yet lost its power."

"Power" was evidently desired and at the same time feared by the hymn-book makers. Church-song manners, like table manners, were apt to be spoiled by undue zest on the part of those participating in the feast.

Among the southern poets represented in the 1889 edition are Mary Palmer Dana, of South Carolina, author of "I'm a pilgrim and I'm a stranger," No. 898, and of "Soft Music," SAH323; John Newland Maffit, of Ireland, who lived in Nashville and elsewhere in the southern states from 1835 to 1850, arranger of "Together let us sweetly live," No. 885; John Leland, of New England, who lived and preached in Virginia from 1775 to 1790, poet of "O when shall I see Jesus," No. 881; William E. Evans, of Virginia, No. 697; and David Nelson, of Tennessee, No. 880.

The southern tune makers of the urban variety were the four Everetts mentioned above and McIntosh. Those allied with the shape-note activities of the rurals were B. C. Unseld, of West Virginia, composer of tune to No. 538; John B. Jackson, of Tennessee, composer of the tune to No. 644 (mistakenly attributed to another fasola tune maker, E. J. King); William Walker, of South Carolina, composer of tune to No. 881;

and Ananias Davisson, of Virginia, composer of tunes No. 317 and No. 310. This last named tune, repeated as No. 350, is not ascribed to Davisson, but is merely called a "Southern tune."

From the 1905 edition of the *Methodist Hymnal* for all Wesleyans there were sixteen fasola hymn omissions. The six camp-meeting texts, including "The Old Ship of Zion," were deleted. And among the other cut-outs were such doleful poems as "Dark was the night," "Thou art gone to the grave," and "Hark, from the tombs." The atmosphere was becoming lighter in Methodist circles.

But the modernizing process was even more evident in the tunes of this 1905 edition. Of the thirty-one fasola-popular tunes of the edition of sixteen years before, only four remained. They were "Lenox," "Nettleton," "Mear," and "Greenville." The tune eliminations included all those by southern fasola composers—John B. Jackson, William Walker, and Ananias Davisson. Even the urban composers of the South were radically reduced. The two Everetts, A. B. and L. C., who together had twenty-nine tunes in the 1859 book and seventeen in the 1889 edition, shrank to three in 1905. And R. M. McIntosh's ten tunes of the 1889 edition shriveled to one in 1905. Thus these three musicians, whom Hall looks on as having done for the South's musical development what Mason, Hastings, and Bradbury did for that of the Northeast, are represented in the South's outstanding church hymnal by a total of four tunes, while the three northern composers have forty-seven tunes in that same book.

Baptist Hymn Books

Apparently one of the earliest hymn-and-tune books used widely by the urban Baptists of the South was the *Baptist*

THE GRAVES OF FOUR PATRIARCHS OF RURAL SONG

UPPER LEFT: *Joseph Funk's gravestone in the cemetery at Singer's Glen in the Shenandoah Valley.* UPPER RIGHT: *The grave of Ananias Davisson, composer of some of the rural South's tunes which were uniquely popular in the early part of the nineteenth century, and the author of the* Kentucky Harmony. *His resting place is in the Union Church graveyard, eight miles from Dayton, Virginia, in the Shenandoah Valley.* LOWER LEFT: *The grave of John Gordon McCurry, author of the* Social Harp, *at Bio, Hart County, Georgia.* LOWER RIGHT: *The gravestone of Benjamin Franklin White, author of the* Sacred Harp, *and his wife, Thurza Golightly White, in Oakland Cemetery, Atlanta, Georgia, a memorial erected by Sacred Harp Singers.*

Hymn and Tune Book (1857).[4] This fat book from the end of the fasola period itself contains but thirty-two songs of that vintage. Of these songs twelve are called "Western Melodies," a term that was used to cover all songs, whether they were recorded in the West or the South, which seemed to be the product of the "Western Revival." Ananias Davisson's "Golden Hill" is among them. Seven songs found in my MPT list appear in the book—MPT 5, 17, 25, 44, 52, 80^a, and 80^b.

The next book in use in southern urban Baptist circles seems to have been the *Service of Song,* published by the Sheldon firm in 1871. It shows a radical reduction in its indigenous songs. We find about the same sprinkling of the fasola-popular hymns and tunes which we found in the Methodist book of 1889. Its nine tunes well liked by the southern fasola folk are "Aylesbury," "Mear," "Balerma," "Nettleton" ("Go Tell Aunt Rhody"), "Brattle Street," "Golden Hill" (Davisson), "China," and two fuguing tunes, "Lenox," and "Northfield."

At the present time (1931) the urban Baptists, like their Methodist brethren, sing largely from an all-American, that is, a north-and-south-used hymnal in which the songs peculiarly popular in the rustic South of long ago get no recognition.[5] Very many congregations, however—those more rural-minded ones?—sing from a book with the somewhat misleading title, *Modern Hymnal,* made in Dallas, 1926, by Robert H. Coleman. In his Foreword the editor declares that "the Grand Old Hymns must be preserved, and the use

[4] New York, Sheldon and Company.

[5] Published in 1902, this Baptist Hymnal has but a dozen or so of the "good old songs." Two of these, "Loving Kindness" and "Happiness," are called "western melodies." Two others, Nos. 400 and 661, appear in our MPT list as Nos. 5 and 12. But all songs of pronounced camp-meeting flavor have disappeared. Suspects of being southern composers are Aaron Chapin (Nos. 65 and 400) and Freeman Lewis (No. 389).

of them encouraged," along with the use of the "worthy newer Gospel Songs." I find, however, but seventeen of those Grand Old Hymns of the specific southern fasola making or adoption, and but seven of these are to be found in the MPT list above (Nos. 13, 18, 20, 22, 28, 72, and 73). An amusing touch, made presumably in the interest of bringing things "up to date," is the transposing of the strong old minor five-tone tunes, "On Jordan's Stormy Banks" (MPT 20, old title, "Promised Land"), and "Come, Humble Sinners" (MPT 18, old title, "Fairfield"), into the major mode, emasculating them thereby. One of the indigenous old songs is "Holy Manna" by Tennessee's William Moore, of whose authorship the users of the *Modern Hymnal* are not informed. Another is "Old-Time Religion."

Presbyterian Hymn Books

The Presbyterian church in the south was supplied for almost the entire second half of the nineteenth century by song-book publishers in Philadelphia. I think we have a right, therefore, even without examining such books themselves, to conclude that they must have avoided all indigenous songs of the southern and western revival. Since 1900 a book called *Chapel Hymns,* also published in Philadelphia, has been in use among the southern Presbyterians. Of the fasola songs, it contains only "Avon," "Lenox," "Balerma," "Loving Kindness," "Nettleton," and "Amsterdam."

The Cumberland Presbyterian church, born in 1806 of the Kentucky-Tennessee revival and camp-meeting spirit, and doubtless singing the fasola-revivalistic songs during its early decades of development, seems to have felt the influence of the hymn-and-tune reformers as early as 1865, when its Nashville board of publication issued a hymn-and-tune book edited by Dr. M. B. DeWitt called *Bible Songs,* a collection which enjoyed considerable popularity in that denomination for decades. The most striking feature of this book, which was expected to appeal, among others, to the country church folk, was the complete absence of the camp-meeting-whoopee type of song. Dr. DeWitt sided evidently with the more dignified urban bloc of his denomination.

In this book the Cumberland Presbyterians eased away gently from the pure and strong fasola tradition. The "good old songs" of the better fasola sort totaled but forty-one of the 223. And of these forty-one there were twenty-one tunes which are to be found in my MPT list. Ananias Davisson and William Caldwell are the only southern tune makers represented.

For the past thirty to forty years this denomination seems to have exerted no definite and strong song-book influence over its congregations. The rural groups have used various collections of "Gospel Song" made by their own publishing house and by others and printed in a seven-shape notation of which I shall speak in Part Two of this book. The city groups have become "protestant regulars" in hymnal matters, like the Baptists and Methodists, and from this standardized church song milieu, as well as from that of the "Gospel Songs," the fasola music has long since disappeared.[6]

Certain Anomalies

Thus we see that southern church folk, to the extent that their organizations have been city-controlled or northern-

[6] Even though the Cumberland Presbyterian church has parted with its ancestral song customs, the primitivity of some of its country congregations in other ways is striking. I was told by Rev. J. L. Hudgins, a veteran preacher of that denomination, that the Shiloh church, an "anti-organ" congregation near McKenzie in western Tennessee, still refused to tolerate lights in its church building and music notation in its gospel hymn books as late as 1910.

The story of the objector to the installing of a chandelier in the place of worship is a southern classic which is attributed on occasion to any country church: During the discussion by the elders, an intransigent member of the board declared: "If we got one of them things, there ain't nobody here could play it."

influenced, have foresworn increasingly, as time has passed, the songs which grew from their own cultural soil, and that they have adopted as their own the standardized Protestant church songs of the rest of the nation. Doubtless the ministers, church musicians, and old-line hymnologists will applaud this as a step in the direction of better church music.

Maybe the serious hymnal makers are right. But even if they are, the *Cokesbury Hymnal,* published by the Methodist Episcopal Church, South, Nashville, 1928, a book more widely used among Methodists and other sects than any other, furnishes what I call a good joke on them, for it includes between its covers six Negro spirituals: "Standin' in the Need of Prayer," "Swing Low, Sweet Chariot," "Lord, I Want to be," "I know the Lord has Laid," "Where Were You," and "Down by the Riverside." The "camp-meeting stuff," as long as it was recognized as such, that is, as what White calls the southern white man's "last year's clothes," musically, poetically, and spiritually, was taboo. But after that same "stuff" had been given the Afro-American flavor and had thus become unrecognizable to the hymnalists as bone of their bone, and after the Negro's songs had been re-introduced to them as "musical antiques," as "folk-songs," then they were welcome again, but in their proper place and under their proper label.

The Primitive Baptists and Their Hymn Books, an Exception

It is interesting to note here that this high-hatting of the South's own songs on the part of the city folk did not kill them. It merely drove them into remote places, remote religiously, culturally, and geographically. We have spoken above of their present-day survival in *Sacred Harp* and *Southern Harmony* circles. We shall find still other persistences of the songs when we discuss the *Harp of Columbia* and the

Christian Harmony in the second part of this book. But all of those survivals are in non-denominational and even non-church environment. I have found but one church milieu in which the South's "good old songs" are still held in such esteem that they practically exclude all other sorts of song, and that is among the Primitive Baptists.

Every time, for over a hundred years past, when a certain group of southern Baptists would take a notion to advance along the line of church activities and tenets, that group would be opposed by another faction which preferred to "ask for the old paths and walk therein." After many decades of these conflicts of opinion—over the introduction of organs into the church, the engaging in foreign missionary work, the paying and educating of preachers, the instituting of Sunday schools, the giving up of the foot-washing rite, etc., etc.—they seem to have agreed to disagree; and as the result of each major conflict a new brand of Baptist came into existence. Dr. E. P. Alldredge, Nashville statistician for the Southern Baptists, tells me there are twelve different sorts of Baptists in Alabama, thirteen in Tennessee, and twelve in Kentucky. The extreme reactionaries in each and every dispute, those who have objected to *every* innovation and retreated from every "worldly" minded group of their brethren are the "Old Line" or "Primitive" Baptists, or simply the "Old Baptists." There are now about 125,000 of them, of whom 81,000 are white and 44,000 are black. They are found largely in Georgia, Alabama, North Carolina, Virginia, and Tennessee.

I have no immediate acquaintanceship with the Negro branch. The white Primitive Baptists are naturally predominatingly country folk. This fact and the fact of their extreme religious conservatism have combined to preserve among them the church-song traditions of their forefathers. They sing the songs on which the earliest Primitive Baptists in their strongest state, Georgia, were brought up.

I attended the annual session of the Big Sandy Primitive Baptist Association in Bruceton, Tennessee, in the summer of 1931 and found them singing southern-made white spirituals almost exclusively. The two books from which they drew these songs were *The Primitive Baptist Hymn and Tune Book,* edited by John R. Daily, published in 1902 and sold by J. D. Shain, Madisonville, Kentucky; and the *Good Old Songs* compiled by Elder C. H. Cayce, published in 1913 by Cayces and Turner in Martin, Tennessee. There were but two or three copies of these books among an assemblage of several hundred under the trees at Bruceton. And this dearth of books, the people singing largely from memory, the out-door services, and the hoary songs all were strikingly reminiscent of the accounts I had read of primitive church conditions over a century before in these same parts.

An examination of the *Primitive Baptist Hymn and Tune Book* (referred to here as PB) showed that though it was printed in the *seven*-shape music notation which succeeded the fasola *four*-shape notation in most of the South, its songs were largely of the early fasola sort. Out of 290 tunes 105 were those which are to be found in book after book of the 1830's and 1840's. And after eliminating all the repeats of one and the same tune, we find eighty-three different old tunes. Among these, forty-one were tunes found in our MPT list; and these forty-one were repeated, here and there through the book, to the extent of bringing their total up to sixty. This may be looked on as a striking proof that the most popular tunes of around a hundred years ago are still in highest favor in these particular surroundings.

Fasola composers represented in PB are William Caldwell

(Tennessee), Joseph Funk (Virginia), Ananias Davisson (Virginia), William Walker (South Carolina), L. P. Breedlove (Georgia), William Moore (Tennessee), and E. J. King (Georgia). Southern composers whose songs sprang up during the post-Civil-War period of gospel hymn influence and who are represented in PB are Aldine S. Kieffer, A. D. Fillmore, J. H. Hall, W. T. Dale, John R. Daily, G. P. Hott, Will H. Ruebush and A. J. Showalter.

The *Good Old Songs* book (GOS), also Primitive Baptist, is an even richer repository of the tunes suggested by its title. For out of about four hundred tunes, three hundred and ten are those which were beloved in early fasola circles. The other ninety are of eighteenth-century type like "Old Hundred," of the "Gospel Hymn" sort, and of the better class of nineteenth-century compositions like those of Lowell Mason. Forty southern fasola composers are mentioned among the makers of these "Good Old Songs." The most often recurring, with the number of songs attributed to each, are: William Walker, thirty-three; William Hauser, twenty; J. P. Rees, thirteen; E. J. King, thirteen; B. F. White, nine; E. Dumas, nine; L. P. Breedlove, six; H. S. Rees, six. All of these are from the Georgia-South Carolina section.

PART II

FASOLA OFFSPRING, THE DORAYME FOLK

CHAPTER XXII

AIKIN'S SEVEN SHAPES; OTHER SETS

Introduction of the Do-re-mi System

The fasola manner was, as we have seen, colonial America's own, inherited from England. We have also seen that the songs which were "sol-faed" in this traditional manner and notated in the four shapes were largely and increasingly indigenous. But we now come to realize that this condition, whatever may have been its worth to America's national music, was not destined to endure. Native song, with the manner of its recording and learning, was not to remain an exception among a people which has habitually discarded its own homespun cultural goods for "store-bought" ones, its domestic civilizational stuff for foreign fabrics.

With the onset of European musical influences around the beginning of the nineteenth century, the now generally used do-re-mi system was introduced on these shores. It spread, of course, from the eastern cities into the country, and slowly. We have seen how the Masons of Massachusetts tried to introduce the novelty among the shape-noters west of the Alleghenies, how they advised even the users of their own *Sacred Harp* to sing *do, re, mi* and "disregard" the shapes of the notes.[1] Less radical was D. Sower of Pennsylvania. He saw clearly that rural America was not going to allow anyone to take away its beloved patent notes, and that if the do-re-mi manner were to gain ground, it would have to do so while holding to the shape-note benefits. So this clever compromiser produced the *Norristown New and Much Improved Music*

[1] See p. 17 above.

Reader (Norristown, Pennsylvania, 1832), using the old foursome of shapes for *fa, sol, la,* and *mi,* and adding for *do, re,* and *si,* shapes varying only slightly from three of the original note forms. Thus his book could be used, as the Gilson pamphlet tells us, "by those who sol-faed with four syllables or with seven." And this caution on Sower's part was quite opportune, for his book came out at just the time when the four-shape notation was all but universal in the rural parts west and south and when four-shape books were multiplying.

Jesse B. Aikin and His Christian Minstrel

At any rate, fourteen years elapsed after the Sower experiment before another attempt was made to substitute seven shapes for the old four. This attempt was made by Jesse B. Aikin of Philadelphia, and its great success is demonstrated by the fact that Aikin's *Christian Minstrel* (Philadelphia, 1846), in which the seven-shapes first appeared, endured for decades and went into as many as 171 editions.[2] Aikin's choice of simple elementary forms for his three additional note-heads has been shown to be fortunate by the fact that his shapes are used today by all the seven-shape rural song-book publishers in the South and have been the standard notation in that territory for over fifty years.

The *Christian Minstrel* is a book six by ten inches, and the twelfth edition, which I have examined, contains 416 pages. In Aikin's Preface he stated clearly his hopes that his book would supplant the "trashy publications" which had, up to that time, "supplied the churches, especially of the South and West. . . ." He also hoped that his new notation would swell the numbers of those who could read music easily. He explained that he had reduced the varieties of musical

[2] A copy of the 171st edition, of 1873, is in the Music Division of the Library of Congress.

measure to three, two-two, three-two, and six-four time; that he had excluded the minor scale from consideration in his rudiments as an unnatural, impractical, confusing, and really non-existent phase of music; that he had but one sort of clef for all four parts, one that has G in the middle (third line) of the staff; and that he had expressed the key of the tune by words and not by symbols.

After the usual theoretical pages we come to the tunes, which occupy 385 pages. Aikin has collected an unusually fine lot of songs which are mainly those by English and American composers of that time and earlier. About twenty of his pieces are drawn from the German composers of church music. Among the more than a hundred composers, Lowell Mason is best represented by eighteen songs. But not one of the songs—tune or words—is claimed by Aikin as his own product.

As to Jesse B. Aikin's life I have been able to ascertain very little. That little may be found on page 352 below.

I have no definite proof that the *Christian Minstrel* was ever widely popular in the rural South. Only nine of those eighty songs which, according to my MPT list, were widely sung in the southern countryside are to be found in the Aikin book, and it did contain hundreds of pieces that are not found in any other of the fourteen books we have examined. The notation of the book was for a time a strange one to the section; and for some time after the seven-shape idea began to grow, or until the 1870's, it was generally believed that his shapes were patented. The result of this belief was that a number of southern teachers shied away from the big Philadelphia book, made their own song books, notated their songs in seven note-shapes, three of which were their own invention, and then used their own influence and energy in introducing these books in their own territory. This competition must have held back the *Christian Minstrel* sales in the South. The chief interest which it has for us lies in its notation.

Alexander Auld and His Ohio Harmonist

The imitators of Aikin got busy without delay. Only a year after the Philadelphia compiler put the *Christian Minstrel* on the market, Alexander Auld, a Pennsylvania German living in Ohio, got out a book which he called the *Ohio Harmonist* (Cincinnati, 1847). Auld himself claimed priority over Aikin in the seven-shape invention. "On Christmas day, 1835," he wrote in the *Musical Million* in 1880, "I invented the three shapes, *do, re,* and *si,* . . . and adapted the seven shapes to the seven sounds of the scale. I exhibited my invention to my classes and it was approved by all . . . except a few round-heads who would prefer calling a spade 'a well known implement of manual labor.'"[3] I have reproduced Auld's shapes on page 337 below. Since his book was not, as far as I have learned, used to any extent in the South, I shall make no further mention of it.

[3] XI, 26.

IMPORTANT SEVEN-SHAPE SONG BOOKS APPEARING BETWEEN 1832 AND 1878

Year of Publication	Name of Book	Author	Author's Home	Place of Printing
1832........	Norristown New and Improved Music Teacher	D. Sower	Norristown, Pa.	
1846........	Christian Minstrel	Jesse B. Aikin	Philadelphia	Same.
1847........	Ohio Harmonist	Alexander Auld	Ohio	Cincinnati.
1848........	Harp of Columbia	W. H. and M. L. Swan	Knoxville, Tenn.	Same.
1848........	Sacred Melodeon	Amos S. Hayden	Ohio	Cincinnati.
1851........	Harmonia Sacra	Joseph Funk & Sons	Mountain Valley	Winchester, Va.
1853........	Western Psalmodist	Andrew W. Johnson	Cornersville, Tenn.	Nashville, Tenn.
1854........	Aeolian Lyrist	Wm. B. Gillham	Columbia, Tenn.	Cincinnati.
1854........	Timbrel of Zion	T. K. Collins, Jr.		Philadelphia.
1863........	Golden Trumpet	Alexander Auld	Ohio	Cincinnati.
1866........	Christian Harmony	William Walker	Spartanburg, S. C.	Philadelphia.
1867........	New Harp of Columbia	M. L. Swan	Bellefonte, Ala.	Nashville, Tenn.
1872........	The Brethren's Tune and Hymn Book	Benj. Funk, H. R. Holsinger	Virginia Pennsylvania	
1873........	New Baptist Psalmist and Tune Book	John R. Graves		Memphis, Tenn.
1876........	Imperial Harmony	Jesse B. Aikin	Philadelphia	New York and Chicago.
1878........	Olive Leaf	William B. Hauser	Wadley, Ga.	Philadelphia.

CHAPTER XXIII

"OLD HARP SINGERS" OF EASTERN TENNESSEE AND THEIR BOOK

The Harp of Columbia

In eastern Tennessee, in its broad valleys as well as in its hill and mountain country, are found numerous groups of "Old Harp Singers." They got their name from the book they use, one that came out first in 1849 in Knoxville and has been reprinted periodically up to the present day. It was the *Harp of Columbia,* later called the *New Harp of Columbia,* compiled by W. H. and M. L. Swan. From these statements alone it may be seen that it holds a record for longevity second only to that of the *Sacred Harp.*

The oldest copy which is at my disposal for examination is that of the seventh edition, 1855. This copy was lent me by Miss Mary Dent Swan, of Chattanooga, who is of the M. L. Swan connection. Its first cover page (facing page 326) reads "Seventh Edition, 5,000 copies, The Harp of Columbia, A New System of Sacred Music; With Notes for Every Sound, and Shapes for Every Note. The Science Made Easy, Rules abbreviated, and Old Characters Abandoned for New Principles. The Seven Letters Variously Representing Nine Lines and Spaces, and the Four Flats and Four Sharps Transposing the Notes to Different Letters, Lines and Spaces, Are all Dispensed with, for the Easy Name and Shape of two Notes, etc. Containing Anthems, Odes and Church Music, Original and Selected, By W. H. & M. L. Swan, Knoxville, Tenn., Published by M. L. Swan, and for Sale by Merchants Generally in East

Tennessee. Printed at Kinsloe's Steam Power Press Printing Establishment. 1855."

The Harp of Columbia has 222 pages, ten of which are devoted to "Elementary Principles" and other preliminaries. Its unique note shapes are reproduced on page 337 following. The book is divided into the then usual three parts, church music, singing school music, and anthems. There is not a key signature in the whole book. The singer had to take the compiler's word for it that "the last note in the bass is always the keynote." If that note was shaped like an hourglass the tune was in major; if it was square the tune was in minor. And from the position of those notes the singer could orient himself and "key" the song.

Swan as Composer of Many Songs

In examining the songs we are at once struck with the large number of songs whose composer is given as "Swan." There are fifty-two of them. The very size of this figure led to the suspicion that "Swan" (probably W. H. Swan), was exaggerating his part in the making of the songs. And when I ascertained that three of the "Swan" songs, "China," "Egypt," and "Solomon's Song," had appeared in the *New England Harmony* (1801) of the rather prominent but much earlier New England composer and compiler, Timothy Swan (1758-1842), my suspicion switched. I wondered if we had perhaps in our W. H. Swan a southern relative or descendant of the Massachusetts Scotchman, an offspring who had added the accomplishments of his forbear to his own without going to the trouble of making any distinction between the two. I shall leave it to others to confirm or to dissipate this suspicion. Among the other songs six are credited to "M. L. Swan" and the number grew in the post-Civil War editions to fourteen. One indication that at least part of the songs claimed by

W. H. Swan and marked "Swan" were composed in that eastern Tennessee region may be found in the names of local towns and rivers given to certain compositions. Such titles are "Athens," "Albany," "Holston," and "Spring Place" (an "Old Harp" singing center near Knoxville). As to the source of some of the other "Swan" songs, it is noticed, bearing in mind the New Englander's "China" and "Egypt," that others with the same "Swan" signature were "Texas," "Iowa," "Delaware," "Peru," "Mexico," "Cuba," "Persia," "France," "Greenland," "Africa," and "Hamburg." Was W. H. consciously carrying on Timothy's geographical-names tradition? And if so, why?

That the eastern Tennessee Swans knew and liked Caldwell's *Union Harmony,* which was also, as we have seen, an eastern Tennessee book and in use for some years before the *Harp of Columbia* came out, is indicated by the forty-four songs of the Caldwell book which reappear in Swan's. The fourteen songs in the *Harp of Columbia* which are ascribed to Caldwell were reduced to seven in the *New Harp of Columbia.* The three songs credited to Jackson, of *Knoxville Harmony* repute, disappeared in the *New Harp.* Of Davisson's songs there are six, William Walker's two, and B. F. White's and J. T. White's one each.

The New Harp of Columbia

In the Preface to the *New Harp of Columbia,* edition copyrighted in 1867, I find the following: "In this, the New Harp of Columbia, the same system of notation is adhered to as in the old Harp." And further on in the same Preface: "Between fifty and one hundred tunes, selected and original, will be found in this that are not in the old Harp. Such tunes as are seldom used have been discarded, and their places filled by others of superior merit."

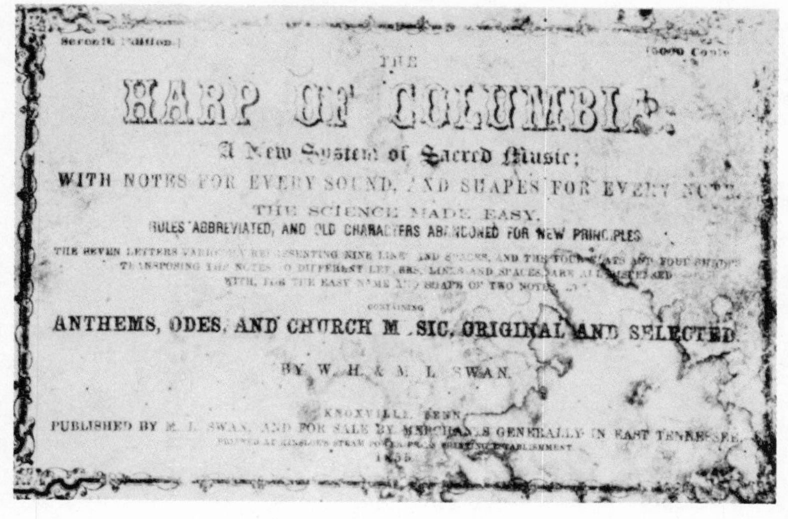

Seventh Edition.]

THE

HARP OF COLUMBIA:

A New System of Sacred Music;

WITH NOTES FOR EVERY SOUND, AND SHAPES FOR EVERY NOTE.

THE SCIENCE MADE EASY.

RULES ABBREVIATED, AND OLD CHARACTERS ABANDONED FOR NEW PRINCIPLES

CONTAINING

ANTHEMS, ODES, AND CHURCH MUSIC, ORIGINAL AND SELECTED.

BY W. H. & M. L. SWAN.

KNOXVILLE, TENN.

PUBLISHED BY M. L. SWAN, AND FOR SALE BY MERCHANTS GENERALLY IN EAST TENNESSEE.

SWAN'S HARP OF COLUMBIA

Cover-page of the Harp of Columbia, *by W. H. & M. L. Swan, seventh edition, Knoxville, Tennessee, 1855, and "Morning Trumpet," a revival "spiritual song" in the* Harp of Columbia.

The *New Harp* is now printed by the Publishing House of the Methodist Episcopal Church, South, at Nashville. Every few years they print off a thousand copies or so and send them to an East Tennessee buyer for the *Old Harp* singers. The plates of the book were inherited from W. T. Berry & Company, the Nashville publishers of the Swan compilation after the Civil War.

Mountain and Valley Singing Conventions of Old Harpers

As I have mentioned above, the *Harp of Columbia* and its successor, the *New Harp of Columbia,* seem to have enjoyed a high degree of popularity in the eastern Tennessee valleys and coves and in the adjoining mountain territory for the entire eighty-two years that have elapsed since its first publication. I have run across its official use at the present time by the "Harp Singer's Convention" of Greene County, Tennessee, which meets once a year at Stone Dam Church near Afton, Tennessee. Leading men are W. S. Bandy, Andy Rader, James Peters, Joe Marshall. Full membership is 244. The name was selected "since nearly all the hymns and tunes with which we were acquainted were written in the New Harp of Columbia." Thus far "No sermons have been preached, . . . no instrumental music has been admitted and no trained choirs or quartets have shared the time."

From the "organization" sheet from which the above quotations have been made, it seems that the Greene County group is the central organization of a still wider activity, for it goes on to state: "The Convention has had a remarkable growth during the twenty-one years (founded in 1907) of its history. Conventions have been held in eighty-two different towns and county churches in East Tennessee, Virginia, and Kentucky. The Greene County Singers have never missed a Fifth

Sunday [in each year] meeting." Harp singings are held three times a year at New Salem Church, New Salem, Tennessee.

O. M. Schantz tells us that the mountain people in the Smoky Mountain National Park region use, in their frequent singings, "a collection of psalm and hymn tunes called the New Harp of Columbia, hence the name of the meetings 'Harp Singings.'"[2]

"Harp Singers" or "Old Harp Singers" is the one by which all groups of users of old song books in the above-mentioned territory are generally known at the present time. And since there has been no other "Harp" used in the eastern Tennessee section, as far as we have been able to learn, it is fair to conclude that Swan's book has given its name to its countless singers for about three generations.

The Swans

Of W. H. Swan's life and identity I have learned little more than that he was probably the uncle of M. L. Swan. From the youngest daughter of M. L. Swan, Ida Morrison Swan, now Mrs. Joe Lenehan, living in Nashville, I have obtained the following, albeit meager, information as to her father. It is meager because her father and mother both died when she was quite young.

Marcus Lafayette Swan (birthplace and date are unknown) sang and played the violin as a youth, but never then used the teaching of music as a profession. September 15, 1853, he married Mary Morrison, a highly educated daughter of well-to-do parents in Bellefonte, Alabama, and made his home in that place. He entered the Confederate army but saw no active service because of his suffering from rheumatism. After the Civil War he returned to Bellefonte, led church music there, and, because of the financial reverses suffered by him, his wife,

[2] *Christian Science Monitor,* June 2, 1930, pp. 1 ff.

and her family during the war, took up the teaching of singing schools as a livelihood. He taught in northeastern Alabama and eastern Tennessee. He died of typhoid fever in Bellefonte, Alabama, in 1869, at the age (so Mrs. Lenehan tells me) of thirty-two. He had made as much as $75,000 on his book, but this money was lost to his heirs soon after his death, by the manipulations of his executors. His grave, in a private burying-ground on the Bellefonte estate, has no gravestone. As to M. L. Swan's forebears, all the information Mrs. Lenehan had was that he was of Scotch-Irish parentage.

From L. L. Swan, a nephew of M. L. living in Chattanooga, I have the following story about his uncle, an anecdote that is too good to be lost: "It seems that Uncle Lafayette had been imbibing a bit one day when he spied on the street a big fellow clad in a new and very loud checked suit. The textile resemblance to the lines and geometrical note shapes of the musician's trade was unavoidable. M. L. approached the fellow, picked out with his finger the 'notes' on his coat and commenced singing them, *'do, mi, sol, sol,'* etc. The man of the new suit, however, his pride grossly insulted, jerked off the coat and threw it to the ground in preparation to cleaning Swan up. The latter, however, far more interested in the practice of his art than in the imminence of a drubbing, followed the musical coat. And by the time its owner had pushed back his shirt-sleeves M. L. was on his knees and busy singing another verse of the musical garment. The big fellow looked on for a few seconds. Then he snatched up his coat and pulled it on with: 'Well, if he's such a dam' fool, I jus' cayn't whup 'im.' "

CHAPTER XXIV

OTHER SEVEN-SHAPE SONG BOOKS

Harmonia Sacra

In 1851 the revised form of the fourth edition of Joseph Funk's *Genuine Church Music* appeared under its new title, *Harmonia Sacra,* printed and bound in his own shop in Mountain Valley, Virginia. The three non-original note shapes used in this book (see page 337 below) were dangerously like Aikin's and had some resemblance also to Auld's.

Since I have already described the book's earlier form, under the title of *Genuine Church Music,*[1] I shall add here merely that the book enjoyed, during the forty-odd years following 1832, nineteen editions comprising a total of about eighty thousand copies; and that it grew in size from the 206 pages of the first edition to a book of 346 pages. All the editions from the fourth on came from the little log print shop and bindery in the Shenandoah Valley hamlet which was first called Mountain Valley and subsequently, shortly after the Civil War, was given its present name, Singer's Glen.

As to the territory in which *Harmonia Sacra*[2] was used I have little to add to what has been said above. It seems that Funk made some attempts shortly before the Civil War to increase its sale in the far South. Charles Beazley, Crawfordsville, Georgia, was a fairly active agent. But the Virginias and North Carolina remained its best market throughout its nineteen editions.

[1] See p. 47 above.

[2] "Hominy Soaker" was the popular Americanizing of the Latin name, the joke of which was not appreciated by Father Funk.

The Western Psalmodist

In 1853 a now-forgotten singing-school teacher, Andrew W. Johnson of Cornersville, Tennessee, published a book called the *Western Psalmodist,* printed in Nashville, "at the Nashville Union Office, No. 69 Cherry Street." Johnson's "new system of notation" is shown on page 337 below. The book has 126 pages, twelve of which are devoted to preliminaries and rudiments. The collection is not notable, and I have found no data as to its use. The Lawson McGhee Library in Knoxville has apparently the only known copy of it. As to the compiler, even his townspeople in Cornersville and his descendants have been unable to tell me anything about him.

The Aeolian Lyrist

In 1854 William B. Gillham, Columbia, Tennessee, published the *Aeolian Lyrist* (printed by Applegate & Co., Cincinnati, and by the Cumberland Presbyterian Board in Louisville) in shapes the three novel ones of which are described as follows:[3] " 'Do' represents an arrow head, 're' represents 'la' with the stem running through the center, and 'si' represents 'mi' with the stem running through the center." From this meager information—I have not seen the *Aeolian Lyrist*—I have reconstructed Gillham's shapes as best I could on page 337 below.

Walker's Christian Harmony

"Singin' Billy" Walker, after his four-shape *Southern Harmony* had been on the market for some thirty years and when it seemed that the future belonged to the seven-shapers, is said to have prayed to God that He might reveal to him a form of notes that would be acceptable to singers. Indeed, a veteran singing-school teacher of northern Georgia, McD. Weams, told me he had been shown the spot where William

[3] By W. T. Dale in the *Musical Million,* XI (1889), 10.

Walker knelt in divine supplication and received the revelation. A different story of the genesis of Walker's shapes was told by his friend, William Hauser, in the *Musical Million* in 1876:[4] "I urged him [Walker] again and again," Hauser declared, "while he was compiling the book, to put it in Aikin's shapes. His last letter on the subject informed me that he tried to get permission to use them, that Aikin consented, but that Collins [Sam C. Collins of the Philadelphia publishing firm] would not. Then he went to work and invented shapes for himself." At any rate, we know that Walker's *Christian Harmony* appeared in 1866 (printed in Philadelphia by Miller's Bible and Publishing House) with a brand-new threesome of notes. "Doe" was an inverted key-stone, "ray" was a quarter-moon and "see" was an isosceles triangle with its base vertical. This was destined to be the last of the shape-note-head variations.

Walker's purpose, as deduced from the Preface, was to provide an improved book that would take the place of the now thirty-year-old *Southern Harmony*. The improvements, according to his Preface, were the adoption of the seven-shape notation and the substantial enlargement of the book by the addition of "more music suitable to church use." Still further examples of "the most beautiful and desirable of modern tunes" were added in the 1873 edition. I cannot find that any other considerable change was made in subsequent years.

In introducing the seven note-syllables and shapes into a territory which had been wedded, through his own books, to the fasola system, he felt it necessary to make an elaborate defense of the move. So he devoted a page following the Preface to telling about the "Seven-Syllable Character-Note Singing, The Quickest and Most Desirable Method Known," and how he came to adopt it.

[4] VII, 55.

He admitted his former preference for the fasola manner. But when he came to teach his "first *normal school,*" he "saw clearly that, as we had *seven distinct sounds* in the scale, we must have, to be consistent, *seven names,*" and he finally chose "the Italian syllables as the most euphonious." "Would any parent having seven children, ever think of calling them by only four names?" seems to have been the question that got no answer and satisfied the objector to the seven-note and seven-shape practice.

A fourteen-page "Rudiments of Music" and a one-page "Dictionary of Musical Terms" are followed by 361 pages of songs and anthems, the latter filling but thirteen pages at the end. Among these songs forty-three bear Walker's name as composer. To his brother David and his son Franklin Boyd Walker is attributed one song each. William Hauser, author of the *Hesperian Harp,* is represented by twenty-two songs, five of which are merely his arrangements. From the *Sacred Harp* authors, B. F. White and E. J. King, he borrowed two and four songs respectively. Leonard P. Breedlove, a Georgia co-worker of White and King, has four songs here. William Caldwell *(Union Harmony)* has five. R. M. McIntosh of Nashville has five. John G. McCurry *(Social Harp)* has three. Ananias Davisson *(Kentucky Harmony)* has two, and John B. Jackson *(Knoxville Harmony)* has one.

The author of the *Christian Harmony* has rendered a service in that he has recorded a number of melodies which he had merely heard sung, knowing nothing further as to their source. Walker's notation is often faulty, and his harmony was often adversely criticized by contemporaries and by those who have followed him. In explaining the unique popularity of his books, all those who seem to have had a right to an opinion attributed it to his judgment in selecting tunes and hymns.[5]

I have found mention of two other books by Walker but have not been able to obtain copies of either. *Southern and Western Harmonist,* a book of one hundred and seventy-six pages, with four-shape notes, published in 1845, is one.[6] *Fruits and Flowers,* a small Sunday-school book published in 1869, is the other.

An estimate of the total sales of Walker's books up to 1876 names 750,000 copies.[7] J. F. Bland, a North Carolina singing teacher, declares that the *Southern Harmony* was among the most popular books in Cleveland and Rutherford counties in his state in the 1870's. W. E. White says that "Here [in the mountain region of North Carolina] with the exception of the primary school books . . . the sales of *Christian Harmony* are more than quadruple that of any other book of the kind. Indeed, the demand for the book is so great that merchants, who do not deal in books, keep it in stock to supply the demand. Music teachers have difficulty in many of the mountain counties in getting [singing] schools to use any other book."[8]

"Thousands and thousands have blessed the name of William Walker who has sent the Southern Harmony into almost every home in the southern land, breaking up the fallow ground and creating . . . a thirsting for sacred music in the masses such as the round-note system never has nor never will accomplish." These are the words of J. A. Downing in the *Musical Million* of 1880.[9] Both of Walker's chief books were popular around Kentucktown (or Kentucky Town), Texas,

[5] See, for example, *Musical Million,* XXVI (1895), 8.

[6] Cf. article by Wm. E. Chute, *Musical Million,* VII (1876), 43.

[7] *Musical Million,* VII (1876), 9.

[8] *Ibid.,* VI (1875), 71.

[9] P. 135.

right after the Civil War.[10] *Christian Harmony* was one of the favorite books of the "Central Arkansas Vocal Musical Convention," which met in Toledo, Cleveland County, Arkansas, in August of 1886.[11] J. H. Morrison, of Hale County, Alabama, tells the *Musical Million* readers of the "devotion of Alabamians to old-fashioned church music such as Father William Walker taught a half century ago."[12] Walker's competitor, the editor of the *Musical Million,* declared editorially in 1887: "To this day his works . . . have a large sale in most of the southern states."[13] *Christian Harmony* was used in the "State Convention" of Louisiana, meeting in Ruston, 1892.[14]

I have personal information that *Fruits and Flowers* was used at Spring Place, Knox County, Tennessee, in 1925. At the present time the Christian Harmony Singing Convention meets at different places around Spartanburg, South Carolina, on the fourth Sunday in August of each year for "all-day singing with dinner on the grounds." D. P. L. Martin, Chesnee, North Carolina, is its president. Other conventions using the same book are held in Rutherford and Buncombe counties, in North Carolina, and in York, Union, and Greenville counties, South Carolina. J. H. Hall, hymnologist and singing teacher, writes in the *Daily News-Record,* Harrisonburg, Virginia, May 10, 1930; "In southern Missouri, organizations have held singings annually for forty-one years. They use the *Christian Harmony* by William Walker." The Alabama State Christian Harmony Musical Association, A. A. Vines, president, held its thirteenth annual three-days convention in Centerville in August, 1932. Singers assembled from nine mid-state counties. The 1931 "Minutes" of the state body announced that there

[10] *Musical Million,* XVII (1886), 42.

[11] *Ibid.,* p. 158.

[12] *Ibid.,* XVIII (1887), 91.

[13] XVIII, 136.

[14] *Ibid.,* XXIII (1892), 12.

would be in these nine counties during the year 1932 fifty-six distinct annual *Christian Harmony* singings with a total of sixty-four full days of song. The oldest local group in the Alabama association is the Warrior River Christian Harmony Musical Association which celebrated its forty-eighth yearly three-day convention in August, 1932, at Harmony Church in Blount County.

The E. W. Miller Company of Philadelphia now sells the *Christian Harmony* at $1.50. This sale is limited largely to people in and around Spartanburg, so Mr. William C. Wetherill of the Miller Company told me.

The Olive Leaf

After Hauser's four-shape *Hesperian Harp* had been used for nearly a third of a century, the veteran teacher and composer joined hands with the much younger Benjamin Turner in getting out the *Olive Leaf,* copyrighted in 1878, notated in Aikin's seven shapes and bearing other signs of the more recent times. Of Hauser's own songs of *Hesperian Harp* vintage, only eight remain. But an orgy of tune making indulged in by Hauser during his post-Civil-War years yielded the *Olive Leaf* forty-eight more songs, making his own songs in this book number fifty-six. William Walker's contributions were reduced to three, Ananias Davisson is represented by only one, William Caldwell and E. J. King disappeared; there are no anthems and but few of those inevitable standbys of pre-Civil-War books like "Idumea," "Imandra," "Rousseau's Dream," and "Royal Proclamation." Naturally, all these eliminations are synonymous with a sharp reduction in five-tone scale tunes, of which I have found but fourteen. Hauser himself composed, in these later years of his life, in a manner that betrayed the workings of the gospel hymn germ. And he used, in the *Olive Leaf,* the songs of a number of others—like Aldine S. Kieffer,[15] T. W. Dennington, and Charles H. Gabriel—all of whom were representative of the same new trend in sacred song.

SEVEN-SHAPE NOTATIONS

	Do	Re	Mi	Fa	Sol	La	Si
AIKIN, 1846 (See p. 320)							
AULD, 1847 (See p. 322)							
SWAN, 1848 (See p. 324)							
FUNK, 1851 (See p. 330)							
GILLHAM, 1854 (See p. 331)							
JOHNSON, 1853 (See p. 331)							
WALKER, 1866 (See p. 331)							

[15] Kieffer's songs are on pp. 192, 222, 239, 260 and 368; Dennington's, p. 314: Gabriel's, p. 317.

CHAPTER XXV

NUMERAL NOTATIONS AND OTHERS USED BY SOUTHERN RURALS

Before continuing the story of the seven-shape books and singing, I want to mention some types of musical "helps to read," other than the shaped-note-head sorts, which had some vogue in the southern states at one time or another. This, largely for the sake of completing the picture which nobody else has yet portrayed. On page 343 below are samples of all the notations mentioned in the following paragraphs.

Harrison's Musical Shorthand

The earliest American alterations of the traditional notation were those of Tufts, spoken of on page 7 above. In the latter part of the eighteenth century Andrew Adgate of Philadelphia, an enterprising promoter of popular music who was linked up with the Uranian Society of that city, published his *Philadelphia Harmony* with notes of the conventional round sort but with their scale relationship indicated by lines running through the note-heads at different angles. During the next three or four decades all the music-notational inventive urge seems to have been expended in the shape-note line. The notes of Charles Woodward found in his *Ecclesiae Harmonia* (second edition copyrighted 1809 in Philadelphia) are a sort of shape-note. But another brand of music-made-easy came out in 1839 in Thomas J. Harrison's *Sacred Harmonicon,* printed by J. A. and U. P. James in Cincinnati. Its notes were merely a succession of figures (1 to 7, *do* being one, *re* being two, etc.), below, between, and above two parallel lines; the lower octave being below the lower line, the middle or usually used octave being between the lines, and the upper octave being above the upper line. The normal-length note (one beat, a quarter note) was the simple figure. Its length was increased by periods before it and decreased by commas under it, it was sharped or flatted by a preceding *s* or *f*, and a rest was simply an *R* with periods and dashes to alter its length. The lowest staff in four-part harmony had the usual name, bass, and was indicated by a *B* between its two lines. The next staff above was designated by an *A* (air), the next by *D* ("double air"), and the uppermost was *C* (counter or treble). The key signature above the upper line was a figure and a letter, the figure indicating the tone on which the octave of the particular key begins and the letter indicating the mode, major or minor. Thus 4G tells us that the tune is in F Major, that is, that it begins on the 4th of the C octave and uses the "grand octave." Likewise 5P tells us that the tune is in G Minor, beginning on the 5th (G) and being in the "plaintive octave" mode. The above terminology will indicate to what lengths Harrison's zeal for simplification carried him, and it will make clear the absence of the usual "dictionary of musical terms" from his *Sacred Harmonicon.* Harrison's musical language was American. By 1851 the book had had seven editions.

Harrison called his notation a sort of musical "short hand." And the appropriateness of the term seems justified when we see such a song as "Mear," four staffs and one line of text, taking up a space only one and a half by five and a half inches of a page of the *Sacred Harmonicon.* With usually two songs to the page, this book is, nevertheless, one of the smallest (four and three quarters by eight and three quarters inches) of its times.

Fillmore and Leonard's Christian Psalmist

Associated with Thomas Harrison in Cincinnati was Elder Augustus D. Fillmore, a Christian (Campbellite) preacher, who afterwards taught singing schools in Kentucky and Tennessee and published song books. Fillmore's first publishing venture was the *Christian Psalmist* (Louisville, 1850, printed by Morton and Griswold) in Harrison's numeral system. In this undertaking he was associated with Silas W. Leonard. The copy which I have examined[1] is of the "eighteenth edition" copyrighted 1850 and 1851 by Silas W. Leonard. But the words "Numeral Edition" on the title-page beneath the title indicate that the *Christian Psalmist* was at that time a popular old (round-note?) book which was also to be had in other notations. Further information is added by William E. Chute: "In 1847 was published in Cincinnati, The Christian Psalmist, by S. W. Leonard and Elder A. D. Fillmore (1823-1870), in round notes, figure notes . . . and patent notes; over 300 hymns, 383 pp. This book went through a large number of editions with revisions and additions. The 18th edition of 1850 has 416 pages and all figure notes. A revised and greatly enlarged edition, published in Louisville, Ky., in 1854, has 844 hymns, 480 pages."[2] Chute says further, "In 1870 was published in Cincinnati by Silas W. Leonard, The New Christian Psalmist, 348 hymns, with figure music, 160 pages."[3] This is the first "tall" tune book we have thus far examined. It is four and one-fourth inches wide by six tall.

Numbers Instead of Note-Heads

In the course of time—I have not been able to find out exactly when, but it was probably in the 1850's—Fillmore

[1] It is from the private library of Dr. George R. Mayfield, Nashville.
[2] *Musical Million,* XV (1884), 76.
[3] *Ibid.,* p. 90.

weakened in his attempts to reform so radically the traditional form of music-symbolizing and invented a notation which retained the numbers but used them instead of the regulation note-heads (with the usual vertical note-handles and flags where needed) on the traditional five-line staff. The first book to have this notation seems to have been the *Christian Choralist,* appearing probably before the Civil War. The second was the *Harp of Zion.* I have a copy of the *New Harp of Zion,* copyrighted by A. D. Fillmore in 1866 and by his son, James H. Fillmore, in 1872, printed in Cincinnati by R. W. Carroll & Company. It is a "long" book of 336 pages, including the usual Rudiments.

Numbers Within Note-Heads

After his father's death in 1870, James H. Fillmore continued teaching and publishing books in the figure notation. But the young man went still one step further in his approach to the round-note standard by placing the figure *within* the round note-head, black in half and whole notes, and white in the black note-heads. Three books *(Songs of Glory, Songs of Gratitude,* and *Praise and Rejoicing*) appeared in this notation between the years 1874 and 1884. And a list furnished me by Mr. Fillmore (who is still the head of the Fillmore Music House of Cincinnati) shows that the total sales of these books were 281,000, of which 94,000 went into the southern states. "They laughed at the figure notation in the North," Mr. Fillmore told me, "but not in the South." The southern market for figure-note books was, according to Mr. Fillmore and to all other information which I have been able to gather, in Kentucky and western Tennessee, territory in which the Filmores, both father and son, had been active teachers of singing schools.

The eighty-one songs in the *New Harp of Zion* which give A. D. Fillmore as composer show that he was a facile tune maker. J. H. Fillmore has but three tunes in that volume. A glance through the subsequent *Songs of Glory,* however, shows that the younger man (now an old man) has been as prolific, along gospel-hymn-making lines, as was his father. I have found the Fillmores' songs in Walker's *Christian Harmony,* Hauser's *Olive Leaf,* and James's *Union Harp.*

Other Devices

Another "Invention for Sight Reading for the Million" is described in Volume IV, page 174, of the *Musical Advocate and Singer's Friend,* a monthly musical journal of music issued in Singer's Glen, Virginia. It consisted simply in designating "do" by thickening the staff line or widening the space where it occurs. This was the device used in 1868 by one V. C. Taylor who, the *Advocate* tells us, "is editor and author of a dozen music books."

Still another scheme[4] to denote the relative scale values was invented in 1883 by C. W. Ray and Charles E. Prior and used in their Sunday-school book, *Spicy Breezes* (192 pages), printed in Philadelphia by John J. Hood. His scheme was to use lines crossing the round note-heads in different directions and combinations. Thus Ray and Prior differed very little from James H. Fillmore.

The Tonic Sol-Fa System

As a much belated successor of John Tufts' letter notation, the Tonic Sol-Fa which was "made in Great Britain" by John Curwen in 1843, came into the United States not long after it gained popularity in England and took root for a time here and there. It is necessary here merely to remind the reader that this system of easy-to-read music notation was essentially a staffless succession in which the tones of the scale were desig-

[4] I have this information from the *Musical Million,* XIV, 105, and XV, 25, 76.

OLD HUNDRED

In sundry notations (other than the shaped note-head sorts heretofore mentioned) devised in America during the past two hundred years.

nated by the initial letters of *do, ray, me* (Curwen's spelling), etc.; that is, by *d, r, m, f, s, l, t* (for ti). It is significant that Theodore F. Seward, a man who, with the Fisk Jubilee Singers and in public school music teaching in eastern cities, had come face to face with the knotty problem of making the traditional notation system understandable to the completely untutored, should be the one to introduce, or try to introduce, this simple system into this country. And it is no less significant that Seward's associate was the West Virginian,

Benjamin C. Unseld, who also had had a part in teaching the Fisk Negroes to sing. Mr. Unseld became a Tonic Sol-Fa enthusiast in the early seventies, was an editor, along with Seward, of the *Tonic Sol-Fa Advocate* in 1881, translated hymn tunes into Tonic Sol-Fa notation for the Negroes in Africa but failed in his attempt to introduce the same notation among the American Negroes at Hampton Institute. The latter part of Unseld's life was spent teaching music in different parts of the South, and he carried his Tonic Sol-Fa faith to the end. But I have found only two mentions of the notation as being in use in that section. One was in Alabama in 1886, where a correspondent of the *Musical Million* wrote that "a few tonic-sol-fa advocates" might be found thereabouts.[5] The other was in North Carolina two years later, where, according to another correspondent of the *Musical Million,* the Tonic Sol-Fa was a force with which the teacher of shape-notes had to contend.[6]

One suggestion (see illustration below) as to graphic helps in solmization was *not* adopted. It was the one offered to the rural reformers facetiously by an Ohio school man of "round-head" persuasion. With a commendable sense of humor, Aldine S. Kieffer, shape-note champion, had a drawing of the suggested "shapes" made and reproduced it in his *Musical Million,* in 1890, Volume XXI, page 153.

"ANIMALISTIC" SCALE

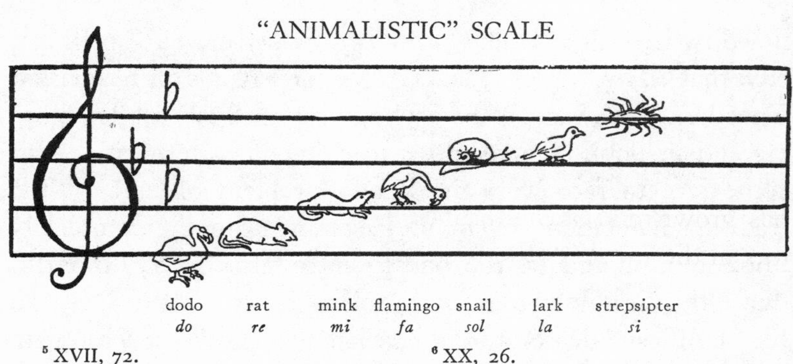

[5] XVII, 72.

[6] XX, 26.

CHAPTER XXVI

NEW STYLES IN SONGS, BOOKS, AND NOTATIONS

"Das Trallern ist bei mir verloren,
Es krabbelt wohl mir um die Ohren
Allein zum Herzen dringt es nicht."
—Goethe, *Faust,* Part II.

The Post-Civil War Period

With the close of the Civil War a new era dawned in the singing practices of the rural South, an era that might be termed that of the gospel-hymn-tinged religious music in shape notation. Naturally the new era was no sudden thing. It came slowly, and the preceding era—that of sedate spiritual songs largely in the four-shape books—receded slowly. It appeared and got a foothold in some communities and sections sooner, whereas other sections were impervious to its novel appeals. And some important groups of singers—notably those who are wedded to the old *Sacred Harp* and to the *New Harp of Columbia*—are, as we have seen, living and singing today in the older era, and are resisting all encroachments of the newer song with a tenacity that is fully comparable to that of the religious zealot of the extreme fundamentalist sort, when confronted with modernism.

I have called the newer trend "gospel-hymn-tinged." It is not "gospel hymn" music as that type is usually understood. It is the old sacred music of the country-South, which has grown and metamorphosed. And one of the early factors in the metamorphosis was the Sunday-school-gospel-hymn epidemic. Later factors were the secular popular songs, the glee club manner, and jazz. But the most important factor from the start in the development of this song as an independent type was doubtless the soon-to-become-practically-universal seven-shape notation of the Aikin brand, which deepened the line between rural and urban music practices and between the established church music style of the big denominations (Baptists, Presbyterians, and Methodists), and that of the little rural denominations. For thus there was that autonomy in shape-note circles that meant a comparatively independent and unauthorized development. I shall try to make clear in the following pages how this came about. And in doing so I shall shift the scene back again to the Shenandoah Valley, the district from which the new movement spread.

Aldine S. Kieffer

Joseph Funk, proponent of the old-time dignity in sacred music, whether in church or in singing school, died in 1862. And when, in 1865, his grandson, Aldine S. Kieffer,[1] was released from a Union prison (through the efforts of his brother-in-law and former companion in singing-school teaching, Ephraim Ruebush, who had been fighting on the Union side) he found the song-book print-shop in Singer's Glen in utter desolation, "a mass of pi" he called it. This publishing plant, in the distribution of Joseph Funk's estate, had fallen to his

[1] Aldine S. Kieffer was the son of Mary (Funk) Kieffer, daughter of Joseph Funk. He was born in 1840 in Saline County, Missouri, where his father died shortly after. His mother took the seven-year-old Aldine back to Singer's Glen, Virginia, where he grew up under the influence of his grandfather. His father, John Kieffer, had been a singing-school teacher, and it was in these schools that the boy learned his first tune, "Christian's Farewell":

> Farewell, my dear brethren, the time is at hand,
> That we must be parted from this social band.

which was then sung to the tune which is now used with "How Firm a Foundation."

Further data as to Kieffer's life may be found in various volumes of the *Musical Million,* especially Vol. XII, p. 177, and Vol. XXXIX, p. 228. See also *History of Virginia* (published by the American Historical Association, New York and Chicago 1924), pp. 179 f.

ALDINE S. KIEFFER

The "Don Quixote of Shape Notes."

sons,[2] who rehabilitated the shop and continued the publication of the editions of *Harmonia Sacra.*

The Musical Million

But the new times belonged to the next generation, and of this younger generation Aldine Kieffer became a leader. One of the first signs of his leadership was his founding of the *Musical Million,* a monthly musical periodical devoted to the cause of rural music, singing schools, singing-school teachers, the songs and song books that they used, and to shape-notes. The *Musical Million* was not an entirely new thing. It had been preceded by Joseph Funk and Sons' *Southern Musical Advocate and Singer's Friend,* which had been born in Singer's Glen in 1859, had suspended during the Civil War, and had resumed in the later sixties only to discontinue definitively in August, 1869. Four months later all the subscribers of the defunct *Advocate* were presented with a six months' subscription to the *Musical Million and Fireside Friend,* whose first issue appeared in January, 1870, published by the Patent Note Publishing Co., with Aldine Kieffer doing the chief editorial work. In 1872 the Patent Note Publishing Company was dissolved and a new company, Ruebush, Kieffer & Co. (Ephraim Ruebush, Aldine Kieffer, and John W. Howe), was organized with headquarters a few miles away from "the Glen" in Dayton. This firm exists today as the Ruebush-Kieffer Co. From 1870 the *Musical Million* appeared uninterruptedly for over forty years. From the start it was of inestimable value in instilling in the growing legions of rural music teachers—and that meant singing-school teachers only—a sense of solidarity and professional self-respect. And the

[2] Then living were John Funk, carpenter and farmer; Timothy Funk, farmer, music teacher, Baptist preacher, and bookbinder; Solomon Funk, farmer, Baptist preacher and music compositor; and Benjamin Funk, school teacher.

direction of its influence was almost exclusively to the south, southwest, and west.

Aldine Kieffer has been called "the apostle of musical democracy," "the defender of popular notation and mass singing," and, by those who ridiculed the shape notation, "The Don Quixote of Buckwheat Notes." And it is true that he never hesitated to attack the wind-mills of the "round-heads." The ridicule that was heaped on Kieffer by those in the round-note camp who chanced to hear of him was more than offset by the love and appreciation of those who believed in the shape-note cause. They named babies after him. I have run across three of them, G. Kieffer Vaughan, of Lawrenceburg, Tennessee; Kieffer Oslin Hammer, of Arley, Alabama, and Kieffer Oslin Cowart, of Winston County, Alabama. "To him is due more credit than to any one other person for getting the character-note system introduced in the Southland and elsewhere," Daniel F. Blake, an old associate of Kieffer's wrote me. Editorially Kieffer defended the notation of the rurals vigorously and continuously for the rest of his life. He was also, perhaps primarily, a poet. Among his most popular song poems are "My Mountain Home," "Grave on the Green Hillside," and the war poem, "To my Blanket." He is the author of the words to "Twilight Is Falling," which, in its musical setting by B. C. Unseld has become as familiar to rural singers all over the South as is "Home, Sweet Home." His early poems are collected in a volume called *Hours of Fancy,* published by Ruebush, Kieffer & Co., Dayton, Virginia, 1881.

The *Musical Million,* its title indicating its appeal to the great masses, grew quickly from an eight-page to the sixteen-page journal that it remained for over three decades. Its first page usually contained one of Kieffer's poems, and then followed a number of pages of "chaste literature" of the solid and often moralizing sort that was usual in those days. The editorial page was dominated by Kieffer, and his articles always took the side of the masses as against the classes, the country against the cities, the country notation as against the "monkish" notation used by the "round-heads," congregational singing as against the "paid choir," singing schools and, later, singing in the public schools as against private vocal instruction, music and other sorts of idealism versus materialism in education, and ten commandments versus those who broke them, etc., etc.[3] A part of each issue was devoted to reports of music teachers "in the field." These reports, though naturally a little heavy with optimism as to the sale of the Ruebush-Kieffer song books, came from all points south and west, that is, all rural points. The reports must have been a strong factor in integrating the hundreds of contributors with the thousands of readers. And those very contributions form, in their sum total, a running history of the rural song movement which is uniquely valuable to the historian of culture.

Little Books for Big

The old before-the-Civil-War tune books were, as we have seen, big and comprehensive. Each was a book for all purposes. This we have observed in the fact that it always contained rudiments, explanations of musical terms, and big collections of songs for church use (in "part one"), for "schools and societies" (in "part two"), and a dozen or so anthems in "part three."

This pattern has now disintegrated. The big thick book has given way to the little thin one, the comprehensive one to the specialized one, the few books to the many, and the

[3] Musical virtuosity received scanty mention in the columns of the *Million*. The great concertizers sometimes got a line or two. Richard Wagner, whose greatest productions came out during the early life of the *Million*, was not mentioned once.

prostrate (long) books to the erect, or tall, ones. Specialization has brought forth separate books. In the place of the old rudiments appeared those called "music readers" and "voice culture" and where the old rudimentary pages have remained at the beginning of a book here and there, they are dignified by some such title as "theoretical statements." In place of the regular old one-page "Dictionary of Musical Terms" has come a separate book with similar title.

Specialization and Sifting

Specialization in the songs themselves resulted in the appearance of separate books for congregational church use, for singing schools, for Sabbath schools, for "day [public or private] schools," and for church choirs. The sedate old church songs have been sifted. Many of the oldest and most doleful in tune and text have disappeared. The war against "minor tunes" has been all but won by those who favor the more optimistic modes. The remaining few songs of the old type ("Mear," "Old Hundred," "Nettleton," "Lenox," and the like), have been preserved in shape-note form and for the rurals largely in the hymnals of those denominations (Methodist, Baptist, and Presbyterian) whose publishing houses issue a special shape-note edition for the use of their country congregations. The older music "for singing schools and societies" also has changed in the manner spoken of above, and it is presented in books made especially for such organizations. But that form of song known as the "fuguing tune" is already on its way toward oblivion, its place being taken slowly by a new sort of vocal excitement which I shall describe later. The old anthems ("Claremont," "Judgment," "Easter," "Farewell," "Heavenly Vision," "Ode to Science," etc., have gone the way of all mundane things and in their place has come a slim book of anthems, independent, for the church choirs, these anthems being the handiwork of contemporary music makers.

The song-book-making activities at Singer's Glen illustrate well the whole trend. The first post-Civil-War book that came from the hand-press of Joseph Funk's sons through the activities of Ruebush and Kieffer was the *Christian Harp,* a little four-and-a-half-by-six-inch book in paper binding, with a hundred songs on 128 pages, intended for Sunday schools and revivals. In this collection the rudiments have shrunk to two pages. The songs are characterized by a new note of optimism. It is felt in the tunes by the prevalence of major modes, and a shallow and instrumentally influenced melodism. This instrumental influence—coming from the melodeon and the Sunday-school reed organ—appears in the melodic jumps (bigger now than formerly), the greater pitch compass of the average song, and the jumpy, syncopated note successions. Not a fuguing tune in the book. A relic of this form is the occasional song in which one voice takes a recess for a measure or two. There are some simple songs for children, in the part following page 65, that have been borrowed from the Kindergarten stock. But awkwardness in the fitting of the traditional phraseology to such childlike tunes is seen in such lines as

> Fight on, ye little soldiers,
> The battle you shall win.

But sometimes the stock phrases fit the new environment as

> Savior, like a shepherd lead us
> Much we need thy tend'rest care.

There are no more than half a dozen of the really old-time sober songs in the book. Three that I am sure of are "Heaven Is My Home," "We Shall Meet," and "Saints Bound for Heaven." There are but two tunes in the book with minor modes. And there are but two by Aldine Kieffer. Of this book 168,000 copies were sold during the ten years following its publication.

Other books of a similar sort issued in succession by the Funks from Singer's Glen and by the Ruebush-Kieffer Company in the Funk notation, up to 1876 were *Song-Crowned King* (1869), *Glad Hosannas* (1871), *Golden City Songsters* (1871), *The Coronet, The Day-School Singer, Glen Chorals, Starry Crown,* and *Melodies of Praise* (1876).

The Case of Singer's Glen

But while all this publishing activity was going on, an important event was approaching and a little behind-the-scenes shape-note drama was about to be played in Singer's Glen. For years before 1877 the Singer's Glen and Dayton folk had been reading the handwriting on the wall. They had seen William Walker recognize Jesse Aikin's ownership of the Aikin shapes. They had realized that the Funk shapes were in reality nothing but Aikin's printed at a different angle. They had seen one successful book after another published in the Philadelphian's notation. And they admitted (to themselves) that the latter shapes were, graphically speaking, superior to Funk's. And, finally, they came to realize that the main reason why Aikin had not insisted on his assumed and perhaps real rights long before was that the publications from the Glen had not, aside from *Harmonia Sacra* and before the seventies, amounted to much.

"But one day in the early fall of 1877," Daniel F. Blake, who was then a typesetter in the Funk plant, told me in a letter, "our mail carrier deposited at the office (in Singer's Glen) a personage whose age must have been close to seventy years; gray hair, almost white, and a Van Dyke beard covered his head and face. He was dressed in a Prince Albert coat and vest, gray trousers, shoes with spats and a high-crowned derby hat; he carried a light overcoat on his arm, a gold-headed cane in one hand and a light travelling grip in the other. That person was JESSE B. AIKIN.

"There had been some correspondence previously, about stopping the printing of books in the Funk shapes, but it had not been satisfactory to either of the interested parties. Now Prof. Aikin had come for a 'show-down.' Kieffer told me that it was a hot, continuous word battle, but he knew from the beginning Funk's shapes would lose. After practically an all-day session had been held, Prof. Aikin got to his feet and said: 'Well, I will go home and have my lawyer get a restraining order forbidding any one using the Funk shapes.' and in a hasty, hasty way, started to leave the room.

"They stopped him and in the next hour an agreement was reached, that as fast as the printed books on hand were sold, they would discontinue printing certain books, no longer selling, and would have plates made of all new books published and of those old ones that were still selling, using Aikin's shapes, and having the plates made . . . by Armstrong [Aikin's electrotyper] in Philadelphia.

"Yes, he intimidated" the Funk's, Ruebush and Kieffer who had used these shapes for so many years and, "innocent of patent and copyright law, never dreamed of being haled into court because their father had conceived and used three shapes for helping the world to sing music easily. . . ."

The readers of the *Million* and the musical public of the South knew nothing of this drama. They had read only, for months before, that "a great centennial work" (so called because of its coincidence with the hundredth anniversary of the United States) was in the offing, namely, "the adoption of one set of character notes" in the entire southern field. But they could hardly have realized at that time the importance of the part in this merging process taken by the Singer's Glen and Dayton people. From the distance of more than fifty years afterwards we can see it better. We can see the force of the most aggressive shape-note book publishing house joined with the force of the one journal of far-reaching influence in the South, the one journal that was, so to speak, the official organ of rural music, as the greatest single factor in the unification of notation. And in this unification we can see the removal of an important hindrance to the union, though perhaps only a moral union, of all the forces in the South's rural singing field. We can see that the rural South, from the day Jesse Aikin left Singer's Glen, was on its way toward learning the same musical language printed in the same musical "script," the well-nigh universal country-song vernacular today and for more than thirty years back.

CHAPTER XXVII

BENJAMIN UNSELD AND THE NORMAL SCHOOLS

The First Normal Music School

But books, boosting, and organization were not all the boons needed by the southern country singers after the Civil War. They needed also singing-school teachers, more and better ones. Aldine Kieffer and his associates saw this need. They saw ignorant men at the head of singing schools, and the pupils of such teachers becoming, in turn, teachers of other schools—a succession that promised no advancement, to say the least. For a correction of a condition similar to this in the Northeast certain fosterers of popular singing—in the wake of Lowell Mason—had established, even before the Civil War, what they called "normal music schools." Aldine Kieffer saw in this sort of movement a means of betterment of the ignorant-teacher situation in the South, and he made up his mind that there should be a normal school in the Shenandoah Valley.

While he was looking for the proper person to head such a school, Theodore F. Seward, editor of the *New York Musical Gazette,* suggested B. C. Unseld, an associate of his, as one qualified for the position. Kieffer met Unseld in 1873, and plans for the South's first normal music school were made. Unseld was found to be in many ways an ideal man for the place. He was a native of the South, of West Virginia German stock, an amiable personality, and a thorough student of music. His only defect, from the character-note viewpoint, was that he was a "round-noter" with a tonic sol-fa hobby. But Unseld and Kieffer compromised on that point by deciding that the proposed normal school should teach both round and shape notes and that even Unseld's hobby might be admitted as a "course" in the school.

Early in August, 1874, the Virginia Normal Music School —now generally looked upon as having been the very first of its sort in the South[1]—began its session at New Market in the Shenandoah Valley with Unseld as principal and P. J. Merges assisting. Its courses were listed as harmony, thorough bass, piano, organ, voice building, reading of round notes, of tonic sol-fa system and of seven-shape notes, practice in church psalmody, glee singing, and oratorio.[2]

The Clash of Notations

The first session, of only a few weeks, saw a clash of notations. And the shape-notes naturally got the worst of it. But Kieffer was not to be downed. So he saw to it that shape-notes were to receive more attention at the second session, in 1875. And when this shape-note emphasis drove away from the normal school those who adhered to the round-notes, Kieffer took his medicine and laid the smaller attendance in part to the fact that the school was held in July before the farmers, "the bulk of the character-note people," had "laid their crops by" and were thus free to attend. With subsequent sessions Kieffer made his point, and Unseld and others learned that they had to teach prospective teachers of the southern rurals in the southern rural musical language.

For eight years Unseld led the Virginia Normal Music School, subsequently held in Dayton. The school then continued under various principals and eventually became identified with the music department of the Shenandoah Collegiate

[1] William Walker claimed (in the introduction to his *Christian Harmony*) to have taught normal schools before this time. Whether or not he stretched the meaning of the word "normal"—as it was often stretched, after that, to cover also ordinary singing schools where some teachers might be in attendance—I have no way of determining.

[2] *Musical* Million, VII, 58.

BENJAMIN S. UNSELD

Composer of "Twilight is Falling," teacher, and principal of the South's first normal school for rural singing teachers.

Institute which is now Shenandoah College of Dayton, Virginia, an institution which, in its emphasis on musical education, if not on shape-notes, is carrying on the traditions of its founders. And it is significant that the music instruction in this college is largely in the hands of the great-grandchildren and the great-great-grandchildren of Joseph Funk.

Wide Influence of the Normal Schools

That those early normal schools were the right thing at the right time and place is proved by their fruitfulness. There has been hardly a singing-school teacher of any standing in the entire southern shape-note field during the past four or five decades who cannot trace his music-educational inspiration directly or indirectly to the Shenandoah Valley normal schools.

Their "direct" influence was, naturally, on those who attended. But when we see that those in attendance were (or became) rural teachers in practically every state and section of the South; and when we see many of those teachers establishing, in due course of time, normal schools of their own, here, there, and everywhere; and when we then see even a third "crop" of singing-school and normal-school teachers springing up from the same seed, then we may understand better what I mean by the "indirect" inspiration which swept far and persistently from the Shenandoah schools.

A few examples may clinch the point. B. C. Unseld himself, influenced largely by his activities in the Valley, deserted the eastern cities and the round-notes and gave the bulk of his life's energies to the rural South. For decades he held other normal schools in North Carolina, Kentucky, Tennessee, and Missouri. And during the last eleven years of his life (he died in 1923) his energies were devoted to the hundreds of rural shape-note singers and singing teachers who studied at the Vaughan Conservatory, Lawrenceburg, Tennessee.

Among Virginia normal students were many who afterward became leaders in every state of the South,[3] numerous teachers of normal schools, ten compilers and publishers of song books, and eleven prolific composers of sacred songs.

By way of illustrating the spread of the idea of normal schools I offer information gleaned from the columns of the *Musical Million*. In 1894 that journal tells of seven normals taught by Daytonians in six states. In 1895 there were six in four states; 1897, seven in six states; 1898, thirteen in eight states, and in 1899 eleven in eight states. All the states south of the Potomac and the Ohio, with the exception of Florida, and as far west as Texas and Indian Territory were represented.

New Song Books Made in Dayton

Unseld was also important as an editor of new books issued from Dayton beginning with 1877. The nature of this series of publications can be understood sufficiently if I give some data as to three books: *Temple Star, Royal Proclamation* and *Star of Bethlehem*. All three might be looked upon as representing a transition stage in composing, compiling, and printing. They all were of the old prostrate, or long, form, six and three quarters by nine and a half inches, with less than two hundred pages. They all retained the earlier section

[3] A few of these leading teachers were, in what might be called the first generation, E. T. Hildebrand, George B. Holsinger, Sam W. Beazley, D. M. Click, A. B. Funk, A. J. Showalter, J. H. Hall, E. P. Hauser, and W. M. Weakley. For a "second generation" I present the following names taken from lists of successful teachers, Dayton inspired, which I found in the *Musical Million* volumes for the early nineties: P. M. Argenbright, W. L. Anderson, J. D. Brunk, J. D. Burkholder, W. C. Blagg, J. M. Bowman, J. C. Brown, D. J. Cook, F. M. Dilley, B. C. Eackle, E. B. Funkhouser, J. B. Gochenour, J. S. H. Good, H. S. Gruver, J. M. Good, Thomas C. Hayes, A. B. Helzel, E. T. Hildebrand, J. H. Howard, J. W. Jones, M. F. Kearnes, S. H. Koontz, G. E. Leonard, A. E. Long, T. J. Sites, J. M. Lutz, S. A. Myers, G. E. Moore, E. W. McMullen, B. C. Miller, J. W. Morris, J. J. O'Neal, J. M. Powell, S. J. Oslin, T. L. Shaver, J. D. Shaver, J. A. Stover, J. H. Showalter, W. S. Snyder, W. H. Ruebush, J. H. Ruebush, J. D. Vaughan, W. S. Weaver, and R. C. Welborne.

devoted to Rudiments. They were all composites of three different sorts of songs. But those sorts were now for (1) singing schools, (2) church singing, and (3) Sunday school singing, with about equal space devoted to each. There was a set of anthems, too, in each. But the old "inevitables" were gone and in their place was a group of anthems composed by contemporary musicians, Unseld, Seward, Bradbury, Root, etc. The first of this trio of books, *Temple Star* (1877), was printed in old dispersed notation, four staffs with the tune on the next staff above the bass, but it now received the new name "soprano." In the second and third books the approach to the present-day usage—bass and tenor on one staff and soprano and alto on another—was made in a number of tunes.

The Temple Star

The *Temple Star* was compiled by Aldine S. Kieffer assisted by B. C. Unseld and J. H. Tenney. Kieffer has thirty-five songs in the collection, to most of which he composed both words and music. Unseld has fifteen and Tenney has ten. Other contemporary and then recent song makers generously represented are Bradbury, Mason, and the southerner, J. G. Douthit. The popular old songs that were to be found in almost every book before the Civil War are almost entirely absent, and those that remain are to be found among the nine (only) songs in the minor mode.

The Royal Proclamation

The *Royal Proclamation* (named for the popular old tune) came out in 1886 under the hands of Kieffer and William B. Blake. Its compilers made a point of selecting songs that were not in the *Temple Star,* so that it would supplement and not supplant the earlier book. The prolific Kieffer has sixteen songs in this book.

The Star of Bethlehem

J. H. Hall, J. H. Ruebush, and Kieffer were the editors of the *Star of Bethlehem,* which appeared in 1889. Jacob Henry Hall was one of the Virginia Normal Music School's "first generation" of pupils. Coming from musical Scotch and German parentage, his first active tonal experience was a mouth organ. Then a German accordeon, the singing schools of Timothy Funk and of H. T. Wartman, the normals of Unseld, and instruction by Dana, Root, Clippinger, and others, made the musician. The *Star of Bethlehem* was his first considerable accomplishment in compiling. But in the years that followed, a large number of his books were published by Ruebush, Kieffer and Company.[4] He has been a successful leader of normal schools, many of which went under the National Normal School of Music title, in twenty states. He is still active in his profession.

James Hott Ruebush is not only a Singer's Glen product—born there in 1863—but also a scion of the Joseph Funk clan.[5] His education was acquired at Otterbein University, the Grand Conservatory (New York), and through private work with such masters as Bartlett, Root, Palmer, and Matthews. In his younger years he taught music at the Shenandoah Collegiate Institute in Dayton and was director of music at Kee Mar College in Hagerstown, Maryland. Since 1908 he has been in Dayton as head of the (now) Shenandoah College (United Brethren) School of Music and as business manager of the college. His musical influence has spread also through the many song books and theoretical works that have been brought out by the Ruebush-Kieffer Company, of which he is now

[4] Mr. Hall is author of *Biography of Gospel Song and Hymn Writers,* (New York, Revell, 1914), a book that stands high in its field. It has furnished me a deal of data in the writing of this book.

[5] Ephraim Ruebush, his father, married Lucilla Kieffer, granddaughter of Joseph Funk and sister of Aldine Kieffer.

the head, and through the numerous normal schools which he has led for the past four decades in practically every state of the South.

The *Star of Bethlehem,* whose general aspects I have already described, contained thirty-one songs composed by Hall, eleven by Kieffer, seven by Ruebush and four by Unseld.[6]

The Southern Shape-Note Boom

I should add here that during the last quarter of the nineteenth century two other groups commenced their attempts to benefit from the southern shape-note boom. One group was that of the big non-denominational publishers in the North and the East. And their efforts are well exemplified by the appearance, in 1876, of a big book called *Imperial Harmony,* compiled by Aikin, Main, and Allen and published by Biglow and Main in New York. The publishers of the famous and uniquely popular *Gospel Hymns* also saw their opportunity among the rural whites in the South and made shape-note editions of their whole series. The other source of shape-note competition was the denominational publishing houses of the South, especially the Methodists, Baptists, and Cumberland Presbyterians, whose publishing concerns hastened to get out shape-note editions of their hymnals and other song books to supply the demands of their rural congregations.

Influence of the Showalters and Their Georgia Publishing House

Outside of Dayton itself, the most important point from which southern rural song spread was Dalton, Georgia, the

[6] Among the other song books issued by the Dayton people during the 1877-1900 period were *Singing School Tribute, Pearls of Truth in Song, Zion Songster, New Starry Crown, New Melodies of Praise, Shining Light, Sweet Fields of Eden, Sharon's Dewy Rose, Last Words, Sabbath Bells, Temperance Harp, Gabriel's Sunday School Songs, Gems of Gladness, Triune Hymnal, Messenger of Song, Choicest Gems and Fountain of Praise.* They issued also a number of instruction books.

adopted home of A. J. Showalter and the town where the A. J. Showalter Company, music-book publishers to the present day, was established in 1885. And it is quite significant, in this connection, that the founder of the concern was not only a native son (born 1857) of the same Rockingham County in the Shenandoah Valley that gave forth so many singers and song books, but that he was also a direct descendant of that German-American, Heinrich Funck (or "Henry Funk" as he englished himself), the first Mennonite bishop in this land and sire of the musical Funks of Virginia.[7]

Anthony Johnson Showalter's father was a singing-school teacher and composer of songs. The boy's first musical study was in the Virginia Normal Music School under Unseld, and he later studied with Palmer, Merges, Root, and others; still later he studied for a period in Europe. He had taught for some time when he was sent to Dalton, Georgia, as an agent of the Ruebush-Kieffer Company. There, a year later, he founded the firm that soon became one of the leading music-publishing firms in the South and still bears his name.

Mr. Showalter's activities were divided among his three interests: composing, song-book making, and teaching, in all

[7] The steps in the descent were Bishop Henry Funk—Henry Funk again—Elizabeth Funk, who became Mrs. Jacob Showalter (originally "Schowalder")—Anthony Showalter—John A. Showalter—A. J. Showalter.—Seven generations beginning with the 1719 arrival of Heinrich Funck at the port of Philadelphia. William J. Showalter, assistant editor of the *National Geographic Magazine* and descendant of the same northern Virginia branch of the Funk-Showalters, is deeply interested in tracing the source of the pronounced musical bent of the family. My own feeling is that, in a family that was so German, so deeply religious, so generally cultured and so numerous, a considerable musical ingredient was inevitable. William J. Showalter also calls my attention to the prominent singer, Edna Blanche Showalter, pupil of David Bispham, concert artist with John Philip Sousa, and principal singer in Savage's production of *The Girl of the Golden West.* Miss Showalter is of the Virginia line.

I have gained the rest of my genealogical information from *A Brief* [874-page!] *History of Bishop Henry Funck,* etc., by A. J. Fretz, Elkhart, Indiana, Mennonite Publishing Company, 1899; and from T. S. Shope, present president of the A. J. Showalter Company, Dalton, Georgia.

A. J. SHOWALTER

An outstanding personality in the making of songs for the rural South. Mr. Showalter's specialty was tune-making. "Leaning on the Everlasting Arms," is his. After supplying his Dalton, Georgia, publishing firm with tunes for nearly four decades, he died, leaving over a thousand of them still unpublished.

of which he was eminently successful. To his fruitfulness as a composer, the more than a thousand of his songs in many books will testify.

Mr. T. S. Shope, now president of A. J. Showalter Company, told me that his firm still had many hundreds of Showalter's songs in manuscript form, which the firm is publishing from time to time. "Showalter used to come to the office before breakfast," Mr. Shope said, "and compose a song or two. After he had written them he would try them on the office piano." Among Showalter's numerous published songs his "Leaning on the Everlasting Arms" has been uniquely popular. Showalter's energy in compiling is seen in the forty-odd song books that his firm has produced in the forty-five years of its existence. It is pertinent to note here that Showalter's cosmopolitan musical background had made him somewhat antagonistic to shape-notes. But here in Georgia he was in a rural environment so devoted to that notation that he found it necessary to put away his prejudices. He published most of his books in both round and shape notations, and at the present time the Showalter Company sells five of the shape-note books to one of the round-note sort. Total sales of song books by this concern have been estimated at five million copies.

Showalter's teaching—that inevitable adjunct to rural song-book selling—took the form of normal schools, very many of them, throughout the southern states but primarily in South Carolina, Georgia, Alabama, Mississippi, Arkansas, and Texas. His popularity as a leader of singing is illustrated by his having been chosen to lead an enormous chorus of country singers at the Southeastern Fair of 1905 in Atlanta. One day of the fair was set aside for music and Showalter was in charge. "He assembled all the singers in the southern states, thousands of country singers, and got $500 for his day's work," McD. Weams, a Georgia singing-school teacher, told me. It seems that this was the outstanding exhibition or field day of all time for the shape-noters. Mr. Showalter died September 15, 1924, in Chattanooga, Tennessee.

An idea of the sort of book Showalter put out may be gained from an examination of his *Work and Worship* (1886) and its elaboration which came out two years later under the title *Class, Choir and Congregation,* the latter having been the firm's most popular book with a total of four hundred thousand copies sold by 1911.

Both *Work and Worship* and *Class, Choir and Congregation* are of the erect form and the size, five and a quarter inches wide by eight inches tall, which has, since the 1880's, become the standard throughout the rural South. This tall form of book came in at the same time the old dispersed (4-staff) harmony gave way to the condensed (2-staff) arrangement. The latter was manifestly easier for instrumentalists to read, though harder for singers. The two books under consideration were among the first in shape-notes to condense their parts. In the earlier book there is no pagination, but the 165 songs are numbered. In the later one the same songs appear with others added, making 278, and there is in this book also a large group of well selected secular songs. Both books have a set of rudiments.

In the songs themselves, the sacred ones, we find little to be enthusiastic about. The gospel-hymn blight has taken almost complete possession. Among the eighteen songs by Showalter there are but few that rise above the general quality level. The twenty-five songs by the co-editor, J. H. Tenney, the "Onward, Christian Soldier" man, are fully as eventless. And the same must be said of the interspersed works of other southern tune makers—Kieffer, Davis, Dale, Leonard, J. B. Vaughan, and the like. And here we find the first excessive use of the "blood" theme. The bloody side of the Christian redemption plan was early emphasized by Lowell Mason in his "There is a fountain filled with blood." Lowry's "Nothing but the Blood of Jesus," Hoffman's "Are you washed in the blood," Excell's "Will you be washed in the blood," Hoffman-Perry's "The Precious blood," and Hoffman-Showalter's "I am washed in His blood"—these are all to be found in the "Index of Subjects" among the "blood of Christ" songs. It is difficult to account for this sanguinary specialization. But it probably did have some "revivalistic" value.

Showalter's "Leaning on the Everlasting Arms" appears in *Class, Choir, and Congregation.* Its unique subsequent popularity seems to have come partly from the Hoffman text, which is happy and religiously comforting, with simple ideas couched in naïve phrases and with the title phrase repeated often enough to form more than half of each stanza; and partly from the effective fit that Showalter gave the words to his tune.

CHAPTER XXVIII

RURAL SHAPE-NOTE SONG BOOKS BY THE MILLION

Publishers of Seven-Shape Song Books

A list of the present-day southern publishing companies who put out song books in the seven-shape notation follows: Bacon, George W., White Pine, Tennessee; Bateman, B. B., Knoxville, Tennessee; Benson, John T., Publishing Co., Nashville, Tennessee; Central Music Co., Little Rock, Arkansas (merged, 1930, with the Hartford Music Co., Hartford, Arkansas); Cornelius, R. H., Fort Worth, Texas; Florida Song Book Co., Tallahassee, Florida; Gainus Bros., Attalla, Alabama; Grisham, R. N., Ellisville, Mississippi; Hartford Music Co., Hartford, Arkansas; Lincoln's New Songland Co., Dallas, Texas; Moore, J. L., Bethlehem, Georgia; Morris and Henson, Atlanta, Georgia; Quartet Music Co., Fort Worth, Texas; Ruebush-Kieffer Co., Dayton, Virginia; Sebren, George W., Asheville, North Carolina; Showalter, A. J., Company, Dalton, Georgia; Showalter Publishing House, Memphis, Tennessee; Sisk Music Co., Toccoa, Georgia; Slater, Will W., Texarkana, Arkansas; Spear and Brock, Athens, Alabama; Stamps-Baxter Music Co., Chattanooga, Tennessee, and Dallas, Texas; Stanley-Gardner Co., Saltillo, Mississippi; Teachers' Music Co., Hudson, North Carolina; Trio Music Co., Waco, Texas, and Oklahoma City, Oklahoma; Vaughan, James D., Lawrenceburg, Tennessee; Vaughan, John B., Music Co., Athens, Georgia; Way of Truth Publishing Co., Brownwood, Texas; Weams, McD. Rome, Georgia; Winsett, R. E., Chattanooga, Tennessee.

This list includes all, as far as I have been able to ascertain, of those southern firms who put out such books. It does not, however, include the various denominational publishing firms or those northern concerns which send shape-note books into the southern territory. There is a great variation in the size and importance of the different firms in the list. About half of them do their own printing and book-binding. The rest are what are called the "little publishers"—those, often teachers, who compile a book periodically and put it in the hands of one of the other bigger firms which does the actual printing. This firm provides the compiler with an edition of a thousand or more books with his own name as "Publisher" on the cover page, and the "one-book" publisher proceeds to dispose of them at his singing schools and conventions. I claim no completeness for the list in the matter of these one-book compilers, for there are very many of them and they vary from year to year.

Extent of Sales

I have referred often in the pages above to the great spread of the seven-shape singing. The large number of song-book-making concerns is evidence in this matter. But a much better idea of the extent of this rural art practice could be gained if we could ascertain the number of different collections of songs appearing annually and the number of copies of each book sold to the singers. But exact or even approximately exact figures are impossible to obtain. Some firms keep no record of total annual sales, and I have found others reluctant to part with such business figures. Out of the twenty-eight firms to whom I addressed question sheets, twelve answered my questions. The twelve firms had been in business all the way from four to forty-seven years, the average firm-age being about fifteen years, and the total number of firm-years being

293. During this time they had all together published 263 different books, or only a little less than an average for each firm of one song collection per year. In this connection we must be reminded that the era which saw many editions of one song book is gone forever. Every book is a brand-new one with a new title. It is true that many old tunes appear in the new book. It is also true that if *Glory Peals* of one year made an unusual hit, it sometimes appears the next year with a different assortment of songs as *Glory Peals, No. 2,*—I have seen them run up into the "No. 10's"—but the usual thing for many years has been "our *new* book for nineteen-hundred-and-blank."

Of these 263 books, 26,400,000 copies have been sold, the twelve publishers assure me. And this reckons out at about 90,000 copies for each of the 293 firm-years, that is, 90,000 copies total average annual sales for the twelve firms. And if, for the other fourteen firms which failed to reply to my question sheet, we doubled the above figure; and if we then added an estimated 20,000 copies of books printed by the church publishing houses, the sum, 200,000 would be as near and as conservative a guess as we could make as to the rural South's yearly consumption of seven-shape song books during the period under consideration.

Those same twelve publishing firms who reported to me estimated their annual sales at that time (1929) in figures that ran all the way from 20,000 to 300,000 books each. The total annual sale for that year, adding all the figures as reported to me, amounted to no less than 1,365,000 books. And the great disparity between this figure and the one for the average yearly sale over the longer period, is explainable either through the assumption that the shape-note song-book business was on a boom during the year under consideration, which was not the case, or through the assumption that some of the publishers allowed a generous ingredient of "hope" to enter into their estimates.

One must not conceive of these publishers, however, as "prominent" business firms in their towns. Some of them are of considerable size and importance, but more often they are to be found housed in a modest residence or a one-door business place of the usual retailer size. This space is usually furnished with a wrapping and mailing table and many shelves piled high with the little five-by-seven-and-one-half-inch, manila-bound books. The printing and book-binding establishment may be in the rear or in another city.

Song Book Publishing in Hartford, Arkansas

The song book people in Hartford, Arkansas, deserve a special word in making clear the spirit and typical habitat of this indigenous industry. Hartford is a sleepy little straggly village a short hour's drive south of Fort Smith and just a ten minutes' jolt east of the Oklahoma line. It nestles between the beautifully towering Poteau Mountain on the south and the equally high Sugar Loaf on the north—two broken links of the Ozarks. Fifty years ago an enthusiastic singing-school master wrote from this dale to the editor of the *Musical Million:* "Round notes are no longer used here. The seven-character notes have swept the field. I have sold about 300 of your [Ruebush-Kieffer] publications." So it seems that the denizens of this secluded settlement, in a district which is less inviting to the thrifty farmer than to the casual folk-lore-seeking visitor from the lowland cities, have for a long time made the best of things, with a song.

For a spell the singers were disturbed. Coal was discovered in the adjacent hills. But after the seams gave out, the town went back to its restful normalcy with nothing but black roads, a few rusting railroad spur-tracks, many slate dumps, and a large number of empty store buildings as the spoils of that industrial interruption.

In 1904 three Arkansas singing-school teachers, David Moore, G. L. Lindsey, and W. M. Ramsey, joined hands in establishing at Hartford a song book publishing partnership, The Central Music Company. This firm has persisted till the present day and now bears the name, Hartford Music Company. E. M. Bartlett is president, all three of its founders are still active, and scores of other teachers are linked up.

Among the activities of the Hartford folks are the making and marketing of a large share of the western South's song books (every year one or two new ones); the conducting of two normal music schools each year, one in June in Hartford and one in January in Bristow, Oklahoma; and the publication of a monthly magazine, *The Herald of Song.*

A dozen widely active music teachers in the shape-note clan form the faculty of the normals, and for a number of years they have brought J. H. Ruebush all the way from Dayton, Virginia, to lend that faculty still further dignity and in the realization, possibly, that they are thus linking it up directly with the oldest in southern shape-note tradition. In the Bristow Normal of the hard winter following the drouth of 1930 there were over a hundred in attendance, over half of them country singing-school teachers.

The *Herald of Song,* a 16-page periodical devoted largely to communications from teachers telling of their singing schools and of conventions here, there and everywhere, combines its influence with that of the normals in integrating the workers in the "gospel song field."

CHAPTER XXIX

WHO MAKES THE SONGS?

Legions of Tune-Crafters

First, every publisher is a song maker. More often he is simply a tune maker and harmonizer, but a number of publishers write both words and music. This activity on their part is perfectly natural, for they have all "come up from the ranks" by the steps of singer, singing-school teacher, tune maker, song-book compiler. As the status of compiler is approached, the prospective book maker gets in touch with a group of his fellow tune-crafters, perhaps a score of them. Each will furnish a few new or near-new (but original) songs for the forthcoming book. Each will be paid, by the compiler, at the rate of a few dollars for each song. The price is, I am told, from five to twenty-five dollars. The manuscript then goes to the "printing publisher" and in a short time the compiler and his associates have a book to use in their singing schools and conventions. And the compiler evolves in the run of some years —according to his ambition and ability—into a printing publisher himself.

The individual tune maker usually starts with a poem. From this as a basis of suggestion, the tune evolves in his mind. It may get no further, in the hands of the non-professional tune maker, than the bare melody, jotted down in pencil, which the compiler has to harmonize for him. The tune maker may, however, do the whole job, harmony and all, as well as the compiler-publisher could. These song producers include all sorts of people. Some of them are real professionals, good melodists and masters of simple harmony, whose songs are in general demand. The ability of some of the shape-note people in practical harmony is astonishing. A number of the publishers possess this ability. And one always finds an expert harmonist coöperating with the larger publishing houses. But the meagerness of the fee per song restricts the professional element to small numbers. Most of the songs are therefore made by people whose livelihood is gained from some other source. One man on my list of composers (page 373) is a dentist who composes a song now and then between patients. A number of others are preachers and revival song leaders. The great majority, however, are singing-school teachers. The number of women tune makers is surprisingly small.

An excellent example of versatility among these tune-crafters is J. M. Henson of Atlanta. Coming from the hill country of northeastern Georgia he became in succession a seven-shape singer, leader, singing-school teacher, tune maker, words maker, harmonizer, song-book compiler and publisher. A short time ago I walked into the modest establishment of the Atlanta publishing firm, the Morris-Henson Company, of which he is a junior partner, and found him setting music type in expert fashion. The next day he was in the "bald-headed row" at a big singing in Kennesaw, Georgia, and encouraging, by his presence and personality, the sale of Morris-Henson books. Mr. Henson's career and present activity are typical. There are scores of equally interesting song men all over the southern field.

There are also many in this legion of tune makers who correspond closely to that secular-song-making sort, those who send their love-song products perennially to the sheet-music publishing houses of the North and the East. Both the secular and the religious producers and product exemplify one fundamental urge, the desire to put down in permanent form and to utter to the big crowd the results of their temporary psycho-musical ventings. But the religious-song producers have the better of it in the matter of the realization of their ambitions. They see their better songs paid for, appearing in large editions, and actually sung in their own towns and sections. While their "popular ballad"-making neighbor helps, in the great number of cases, to fill the "legitimate" song publisher's waste basket or, still more unfortunately, gets a dearly bought (by himself) "edition" of his song from the illegitimate "publisher" for his own waste basket.

Contemporary Contributors of Songs to the Shape-Note Books

I have compiled the accompanying list of present-day rural song makers from information furnished largely by song-book publishers. My purpose in giving it here in full is to impress on the reader the actual democracy and the extent of this folk-activity in making songs.

Achord, D. H., Tennessee
Acuff, J. W., Texas
Alford, Burns, Texas
Allphin, N. W., Texas
Ambrester, C. W., Alabama
Arnold, Robert S., Arkansas
Askew, J. W., Georgia
Bacon, George W., Tennessee
Baldwin, Chas. O., Kentucky
Barnard, T. W., Alabama
Barrentine, Carlis, Alabama
Bartlett, E. M., Arkansas
Bartlett, J. F., Texas
Bateman, B. B., Tennessee
Baxter, J. R., Jr., Tennessee
Baxter, P. H., Alabama
Bearden, J. O., Texas
Beazley, Sam W., Illinois
Berrie, Rev. S. A., Arkansas
Benton, Thos., Texas
Bethea, Otis, Florida
Black, R. T., Alabama
Bradford, Grady G., Georgia
Bridges, C. E., Louisiana
Brock, Dwight M., Tennessee
Broome, J. W., Georgia
Brown, A. B., Oklahoma
Butrum, L. E., Kentucky
Cassady, V. P., Kentucky
Carden, W. C., Arkansas
Carr, J. H., Arkansas
Chambliss, T. N., Arkansas
Chamlee, W. J., Arkansas
Clements, J. B., Alabama
Cobble, John E., Tennessee
Cole, Joe, Texas
Collins, H. C., Georgia
Combs, Hollace, Texas
Combs, M. O., Texas
Combs, W. W., Texas
Cornelius, R. H., Texas
Cox, Silas L., Oklahoma
Craft, Robert S., Arkansas
Crawford, Ernest, Tennessee
Crawford, J. W., Georgia
Culpepper, E. D., Tennessee
Daniel, Roland J., Alabama
Daniel, W. M., Alabama
Davis, W. H., Texas
Dean, Emmett S., Texas
Deaton, Otis, Texas
Denson, Whit, Alabama
DeVaughan, W. M., Alabama
Dickinson, G. B., Alabama
Edmiaston, B. B., Texas
Edmiaston, W. E., Colorado
Elliott, H. W., Texas
Ely, J. T., Texas
Erwin, H. L., Tennessee
Etheridge, D. C., Louisiana
Evridge, W. D., Texas
Farris, Thos. J., Arkansas
Ferguson, M. L., Texas
Ferrell, M. F., Texas
Finley, H. C., Tennessee
Formby, Floyd A., Arkansas

Fossett, V. O., Alabama
Francis, O. L., Texas
Franklin, J. B., Texas
Frye, Harkins, W. Va.
Fulkerson, O. C., Illinois
Gaines, D. C., Kentucky
Gaines, J. W., Tennessee
Garner, Milton, Oklahoma
Godley, A. G., Texas
Golden, Wm. M., Miss.
Graves, W. J., Texas
Green, L. E., Texas
Greer, J. M., Georgia
Grice, O. V., Arkansas
Hagan, J. M., Kentucky
Hall, J. H., Virginia
Hammill, L. A., Tennessee
Hamilton, D. C., Oklahoma
Hammett, H. B., Arkansas
Harris, John R., Oklahoma
Harrison, V. V., Alabama
Hazelwood, Austin, Alabama
Hensen, J. M., Georgia
Holland, Sam, Alabama
Irwin, Andrew, Texas
Irwin, Otho, Texas
Ivey, G. G., Georgia
Ivie, L. E., Georgia
Jacobs, J. D., Tennessee
Johnson, E. L., Louisiana
Jones, C. P., Tennessee
Jones, Mrs. L. B., Texas
Jones, S. W., Texas
Kelley, H. A., Arkansas
Kendrick, W. T., Arkansas
Kesseler, Mrs. John, Texas
Lambert, Jesse J., Oklahoma
Lasiter, L. N., Texas
Lincoln, H. N., Texas
Malloy, J. T., Mississippi
Manley, L. J., Oklahoma
McDaniels, Rev. J. H., Tenn.
McDonald, J. W., Texas
McDonald, W. C., Louisiana
McCollum, S. J., Arkansas
McCord, Calvin, Arkansas
McCord, Earl E., Arkansas
McKinney, W. O., S. C.
McKinney, B. B., Texas
McKissak, Arvad E., Tenn.
Meeks, J. W., Texas
Merritt, B. W., Georgia
Moody, Chas. E., Georgia
Moore, J. C., Florida
Moore, J. L., Georgia
Moore, L. T., Arkansas
Morris, Grady C., Alabama
Morris, Homer F., Georgia
Murray, R. W., Alabama
Pace, A. M., Tennessee
Paris, J. B., Texas
Parris, O. A., Alabama
Parrish, Ben H., Texas
Peck, Emory, Georgia
Powell, R. L., Texas
Presley, Luther G., Arkansas
Purser, W. R., Texas
Ramsey, Thos., Texas
Ramsey, Will M., Arkansas
Ramsey, Mrs. Will M., Ark.
Rhodes, G. T., Tennessee
Richardson, W. T., Texas
Robinson, Dr. D. T., Ala.
Robinson, K. C., Tennessee
Roper, E. A., N. C.
Ross, Dr. G. Duff, Texas
Ruebush, J. H., Virginia
Ruebush, Will H., Virginia
Rust, R. L., Texas
Seabren, A. B., Tennessee
Seabren, G. W., N. C.
Sewell, J. N., Alabama
Showalter, J. Henry, Ohio
Sisk, Rev. J. L., Georgia
Sisk, Theodore, Georgia
Sitzler, N. S., Tennessee
Slater, J. F., Texas
Smith, Robert R., Oklahoma
Smothermon, P. F., Texas
Stafford, C. C., Texas
Stamps, V. O., Texas
Stevens, Thos. M., Alabama
Steward, J. H., Tennessee
Taylor, Austin, Texas
Taylor, Ben. M., Texas
Taylor, John F., N. Mexico
Teddlie, Tillit S., Texas
Thomas, J. M., Texas
Thomas, Mrs. Jessie S., Ala.
Thomas, L. B., Tennessee
Thornton, C. B., Tennessee
Torbett, J. S., Texas
Vaughan, James D., Tenn.
Vaughan, Chas. W., Tenn.
Warren, Noel, Arkansas
Weaver, J. R., Texas
Webb, A. C., Arkansas
Wesson, W. Henry, Arkansas
Williams, Austin, Texas
Williams, C. D., Texas
Williams, J. E., Texas
Williams, Rev. Morgan, Ky.
Williamson, Edgar P., Ala.
Wilson, E. V., Tennessee
Wilson, J. A., Georgia
Wood, W. W., Texas
Woodard, M. H., Alabama
Wright, J. B. F., Texas
Yandell, M. L., Texas
York, Jesse, Oklahoma

Fifteen Hundred Song Poems a Year

The words writers are fewer than the tune makers. The reason for this condition will be understood when we recall the singing-school musical genesis of most of the song-crafters. Some few composers write most of their song texts. Many a song shows the musician's wife as the text creator. Indeed, this is where the women in general shine more brightly than in the musical part of sacred song making. But since each tune must have its hymn-poem and since the southern demand for the latter is greater than the supply, the tune makers have to call on words writers of other sections. And this situation explains such phenomena as James Rowe, Alfred Barratt, and others—northerners largely, prolific words writers, purveyors to the southern tune makers.

Seeing the name James Rowe at the left of the title of numerous songs in the seven-shape books, I became curious to learn more of such a generally useful personality. My letter to him elicited a reply from which the following extracts have been made.

"I was born in Devonshire [England] sixty-four years ago. I came to this country forty years ago and began to earn a living as a crayon artist, and—being SOME artist—failed." Then ten years in the employ of a railroad and a period as superintendent of the Hudson River Humane Society. "It was at this time that I began my career as a gospel hymn writer, in this way: I used to contribute a poem weekly to the Albany *Sunday Press*. One of my poems, 'Speak It Out', was used with a little change by E. O. Excell, a gospel hymn publisher, as a gospel hymn poem. After it was published I began to get orders for poems from Charles H. Gabriel and many others. In 1911 I went to Waco, Texas, and edited a monthly journal for the Trio Music Company. Remained there ten months and was obliged to return to my old home at Saratoga Springs, N. Y., because of my wife's ill health. In 1913 I began to write sentiments of all kinds for Christmas card producers; also wrote humorous matter for humorous journals. . . . I then went to Chattanooga to look after the Showalter interests . . . mailing out hymn books part of my time and writing poems, etc., the rest of it. While there I wrote—fitted to music—one thousand poems for A. J. Showalter, composer of the music of Leaning on the Everlasting Arms. I remained at Chattanooga eighteen months and then went to Lawrenceburg, Tenn., to edit a weekly paper for James D. Vaughan. I remained there two years and then, because of wife's health, returned to New York state; but continued to edit the weekly and contribute a humorous column and poem weekly.

"I am now settled at Wells, Vermont. I contribute jokes, verses and editorials to the Herald of Song, a publication issued monthly by the Hartford Music Company of Hartford, Arkansas.

"The best answer I can make to your question as to which publishers have used my poems is,—nearly every hymn-book publisher in America. Up to last January [1929] I had written 19,000 hymn poems. Since then I have kept no account, though Morris-Henson Company alone bought 200 of my poems since then.

"I have always maintained that the teacher who goes out into the field and teaches gospel song writing and singing is doing as much good in the world as the preacher; and since there are thousands of such teachers today, only God knows how much good is being done.

"My most popular songs are I Walk With the King, Love Lifted Me, I Would Be Like Jesus, and What a Wonderful Gathering, I believe, for they (and many others) are on Victrola records and big sellers.

"I am the author of one volume of poems, Ready for Mornin', published by James D. Vaughan, Lawrenceburg, Tennessee, a number of cantatas, children's plays, etc., etc.

"There you are, sir. That's about all I can tell you, I think, except that I can write a sacred poem on a blackboard in front of a congregation while it is singing one of my songs. I did this 'stunt' for thirteen nights at Rutherford, N. Y., and at Patterson, N. Y."

Another wholesale poetry purveyor to the southern songsters is Alfred Barratt, a Presbyterian minister born in England but now living in Punxsutawney, Pennsylvania.

"I began writing hymns at the age of twenty," the Reverend Mr. Barratt wrote in reply to my questions; "My first hymn was a simple one for the children. Professor Bramhall was at my home for dinner and we were talking about hymns. I showed a few of my compositions he selected 'Sing for Jesus'—he gave me $1.50 for this poem. It very soon became a favorite in all parts of England. I have written 1,734 hymns, each breathing a cheerful optimistic spirit. . . . I have written three today and wrote three yesterday. . . . 'Shining for Jesus' Music by James A. Meale has penetrated almost every corner of England. . . . I have taken more than a score of prizes with my hymns in English contests for Children's Day services."

After explaining that the price of song poems in the South is about one-half of what the northerners pay, Rev. Barratt continues: "A great many composers send me a piece of music and ask me to write words to go with their tunes. Others purchase the poems that I submit to them. The publishers do not purchase large quantities of hymns from me. They send large numbers of tunes to me for words. Before Mr. Showalter died and also before Mr. Mosely [T. B. Mosely, music editor for the Showalter firm after the death of its founder] died I was kept very busy writing words for their wordless tunes. Since the death of these two great composers I have had others take their places, and my poems are coming to the South in large quantities on the wings of song. I cannot tell you the favorites because every man seems to look upon his own composition as a favorite."

Among the prominent women writers of song texts is Mrs. Clint Shelton, of Greenville, Kentucky. During the past ten years she has written several hundred poems which have appeared in the rural books. She has also "revised a good deal of verse for others." She is very sure that her calling to this occupation of giving "to the world the gospel message in sacred song" was of divine origin, according to her letters to me.

Other furnishers of song texts are Dr. T. O. Chisolm, Vineland, N. J.; Gertrude Stoddard Dennstedt, Albert Lee, Minn.; Luther G. Presley, Pangburn, Ark.; N. W. Allphin, Fort Worth, Tex.; E. M. Bartlett, Hartford, Ark.; Thomas Benton, Nacogdoches, Tex.; J. M. Henson, Atlanta, Ga.; G. L. Lindsey, Hartford, Ark.; Charles E. Moody, Calhoun, Ga.; Agnes Ruth Riddles, Geneva, Ala.; Dr. E. Jackson, Dalton, Ga.; J. W. Preston, Holly Pond, Ala.; Mrs. J. M. Hunter, North East, Md.; Mrs. Lizzie De Armond, Swarthmore, Pa.; J. Graydon Hall, Birmingham, Ala.; Newton D. Keeling, Derby, Conn.; and James Wells, Dalton, Ga.

The words writers are unanimous in their condemnation of a certain large class of "potes" who send them their effusions for "revision." One writes, "You ought to see some of their work, . . . not one line could be used. They know absolutely nothing about rhymes or rhythm; in fact, some of them can hardly write their own names. The 'revised' poems, however, have their names attached as authors, because they increase the publishers' sales, for they [the "potes"] are good at composing tunes. Thousands of hymns [texts] published never belonged to the ones whose names are attached. Even the tunes and harmony were rewritten. . . . Mr. X and I have rewritten and recomposed at least 5,000 of such."

TWO NOTABLE MEN IN RURAL SONG

LEFT: *James Rowe, who has written two thousand poems for southern shape-note song books.* RIGHT: *Rev. Alfred Barratt, who has written 1,734.*

Words writers' advertisements appearing in the southern shape-note monthly publications indicate that the usual price is $1.00 to $1.50 per song, or six songs for $5.00. This last appears to be the "wholesale" price. Poems are "corrected" for the trade at fifty cents each.

How many songs, produced thus, are published annually in the shape-note books? An estimate is all that is possible. The publishers listed above, big publishers and little ones together, issue probably no less than twenty-five books per year. These are uniformly five and a quarter by seven and three quarters inches in size with from one hundred and fifty to two hundred songs each. Among these songs there are usually about sixty new ones, about seventy that are well-liked songs brought forward from recent issues, and around fifty standard church songs or "service songs." There are no anthems and no songs specifically designated as for singing schools. Multiply the sixty (average) new songs in each book by twenty-five—the number of different books per year—and we have an estimated fifteen hundred new songs, all the music of which is made by southerners, appearing every twelve months. The seventy (approximately) "slightly used" songs in each new book, written by southerners and taken over from various southern song books of a few years previous, give a total annual figure of about seventeen hundred and fifty for such songs. This figure indicates clearly that the southern song crop does not die after merely one year of singing.

CHAPTER XXX

RURAL SONG MEETS PEOPLE'S TASTES

Popular Qualities of Mode and Tempo

When one sees this quantity output of song, one will not be too expectant as to its intrinsic quality. The songs fall somewhat into musical types, melodic, rhythmic, and structural. Indeed, if this were not the case, if they were individualistic, rising far above the norm or falling far below it, they would fail to appeal to the singers and would go into the discard after their one-book and one-year trial.

The melodies are all in the major mode. Minor has long since disappeared. The seven-shape publishers reproduce many an old standard hymn as "filler" in their books but never one in the "plaintive" mode. The tunes run pretty uniformly along the popular progressions, using tonic, dominant, and subdominant chords. The melodic progressions are usually by diatonic steps which are prevailingly seconds and thirds, but with a goodly intersprinkling of the bigger intervals up to the octave.

One would expect to find far more sameness, melodic interdependence from song to song, than one actually does find. Tune cribbing is rare; remarkably so, when one considers the musical limitations set for the composers, sometimes by their own capacities and always by the capacities of the singers, and when one bears in mind that the tune makers are so numerous and so prolific. Under such circumstances it is strange that we do not meet oftener such songs as Henson's "O Glorified City" (*Crowning Hymns Number Ten,* No. 146), which conceals rather effectually and effectively Bradbury's older "Sweet Hour of Prayer."

The perennial attractiveness of the five-tone mode is illustrated by my findings of fifteen songs built of this melodic material and six other songs which are essentially five-tone melodies in one book, Morris-Henson Company's *Crowning Hymns Number Ten* (1930).[1] All but one of these songs are new or quite recently composed. The one old five-tone song is "Harmony Grove" ("Amazing Grace"), which is attributed to William Walker. I have found the tendency to fall into the five-tone mode to be quite general among the southern tune makers of the present as it was among their ancestors before the Civil War. The particular variety of this pentatonic mode they use is always the one which includes *do re mi sol* and *la* with the feeling-content which we call "major."

The sprightly optimism of the rural seven-shape tunes is one of their outstanding features. We have seen one sign of this in their universally "major" modes. Another sign is their lively gait and their making jiggy songs in what their musical ancestors before the Civil War called "12s and 11s." T. B. Moseley's "Heaven" (composed in 1927), beginning

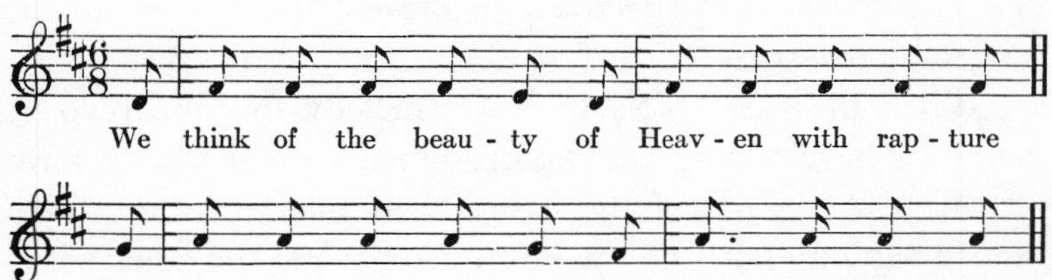

reminds one strikingly of the sacred "dance tunes" of three and four generations before.

Another rhythmically interesting feature is found in those

[1] Nos. 27, 89, 102, 119, 144, 148, 149, 151, 154, 164, 168, 171, 172, 179. The essentially five-tone melodies are Nos. 52, 54, 61, 72, 162, 188.

songs in places where the successive notes, instead of being of perfectly uniform length, commence taking time values from each other. One of the results of this give-and-take is syncopation, once the trade-mark of the rag-timers and still an ingredient of most of the secular popular music. An example is P. B. Jones's "Feasting on Love":

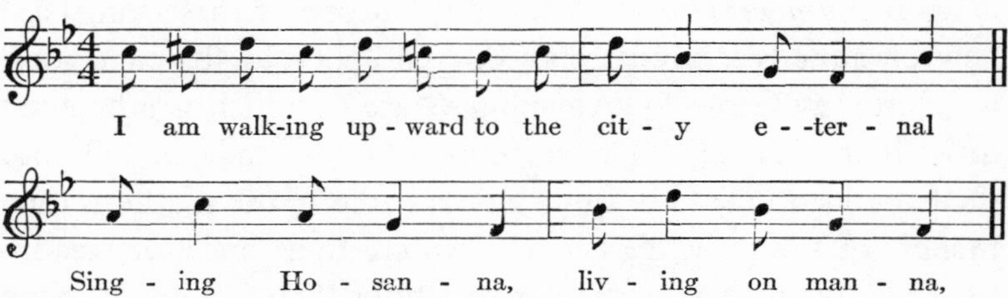

But such quick successions of syllables do not persist throughout the song, that is, not in one and the same voice. After a few measures the melody part often has a way of going into longer notes, while the rhythmic pace and the melodic trend are carried on by one of the other voices. In fact, this passing of parts of the melody to bass, tenor, and alto as well as to the soprano, is one of the marks of almost every song. And it serves to make the different parts equally attractive to the singers and thus effectively to prevent the drift of all the singers to one part.

When the bass voices have the melody the upper voices naturally have to sing an accompaniment. In the older form of this accompaniment the basses went their own way with somewhat long notes on the heavy accents and the other voices came in on the more lightly accented beats of the measure, somewhat as follows:

Upper voices 4/4 | Hal - le - lu - jah, | hal - le - lu - jah,

Bass melody 4/4 Hal - le - | lu - jah, hal - le - | lu - jah,

This mannerism may have come to the seven-shapers by way of the barber shop and the old-time type of college glee club concert, with such omnipresent things as "Sweet Adeline" as an art vehicle.

But the seven-shape singers have now gone beyond this style and are now in the midst of that type of instrumentally motivated vocal accompaniment which they call "after-beats" and "after-time" or, more facetiously, "back-fire" or "static." The peculiarity has long been a rhythmic staple with the brass band people. It has also been used for a long time by college glee clubs in their "oom-pah oom-pah" songs. But its use by the sacred-song singers and makers of the group we are discussing is only about a decade old. Indeed, the very first song of this type is said to have been "I Will Take Care of Thee, My Child," written by some northerner by the name of Miller and appearing in one of James D. Vaughan's books in 1919. "Back-fire" occurs, usually with a bass melody, when the accompanying voices sing a little short snappy syllable on the second half of each beat in the measure, just as the alto horns do in the brass bands. Byron T. Whitworth's "Over All the World" (*Crowning Hymns, Number Ten,* No. 98); may serve as a graphic illustration of the seven-shape "back-fire":

Upper voices 4/4 — Christ will reign yes, | o-ver all the world

Bass Solo 4/4 — He'll come to | reign o'er all the | world . . . . Oh, let the | *etc.*

The manner is now so popular that it is arousing a good deal of opposition from musical conservatives among the seven-shapers themselves. But a very animated discussion of the matter, going on in the columns of the Hartford *Herald of Song* for some months during the year 1930, came to an end with

Marvin P. Dalton's question: "How long would our conventions last if we used only songs with ordinary rhythm?" His own answer, "Not long," is one that all seemed to agree to, and this fact will probably give the after-beats a lease on life.

In the matter of general structural characteristics of these melodies there are two features to mention. We have spoken of the habit of passing over the "leads" to all the parts, bass especially. In this we may see a striving for variety, the same desire which animated William Billings one hundred and fifty years ago and brought into the world the "fuguing tunes." The Billings style is now entirely dead excepting in the southern *Sacred Harp* circles, but that same variety which the fuguing tunes and the equally old-fashioned "anthems" fostered has been salvaged by the rural seven-shapers. The second structural feature is that the "chorus" which was such an inevitable but musically barren thing, a mere repeat of melodic parts gone before, in the Sunday school gospel hymns of fifty years ago, has developed. The songs of the present-day rurals have a "refrain" that is really different from the "verse" and adds something new to it instead of being merely a repeat of it.

Greater Optimism than Formerly in the Words

There is little to say of new tendencies in the textual material of the songs under consideration. In the matter of the texts the seven-shapers are, as they themselves proclaim, "in the Gospel Song field." And the gospel hymns have doubtless received already more attention from their hymnologists than they deserve. But these do-ray-me songs differ also in the matter of their poetry, from the Sunday school type of gospel hymn. For example, that unique tone of wholesome lightness and happiness, pointed out as it appears in the music, pervades also the almost worldly texts. The subjects or themes are naturally the same as ever. The songs treat now, as they did a century ago, of the brevity of life, the rescue from sin, the virtues of right living, the companionship of Christ (the Lord, Pilot, Friend, Guide, etc.), the march to heaven, and heaven itself. But there is now also an emphasis on this life, as contrasted to the greater stress laid formerly on the life beyond. The pioneer Christians looked on this world as a pitch-dark place. Now it is "shadow and shine." Heaven is still the goal filled with "gladness and peace," but with Christ "walking and talking" with the earthly pilgrim, why worry? Earthly possessions were not attractive apparently to the old-timers. "Religion is a fortune and heaven is a home," they sang. But now there is no inherent stigma attached to "earthly wealth and fame" and even "a palace fair." And where these boons do not put in an appearance, there is, of course, still the compensation of the "home on high." They still sing of being the "blood-bought princes of the royal host," but the "blood flood" which ran so high in the Gospel Hymn Era has fortunately ebbed. "Carnal mirth," "civic mirth," and almost all forms of merriment were once taboo, if we are to judge by the song texts of the early nineteenth century. Now a differentiation is made; those "pleasures found in sin" are the only ones that dare not "our attention win." And finally, the grave is not that thing whose horrors the old-time singers dwelt on, seemingly throughout life. J. Henry Showalter's attitude toward death as found in his "Not for Long" exemplifies the new optimism:

The storm will come and thunders rumble;
The flow'rs will bloom and bees will bumble,
Then out of life we'll take a tumble,
We won't be here long.

Thro' hopes and fears a few more years,
Thro' joy and sorrow, sunshine, tears,
Tho' growing weaker, jumping gears,
We won't be here long.

Favorite Songs

In the face of the plethora of these songs, the ever-flowing stream which changes its aspects quickly and in which few individual creations subsist for more than a few years, it would be an herculean if not an impossible task to make a "Most Popular Song" list by the same method we used in sifting the sturdy, lasting songs of one hundred years ago. So the best I have been able to do is to get authoritative opinion as to what songs are most widely sung among the seven-shapers at the present time, 1930. I addressed the question to the prominent publisher-musicians as to which half-dozen songs they would call the most popular now. Not all of them answered. The resultant information is, therefore, not as complete as I should wish. And while there was evident, in the answers, that natural tendency to favor, in this "popularity contest," those songs of writers allied with the publisher who made the particular list, still I felt also their desire to be fair. I therefore list the songs of their choice without any claim for its completeness and merely as material showing in a general way the song-likings of these people today.

The favored songs were "Everybody Will Be Happy" (by E. M. Bartlett), "Give the World a Smile" (M. L. Yandell), "Gloryland Way" (J. S. Torbett), "Harp of a Thousand Strings" (A. M. Pace), "He Bore It All" (V. O. Stamps), "He Knows How" (Charles W. Vaughan), "He Keeps My Soul" (Ernest Rippetoe), "If I Could Hear My Mother Pray Again" (James W. Vaughan), "It Won't Be Very Long" (E. M. Bartlett), "Kneel at the Cross" (Charles E. Moody), "Love Took It Away" (J. M. Henson), "Never Grow Old" (James C. Moore), "Over in the Gloryland" (Emmett Dean), "Some Glad Day After a While" (Will M. Ramsey), "Swing Out on the Promises" (E. M. Bartlett), "Sweetest Mother" (?), "We

Shall Rise" (J. E. Thomas), "Watching You" (J. M. Henson), "When the Sweet By and By Is Ended" (E. M. Bartlett), "When Jesus Comes" (J. W. Gaines), and—the only song of any considerable age—"Twilight Is Falling," by B. C. Unseld.

CHAPTER XXXI

MUSICAL PERIODICALS AND OTHER PROPAGANDA

Southern Musical Periodicals

The list of southern musical periodicals below is far from complete, and data as to the years of publication are even less satisfactory. But what there is of it may convey a fair general idea of one of the main avenues of publicity used by the little and big southern publishers of singing books for the rurals. A perusal of the list shows also that the 1880's and the 1890's saw the greatest activity along this line. Most of the periodicals were of sixteen pages and contained a few pages of sacred music. The only ones still appearing regularly are the *Herald of Song* and *Vaughan's Family Visitor*. The usual subscription was fifty cents a year, sometimes even less. The *Musical Million* (1870-1915) stood out uniquely in the matter of the size of its subscription list, the quality of its journalism, and its longevity.

The popular means of establishing contact between songbook maker and singer in these days of better roads and Fords is a more personal one. Wherever singers gather, a representative of the book makers is sure to be present. If it is a singing school, the teacher is pretty sure to be "lined up" with some publisher, if he is not one himself. If it is a "singing" or convention, either the publisher (or several of them) will be on hand with a package of his latest books for distribution and eventual sale, or he sends a sort of "good will" group in the form of a male quartet and a piano accompanist. The quartet lends variety to the day's musical trend by contributing now and then a song (from their manager's book). This is often

SOUTHERN MUSICAL PERIODICALS (MONTHLY, AND FOSTERING SHAPE NOTATION UNLESS OTHERWISE SPECIFIED)

Term of Publication	Name	Publisher	Place	Remarks
1847-?......	Musician and General Intelligencer	A. D. Fillmore	Cincinnati, O.	Fostered numeral notation.
1859-1869...	Southern Musical Advocate and Singer's Friend	Joseph Funk and and Sons	Mountain Valley, Va.	Suspended during Civil War.
1870-1915...	Musical Million	Aldine S. Kieffer	Dayton, Va.	
1869 (?)-?...	Southern Journal of Music	Wm. M. McCarrell	Louisville, Ky.	Probably round notation favored.
1875-1884...	Southern Musical Journal	Ludden & Bates	Savannah, Ga.	Probably round notation favored.
1879-1889...	Musical Leader	John B. Vaughan	Elberton, Ga.	8 pages.
1883-	Etude	Theodore Presser	Lynchburg, Va.	For pianists. Moved to Philadelphia 1884. Round notes.
1883-?......	Musical and Educational Journal	E. D. Irvine & Co.	Macon, Ga.	Succeeded "Sou. Musical Journal" (above).
1884-1894...	Our Musical Visitor	A. J. Showalter	Dalton, Ga.	
1884-?......	Musical Guest	L. B. Shook	Dallas, Tex.	
1884-?......	Pound's Welcome Visitor, soon changed to Musical Tidings	Edwin T. Pound	Barnesville, Ga.	
1885-?......	Musical Review	W. C. Hafley	Athens, Tenn.	
1889-1896...	Musical Worker	R. M. McIntosh	Oxford Co., Ga.	Round notation, not hostile to shape.
1890-1894...	Music Teacher	A. J. Showalter	Dalton, Ga.	Evidently merely a new name for "Our Musical Visitor" (above).
1891-1894...	Tempo	S. J. Oslin & J. H. Ruebush	Fort Smith, Ark.	
1891-?......	Musical Advocate	R. M. McIntosh & J. W. Burke	Macon, Ga.	Round notation, not hostile to shapes.
1891-1900...	Musical Messenger	Fillmore Bros.	Cincinnati, O.	Numeral notation.
1894-?......	North State Voice, later, North State Vocalist	E. C. Hamilton	Liberty, N. C.	
1897-?......	Our Songland, in 1900 changed to Songland & Home	H. N. Lincoln	Dallas, Texas	
1898-?......	Musical Idea	Dolby & Dolby	Greenville, Tenn.	For band and orchestra musicians.
1898-?......	Musical Educator	J. L. McMaster & Chas. E. Duskin	Clarksville, Tex.	
1898-?......	Musical Trio	F. L. Eiland	Waco, Tex.	
1898-?......	Musical Observer	J. A. Wray	Dallas, Tex.	
1900-?......	Western Chorus	?	? Ark.	
1905-1915...	Musical Advocate	Will M. Ramsey	Little Rock, Ark.	
1912-to date.	Vaughan's Family Visitor	Jas. D. Vaughan	Lawrenceburg, Tenn.	
1922-to date.	Herald of Song	Hartford Music Co.	Hartford, Ark.	
1927-to date.	Stamps-Baxter News	Stamps-Baxter Music Co.	Chattanooga, Tenn. and Dallas, Tex.	Publ. "now and then".

done in professional style. And the pianist accompanies everything and adds a solo or two on his own account, played with many of the popular ornaments which one hears in less avowedly "sacred" environment. These traveling quartets, really quintets, are largely self-supporting. Conventions take up only a part of their time. In between they give concerts, do evangelistic singing, make talking-machine recordings, and do radio broadcasting, or they disperse and teach singing schools and normals—but their whole activity is among the rurals or for rural record buyers and rural listeners-in. The cities (that is, the urban elements in the cities) know them not. The whole organism of cosmopolitan concert managers, concertizers, concert goers is about one hundred per cent ignorant of their existence. And yet, they provide millions of southern countryfolk with practically all the musical entertainment they ever have a chance to enjoy, aside from their own community singing.

Talking-Machine Records

Talking-machine recording also is becoming an increasingly important means of the dissemination of rural sacred song of the shape-note genesis. The recording is done not only by the quartets mentioned above but also by trios, duettists, and soloists, the latter often with guitar accompaniment. And with these solo performances we arrive at a sort of song that merges by imperceptible steps with the traditional ballad ("love song" or "ballet") singing of the lonesome places in the southern mountains. Indeed, the difference between the sacred song and the sentimental or the secular ballad, as represented for example by the rural solo singing, of "Not for Long," "A Drunkard's Child," and "Hobo Bill's Last Ride," is neither a musical one nor an artistic one, but merely a difference in subject matter. All records of these sorts are grouped by the talking machine companies under one heading. They call them all "native American melodies," or "old-time southern tunes." They all seem to appeal to the same public, as one sees representatives of that public in the music stores' phonograph booths. And the music dealers and radio directors assure me that this listening public is surprisingly large. This seems to point rather to the "persistence" of the primitive in music appreciation, rather than a "return" to it. But I have strayed from the subject. We were talking about group singing and its propaganda.

The Singing School

O tell me, young friends, while the morning's fair and cool,
O where, tell me where shall I find your singing school.
You'll find it in a large church beside the flowing spring,
You'll find half a hundred and faw sol law they sing.

The beginning of all group singing is in the singing school, the cradle of musical democracy in the South. On page 7 above I devoted a few paragraphs to telling of the northern singing schools of a hundred and fifty years ago, and much that was said there is true of the southern schools of recent decades and of today. In P. M. Claunts' advice[1] to would-be singing-school teachers of around the year 1900 we get a good view of the institution which has changed little since then.

Mr. Claunts' list of the teacher's impedimenta includes a four-by-five-foot blackboard, a music chart (showing graphically the diatonic and chromatic steps and how they appear with changes of key), a quire of heavy white paper, say twenty-four by thirty-six inches; a blue drafting pencil, box of crayon, box of tacks, one tack hammer, one baton, two three-foot pointers, a good supply of music books, tablets and pencils sufficient for a large school and "a soul burning with love for

[1] *Musical Million,* XXIX, 17; XXX, 4 f.

the work." In the town or neighborhood where the teacher is soliciting a school he should "meet the best people who are interested in building up their church. Show them that music teaching is a business, that you are worthy and competent to earn a good salary and that . . . you are not in a charity line. . . . Pay your board. Have an appointment for a public singing well announced (by the heavy-paper, blue-pencil, and tack-hammer method, we presume). In introducing yourself "don't be too gay. Be unassuming."

At the first lesson, Mr. Claunts admonishes, have your class nicely arranged, tablet and pencil in hands of each pupil. "Explain the helpfulness of such things. They will then buy them." Then the work begins. The teacher explains the musical staff, symbols, measures, note shapes and names (solmization), scales, etc.; and impresses them by the question-and-answer method and by much choral singing. And before the ten-day term is over, the group—a dozen to many dozens, all ages but mainly young folk—will be do-ray-mee-ing their different parts to the songs in one of the little manila-bound books which we have described above. When the school closes, another squad of singers has been prepared either to go on and deepen their elementary musical attainments at other singing schools later on, or to take part directly in church and revival choruses and to swell the singing throngs at the many big "singings" or conventions.

Seven-Shape Singers' Conventions

The shape-note singers' conventions fall naturally into two varieties. Those of the four-shapers and the seven-shapers. I have described the former in connection with my consideration of the *Southern Harmony* and the *Sacred Harp*. In taking up here the matter of the seven-shape singing conventions, I shall confine myself to telling how they differ from the others.

In general it may be said that the conventions of the seven-shape people are progressive as contrasted to the non-progressiveness of the *Sacred Harp* branch. I have already made clear the modern tendencies of the seven-shapers. And it is probably this music—developing and keeping up with the times—that is at the bottom of the whole difference. The singers are younger than those of *Sacred Harp* persuasion. And this condition stands in causal relationship, presumably, with the fact that the music of today appeals to youth more deeply than does that of a hundred years ago. Another thing about the songs that attracts the young folk is the texts. We have seen that these texts are nominally religious but that their religious aspect is far removed from the sadness which pervades the old-time *Sacred Harp* song texts. Youth wants entertainment, fun. The quartets, soloists, comic songs, and good humor of the seven-shape singings provide it. And thus we often find the singing "classes" comparatively smaller, and the non-singing but applauding listeners more numerous than at the four-shape gatherings. The present young generation likes instrumental music; hence the presence and active participation of pianists and the approval and applause they win. In the *Sacred Harp* meetings "Brother So-and-so will lead a lesson" (a series of songs). In the "little-book" gatherings it is: "Brother So-and-so will now entertain us," or he will "sing for us," although he really sings "with" us.

Another phase of the music has far-reaching influence over the singers' conventions. The phase I refer to is its heterogeneity. We have seen that the *Sacred Harp* people are singing, in the main, the same songs that their forefathers enjoyed a century and more ago. And we have seen also that the four-shape singers from Georgia to Texas use the same book, and that it is this book that draws the singers into one great family and thus makes the great state organizations with their three-day conventions possible and usual. We have seen, in other words, the common book and the common body of song as the basis of a community of interest and action.

In the little-book circles just the opposite situation is met with. Twenty-five different books (35 cents each), with fifteen hundred new songs appearing each year, is no foundation on which a big homogeneous singing association can be built. Where a dozen different books are used in a dozen neighboring counties, the "one great family" idea is difficult to realize. Hence the seven-shape singing convention draws singers from a more restricted area, and its meetings are far more numerous. The county convention is the usual type now. Sectional conventions are rare, and state conventions have practically disappeared from among the seven-shape activities. The State Musical Convention of Arkansas, A. M. Wilkinson, president, drawing singers from twenty-five counties, is the only big meeting left.

And the three-day convention is no more in seven-shape practice. The Sunday all-day singing is the rule, sometimes with "dinner on the grounds," sometimes not. And many times the singers give way to church services in the forenoon and restrict their sessions to the afternoon.

The hindrance to singing, caused by the many-different-books and ever-new-books condition, though great, is mitigated by the seven-shapers' astonishing sight-reading ability. They "turn loose" on any and all new songs and read shape notes "like a crow picks up corn." I never heard, for example, more rousing song than at Kennesaw, Georgia, in the fall of 1929, where a church full of people were using a book which not one of them had ever seen before that day.

But despite the absence of the big units in the seven-shape singing fraternity, the smaller units cover almost the entire Southland. And they honeycomb the four-shape area as elsewhere. An estimate of the numerical strength ratio of the seven-shape to the four-shape singings (and therefore of the singers themselves) would run all the way from ten-to-one to fifty-to-one.

Geography of Shape-Note Singing

In the 1880's the *Musical Million,* that brave advocate of rural singing, published monthly lists of its new subscribers by states. In the conviction that these lists are a good indication as to the interest at that time in the art in the various sections, I have compiled the figures for 1880 and 1881, and for the southern states only. In these two years the total number of new subscribers was approximately three thousand.

The 570 subscribers of the Virginias would point to that territory which had Dayton, Virginia, as its shape-note musical center as highly interested in the movement. But when one realizes that some of this was due to the personal and institutional activities of the publishers of the *Million* and its many teachers and books, reducing competition from other shape-note sources, then it becomes apparent that that section was not the place of *greatest* interest.

North Carolina and South Carolina show good figures, 422 together. In fact, these totals are even more significant when one takes into consideration the narrowness of North Carolina and the smallness of the western half, which was roughly all that the "round heads" would allow to the shape-noters unmolested. In South Carolina the shape-note area was probably even smaller. For it was the northwestern corner of that wedge-shaped commonwealth that was remote enough from the coast and its hinterland cities to make it good shape-note grazing.

Georgia's figure, 540, shows that that state was fertile ground for the Dayton propagandist journal. Alabama's 222 is a respectable figure for a state of which only the northern half was undisputably in the hands of the rural whites.

I cannot find a satisfying reason for the rarity of *Millions* in Tennessee and their even greater rarity in Kentucky. It may be that Kentucky was fed from Cincinnati and Louisville, rather than from Dayton, and it seems possible that Tennessee's shape-note appetite may have been appeased largely by the big church publishing houses in Memphis and Nashville.

To understand Mississippi's figure, less than half the size of that of its sister state to the east, we shall have to remember those great flat stretches of field and forest where the Negroes and their influence on economic conditions induced the poorer whites—spreading westward from Georgia and Alabama—to move on. The northern part of the state is its "singing" part.

Arkansas's infertility and hilliness may have effectively driven its rural white population to song. For that sparsely peopled state, the figure of 167 is not bad.

The 664 figure for Texas, the biggest single area under discussion—and here we mean simply northeastern Texas—indicates that its population had taken its shape-note singing practices along when it came from the East, and that it had not forgotten them. It is the regular thing, I have found, among the rural singing families of Georgia and Alabama to have an uncle or a brother or a son in Texas. It is probably this continuous flow from the older shape-note sections that made Texas the banner state as far as the *Million* figures go. It is true, too, that many Dayton emissaries went out there and did some of their best work in propagandizing, during the particular years from which our figures are taken.

Shape-note singing activities covered a somewhat greater area formerly than now. In the three decades following the Civil War, reports appeared in the *Musical Million* of such singing in Southern Missouri, Florida, and parts of Louisiana, for example, where it seems to have been reduced or to have disappeared. One reason, perhaps the main one, for the reduction in area is, without doubt, the growth of cities and the extension of urban musical customs into the terrain of the rurals. Cities are springing up everywhere excepting in the impossible mountainous parts. Towns are growing and becoming citified. This means, in such parts, fewer singers, schools, and conventions, and defection in the ranks of those who would persist. Conditions make them feel "countrified." This rural singing is still strong, therefore, mainly in those parts where it got a foothold a hundred and more years ago and where the disintegrating forces have not yet appeared.

As to its original territory, I have called attention to its coming down the mountain valleys, the slopes east of the Appalachians, and spreading to the south and the southwest. I have also mentioned that it was fostered by the Anglo-Saxons, but even more enthusiastically by the Germans and the Scotch-Irish, and that the settlements of these thrifty people were made, not in the alluvial coastal plains—these were already in the hands of the Anglo-Saxon patricians and they were worked by Africans—but in the hill country that was still easy to occupy, if not easy to till profitably. So it was among this democratic people, every honest man of whom was his neighbor's peer, and in this land of hills, valleys, mountains, and coves where a caste system was impossible, that this democratic music made its first stand and is still standing.

If one could find a map of the Southeast, including states as far west as Texas and Oklahoma, which showed those lowland parts that are suitable to plantation farming, big-scale fruit growing, stock ranching, manufacturing, mining and oil pumping, and if one then blocked out all those portions, what remained would be a fairly good map of the rural indigenous singing sections, the southern "song belt." And it would, incidentally, coincide quite well with that part of the southeast which is five hundred feet and more above sea level.

CHAPTER XXXII

"GOD'S MUSIC" IN THE COUNTRY CHURCHES

The Use of Shape-Notes in Rural Churches

The 130-year-old note shapes have enjoyed a much wider acceptance even than is represented by the singing schools, conventions, and home circles. They have been and are still widely used also by many church denominations in their devotional activities, especially by those denominations which are, for one reason or another, of the rural type.

The tenacious conservatism of rurals, especially in the matter of their "Weltanschauung," has been widely recognized from those early times when the words "pagan" and "heathen" began to signify those of the country parts who were slow in accepting the urban religious innovations, up to present times when the studies of the social scientists have shed further light on the subject. Remoteness from the source of religious authority and differing conditions of life and thought accompanying that remoteness seem to have been active factors in bringing about most religious schisms. These factors have been most active in America, where separation from English and continental European hierarchies began with the earliest colonists and where the factors continued, especially after the Revolutionary War, to split one American church group after another, and largely along country-city lines.

I have mentioned one phase of this country-city splitting, as seen in the Baptist Church, on pages 313 ff above. A similar continuous dividing and subdividing among the Methodist churches has been even more important. M. Phelan, in his

Handbook of All Denominations,[1] lists a dozen or more offshoots of the northern and southern Methodist Episcopal churches existing today in opposition to some doctrinal or administrational tenet of the big city-controlled groups. And the United States *Census of Religious Bodies* bulletins show these offshoots to be conservative and rural.

Among those Baptist, Methodist, and other denominations which may be gathered together under the rubric "The Southern Country Church" are the Primitive Baptists (white and black), Landmark Baptists (in Texas and Oklahoma), Freewill Baptists (white and black, strongest in North Carolina but all over the South), "Regular" Baptists (Kentucky and North Carolina), United Baptists (Kentucky and Virginia), German Baptists or "Dunkers" (Virginia), at least twelve varieties of Methodists, Church of God, or "Holy Rollers" (in Southeast), Assemblies of God, many other "Holiness" sects (white and black), Nazarenes, large sections of the Cumberland Presbyterians, Church of Christ (conservative branches), and the Mennonites in Virginia.

Among the numerous reasons for separation from their urban brethren's organizations are their adherence to sanctification, baptism by immersion, divine healing, speaking in "strange tongues," foot-washing, simplicity in dress, and belief in the imminent personal coming of Christ; and their opposition to armed warfare, organs and artificial lighting in their churches, foreign missions, Sunday schools, governing boards, insurance, and automobiles.

Some of these sects were born in Europe. Others have come into existence, one after another, during the past one hundred years. But the great period of religious separation, even among the country sects themselves, seems to have been during the fifty years following 1880.

[1] Nashville, Cokesbury Press, 1929.

The membership of these denominations runs from a few hundred to a few hundred thousand each, with a total membership in the southern country church of somewhere between one and two million.

There may be some differences among these various-similar groups as to whether they prefer the old fasola songs or the newer dorayme ones of gospel hymn flavor, but there is no question as to notation. They all, as far as I have observed, use the seven-shape notation of pure sacred song tradition. I shall try to explain how some of the sects mentioned above adopted the music custom.

The German Baptist Brethren, or Dunkers

The German Baptist Brethren, or "Dunkers," came to William Penn's haven of real religious freedom in the early part of the eighteenth century. They were a comparatively new sect and hence had no deep denominational roots or church-musical traditions behind them. The old conventional notation was a part of that church formalism which was taboo among these pietists and from which they had separated and emigrated. It was "the Devil's music," as they still call it in the Valley of Virginia. So when they did ultimately see the practical advantage of tunes in their hymn books, that form of notation which was allied with sacred song and not at all with worldly forms of music was the one they espoused.

Lauren T. Miller of the Brethren Publishing House, Elgin, Illinois, informs me as follows:

"The first Brethren hymnal, published in 1879,[2] was in shape notes. In those days and prior to that time the majority of the singing school song book publishers used the shape-

[2] A note in the *Musical Million,* XV (1886), 109, says that Benjamin Funk and H. R. Holsinger published the *Brethren's Tune and Hymn Book,* 329 pages, in Funk's notation; the hymns (words) being identical with those of the *Brethren's Hymn Book,* by James Quinter, 1867.

note system. So it came about that our people learned this system and not that of the round notes, and, of course, wanted in our publications the system they understood. The second Brethren hymnal published in 1901 was also in shape notes only. So also were the first Sunday-school song books. . . . The new Brethren hymnal published in 1925 was put out in both shaped and round notes.

"Our latest records show that for one of the Sunday-school song books the orders for shape notes are about six to one of the round. . . . For the new hymnal the two editions (notations) score about even. The pendulum seems to be swinging toward the use of the round notes.

"The orders from Virginia, West Virginia and Tennessee are almost invariably for shape notes. In Florida, where the majority of the Brethren folks are recently from the North, the round notes are gaining ground." Mr. Miller noted the same tendency in the Middle-West and the western states, "though quite a few still prefer the shape notes."

The Mennonites

A much larger German sect, the Mennonite (German, Die Mennoniten, early followers of Menno Simon), came to Pennsylvania on the same immigrational wave that brought the Dunkers. As to their use of shape notation I quote from a letter to me from Harold S. Bender, president of the Mennonite Historical Board, Goshen, Indiana:

"Our denominational hymn books contained no notes at all until 140 years ago. It was felt by many that 'notes' were worldly. The most conservative branch, still known as 'Old Order Amish,' still refuses to tolerate 'notes.' However, all the hymnals issued since the first note-edition have used the shape notes exclusively until the last edition, which was issued in two forms. This means that the shape notes have been used in all our churches until very recently."

Levi Mumaw, secretary of the Mennonite Central Committee in Scotdale, Pennsylvania, reports for the present shape-note situation that their "congregations throughout the states of Pennsylvania, Maryland, Virginia, Ohio, Indiana, Illinois, Kansas and the northwestern states are using shape notes. . . . During the past two years we have marketed a new hymnal. Out of the about 28,000 copies sold during this time, not more than 3,500 were of the round-note edition. We offer either notation in our publicity campaigns.

"Our colleges located in Harrisonburg, Virginia; Goshen, Indiana, and Hesston, Kansas, are using the round notes in their music courses, but this has not affected the use of character notes in our congregations. . . . We have no congregations south of Virginia except a few in Missouri, Oklahoma, and Texas."

The United Brethren

The United Brethren was another German church that used shape notes at one time. I find mention in the *Musical Million* of a volume entitled *Notes of Triumph,* containing 192 pages, published in character notes in 1886 by the United Brethren Publishing House (now the Otterbein Press) at Dayton, Ohio, and edited by E. S. Lorenz and I. Balzell.[3] This would indicate shape-notes for this church from the start. (For it is manifestly impossible to go over from a round-note tradition to the shapes. At any rate, we have no record of any such procedure.) But the present-day "U.B's" seem to have become conformistic in musical practice as in most other ways. W. R. Funk, a scion of the old Pennsylvania family spoken of above, who is present head of the Otterbein Press, wrote

[3] XVII (1886), 41.

me recently that he knew "nothing at all about the shape notation. We print a good deal of music here, but never any of that kind. I have seen the notation, but never used it either in our business here or personally."

The Henry and Joseph Funks of Pennsylvania and Virginia were Mennonites. Joseph Funk's *Choral-Music, Genuine Church Music,* and *Harmonia Sacra* are illustrative of the shape-note musical influences that played on the German sects in the first part of the nineteenth century. And that the effect of those influences has not yet died is shown not only in the church usages just mentioned but also in the Old Folks' Singings that are still held here and there in the Virginias, events that bring out great throngs of the older singers and younger ones as well—everybody with a *Harmonia Sacra* under his arm.

An Old Folks' Singing Near Harrisonburg, Virginia

I attended one of these Old Folks' Singings at Weaver's Mennonite Church near Harrisonburg, Virginia, on New Year's Day, 1930. All day long they sang, the women filling one side of the big church sitting there in their little white lace "prayer caps" (their black poke bonnets of Old-World-traditional form had been removed); the men on the other side of the three-foot-high fence, with no moustaches and no buttons on coat sleeves—for these were symbols of that military usage from which these non-resistant people dissented. Neither men nor women wore gaudy colors or showy jewelry. The men wore white collars, usually celluloid, but no neckties. But the long chin beards of many of the older men made the question of cravats or no cravats simply an academic one.

There was no organ. The Mennonites do not use them. Different leaders conducted the singing just as we have seen in the conventions farther south. The harmonic balance and

MENNONITE AND DUNKARD SHAPE-NOTE SINGERS

TOP: *The Mennonites gather for an "Old Folk's Singing" at Weaver's Church near Harrisonburg, Virginia.* LOWER LEFT: *J. Henry Showalter and,* LOWER RIGHT: *George B. Holsinger, a Mennonite and a Dunkard, both of Virginia, who have made notable contributions to sacred song.*

the volume were even and pleasing, and the quality of tone was far better than I have ever heard in any of the *Sacred Harp* singings or in those of the far-southern seven-shapers. These Virginia German women, for example, did not emit the squeaky, high, all-permeating tones that their enthusiastic sisters to the southwest indulge in so generally. The basses were exceptionally strong.

The singers were not all Mennonites. The presence of Dunkers, United Brethren, and others showed the unifying influences of these singings. The old institution, "dinner on the grounds," brought in baskets by everybody, was enjoyed in the basement of Weaver's Church. And the excellent quality of the food suggested to me one good reason for the unique persistence and spread of this German element and its musical zeal in American life.

The German-American sects of which we have just spoken and some other groups like the Primitive Baptists stick pretty closely to the older fasola and other sedate types of song. But the numerous little and big groups of more recent organization, the many "holiness" sects, for example, have cast their lot generally with the dorayme folk and use the little manila-bound collections of new and near-new gospel songs as they come from the presses of this and that country publisher.

A Holy Rollers' Convention

I once breathed the unique church atmosphere in which these lively songs were an element. It was while attending a national convention or assembly of the Church of God, or "Holy Rollers," a sect that may be looked upon as representing in its practices the religious conditions obtaining to a large extent among the pioneers of over a hundred years ago. The convention, that is, a big protracted meeting with hyper-zealots in attendance from many states, was held in Cleveland, eastern Tennessee, in September of 1929. The little shape-note song book, compiled in Chattanooga and printed in Rome, Georgia, was used mainly by the leaders and the choir occupying the stage of the big tabernacle. This "choir" consisted of a score of singers led by a piano player and a half dozen players of guitars and mandolins, standing in a row.

"Songs were, during the first hour or so of the meeting, merely incidental, as in the usual service. But when the two alternating women preachers had come to the end of their part in the occasion and the "altar service" was being prepared for by the removal of many chairs and the making of a sort of arena in front of the stage for the use of the "mourners" and their attentive exhorters, then the songs' function, as a rhythmic, tom-tom-like noise for inducing the desired ecstasy, became apparent. For from that time on there was no let-up. The spirit moved some to dance, others to speak in the unknown tongue, to shout, to jerk, or to fall in a dead trance. Mourners in ever-increasing numbers fell on their knees, elbows in a folding chair, at the altar, while the exhorters clapped hands to the time of the music, urged the kneeling ones to "come through," I imagined, and were quite beside themselves at the appearance of even a faint smile on the face of the praying sinner.

After half an hour of this, the singing came to an end. Also the instrument strummers, worn out, dropped out one by one, leaving only the piano player and a tambourine whacker, whom I could not see, to carry on the steady and almost terrifying rhythmic noise. Terrifying because it impressed me as being the production of the wild, subconscious human animal, one which we seldom come upon in such frightfully self-regimented herds. But the extreme mesmeric orgies of such primitive groups have been often enough described. And after all, my purpose is simply to make clear how the indigenous song merges into the hypnotic rhythmizing used in this indigenous type of religious practice.

The din, or, as they would call it "the joyful noise," rose till I could discern only the heavy bass tones of the piano and the rattle of the tambourine. And after a time even the piano man gave out, leaving only that still unseen thumper of the tambourine to lead the regularity of the noise. I walked in the direction of the tambourine sound. Across the now deserted stage and over to its left I found him—a Negro standing beside another, a hand-clapping one, before the black section of the convention, a group of perhaps a hundred, whose presence I had not suspected before. And as I watched, even the tambourine became silent and the human noise went on, *a cappella,* so to speak.

Other Country Congregations

A preference for shape-note books, though not always for the indigenous songs, exists in rural congregations of the centrally controlled bigger denominations, Baptists, Methodists, and Presbyterians. The Baptists and Methodists meet this preference by publishing all their song books and hymnals in both round and shape notations, leaving the individual congregation to make its own choice. The Presbyterians have divided somewhat along the country-city line. The rural branch, known as the Cumberland Presbyterian Church, puts out largely shape-note song books from its Nashville publishing house. The authorities of the Methodist Publishing House in Nashville tell me that the southern demand for shape-note editions exceeds that for the round-note books.

NEGRO COUNTRY CHURCHES

The Negro's churches of practically all denominations are essentially "country" churches, and their music must therefore be considered here.

Just as the Negroes have taken on the religious denominational aspects of the whites, so also have they adopted, in a measure, the whites' song habits and styles. We have spoken of the early stages of this adoptive and adaptive process, those stages which resulted in the early Negro spirituals. A subsequent stage may be looked on as beginning around Civil-War times and lasting to the present. After the Civil War the Negroes were torn between two song tendencies. They wanted to keep on singing their "slave songs." But they felt also that they *should* sing the songs, the gospel hymn sort, which were coming into fashion among the whites. Both pulls doubtless got many adherents, but for decades the Negroes, by and large, seem to have assimilated very little of this song manner. It was so far from their feeling as to what religious singing should be, so far from what they liked racially.

It has been only comparatively recently that the gospel song influence, bearing in on them continually from country white churches, singing schools, and singing conventions, and feeding their desire to be like the white folks, has made itself felt in any large section of the Afro-American population. But just to the extent to which this influence has permeated, it has brought along all the paraphernalia of the country white songsters. So that now numerous Negroes are singing in the white rural manner. They use the seven-shape notation and have their own little thirty-five-cent manila-bound song books, their own singing schools, conventions, teachers, composers, and, to some extent, publishers.

I make no pretense to anything but sporadic information as to singing schools and conventions. Marvin Poole, a Negro evangelist, told me of a singing convention held monthly on Sunday afternoons in Knoxville, Tennessee, where individual "vocal choirs" of ten to fifteen singers compete. They sing the *do-re-mi* syllables first—as in the *Sacred Harp* practice—and then the words. Poole said that some can sing the notes who cannot read the words. Homer F. Morris, the Atlanta publisher, tells me the Negroes have a state singing convention in Georgia. Poole also told me of the singing convention at Union, South Carolina, called the Pacolet River Association. P. A. Massingale, a Texas Negro teacher and composer, told me that there are many district conventions held by the Negroes in his state, and W. M. Ramsey vouches for the popularity of shape-note singing among the Negroes of Arkansas' cotton swamps.

Among the Negro song makers who have contributed to the books published by their own race and by the white people are J. W. Sykes (Ga.), T. M. Garrett (Tex.), P. A. Massingale (Tex.), C. P. Jones, (Cal.), G. T. Rhodes (Tenn.), W. C. Tinsley (Pa.), Carrie Booker Person (Ark.), Fred. Work (Ill.), Lucy Campbell (Tenn.), Thomas A. Dorsey (Ill.), E. C. Deas (Ill.), Willa A. Townsend (Tenn.), J. D. Bushell (N. Y.). James Wood of Georgia is a Negro song book compiler. The Colored National B. Y. P. U. Board (Nashville) publishes a shape-note book every other year, obtaining most of its songs from one of the independent white publishers. The Sunday School Publishing Board (Negro Baptist) in Nashville publishes the Baptist Standard Hymnal and Sunday school song books in both notations, selling about one-third of them in shape notation. In Arkansas they cannot sell a single book in round notes. The migration of Negroes into the North has brought a considerable demand for shape notes from many northern states, according to leaders in this Sunday School Publishing House.

CHAPTER XXXIII

SHAPE NOTES AND DORAYME SONGS AMONG THE INDIANS

"No more shall the sound of the war-whoop be heard"

ONCE the whites struck up a song when they had killed the Indians into submission. Now—a century later— the First Americans are singing songs in praise of the Pale Faces' God in the patterns of their white subjugator and in the notation made by Little, Smith, and Aikin.

THE WHITE MAN'S SINGING SCHOOLS AND MISSION STATIONS

The Indians of the South are in Okhahoma, North Carolina, and Florida. I have not investigated the Indians in Florida, and so do not know whether they also should be considered as "singing Indians." In North Carolina and Oklahoma the musical influences seem to have come to the Indians from two somewhat similar sources, the white man's singing schools and his mission stations.

In the early 1880's there was, according to many notes which I have found in the *Musical Million* of those years, much teaching of singing schools among the landless and migratory whites of Oklahoma, then Indian Territory. But I have found no mention of the singing of the Indians themselves before 1884, when William P. Blake, a missionary to the Creeks, reported that "the singing of the Indians is a feast to the soul. Generally but one part is sung, soprano. Sometimes the bass is added, and there may be a sprinkling of alto and tenor, though the parties who sing know it not. But the voices, blended as they are, rise and swell and gather volume as they go, until the soul is lifted up and you feel to go with the melody. The Creeks love singing. Usually half a dozen hymns at least are sung at each service. Then during protracted efforts, a whole night is spent in singing, praying and talking, or preaching. And you listen to the last song in the morning and say it sounds as fresh and full as the first one on the night before."[1]

In the same year Charles H. Gabriel held a singing convention in Muscogee (Indian Territory) at which around twenty Indians were in attendance. In 1887 W. S. Young—evidently a Baptist missionary and singing teacher—wrote to the *Musical Million* from Maxey, Choctaw Nation, as to his typical work, of a Sunday. Before and after the sermon the Choctaws sang from the shape-note song books. Following a dinner on the grounds "we reassembled and after singing a number of pieces from Sabbath Bells the writer gave them a lesson in [shape] notation and dynamics with blackboard exercises."

Ten years later (1897) S. J. Oslin, an itinerant singing-school teacher and song maker of some note, tells that Indians attended the Canadian Musical Convention at Enterprize (Haskell County, near the Canadian River), though the meeting was primarily for whites.[2] And a year later Will M. Ramsey reports, in the same periodical, successful singing schools held among the Choctaws and Chickasaws.

Abel B. Brown, Full-Blooded Chickasaw

The period from around 1900 to the present seems to have been one of real growth in the active participation of the Indians in song. One of the earliest and most courageous Indian workers was Abel B. Brown, full-blooded Chickasaw. I have

[1] *Musical Million,* XV (1884), 91.
[2] *Musical Million,* XXVIII (1897), 86.

his story from Milton Garner, Sulphur, Oklahoma, a singing teacher who has spent a lifetime among the Indians of Oklahoma.

"It was in the early part of the year 1901," Mr. Garner wrote me, "when I was singing on a school quartet that I met a little Chickasaw boy about seven years of age. This boy had never heard a gospel song, or any other song, in any language other than his own. He could not speak the English language at that time. It was noticeable that the Indian boy was very much interested, and he pleaded for an opportunity to learn to sing as the white folks did." Mr. Garner became interested in the boy, and his help and the boy's enthusiasm have resulted in the Rev. Abel B. Brown, a prominent Baptist minister whom Mr. Garner designates further as "one of the outstanding [singing] teachers, [song] writers and gospel singers of Oklahoma."

Abel B. Brown's importance in introducing the white man's music among his people induces me to quote further from Mr. Garner's story of this Indian's life:

"He was born Feb. 28, 1892, near where the city of Ada now stands. Like all boys of those times, he was denied the advantages of education, excepting those limited common-school branches that were offered in the white man's subscription school, or in the tribal schools which were over-crowded. He attended those schools and later, for one year, the Oklahoma Baptist University. His desire for a musical education was at all times uppermost in his mind. And even before he could speak the English language his one greatest desire was to have a song book of his very own,—yes, a white man's song book. Realizing the possibilities of his success in this work, his parents relented and secured for him the longed-for book. He attended singing school at every opportunity. And in 1910, at the age of eighteen years, he taught his first singing school at Durwood, Oklahoma.

"In speaking of this beginning, Mr. Brown says that none of his pupils could speak the English language, and that they asked him how he expected them to sing the white man's songs when they could not talk the white man's talk. It took the courage of a warrior to take this new thought to a people who insisted that 'white man's songs are for white man; Indians don't need them.' "

But Brown won out; and today "fully one-half the members of the Chickasaw and Choctaw tribes are singing the white man's songs, reading the shaped notes as readily as they would read a book. At least twelve teachers of music are working regularly among their people, and there are, in addition, scores of choristers or conductors who are keeping up the interest in the various Indian community centers.

"While he has been busily engaged in teaching others, Mr. Brown has not neglected his own musical advancement. He has continued to study and is today considered one of the outstanding song writers of the South. Each year his musical contributions are demanded by the song book publishers of the Southland. He is pastor of the Sandy Baptist Church near Sulphur and moderator of the Chickasaw Baptist Association."

Jesse York, a Mississippi Choctaw, and Others

Jesse York, a "Mississippi Choctaw," is also one of Oklahoma's outstanding singing teachers and song writers. He has taught widely among his people and he assured me that shape notes are the only ones used by any of the Indians in their "Big Injun" Singing Conventions. His songs may be found in the books of the Trio Publishing Company of Waco, Texas, and elsewhere.

Still other Indian song writers and teachers are Hamp J.

Porter (Oklahoma Choctaw), George W. Anderson (Chickasaw), William A. Lewis (Mississippi Choctaw), and Ed. Jackson (Choctaw). Much of the Indians' development in music must be credited to the white teachers mentioned above and to Milton Garner, Emmett S. Dean, B. B. Edmiaston, W. E. Edmiaston, P. M. Claunts, and other pioneers of rural song teaching.

Extent of the Indians' Musical Work

In explanation of the different tribal names mentioned above and of parts of Oklahoma which the different tribes occupy, I quote again from Mr. Garner:

"The Chickasaw and the Choctaw tribes are the leaders in musical activities among the Indians of Oklahoma. They are two of what are known as the 'five civilized tribes,' the others being the Cherokees, Creeks, and Seminoles. Of the Choctaws we have two separate and distinct branches, the Mississippi Choctaws and the Oklahoma Choctaws. The latter are descendants of those who came to this section in 1830, while the former are descendants of those who remained in the state of Mississippi and removed to Oklahoma in comparatively recent years.

"The Indians' musical work among their own people is confined to the territory formerly occupied by them under their tribal form of government and known as the Choctaw Nation and the Chickasaw Nation, embracing that part of Oklahoma extending from the western boundary of Arkansas westward to the 98th meridian and from the Red River on the south northward to the South Canadian and Arkansas rivers on the north. This territory is now the counties of Haskell, Pittsburg, Le Flore, McCurtain, Pushmataha, Latimer, Choctaw, Bryan, Atoka, Coal, Johnston, Marshall, Love, Carter, Jefferson, Stephens, Murray, Pontotoc, Garvin, McClain, Grady and the southern portion of Hughes—all in Oklahoma."

Jesse York tells me that "the Wichita Indians covering northern Oklahoma and the Cherokee Indians in the northeastern part of the state also sing the shape notes."

Indian Singing Organizations in Southeastern Oklahoma

The singing organizations in southeastern Oklahoma differ somewhat from the groupings of the white singers that we have been observing, in that they are more closely allied with church work. According to Mr. Garner, they have their "singing classes at the local churches, at district or associational conventions, and at the joint conventions of the several districts, which are held semi-annually. Their song work is very closely allied with their Sunday-school work, in fact, their Sunday-school conventions and their singing conventions are often held jointly, or you might say it is one organization, and it is supported in a great measure by the churches. These meetings are usually of three or four days' duration and are really great gatherings. We still follow the old-time custom, in a way, inasmuch as these meetings are on the camp-meeting order, the entire family attending, bringing their camp equipment, pitching camp and living at the church during the entire session. A major part of the time is devoted to singing which is engaged in by most of the young people and many of the aged ones. At most of these meetings prizes are offered for efficiency and some very interesting contests are held. The outstanding organization of the district is the Chi-ka-sha convention of which Abel B. Brown is president."

On a sultry evening in August of 1930 I attended a singing school taught by Abel Brown, the full-blooded Chickasaw, at the district school house in Fairview, a few miles west of Sulphur, Oklahoma. In front of the coatless teacher and standing around on the podium with him were perhaps seventy singers and onlookers. They were young and old, white and red. The pupils were mainly young and in the foreground. In the rear sat the old Indian men, and the women with their babies, silently. Here was one place where caste and race were apparently forgotten. A sixteen-year-old white girl—lipstick, rouge, short skirt, bare sun-tanned legs—held one side of a song book along with an unpainted Indian maiden. A pale-faced young white man stood beside his girl and sang, but with that reticence determined by adolescence; while beside them two chunky Chickasaw girls sang alto lustily. Their skirts were longer. A pair of Indian boys were singing tenor. But for their color, the slender fellows reminded one of the better type of college freshman.

For half an hour Abel Brown stood at the blackboard and explained "scale" (not "scales." Their ancestral language has no s-plurals, and so their English is without them), whole step, half step, major, minor, staff, signature, length of note, etc. The little girls were busy with pencils and note books. Then came his questioning and free answering from the pupils. And the rest of the evening was taken up with singing.

Afterwards, the excellent singer and intelligent fellow (white) with whom I had divided a song book asked me to wait a minute. He would like to introduce his family. And he proudly brought forward a most comely Indian woman and four neatly dressed children with clear, open faces, who seemed a bit more Indian than white. This was new to me, and refreshing. It was even more novel to talk with whites who were proud of their Indian associations; and to hear of others, without a drop of Indian blood in them, who had tried to get into the Indian tribe as real members.

INDIAN SHAPE-NOTE SINGERS AND COMPOSERS

UPPER LEFT: *A B. Brown is a Chickasaw singing-teacher.* UPPER RIGHT: *Jesse York, a "Mississippi Choctaw," does teaching and composing.* BELOW *is one of Professor York's singing schools.*

Singing Among the Indians of North Carolina

Singing among the Indians of North Carolina has a less flourishing aspect. E. C. Snoddy of the Cherokee Indian Normal School at Pembroke, North Carolina, informs me as follows:

"There are two groups of Indians in North Carolina: a Cherokee reservation in the western part of the state, and a group of about 17,000 Indians who are living in Robeson County, and who are mixed with other races. These Robeson County Indians, sometimes called Cherokee, and sometimes called Croatan, have lost a great deal of their racial identity, but still maintain separate churches and schools. They are a rural people and in their schools and churches their singing is almost wholly in shape notes. They have singing contests among their churches every fifth Sunday. These contests will ordinarily have about four or five groups or choirs from that many churches, and each choir will have ten to fifteen singers.

"Each choir sings separately. They have no instruments, and give no prizes. The books they use are secured from some advertisement in the back of a Sunday school quarterly, or are merely picked up from some itinerant preacher or teacher. Mr. Ruebush's publications are the most frequently used, and have been known here about twenty years, I am told."

Professor Snoddy referred me, for information as to the beginnings of this singing activity in Robeson County, to John R. Oxendine, an Indian singing teacher; and from him I have a letter from which I quote:

"You was wanting information when shape note music was first practice with us and who first introduced it among the Indians. Mr. Jim Pravatt was the first man that taut shape note music among us in 1914 and 15, at Mt. Olive church. then I taken up the work and taut shape note music among my people. And all so L. M. Lowrie. We both has bin teaching shape not music among our people. the use of shape note music is now a wide spread among my people. You allso wanted to know ef any among us that writes songs for the various song book publishers. non at all."

Of singing among the Cherokee Indians on the reservation in the mountains in the western end of North Carolina I have no information.

Shape-Note Singing in Wisconsin and Michigan

The Southern Indians are not the only ones who indulge in shape-note gospel song. L. A. Dokken, missionary to the Potowatome Indians at Soperton, Wisconsin, writes me that "the Indians here are deeply interested in singing and the shape notes seem to appeal to them very much." Their song books come from the South. Southern song books were used also by the Michigan Chippewas in the summer of 1930 at their "Annual Indian Grand Tribal Reunion and Camp Meeting" held at Indian Grove north of Oscoda, under the leadership of the Indian evangelist, the Reverend Simon Greensky (!).

Some readers may wonder about these names, Greensky, Brown, and York. Their wonderment will possibly be all the greater when they recall how the concert-stage "Chief Os-ke-non-tons and Chief Yowlaches strut in white buckskin and trappings of beads, eagle feathers, and fringe, to the great glee of their publicity agents and to the profit of their managers. I asked Abel Brown about his name. It came, as he explained, from a white family with which his ancestors had been associated. His Indian family name, no longer used, was once Abbe, meaning "killer," which in its variations as given to various individuals (Abbetanta, Tahoby, etc.), eventually became known among the whites as "Tubby," and was then given up.

CHAPTER XXXIV

STRUGGLE FOR EXISTENCE

All we'll have is character notes,
For 'tis our joy and pride
To keep the Aikin shapes afloat
And round-heads cast aside.

Our little children want to sing
With round notes they are blind.
To characters alone we'll cling
And leave the rest behind.

I was once a round-note man,
And thot they were the best;
I could not tell the reason why,
And neither can the rest.[1]

Shape-Noters on the Defensive

The shape-noters have from the start had to defend their practices. When it was a matter merely of one notation against another, the controversy took the form of mutual ridicule. The adherents to the traditional notation called the rural innovation "buck-wheat grains," "three-cornered sounds," "measle-toed," and "square-toed" music, and declared that it was fit only for ignorant whites and darkies. The character-note champions then came back at the "round-heads," calling their system "monkish" music[2] and "the foreign language of music" for the few snobs; always defending themselves with the reasoning that if notes were to symbolize at once the relative pitch and the relative tonality character of the various

[1] A rural rhymster of Missouri in *Musical Million,* XVII (1888), 41.

[2] They were convinced that the shapes had removed from their notation all suspicion of having its roots in the system attributed to Guido d'Arezzo.

tones, then the shapes were better, for they eliminated, by showing the singer the tonal relationship or melodic and harmonic function at a glance, the element of "calculation."

This argument could not be refuted. But the shape-noters were still radicals in their opponents' eyes. And when in the 1870's and 1880's the shape-note song-book production became an actual economic power that had to be reckoned with and when the big denominations and their publishing boards began to feel that power, then the rural singing cult was looked on as downright harmful and their art as "a dangerous delusion."[3] But the churches saw soon and wisely that they should fight the devil with fire. And the shape-note editions of their church song books appeared, as we have seen above. But though this move extended the influence of the church song books and improved their own church singing, still it seems to have had little effect on song activities outside the churches. There the rurals sang what, where, when, how, and with whom they pleased. No authority over them. Autonomous.

Fifty years ago a Georgia church convention passed resolutions deploring the all-day Sunday singings which, though of sacred song, were not accompanied by "preaching and exhortation." Today we see such Sabbath-day conventions still frowned on by some church authorities, condoned by others, and welcomed by the most liberal. The frowners do not approve of the "glee club" aspect of the shape-note song. They also object to the singers' staging their conventions at hours that conflict with the Sunday morning church service period. And here again a compromise has been reached in some localities by the church's offering the use of its building on Sunday afternoon in exchange for the singers' respect for its forenoon service period.

[3] The quotation is from R. M. McIntosh, for thirty years musical editor for the publishing house of the Methodist Episcopal Church South and one of the South's outstanding figures in orthodox sacred music circles during the period 1870-1900.

For a hundred years the fasola and dorayme folk struggled for their tonal existence against the "round-heads" and other natural but tangible enemies. For three decades or more since then they have struggled against two other foes, both of them intangible and hence apparently invincible. The first of these is the complete ignoring of the entire rural song activity by all excepting those directly participating in it. The other is the progressive invasion of the country by the city.

The Indifference That Kills

If the surest way to kill a minority human undertaking is for the powerful majority to ignore it, the southern country singers' institution is doomed. For in the big outside world, the great masses of people with non-specialized cultural interests as well as its scholarly people—musicians, historians, sociologists, anthropologists, hymnologists—are alike in their ignorance (I do not use the word in its aspersive sense) of this long-lived, widespread, and organically developed activity.

Of the rank and file of professional musicians, one can expect little else. Their failure to see the tonal art *as a whole* has made them either ignore the roots of that art entirely or give them merely fleeting recognition. If the musician recognizes that "folk-music is the primary source of art-music," he is apt to do so somewhat as the fundamentalist recognizes Adam or as the amateur scientific observer does the *pithecanthropus erectus* or the *amoeba,* as something very dim and far away.

The great spectacular musical achievements in Europe and during the past three centuries are for him and for his prospective audiences all there is of importance in music. Oh, to be sure, folk-music is still to be found, in Europe, maybe. A few composers have dressed up some of the Old World's folk-tunes so that they can appear on our programs, and with appropriateness. As for American folk-music? Well, many people will agree supinely with London's Ernest Newman: "If that [the Negro Spiritual sort of music as sung by Paul Robeson] is a sample of American folk-music, then America has the most miserable folk-music in the world." These words were copied in one of America's most prominent musical journals, and its editor agreed that Mr. Newman had spoken a timely and true word.

But if the musicians agree that even the Negro-American folk-music is worthless, then what is there of the indigenous sort left for their admiration? They agree generally that there is no white man's folk-music on these shores that can lay claim to being a widely possessed body of national music and an intrinsically worth-while one. So the professing musician can hardly be looked on as desiring to delve into his own native field, for it seems to him musically barren. And the fact of his ignorance of the southern angle of that field becomes thus understandable.

Attitude of Hymnologists, Musical Historians, Folklorists, Amateurs

The reason why the hymnologists have remained aloof from all observation of this corner of their field is perhaps that they are, practically first and last, concerned with the *words* of sacred song, and of those sacred "art songs" more particularly that fill and have filled the popular church hymnals. The spiritual songs of the folk, outside of the churches, and the social-cultural, religious, and musical meaning of such songs have not engaged their attention.

The historians' interests are becoming more domestic and broader. These scholars are now branching into the cultural phases of history. But books of song still have their inherent disadvantages to many historians as source material.

We call the musical historian "musicologist." But he is rare. Such scholars in the tonal field as the late Oscar G. Sonneck and the living Carl Engel are of the genus which does not seem to multiply on these shores. And none of the musicologists has become interested in the shape-note-singing phenomenon.

Another small group, the folklorists, are unfeignedly greedy for this sort of material. As yet, however, their folk-song researches have been largely in the secular field. Their interest goes beyond the individual and seeks types, and in this they touch elbows with the sociologist in his search for "patterns" and with their own brothers, the anthropologists, who go questing for "survivals in culture." The material which I am uncovering in the South will doubtless interest the folklorist, though he has not delved into it as yet.

How about the amateurs in music? The professed lovers of the art? If such are men, their numbers are (in the South at least) small. If such are women, they gravitate to the Music Club. The South is the nation's Music Club Center *par excellence*. There are more music clubs in the southern towns and cities than in all the rest of the Union together. Texas is the nation's banner Music Club state. The clubwomen profess an interest in folk-music. But that interest has not begun, as I have observed, with the folk-music of the South.

General and Complete Ignorance of This Field of Rural Song

We should hardly expect people generally, those non-specialized interests and those outside of the southern states, to know of the singing of these rural whites. The actual chastity of the non-southerner's mind in this regard is well illustrated by the incident, told me by an East Tennessee singing-school teacher. It was about a woman tourist from the North who happened to come within hearing distance of a rural singing convention where four hundred *Old Harp* singers were making the air ring. She listened, entered the church, marveled. Her first comment was: "Well! I didn't know the whites of the South were singers. I thought only the Negroes sang down here."

That the non-musical city dweller of the South itself is also generally innocent of anything but a fragmentary knowledge of this rural institution, may be hard to believe, but it is nevertheless a fact which he himself will readily admit.

If this urban is a native of the South, he has probably heard of it as a "poor white" amusement. And the poor whites have naturally never been the favorite object of study on the part of the less poor. The term "poor white" is somewhat synonymous, in general parlance, with "rural white." Rural whites are, of course, the immediate forebears of the great majority in every inland southern city, indeed, of a considerable part of these cities' best citizenry. But this is a fact of which these descendants seldom prate. Hence the will to "forget" the specifically rural customs of their ancestors.

And even if the city-dwelling southerner of rural parentage does in some cases look on the music practices of his country kinfolk as innocent and not to be laughed at, still he regards them as diversions that are unimportant genetically and culturally. This attitude is more than likely the result of his never having learned that the activity represents anything in the cultural tradition of his race more significant than, let us say, barbecues or home-comings. Nor have his historical-cultural concepts of rural music been changed to any extent by the feature stories, appearing occasionally in his newspapers, that tell of some singing convention, in paragraphs that are a mixture of fact and fancy, never going beneath the surface. The people of the large towns are not alone in this somewhat voluntary ignorance of rural song either. The attitude extends to the county seats and to those homes of the small-town élite which face the courthouse, whence, of a Sunday, the strains of the country singing peal forth. The libraries, too, come near to completely ignoring the rural songfolk. In a Georgia county out to the entire South in a steady stream for nearly fifty years, books that were locally compiled, printed, and bound, filled with songs that were composed largely by citizens of that town and its near-by villages, I walked into the public library. The librarian knew nothing of this musical activity. But since I was interested in music, would I like to see their department of music? Yes. It contained Grove's *Dictionary,* a half dozen other books, and the Methodist Hymnal. The Spartanburg (South Carolina) public library has William Walker's *Southern Harmony*. The Lawson McGhee Public Library of Knoxville has a *Knoxville Harmony* and a *Western Psalmodist,* and is collecting, with the aid of the author of *White Spirituals,* a complete set of the old rural song books.

Of the fifty-four early tune books of the fasola and dorayme folk (see lists on pages 25 and 323), more than half are absent from the list of American tune books in Grove's *Dictionary, American Supplement,* pages 385 ff.

Urbanization as a Factor

Another deadly enemy of this country-singing institution is urbanization. The rural South is rapidly becoming less rural. The line between the city and the country is fading, and the institutions of the former are invading the latter. (Such phenomena as the Tennessee anti-evolutionary legislation may be looked on, it seems to me, as skirmishes merely, in which the country has won a temporary advantage over its ultimate conqueror.) And to the extent that the country becomes urbanized, to just that same extent are its traditional rural practices losing ground.

In conceiving just what this penetration of the country by the city means, in its musical phases, we shall have to review first the obvious musical attitudes of the population centers. And in doing so, the first fact that strikes us as fundamental is that *city folk do not sing*. Even individual singing is extremely rare in our big towns, and group singing is practically extinct. The southern city's most unpopular and unstable musical organization is its choral society, if indeed it has one at all. The fewest of people are interested, it seems, in joining a club merely for the joy of singing with others. And as for listening to choral music, not even noted touring ensembles like the Saint Olaf Choir have been able to draw adequate audiences in the Southeast, and the mere mention, among singing folk, of that recent war-time institution known as community singing brings a smile. That was merely to help win the war. It is no longer needed. Nor is the essential vocal-musical silence of the city folk broken to an extent by the church choirs, for the most optimistic choirmaster will hardly assert that his angle of the musical art is a growing and thriving one, and the most optimistic pewholder will admit that his lack of enthusiasm for choral music, as such, has come from his uniformly disappointing musical experiences during church service.

City Folk as Listeners Only

Since the city dweller has ceased to sing, there are two other ways in which he has found some musical satisfaction. He has learned to play an instrument, or he has folded his hands and become a mere listener. The cities have always been the first to welcome instruments and instrumentalists. The urbans have learned by much listening that while the human voice at its best is uniquely appealing, instruments have added to the world's wealth of tone a variety in sound color and a degree of technical accomplishment that cannot be equalled in the realm of vocal music. The recognition of this fact has led to the wide popularity of the piano, the installation of bigger and better organs in churches and theaters, the establishment of bands and orchestras, and the multiplication of individual players of this and that instrument from the mouth harp to the oboe. The whole movement may be looked on as one in which a good deal of the slack left by the singers-become-silent has been taken up. It may also be considered, I think, as a positive factor in the discouragement of singing.

The country folk could get no instruments in the early times. Their church tenets made a virtue—a mandate even—of their deprivation. And their whole art of music grew up as an exclusively vocal development. The charm of harmony, since it could not be delegated to an instrument, had to be produced vocally. The bare melody of the early colonists grew thus into the four-part songs that we hear in the rural South today, with each part lustily sung. How can the impinging of urban instrumentalism upon such purely vocal customs be other than destructive? The beginnings of such disintegration may be seen in the introduction of pianos into the shape-note conventions.

But the great mass of city people are neither singers nor players, but simply listeners. "I can't carry a tune or play an instrument, but I dearly love music," is an often-heard declaration. Hence the fostering of "music appreciation." Hence also the mass production of music-reproducing and music-projecting mechanisms. Hence the musical talkies. Hence sheet-music stores have become piano stores, piano stores have become talking-machine and radio stores. Hence instrumentalists are idle and their professional associations are appealing to the nation to save itself (and them) from the machine's threat against the existence of personal music.

But this already fixed habit among the urbans of looking on the human being as a mere passive listener, someone to be amused, has an even farther reaching effect. Hearers are becoming increasingly imperious as to what is offered their ears, and less and less friendly to homely music production for production's sake alone. To the "pure" listener, chaste of any social notions, the country singing—shrill-voiced women and "bellowing" men—is "low caste" song or "dreadful trash." The quotations are from a letter to me written by an educated musician in the country song belt of South Carolina. To him the prohibition of this singing activity, the extinction of all native music-making which gives satisfaction merely to those who are actively engaged in it, is imperative. The process of making the world safe for his tympanum is musical "progress."

The pampered listener's attitude has been increasingly orthodox and authoritative ever since our early cultural illuminati discovered European art-music and got their first conviction of American artistic inferiority. Miss Brown's arraignment of the folk-music institutions of eighty years ago (see page 19) has a familiar ring today.

To the existence of the composer of music, to say nothing of that of the country song cobbler, most people of our cities are highly indifferent. Europe has for time-out-of-mind supplied satisfactorily the demands of particular listeners. The jazz makers of New York are supplying those who are not so particular. So all concern with the source of supply of tonal productions would seem to be unnecessary. It is obvious, however, that such an attitude fails to consider the vital value of the music-creative activity, as such. It is also clear that this nation-wide resignation to the substitution, in musical life, of lap dogs and adoption, for parenthood, has resulted in turning over many of the ingenuous composers and their creative urge to the commercial exploiters with their "song competitions" and "lyric contests."

The cities, then, with their present cult of listening silence for themselves and for all others, excepting the few musical incomparables, and with their conception of the composer as merely a purveyor to his imperious majesty, The Listener, can have but one effect on music in the conquered countryside, and that is one of complete blight.

"Friendly and Neighborly Modesty"

It is not the purpose of this work to map out a program for those who would attempt to obviate the seemingly inevitable disintegration in question or to salvage after the wreck. Our principal task is completed, now that we have told the story of the institution and called attention to some of the factors in its impending destruction. But for the information of those who may be interested in the attempt to switch the "destruction" process into one of metabolism, I wish, before closing, to list a few heterogeneous "exhibits" which will, perhaps, when taken together, throw an additional gleam of light on the present period of transition.

Henry Fillmore, whose forebears have been singing-school teachers in Kentucky and Tennessee since a hundred years ago, is one of Cincinnati's best band and orchestra leaders.

Will H. Ruebush, scion of the Virginia Funk family, which has fostered rural music for one hundred and fifteen years, is the World-War bandmaster who took first honors in the school for American conductors founded in France, during the period of hostilities, by General Pershing and Walter Damrosch.

The four Higgins sisters (facing page 430), products of

North Carolina's rural singing schools and of Will Ruebush's sympathetic coaching, won first prize in the "Vocal Music in the Home" national contest at a recent Boston biennial meet of the National Federation of Music Clubs. They are now concertizing on the Pacific coast.

A male quartet, headquartering at the Vaughan School of [rural] Music in Lawrenceburg, Tennessee, has toured during the past year from the Great Lakes to the Gulf and from the east to the west coast.

A present-day representative of the Swans *(Harp of Columbia)* of three generations back, is Mrs. George T. Colyar, a prominent choirmaster and organist of Nashville.

An outstanding organizer in Tennessee's public school music circles told me that the establishment of effective choruses in the new county high schools of that state—that is, in the shape-note singing regions—was astoundingly easy.

The director of music in a Nashville college for teachers told me his best sight readers of music had learned in the shape-note singing schools.

A "lyric writing contest," put on by a southern city newspaper and its advertiser, a talkie concern, brought out two hundred poetic offerings. A very bad poem, filled with jazz-worn phrases, won, and received the newspaper's testimony that it was "a worth while lyric," showing "originality and discrimination."

The two children of the late John B. Vaughan, Georgia composer, dorayme singing-school teacher and song-book publisher, are students at the University of Georgia. One is "very good in harmony" and the other is "best at piano," their mother writes me. She is publishing and marketing song books to put them through college.

Joseph Maddy, creator of the National High School Or-

THE HIGGINS SISTERS

Left to Right, seated, *Sallie and Ida May;* standing, *Katherine and Allie.*

chestra and organizer of various All-State High School Orchestras in the South and the All-Southern High School Orchestra, told me the boy and girl players in Dixie "have had a poor start [in public school music instruction], but they make astounding progress once they do get into proper instrumental work."

As one who knows both northern and southern college students, I can testify that the southern student still sings. Poorly enough, but unashamedly, and much more than do northern students. The southern mechanic, on his back under a Ford, sings "If I had the wings of an angel." My cook and everybody's cook sings her religious songs in the kitchen. Her primitive melodic idiom, however, is giving way to the gospel song dialect.

A music club in a southern town that is known principally for its decades of folk-music propaganda—rural normal music schools, song-book publishing, a long-lived music journal, talking-machine recording, radio broadcasting, etc.—recently gave a program on the "Folk Music of Europe," according to a news story, featuring the rendition of "Robin Adair," "Believe Me If All Those Endearing Young Charms," a pianistic "Folk Dance," and "refreshments were served from a decorated table."

The president of Lincoln University in the mountains of eastern Tennessee reported on the initial reaction of the mountain folk to the university's activities in providing them with radio receiving sets: "Dozens of appeals for sets are being received" and "sermons and religious programs are most popular."

The Italian head of a southern city conservatory of music told me that his institution's greatest hindrance was the advent of new students of mature years and of sometimes exceptionally fine voices who do not know a musical note from a mathematical symbol.

Direct from a shape-note singing school just outside the smoke screen of Atlanta, where I had heard half a hundred boys and girls animatedly discussing questions of elementary harmony, I walked into the Atlanta studio of a private vocal teacher. He was laboring ineffectually with an uninterested young man on the subject of the different note lengths. This teacher told me he had never heard of shape-notes.

The American evangelistic song leader is an almost exclusively southern institution. Millions of those who have indulged in that form of religious activity will recognize one or the other of the following names: Charles M. Alexander, Homer Alexander Hammontree, Homer A. Rodeheaver, Sam Beazley, Will M. Ramsey, Charles D. Tillman, and Powell Lee. They have coöperated with most of the noted evangelists of the past three or four decades. They are all shape-note southerners.

Dr. H. M. Poteat, professor at Wake Forest College in North Carolina, amateur singer and good Baptist, declares, in the second chapter of his *Practical Hymnology,* 1921, that the southern country gospel song industry is "commercialized" and that its boosters lack "piety and religious enthusiasm." They "stir up pep" and thrive on conventions where "the people come together from all parts of the surrounding country, bring the babies and abundant baskets of dinner and spend the day . . . whooping and squalling and bellowing songs out of sundry cheap books," songs which do not "elevate the public taste" but, on the contrary, "pander to it." Then the author—in this chapter which he has used as material for lectures before Baptist assemblies and Federated Music Club conventions—illustrates the country singer's love and enthusiastic singing of well known choruses by pointing to the similar sort of chorus which is found in the Tin Pan Alley song, "They are Wearing Them Higher in Hawaii."

Enough of these "case studies."

When a recent flare-up of the anti-evolutionary wrangle had subsided somewhat, Professor Robert A. Millikan was quoted as of the opinion that the whole unfortunate matter held a lesson in friendly and neighborly modesty—as opposed to cocksureness—for both scientist and layman, modernist and fundamentalist. Here is a hint, the best one I know of, for those who are approaching the task which has to do with the musical fundamentalist of the South and his wide field of native music.

BIBLIOGRAPHY

Arlt, Gustave Otto. Status of Research in Folk Melodies. Unpublished Master's Dissertation, The University of Chicago, 1929.

Benson, Louis F. *The English Hymn.* Philadelphia, The Presbyterian Board of Publication, 1915.

Burrage, Henry S. *Baptist Hymn Writers and Their Hymns.* Portland, Maine, Brown, Thurston and Company, 1888.

Campbell, John C. *The Southern Highlander and His Homeland.* New York, Russell Sage Foundation, 1921.

Campbell, Olive Dame, and Sharp, Cecil J. *English Folk-Songs from the Southern Appalachians.* New York, G. P. Putnam's Sons, 1917.

Cox, John Harrington. *Folk-Songs of the South.* Cambridge, Mass., Harvard University Press, 1925.

Dett, R. Nathaniel. *Religious Folk-Songs of the Negro as Sung at Hampton Institute.* Hampton, Va., Hampton Institute Press, 1927.

Elson, Louis C. *History of American Music.* New York, The Macmillan Company, 1895.

Fretz, A. J. *A Brief History of Bishop Henry Funck and Other Funk Pioneers,* etc. Elkhart, Ind., Mennonite Publishing Company, 1899.

Gilson, F. H. *The History of Shaped or Character Notes.* Boston. 1889. (The only available copy is in the Library of Congress.)

Gould, Nathaniel D. *History of Sacred Music in America.* Boston, 1853.

Grissom, Mary Allen. *The Negro Sings a New Heaven.* Chapel Hill, N. C., The University of North Carolina Press, 1930.

Grove's *Dictionary of Music and Musicians, American Supplement.* New York, The Macmillan Company, 1928.

Hall, Jacob Henry. *Biography of Gospel Song and Hymn Writers.* New York, Fleming H. Revell Company, 1914.

——— A series of articles on the old-time shape-note singing activities, appearing in the *Daily News-Record,* Harrisonburg, Virginia, during the spring of 1930.

History of Virginia, Vols. IV and VI. New York and Chicago, American Historical Association, 1924.

Howard, John Tasker. *Our American Music.* New York, Thomas Y. Crowell Company, 1931.

James, J. S. *A Brief History of the Sacred Harp.* Douglasville, Ga., New South Book and Job Print, 1904.

Johnson, Guy B. *Folk Culture on St. Helena Island.* Chapel Hill, N. C., The University of North Carolina Press, 1930.

——— "The Negro Spiritual, a Problem in Anthropology," *The American Anthropologist,* XXXIII (No. 2), 157-71.

——— See also Odum, Howard W.

Johnson, James Weldon. *The Book of American Negro Spirituals.* New York, The Viking Press, 1925.

——— *Second Book of Negro Spirituals.* New York, The Viking Press, 1926.

Journal of American Folk-Lore. American Folk-Lore Society.

Kieffer, Aldine S. *Hours of Fancy.* Dayton, Va., Ruebush, Kieffer & Co., 1881.

Krehbiel, Henry E. *Afro-American Folksongs.* New York, Schirmer, 1914.

Krohn, Ernst Christopher. *A Century of Missouri Music.* St. Louis, privately printed, 1924.

Landrum, J. B. O. *Colonial and Revolutionary History of Upper South Carolina.* Greenville, S. C., Shannon & Co., 1897.

——— *History of Spartanburg County* (South Carolina). Atlanta, Franklin Printing and Publishing Company, 1900.

Lightwood, James T. *Hymn-Tunes and Their Story.* London, Charles H. Kelly, 1905.

Logan, John R. *Sketches of the Broad River and King's Mountain Baptist Association from 1800 to 1882.* Shelby, N. C., Babington, Roberts & Co., 1887.

Marsh, J. B. T. *The Story of the* (Fisk) *Jubilee Singers.* Boston, 1880.

Mersmann Hans. *Grundlagen einer musikalischen Volksliedforschung.* Leipzig, 1930.

Metcalf, Frank J. *American Writers and Compilers of Sacred Music.* New York, The Abingdon Press, 1915.

Musical Million, The. A Monthly Periodical. Dayton, Va., 1870-1915.

Ninde, Edward S. *The Story of the American Hymn.* New York, The Abingdon Press, 1921.

Odum, Howard W., and Johnson, Guy B. *The Negro and His Songs.* Chapel Hill, N. C., The University of North Carolina Press, 1925.

Phelan, M. *Handbook of All Denominations,* Nashville, Tenn., Cokesbury Press, 1929.

Pound, Louise. "Ancestry of a 'Negro Spiritual,'" *Modern Language Notes,* XXXIII (1918), 442-44.

Sandburg, Carl. *The American Songbag.* New York, Harcourt, Brace and Company, 1927.

Smith, Reed. *South Carolina Ballads.* Cambridge, Mass., The Harvard University Press, 1928.

Tillett, Wilbur F. *The Hymns and Hymn Writers of the Church.* Nashville, Tennessee, Smith and Lamar, 1911.

Wade, John Donald. *John Wesley.* New York, Coward-McCann, Inc., 1930.

Wallaschek, Richard. *Primitive Music.* London, 1893.

Wayland, John W. "Joseph Funk, Father of Song in Northern Virginia," *Pennsylvania-German,* Vol. XII (October, 1911), No. 10.

——— *A History of Rockingham County, Virginia.* Dayton, Va., Ruebush-Elkins Company, 1912.

LIST OF ABBREVIATED TITLES

BH, Baptist Hymn and Tune Book
CM, Christian Minstrel
CO (COH), Columbian Harmony
DIT, Thirty-six South Carolina Spirituals (Diton)
DT, Religions Folk-Songs of the Negro (Dett)
FIS, Seventy Negro Spirituals (Fisher)
FK, Story of the [Fisk] Jubilee Singers (Marsh)
GCM, Genuine Church Music
GOS, Good Old Songs
GRIS, Negro Sings a New Heaven (Grissom)
HH, Hesperian Harp
HO (HOC) Harp of Columbia
JH, 1, Book of American Negro Spirituals (Johnson)
JH, 2, Second Book of American Negro Spirituals (Johnson)
KN (KNH), Knoxville Harmony
KR (KRE), Afro-American Folk-Songs (Krehbiel)
KYH, Kentucky Harmony
MEL, Mellows (Kennedy)
MOH, Missouri Harmony
OD, Negro and His Songs (Odum and Johnson)
OL, Olive Leaf
OSH (OS), "Original" Sacred Harp
PB, Primitive Baptist Hymn and Tune Book
SAH, Sacred Harp
SCA (SC), On the Trail of the Negro Folk-Songs (Scarborough)
SK (SKH), Supplement to the Kentucky Harmony
SO (SOH), Southern Harmony
SOC (SOCH), Social Harp
SS, Slave Songs of the United States (Allen, Ware, Garrison)
TZ, Timbrel of Zion
UH, Union Harmony
VH, Virginia Harmony
WES, Wesleyan Hymn and Tune Book
WH, American Negro Folk-Songs (White)
WK, Folk Songs of the American Negro (Work)
WP, Western Psalmodist

INDEX

For titles of hymn books and song collections, see alphabetical list below, under "Tune books, shape-note". See also List of Abbreviated Titles, p. 437 above.

A CATALOGUE OF SELECTED DOVER BOOKS IN ALL FIELDS OF INTEREST

DESIGN BY ACCIDENT; A BOOK OF "ACCIDENTAL EFFECTS" FOR ARTISTS AND DESIGNERS, James F. O'Brien. Create your own unique, striking, imaginative effects by "controlled accident" interaction of materials: paints and lacquers, oil and water based paints, splatter, crackling materials, shatter, similar items. Everything you do will be different; first book on this limitless art, so useful to both fine artist and commercial artist. Full instructions. 192 plates showing "accidents," 8 in color. viii + 215pp. 8⅜ x 11¼. 21942-9 Paperbound $3.50

THE BOOK OF SIGNS, Rudolf Koch. Famed German type designer draws 493 beautiful symbols: religious, mystical, alchemical, imperial, property marks, runes, etc. Remarkable fusion of traditional and modern. Good for suggestions of timelessness, smartness, modernity. Text. vi + 104pp. 6⅛ x 9¼. 20162-7 Paperbound $1.25

HISTORY OF INDIAN AND INDONESIAN ART, Ananda K. Coomaraswamy. An unabridged republication of one of the finest books by a great scholar in Eastern art. Rich in descriptive material, history, social backgrounds; Sunga reliefs, Rajput paintings, Gupta temples, Burmese frescoes, textiles, jewelry, sculpture, etc. 400 photos. viii + 423pp. 6⅜ x 9¾. 21436-2 Paperbound $5.00

PRIMITIVE ART, Franz Boas. America's foremost anthropologist surveys textiles, ceramics, woodcarving, basketry, metalwork, etc.; patterns, technology, creation of symbols, style origins. All areas of world, but very full on Northwest Coast Indians. More than 350 illustrations of baskets, boxes, totem poles, weapons, etc. 378 pp. 20025-6 Paperbound $3.00

THE GENTLEMAN AND CABINET MAKER'S DIRECTOR, Thomas Chippendale. Full reprint (third edition, 1762) of most influential furniture book of all time, by master cabinetmaker. 200 plates, illustrating chairs, sofas, mirrors, tables, cabinets, plus 24 photographs of surviving pieces. Biographical introduction by N. Bienenstock. vi + 249pp. 9⅞ x 12¾. 21601-2 Paperbound $4.00

AMERICAN ANTIQUE FURNITURE, Edgar G. Miller, Jr. The basic coverage of all American furniture before 1840. Individual chapters cover type of furniture—clocks, tables, sideboards, etc.—chronologically, with inexhaustible wealth of data. More than 2100 photographs, all identified, commented on. Essential to all early American collectors. Introduction by H. E. Keyes. vi + 1106pp. 7⅞ x 10¾. 21599-7, 21600-4 Two volumes, Paperbound $11.00

PENNSYLVANIA DUTCH AMERICAN FOLK ART, Henry J. Kauffman. 279 photos, 28 drawings of tulipware, Fraktur script, painted tinware, toys, flowered furniture, quilts, samplers, hex signs, house interiors, etc. Full descriptive text. Excellent for tourist, rewarding for designer, collector. Map. 146pp. 7⅞ x 10¾. 21205-X Paperbound $2.50

EARLY NEW ENGLAND GRAVESTONE RUBBINGS, Edmund V. Gillon, Jr. 43 photographs, 226 carefully reproduced rubbings show heavily symbolic, sometimes macabre early gravestones, up to early 19th century. Remarkable early American primitive art, occasionally strikingly beautiful; always powerful. Text. xxvi + 207pp. 8⅜ x 11¼. 21380-3 Paperbound $3.50

ALPHABETS AND ORNAMENTS, Ernst Lehner. Well-known pictorial source for decorative alphabets, script examples, cartouches, frames, decorative title pages, calligraphic initials, borders, similar material. 14th to 19th century, mostly European. Useful in almost any graphic arts designing, varied styles. 750 illustrations. 256pp. 7 x 10. 21905-4 Paperbound $4.00

PAINTING: A CREATIVE APPROACH, Norman Colquhoun. For the beginner simple guide provides an instructive approach to painting: major stumbling blocks for beginner; overcoming them, technical points; paints and pigments; oil painting; watercolor and other media and color. New section on "plastic" paints. Glossary. Formerly *Paint Your Own Pictures*. 221pp. 22000-1 Paperbound $1.75

THE ENJOYMENT AND USE OF COLOR, Walter Sargent. Explanation of the relations between colors themselves and between colors in nature and art, including hundreds of little-known facts about color values, intensities, effects of high and low illumination, complementary colors. Many practical hints for painters, references to great masters. 7 color plates, 29 illustrations. x + 274pp.
20944-X Paperbound $2.75

THE NOTEBOOKS OF LEONARDO DA VINCI, compiled and edited by Jean Paul Richter. 1566 extracts from original manuscripts reveal the full range of Leonardo's versatile genius: all his writings on painting, sculpture, architecture, anatomy, astronomy, geography, topography, physiology, mining, music, etc., in both Italian and English, with 186 plates of manuscript pages and more than 500 additional drawings. Includes studies for the Last Supper, the lost Sforza monument, and other works. Total of xlvii + 866pp. 7⅞ x 10¾.
22572-0, 22573-9 Two volumes, Paperbound $10.00

MONTGOMERY WARD CATALOGUE OF 1895. Tea gowns, yards of flannel and pillow-case lace, stereoscopes, books of gospel hymns, the New Improved Singer Sewing Machine, side saddles, milk skimmers, straight-edged razors, high-button shoes, spittoons, and on and on . . . listing some 25,000 items, practically all illustrated. Essential to the shoppers of the 1890's, it is our truest record of the spirit of the period. Unaltered reprint of Issue No. 57, Spring and Summer 1895. Introduction by Boris Emmet. Innumerable illustrations. xiii + 624pp. 8½ x 11⅝.
22377-9 Paperbound $6.95

THE CRYSTAL PALACE EXHIBITION ILLUSTRATED CATALOGUE (LONDON, 1851). One of the wonders of the modern world—the Crystal Palace Exhibition in which all the nations of the civilized world exhibited their achievements in the arts and sciences—presented in an equally important illustrated catalogue. More than 1700 items pictured with accompanying text—ceramics, textiles, cast-iron work, carpets, pianos, sleds, razors, wall-papers, billiard tables, beehives, silverware and hundreds of other artifacts—represent the focal point of Victorian culture in the Western World. Probably the largest collection of Victorian decorative art ever assembled—indispensable for antiquarians and designers. Unabridged republication of the Art-Journal Catalogue of the Great Exhibition of 1851, with all terminal essays. New introduction by John Gloag, F.S.A. xxxiv + 426pp. 9 x 12.
22503-8 Paperbound $5.00

A HISTORY OF COSTUME, Carl Köhler. Definitive history, based on surviving pieces of clothing primarily, and paintings, statues, etc. secondarily. Highly readable text, supplemented by 594 illustrations of costumes of the ancient Mediterranean peoples, Greece and Rome, the Teutonic prehistoric period; costumes of the Middle Ages, Renaissance, Baroque, 18th and 19th centuries. Clear, measured patterns are provided for many clothing articles. Approach is practical throughout. Enlarged by Emma von Sichart. 464pp. 21030-8 Paperbound $3.50

ORIENTAL RUGS, ANTIQUE AND MODERN, Walter A. Hawley. A complete and authoritative treatise on the Oriental rug—where they are made, by whom and how, designs and symbols, characteristics in detail of the six major groups, how to distinguish them and how to buy them. Detailed technical data is provided on periods, weaves, warps, wefts, textures, sides, ends and knots, although no technical background is required for an understanding. 11 color plates, 80 halftones, 4 maps. vi + 320pp. 6⅛ x 9⅛. 22366-3 Paperbound $5.00

TEN BOOKS ON ARCHITECTURE, Vitruvius. By any standards the most important book on architecture ever written. Early Roman discussion of aesthetics of building, construction methods, orders, sites, and every other aspect of architecture has inspired, instructed architecture for about 2,000 years. Stands behind Palladio, Michelangelo, Bramante, Wren, countless others. Definitive Morris H. Morgan translation. 68 illustrations. xii + 331pp. 20645-9 Paperbound $3.00

THE FOUR BOOKS OF ARCHITECTURE, Andrea Palladio. Translated into every major Western European language in the two centuries following its publication in 1570, this has been one of the most influential books in the history of architecture. Complete reprint of the 1738 Isaac Ware edition. New introduction by Adolf Placzek, Columbia Univ. 216 plates. xxii + 110pp. of text. 9½ x 12¾.
21308-0 Clothbound $10.00

STICKS AND STONES: A STUDY OF AMERICAN ARCHITECTURE AND CIVILIZATION, Lewis Mumford.One of the great classics of American cultural history. American architecture from the medieval-inspired earliest forms to the early 20th century; evolution of structure and style, and reciprocal influences on environment. 21 photographic illustrations. 238pp. 20202-X Paperbound $2.00

THE AMERICAN BUILDER'S COMPANION, Asher Benjamin. The most widely used early 19th century architectural style and source book, for colonial up into Greek Revival periods. Extensive development of geometry of carpentering, construction of sashes, frames, doors, stairs; plans and elevations of domestic and other buildings. Hundreds of thousands of houses were built according to this book, now invaluable to historians, architects, restorers, etc. 1827 edition. 59 plates. 114pp. 7⅞ x 10¾.
22236-5 Paperbound $3.50

DUTCH HOUSES IN THE HUDSON VALLEY BEFORE 1776, Helen Wilkinson Reynolds. The standard survey of the Dutch colonial house and outbuildings, with constructional features, decoration, and local history associated with individual homesteads. Introduction by Franklin D. Roosevelt. Map. 150 illustrations. 469pp. 6⅝ x 9¼. 21469-9 Paperbound

THE ARCHITECTURE OF COUNTRY HOUSES, Andrew J. Downing. Together with Vaux's *Villas and Cottages* this is the basic book for Hudson River Gothic architecture of the middle Victorian period. Full, sound discussions of general aspects of housing, architecture, style, decoration, furnishing, together with scores of detailed house plans, illustrations of specific buildings, accompanied by full text. Perhaps the most influential single American architectural book. 1850 edition. Introduction by J. Stewart Johnson. 321 figures, 34 architectural designs. xvi + 560pp.
22003-6 Paperbound $4.00

LOST EXAMPLES OF COLONIAL ARCHITECTURE, John Mead Howells. Full-page photographs of buildings that have disappeared or been so altered as to be denatured, including many designed by major early American architects. 245 plates. xvii + 248pp. 7⅞ x 10¾. 21143-6 Paperbound $3.50

DOMESTIC ARCHITECTURE OF THE AMERICAN COLONIES AND OF THE EARLY REPUBLIC, Fiske Kimball. Foremost architect and restorer of Williamsburg and Monticello covers nearly 200 homes between 1620-1825. Architectural details, construction, style features, special fixtures, floor plans, etc. Generally considered finest work in its area. 219 illustrations of houses, doorways, windows, capital mantels. xx + 314pp. 7⅞ x 10¾. 21743-4 Paperbound $4.00

EARLY AMERICAN ROOMS: 1650-1858, edited by Russell Hawes Kettell. Tour of 12 rooms, each representative of a different era in American history and each furnished, decorated, designed and occupied in the style of the era. 72 plans and elevations, 8-page color section, etc., show fabrics, wall papers, arrangements, etc. Full descriptive text. xvii + 200pp. of text. 8⅜ x 11¼.
21633-0 Paperbound $5.00

THE FITZWILLIAM VIRGINAL BOOK, edited by J. Fuller Maitland and W. B. Squire. Full modern printing of famous early 17th-century ms. volume of 300 works by Morley, Byrd, Bull, Gibbons, etc. For piano or other modern keyboard instrument; easy to read format. xxxvi + 938pp. 8⅜ x 11.
21068-5, 21069-3 Two volumes, Paperbound $10.00

KEYBOARD MUSIC, Johann Sebastian Bach. Bach Gesellschaft edition. A rich selection of Bach's masterpieces for the harpsichord: the six English Suites, six French Suites, the six Partitas (Clavierübung part I), the Goldberg Variations (Clavierübung part IV), the fifteen Two-Part Inventions and the fifteen Three-Part Sinfonias. Clearly reproduced on large sheets with ample margins; eminently playable. vi + 312pp. 8⅛ x 11. 22360-4 Paperbound $5.00

THE MUSIC OF BACH: AN INTRODUCTION, Charles Sanford Terry. A fine, nontechnical introduction to Bach's music, both instrumental and vocal. Covers organ music, chamber music, passion music, other types. Analyzes themes, developments, innovations. x + 114pp. 21075-8 Paperbound $1.50

BEETHOVEN AND HIS NINE SYMPHONIES, Sir George Grove. Noted British musicologist provides best history, analysis, commentary on symphonies. Very thorough, rigorously accurate; necessary to both advanced student and amateur music lover. 436 musical passages. vii + 407 pp. 20334-4 Paperbound $2.75

JOHANN SEBASTIAN BACH, Philipp Spitta. One of the great classics of musicology, this definitive analysis of Bach's music (and life) has never been surpassed. Lucid, nontechnical analyses of hundreds of pieces (30 pages devoted to St. Matthew Passion, 26 to B Minor Mass). Also includes major analysis of 18th-century music. 450 musical examples. 40-page musical supplement. Total of xx + 1799pp.
(EUK) 22278-0, 22279-9 Two volumes, Clothbound $17.50

MOZART AND HIS PIANO CONCERTOS, Cuthbert Girdlestone. The only full-length study of an important area of Mozart's creativity. Provides detailed analyses of all 23 concertos, traces inspirational sources. 417 musical examples. Second edition. 509pp. 21271-8 Paperbound $3.50

THE PERFECT WAGNERITE: A COMMENTARY ON THE NIBLUNG'S RING, George Bernard Shaw. Brilliant and still relevant criticism in remarkable essays on Wagner's Ring cycle, Shaw's ideas on political and social ideology behind the plots, role of Leitmotifs, vocal requisites, etc. Prefaces. xxi + 136pp.
(USO) 21707-8 Paperbound $1.50

DON GIOVANNI, W. A. Mozart. Complete libretto, modern English translation; biographies of composer and librettist; accounts of early performances and critical reaction. Lavishly illustrated. All the material you need to understand and appreciate this great work. Dover Opera Guide and Libretto Series; translated and introduced by Ellen Bleiler. 92 illustrations. 209pp.
21134-7 Paperbound $2.00

BASIC ELECTRICITY, U. S. Bureau of Naval Personel. Originally a training course, best non-technical coverage of basic theory of electricity and its applications. Fundamental concepts, batteries, circuits, conductors and wiring techniques, AC and DC, inductance and capacitance, generators, motors, transformers, magnetic amplifiers, synchros, servomechanisms, etc. Also covers blue-prints, electrical diagrams, etc. Many questions, with answers. 349 illustrations. x + 448pp. 6½ x 9¼.
20973-3 Paperbound $3.50

REPRODUCTION OF SOUND, Edgar Villchur. Thorough coverage for laymen of high fidelity systems, reproducing systems in general, needles, amplifiers, preamps, loudspeakers, feedback, explaining physical background. "A rare talent for making technicalities vividly comprehensible," R. Darrell, *High Fidelity*. 69 figures. iv + 92pp. 21515-6 Paperbound $1.25

HEAR ME TALKIN' TO YA: THE STORY OF JAZZ AS TOLD BY THE MEN WHO MADE IT, Nat Shapiro and Nat Hentoff. Louis Armstrong, Fats Waller, Jo Jones, Clarence Williams, Billy Holiday, Duke Ellington, Jelly Roll Morton and dozens of other jazz greats tell how it was in Chicago's South Side, New Orleans, depression Harlem and the modern West Coast as jazz was born and grew. xvi + 429pp.
21726-4 Paperbound $3.00

FABLES OF AESOP, translated by Sir Roger L'Estrange. A reproduction of the very rare 1931 Paris edition; a selection of the most interesting fables, together with 50 imaginative drawings by Alexander Calder. v + 128pp. 6½x9¼.
21780-9 Paperbound $1.50

AGAINST THE GRAIN (A REBOURS), Joris K. Huysmans. Filled with weird images, evidences of a bizarre imagination, exotic experiments with hallucinatory drugs, rich tastes and smells and the diversions of its sybarite hero Duc Jean des Esseintes, this classic novel pushed 19th-century literary decadence to its limits. Full unabridged edition. Do not confuse this with abridged editions generally sold. Introduction by Havelock Ellis. xlix + 206pp. 22190-3 Paperbound $2.00

VARIORUM SHAKESPEARE: HAMLET. Edited by Horace H. Furness; a landmark of American scholarship. Exhaustive footnotes and appendices treat all doubtful words and phrases, as well as suggested critical emendations throughout the play's history. First volume contains editor's own text, collated with all Quartos and Folios. Second volume contains full first Quarto, translations of Shakespeare's sources (Belleforest, and Saxo Grammaticus), Der Bestrafte Brudermord, and many essays on critical and historical points of interest by major authorities of past and present. Includes details of staging and costuming over the years. By far the best edition available for serious students of Shakespeare. Total of xx + 905pp.
21004-9, 21005-7, 2 volumes, Paperbound $7.00

A LIFE OF WILLIAM SHAKESPEARE, Sir Sidney Lee. This is the standard life of Shakespeare, summarizing everything known about Shakespeare and his plays. Incredibly rich in material, broad in coverage, clear and judicious, it has served thousands as the best introduction to Shakespeare. 1931 edition. 9 plates. xxix + 792pp. (USO) 21967-4 Paperbound $3.75

MASTERS OF THE DRAMA, John Gassner. Most comprehensive history of the drama in print, covering every tradition from Greeks to modern Europe and America, including India, Far East, etc. Covers more than 800 dramatists, 2000 plays, with biographical material, plot summaries, theatre history, criticism, etc. "Best of its kind in English," *New Republic.* 77 illustrations. xxii + 890pp.
20100-7 Clothbound $8.50

THE EVOLUTION OF THE ENGLISH LANGUAGE, George McKnight. The growth of English, from the 14th century to the present. Unusual, non-technical account presents basic information in very interesting form: sound shifts, change in grammar and syntax, vocabulary growth, similar topics. Abundantly illustrated with quotations. Formerly *Modern English in the Making.* xii + 590pp.
21932-1 Paperbound $3.50

AN ETYMOLOGICAL DICTIONARY OF MODERN ENGLISH, Ernest Weekley. Fullest, richest work of its sort, by foremost British lexicographer. Detailed word histories, including many colloquial and archaic words; extensive quotations. Do not confuse this with the Concise Etymological Dictionary, which is much abridged. Total of xxvii + 830pp. 6½ x 9¼.
21873-2, 21874-0 Two volumes, Paperbound $7.90

FLATLAND: A ROMANCE OF MANY DIMENSIONS, E. A. Abbott. Classic of science-fiction explores ramifications of life in a two-dimensional world, and what happens when a three-dimensional being intrudes. Amusing reading, but also useful as introduction to thought about hyperspace. Introduction by Banesh Hoffmann. 16 illustrations. xx + 103pp. 20001-9 Paperbound $1.00

POEMS OF ANNE BRADSTREET, edited with an introduction by Robert Hutchinson. A new selection of poems by America's first poet and perhaps the first significant woman poet in the English language. 48 poems display her development in works of considerable variety—love poems, domestic poems, religious meditations, formal elegies, "quaternions," etc. Notes, bibliography. viii + 222pp.
22160-1 Paperbound $2.50

THREE GOTHIC NOVELS: THE CASTLE OF OTRANTO BY HORACE WALPOLE; VATHEK BY WILLIAM BECKFORD; THE VAMPYRE BY JOHN POLIDORI, WITH FRAGMENT OF A NOVEL BY LORD BYRON, edited by E. F. Bleiler. The first Gothic novel, by Walpole; the finest Oriental tale in English, by Beckford; powerful Romantic supernatural story in versions by Polidori and Byron. All extremely important in history of literature; all still exciting, packed with supernatural thrills, ghosts, haunted castles, magic, etc. xl + 291pp.
21232-7 Paperbound $2.50

THE BEST TALES OF HOFFMANN, E. T. A. Hoffmann. 10 of Hoffmann's most important stories, in modern re-editings of standard translations: Nutcracker and the King of Mice, Signor Formica, Automata, The Sandman, Rath Krespel, The Golden Flowerpot, Master Martin the Cooper, The Mines of Falun, The King's Betrothed, A New Year's Eve Adventure. 7 illustrations by Hoffmann. Edited by E. F. Bleiler. xxxix + 419pp. 21793-0 Paperbound $3.00

GHOST AND HORROR STORIES OF AMBROSE BIERCE, Ambrose Bierce. 23 strikingly modern stories of the horrors latent in the human mind: The Eyes of the Panther, The Damned Thing, An Occurrence at Owl Creek Bridge, An Inhabitant of Carcosa, etc., plus the dream-essay, Visions of the Night. Edited by E. F. Bleiler. xxii + 199pp. 20767-6 Paperbound $1.50

BEST GHOST STORIES OF J. S. LEFANU, J. Sheridan LeFanu. Finest stories by Victorian master often considered greatest supernatural writer of all. Carmilla, Green Tea, The Haunted Baronet, The Familiar, and 12 others. Most never before available in the U. S. A. Edited by E. F. Bleiler. 8 illustrations from Victorian publications. xvii + 467pp. 20415-4 Paperbound $3.00

MATHEMATICAL FOUNDATIONS OF INFORMATION THEORY, A. I. Khinchin. Comprehensive introduction to work of Shannon, McMillan, Feinstein and Khinchin, placing these investigations on a rigorous mathematical basis. Covers entropy concept in probability theory, uniqueness theorem, Shannon's inequality, ergodic sources, the E property, martingale concept, noise, Feinstein's fundamental lemma, Shanon's first and second theorems. Translated by R. A. Silverman and M. D. Friedman. iii + 120pp. 60434-9 Paperbound $1.75

SEVEN SCIENCE FICTION NOVELS, H. G. Wells. The standard collection of the great novels. Complete, unabridged. *First Men in the Moon, Island of Dr. Moreau, War of the Worlds, Food of the Gods, Invisible Man, Time Machine, In the Days of the Comet.* Not only science fiction fans, but every educated person owes it to himself to read these novels. 1015pp. (USO) 20264-X Clothbound $6.00

LAST AND FIRST MEN AND STAR MAKER, TWO SCIENCE FICTION NOVELS, Olaf Stapledon. Greatest future histories in science fiction. In the first, human intelligence is the "hero," through strange paths of evolution, interplanetary invasions, incredible technologies, near extinctions and reemergences. Star Maker describes the quest of a band of star rovers for intelligence itself, through time and space: weird inhuman civilizations, crustacean minds, symbiotic worlds, etc. Complete, unabridged. v + 438pp. (USO) 21962-3 Paperbound $2.50

THREE PROPHETIC NOVELS, H. G. WELLS. Stages of a consistently planned future for mankind. *When the Sleeper Wakes,* and *A Story of the Days to Come,* anticipate *Brave New World* and *1984,* in the 21st Century; *The Time Machine,* only complete version in print, shows farther future and the end of mankind. All show Wells's greatest gifts as storyteller and novelist. Edited by E. F. Bleiler. x + 335pp. (USO) 20605-X Paperbound $2.50

THE DEVIL'S DICTIONARY, Ambrose Bierce. America's own Oscar Wilde—Ambrose Bierce—offers his barbed iconoclastic wisdom in over 1,000 definitions hailed by H. L. Mencken as "some of the most gorgeous witticisms in the English language." 145pp. 20487-1 Paperbound $1.25

MAX AND MORITZ, Wilhelm Busch. Great children's classic, father of comic strip, of two bad boys, Max and Moritz. Also Ker and Plunk (Plisch und Plumm), Cat and Mouse, Deceitful Henry, Ice-Peter, The Boy and the Pipe, and five other pieces. Original German, with English translation. Edited by H. Arthur Klein; translations by various hands and H. Arthur Klein. vi + 216pp.
20181-3 Paperbound $2.00

PIGS IS PIGS AND OTHER FAVORITES, Ellis Parker Butler. The title story is one of the best humor short stories, as Mike Flannery obfuscates biology and English. Also included, That Pup of Murchison's, The Great American Pie Company, and Perkins of Portland. 14 illustrations. v + 109pp. 21532-6 Paperbound $1.25

THE PETERKIN PAPERS, Lucretia P. Hale. It takes genius to be as stupidly mad as the Peterkins, as they decide to become wise, celebrate the "Fourth," keep a cow, and otherwise strain the resources of the Lady from Philadelphia. Basic book of American humor. 153 illustrations. 219pp. 20794-3 Paperbound $1.50

PERRAULT'S FAIRY TALES, translated by A. E. Johnson and S. R. Littlewood, with 34 full-page illustrations by Gustave Doré. All the original Perrault stories—Cinderella, Sleeping Beauty, Bluebeard, Little Red Riding Hood, Puss in Boots, Tom Thumb, etc.—with their witty verse morals and the magnificent illustrations of Doré. One of the five or six great books of European fairy tales. viii + 117pp. 8⅛ x 11. 22311-6 Paperbound $2.00

OLD HUNGARIAN FAIRY TALES, Baroness Orczy. Favorites translated and adapted by author of the *Scarlet Pimpernel.* Eight fairy tales include "The Suitors of Princess Fire-Fly," "The Twin Hunchbacks," "Mr. Cuttlefish's Love Story," and "The Enchanted Cat." This little volume of magic and adventure will captivate children as it has for generations. 90 drawings by Montagu Barstow. 96pp.
22293-4 Paperbound $1.95

THE RED FAIRY BOOK, Andrew Lang. Lang's color fairy books have long been children's favorites. This volume includes Rapunzel, Jack and the Bean-stalk and 35 other stories, familiar and unfamiliar. 4 plates, 93 illustrations x + 367pp.
21673-X Paperbound $2.50

THE BLUE FAIRY BOOK, Andrew Lang. Lang's tales come from all countries and all times. Here are 37 tales from Grimm, the Arabian Nights, Greek Mythology, and other fascinating sources. 8 plates, 130 illustrations. xi + 390pp.
21437-0 Paperbound $2.50

HOUSEHOLD STORIES BY THE BROTHERS GRIMM. Classic English-language edition of the well-known tales — Rumpelstiltskin, Snow White, Hansel and Gretel, The Twelve Brothers, Faithful John, Rapunzel, Tom Thumb (52 stories in all). Translated into simple, straightforward English by Lucy Crane. Ornamented with headpieces, vignettes, elaborate decorative initials and a dozen full-page illustrations by Walter Crane. x + 269pp. 21080-4 Paperbound $2.00

THE MERRY ADVENTURES OF ROBIN HOOD, Howard Pyle. The finest modern versions of the traditional ballads and tales about the great English outlaw. Howard Pyle's complete prose version, with every word, every illustration of the first edition. Do not confuse this facsimile of the original (1883) with modern editions that change text or illustrations. 23 plates plus many page decorations. xxii + 296pp.
22043-5 Paperbound $2.50

THE STORY OF KING ARTHUR AND HIS KNIGHTS, Howard Pyle. The finest children's version of the life of King Arthur; brilliantly retold by Pyle, with 48 of his most imaginative illustrations. xviii + 313pp. 6⅛ x 9¼.
21445-1 Paperbound $2.50

THE WONDERFUL WIZARD OF OZ, L. Frank Baum. America's finest children's book in facsimile of first edition with all Denslow illustrations in full color. The edition a child should have. Introduction by Martin Gardner. 23 color plates, scores of drawings. iv + 267pp. 20691-2 Paperbound $2.50

THE MARVELOUS LAND OF OZ, L. Frank Baum. The second Oz book, every bit as imaginative as the Wizard. The hero is a boy named Tip, but the Scarecrow and the Tin Woodman are back, as is the Oz magic. 16 color plates, 120 drawings by John R. Neill. 287pp. 20692-0 Paperbound $2.50

THE MAGICAL MONARCH OF MO, L. Frank Baum. Remarkable adventures in a land even stranger than Oz. The best of Baum's books not in the Oz series. 15 color plates and dozens of drawings by Frank Verbeck. xviii + 237pp.
21892-9 Paperbound $2.25

THE BAD CHILD'S BOOK OF BEASTS, MORE BEASTS FOR WORSE CHILDREN, A MORAL ALPHABET, Hilaire Belloc. Three complete humor classics in one volume. Be kind to the frog, and do not call him names . . . and 28 other whimsical animals. Familiar favorites and some not so well known. Illustrated by Basil Blackwell. 156pp. (USO) 20749-8 Paperbound $1.50

EAST O' THE SUN AND WEST O' THE MOON, George W. Dasent. Considered the best of all translations of these Norwegian folk tales, this collection has been enjoyed by generations of children (and folklorists too). Includes True and Untrue, Why the Sea is Salt, East O' the Sun and West O' the Moon, Why the Bear is Stumpy-Tailed, Boots and the Troll, The Cock and the Hen, Rich Peter the Pedlar, and 52 more. The only edition with all 59 tales. 77 illustrations by Erik Werenskiold and Theodor Kittelsen. xv + 418pp. 22521-6 Paperbound $3.50

GOOPS AND HOW TO BE THEM, Gelett Burgess. Classic of tongue-in-cheek humor, masquerading as etiquette book. 87 verses, twice as many cartoons, show mischievous Goops as they demonstrate to children virtues of table manners, neatness, courtesy, etc. Favorite for generations. viii + 88pp. 6½ x 9¼.
22233-0 Paperbound $1.25

ALICE'S ADVENTURES UNDER GROUND, Lewis Carroll. The first version, quite different from the final *Alice in Wonderland,* printed out by Carroll himself with his own illustrations. Complete facsimile of the "million dollar" manuscript Carroll gave to Alice Liddell in 1864. Introduction by Martin Gardner. viii + 96pp. Title and dedication pages in color. 21482-6 Paperbound $1.25

THE BROWNIES, THEIR BOOK, Palmer Cox. Small as mice, cunning as foxes, exuberant and full of mischief, the Brownies go to the zoo, toy shop, seashore, circus, etc., in 24 verse adventures and 266 illustrations. Long a favorite, since their first appearance in St. Nicholas Magazine. xi + 144pp. 6⅝ x 9¼.
21265-3 Paperbound $1.75

SONGS OF CHILDHOOD, Walter De La Mare. Published (under the pseudonym Walter Ramal) when De La Mare was only 29, this charming collection has long been a favorite children's book. A facsimile of the first edition in paper, the 47 poems capture the simplicity of the nursery rhyme and the ballad, including such lyrics as I Met Eve, Tartary, The Silver Penny. vii + 106pp. (USO) 21972-0 Paperbound $1.25

THE COMPLETE NONSENSE OF EDWARD LEAR, Edward Lear. The finest 19th-century humorist-cartoonist in full: all nonsense limericks, zany alphabets, Owl and Pussycat, songs, nonsense botany, and more than 500 illustrations by Lear himself. Edited by Holbrook Jackson. xxix + 287pp. (USO) 20167-8 Paperbound $2.00

BILLY WHISKERS: THE AUTOBIOGRAPHY OF A GOAT, Frances Trego Montgomery. A favorite of children since the early 20th century, here are the escapades of that rambunctious, irresistible and mischievous goat—Billy Whiskers. Much in the spirit of *Peck's Bad Boy,* this is a book that children never tire of reading or hearing. All the original familiar illustrations by W. H. Fry are included: 6 color plates, 18 black and white drawings. 159pp. 22345-0 Paperbound $2.00

MOTHER GOOSE MELODIES. Faithful republication of the fabulously rare Munroe and Francis "copyright 1833" Boston edition—the most important Mother Goose collection, usually referred to as the "original." Familiar rhymes plus many rare ones, with wonderful old woodcut illustrations. Edited by E. F. Bleiler. 128pp. 4½ x 6⅜. 22577-1 Paperbound $1.00

TWO LITTLE SAVAGES; BEING THE ADVENTURES OF TWO BOYS WHO LIVED AS INDIANS AND WHAT THEY LEARNED, Ernest Thompson Seton. Great classic of nature and boyhood provides a vast range of woodlore in most palatable form, a genuinely entertaining story. Two farm boys build a teepee in woods and live in it for a month, working out Indian solutions to living problems, star lore, birds and animals, plants, etc. 293 illustrations. vii + 286pp.

20985-7 Paperbound $2.50

PETER PIPER'S PRACTICAL PRINCIPLES OF PLAIN & PERFECT PRONUNCIATION. Alliterative jingles and tongue-twisters of surprising charm, that made their first appearance in America about 1830. Republished in full with the spirited woodcut illustrations from this earliest American edition. 32pp. 4½ x 6⅜.

22560-7 Paperbound $1.00

SCIENCE EXPERIMENTS AND AMUSEMENTS FOR CHILDREN, Charles Vivian. 73 easy experiments, requiring only materials found at home or easily available, such as candles, coins, steel wool, etc.; illustrate basic phenomena like vacuum, simple chemical reaction, etc. All safe. Modern, well-planned. Formerly *Science Games for Children.* 102 photos, numerous drawings. 96pp. 6⅛ x 9¼.

21856-2 Paperbound $1.25

AN INTRODUCTION TO CHESS MOVES AND TACTICS SIMPLY EXPLAINED, Leonard Barden. Informal intermediate introduction, quite strong in explaining reasons for moves. Covers basic material, tactics, important openings, traps, positional play in middle game, end game. Attempts to isolate patterns and recurrent configurations. Formerly *Chess.* 58 figures. 102pp. (USO) 21210-6 Paperbound $1.25

LASKER'S MANUAL OF CHESS, Dr. Emanuel Lasker. Lasker was not only one of the five great World Champions, he was also one of the ablest expositors, theorists, and analysts. In many ways, his Manual, permeated with his philosophy of battle, filled with keen insights, is one of the greatest works ever written on chess. Filled with analyzed games by the great players. A single-volume library that will profit almost any chess player, beginner or master. 308 diagrams. xli x 349pp.

20640-8 Paperbound $2.75

THE MASTER BOOK OF MATHEMATICAL RECREATIONS, Fred Schuh. In opinion of many the finest work ever prepared on mathematical puzzles, stunts, recreations; exhaustively thorough explanations of mathematics involved, analysis of effects, citation of puzzles and games. Mathematics involved is elementary. Translated bv F. Göbel. 194 figures. xxiv + 430pp. 22134-2 Paperbound $3.50

MATHEMATICS, MAGIC AND MYSTERY, Martin Gardner. Puzzle editor for Scientific American explains mathematics behind various mystifying tricks: card tricks, stage "mind reading," coin and match tricks, counting out games, geometric dissections, etc. Probability sets, theory of numbers clearly explained. Also provides more than 400 tricks, guaranteed to work, that you can do. 135 illustrations. xii + 176pp.

20335-2 Paperbound $1.75